VEILED VISIONS

VEILED

DAVID FORT GODSHALK

THE UNIVERSITY OF NORTH CAROLINA PRESS

CHAPEL HILL AND LONDON

THE 1906 ATLANTA RACE RIOT

AND THE RESHAPING OF AMERICAN

RACE RELATIONS

VISIONS

Designed by Rebecca Giménez
Set in Minion and Rockwell by Keystone Typesetting, Inc.
Manufactured in the United States of America

Publication of this work was aided by a generous grant from
the Z. Smith Reynolds Foundation.

The paper in this book meets the guidelines
for permanence and durability of the Committee
on Production Guidelines for Book Longevity
of the Council on Library Resources.

Library of Congress Cataloging-in-Publication Data
Godshalk, David Fort.
Veiled visions : the 1906 Atlanta race riot and the reshaping
of American race relations / by David Fort Godshalk.
p. cm.
Includes bibliographical references and index.
ISBN 0-8078-2962-5 (alk. paper)
ISBN 0-8078-5626-6 (pbk. : alk. paper)
1. Atlanta (Ga.)—Race relations—History—20th century.
2. Race riots—Georgia—Atlanta—History—20th century.
3. Racism—Georgia—Atlanta—History—20th century.
4. African Americans—Civil rights—Georgia—Atlanta—
History—20th century. 5. Southern States—Race relations—
History—20th century. 6. United States—Race relations—
History—20th century. I. Title.
F294.A89N439   2005
305.896'0730758231—dc22   2005005914

Portions of Chapter 7 appeared earlier, in
somewhat different form, as "William J. Northen's Public
and Personal Struggles against Lynching," in *Jumpin'*
Jim Crow: Southern Politics from Civil War to Civil Rights, ed.
Jane Dailey, Glenda Elizabeth Gilmore, and Byrant Simon
(Princeton: Princeton University Press, 2000), and
are reprinted here with permission.

cloth   09 08 07 06 05   5 4 3 2 1
paper   09 08 07 06 05   5 4 3 2 1

FOR MY PARENTS,

DAVID AND ROLFE GODSHALK,

AND MY SISTERS,

JUNE, MERRELL, AND ROLFE

He looked now for the first time sharply about him,

and wondered he had seen so little before. He grew slowly to

feel almost for the first time the Veil that lay between him and the

white world; he first noticed now the oppression that had not

seemed oppression before, differences that erstwhile seemed natural,

restraints and slights that in his boyhood days had gone unnoticed

or been greeted with a laugh. . . . And he sat long hours

wondering and planning a way around these crooked things.

—

Atlantan W. E. B. Du Bois, *The Souls of Black Folk*, 1903

CONTENTS

MAPS & ILLUSTRATIONS

ACKNOWLEDGMENTS

THE SUPPORT I HAVE ENJOYED and the generosity I have encountered while completing this work have been life changing and awe inspiring. Even during the loneliest nights at my computer, I have repeatedly found in writers and fellow scholars those "smiling men and welcoming women" who so comforted W. E. B. Du Bois during his studies. Their ideas and musings have nourished me and enriched my life during the fifteen years I have devoted to this project. My contemporary comrades and those who have touched me across time and space have made possible the insights this book offers. Any mistakes and gaps are my own.

Public and private institutions have also sustained me at key points in my research and writing. This project could never have been completed without the financial support of Shippensburg University and Yale University. An Andrew W. Mellon Postdoctoral Teaching Fellowship at Emory University allowed me to enrich my understanding of Georgia and meet many future friends. During an all-too-brief year, the students and staff at Morris College welcomed me into their lives. After providing "William J. Northen's Public and Personal Struggles against Lynching" a forum, Princeton University Press has permitted me to republish portions of it in Chapter 7. My participation in Don Doyle's 2003 NEH seminar at Vanderbilt University allowed me to enjoy the companionship of a brilliant collection of scholars, while Sundays at Nashville's Bluebird Cafe reawakened within me a love of writing for writing's sake.

I have also benefited from the resources and committed staffs of numerous libraries and organizations—especially the Atlanta History Center, the Beinecke Library of Yale, the Georgia Archives and History Division, the Library of Congress, the Richard J. Daley Library of the University of Illinois at Chicago, the Robert W. Woodruff Library of the Atlanta University Center, the Robert W. Woodruff Library of Emory University, the Special Collections Archives of the W. E. B. Du Bois Library of the University of Massachusetts Amherst, and, finally, Tulane's Amistad Research Center. Always with a smile and often with a quip, the library staff at Shippensburg University enthusiastically and skillfully answered hundreds of questions and processed thousands of requests. I also appreciate the hospitality that I received at the initial stages of this research from First Congregational Church of Atlanta, especially from Kathleen Redding Adams and Lavaughn Elkins, two historians who patiently went out of their way to introduce me to their church.

David Perry of the University of North Carolina Press evidenced a remarkable faith in this manuscript, helped guide it along the publication process, and provided me with valuable writing lessons. As readers for the press, Dan T. Carter and an anonymous reviewer helped me refine my arguments and prompted me to delete countless confusing digressions. Arriving late to this project, Rebecca Hawthorne, John Rohrbaugh, and Adriane Smith helped me verify quotations, check facts, and make maps. Professor Janet Ruby and her upper-level art classes helped me visualize my book and offered me wonderful ideas regarding prospective book jacket designs. Stephanie Wenzel proved to be a patient, meticulous, and perceptive project editor.

When I first began this project as a dissertation, Dale Couch, Gary Fink, Robin D. G. Kelley, Kathryn Nasstrom, Virginia Shadron, and Allen Tullos provided perceptive insights and important leads. Clifford Kuhn, who knows as much about Atlanta as anyone I've met, has patiently corrected many of my misperceptions and errors while guiding me to important sources. At Yale, I found a home away from home among a coterie of friends whose brilliance was overshadowed only by their bonhomie and compassion. These include Mia Bay, Nemata Blyden, Jonathan Cedarbaum, Debbie Elkin, David Moss, Daniel Nakano, Karen Sawislak, Carol Sheriff, Anne Standley, Martha Vail, Beth Wenger, and Charles Yang. My dissertation committee provided me with invaluable guidance and the perfect combination of support and constructive criticism. Howard Lamar's gentleness and innumerable kindnesses showered rays of hope and warmth on even the darkest New Haven days. David Brion Davis's breadth of knowledge and openness to diverse perspectives continue to inspire. Only after years of additional research and thought have I come to appreciate fully the profundity of Melvin Ely's suggestions regarding how I might transform my dissertation into a book.

During conferences and private conversations, numerous individuals have offered me fresh perspectives, pointed me in a truer direction, and reminded me of how much work remained to be completed. These include Edward Ayers, Gail Bederman, John Blassingame, Elsa Barkley Brown, William Carrigan, Bruce Fort, Aaron Frith, Earl Lewis, Robert McMath, Lester Rodney, Manisha Sinha, Clive Webb, Deborah Gray White, and George C. Wright.

I feel privileged to be a part of the History-Philosophy Department at Shippensburg University. I cannot imagine having more supportive colleagues or better comrades. No author could ask for more committed editors or truer friends than Charles Loucks and Mary Stewart. They are truly this project's coeditors. Charles has read many of these chapters more than a dozen times, always bringing a fresh eye and infectious enthusiasm. Even when I've faced my most difficult challenges, Mary has always lifted my spirits, lent a helping hand, and provided matchless counsel. The extensive Stewart clan has welcomed me into their homes in locations stretching from Manhattan to Atlanta. Close friend Chandrika Paul graciously and expertly helped proofread my text, endnotes, and bibliography. Other Shippensburg friends who've offered crucial support include Paul Adams, Kwabena Akurang-Parry, James Barnhart, Douglas Birsch, Steven Burg, Beverly Butler, Dennis Castelli, Anthony Ceddia, Catherine Clay, James Coolsen, Angelo Costanzo, Betty Dessants, James Edwards, Paul Gill, Sara Grove, Lee and Anne Hockersmith, Sarah and Sandy Hughes, Signe Kelker, Shirley Mellinger, Jack Morrison, John Quist, Vera Reber, Janice Reed, Christine Senecal, and George Snow.

I cannot imagine better undergraduate training grounds for a future academic than the University of South Carolina's History Department and its unique Honors College. Carolyn Matalene made me a writer and helped me appreciate the complexities and potential beauty of words. Walter Edgar shared with me his passion for southern history, and John G. Sproat provided crucial support for me while I was applying to graduate schools.

Fifteen years ago, a shy graduate student contacted Jacquelyn Dowd Hall after hearing that she was embarking on a study of Progressive Era Atlanta. Her willingness to *listen* to my ideas boosted my confidence in this project, and she graciously introduced me to some of the most decent and committed graduate students imaginable—including Laura Edwards, Glenda Gilmore, Leah Hagedorn, and Karen Leathem.

Since graduate school, Glenda as well as Dan and Jane Carter have served as valued friends and mentors, ceaselessly believing in and supporting this book. Glenda's generosity has been limitless. Her queries about my progress and her guidance at key moments proved crucial. My participation in the *Jumpin' Jim Crow* project on her invitation helped me rediscover myself as a historian and allowed me to benefit from Jane Dailey and Bryant Simon's sage editorial advice. Dan and Jane's gusto for life and their commitment to social justice brought into my humble hamlet a breath of fresh air just as I was finishing this project.

In addition to the kindness of strangers and friends, I have also benefited from the insights of countless fellow historians, whose scholarship has enriched my own work. Three contemporary historians—Mark Bauerlein, Allison Dorsey, and Gregory Lamont Mixon—have written finely crafted studies of Atlanta that culminate in the riot and its immediate aftermath. I have also benefited from biographical studies published by, among others, Dominic Capeci Jr., Leroy Davis, Louis Harlan, Jack Knight, David Levering Lewis, Jacquelyn Rouse, and Emma Lou Thornbrough. I have also learned much about Atlanta's and America's social and political history from the writings of Clarence Bacote, Ronald Bayor, Gail Bederman, Bobby Donaldson, Karen Ferguson, Kevin Gaines, Georgina Hickey, Evelyn Brooks Higginbotham, Tera Hunter, Sarah Judson, Nancy MacLean, Deborah Gray White, and Joel Williamson. One of the most bittersweet aspects of completing this book is saying goodbye to so many historical figures whose lives and writings have taught me so much and so deeply moved me—including those of Jesse Max Barber, W. E. B. Du Bois, Lugenia Burns Hope, William J. Northen, Henry Hugh Proctor, and Booker T. Washington.

My great-grandmother Jessie Merrell Saunders Cole cultivated my love for reading, and my grandfather Al Fort has helped me see the world through new eyes. Most of all, I appreciate the dedication of my parents, Rolfe and Dave, teachers par excellence, who introduced my siblings and me to the world of ideas and who have generously and unstintingly supported all of our endeavors. This book is dedicated to them and to my sisters—June, Merrell, and Rolfe Janie—who have challenged so many of my ideas and always welcomed me into their families.

ABBREVIATIONS

The following abbreviations are used in the text:

AME: African Methodist Episcopal

ANDP: Atlanta Neighborhood Development Partnership

ATBA: Atlanta Anti-Tuberculosis Association

AUL: Atlanta Urban League

CC: Community Chest

CIC: Commission on Interracial Cooperation

CODA: Corporation for Olympic Development in Atlanta

EMA: Evangelical Ministers' Association

First Church: First Congregational Church of Atlanta

GERC: Georgia Equal Rights Convention

HDDC: Historic District Development Corporation

KKK: Ku Klux Klan

NAACP: National Association for the Advancement of Colored People

NACW: National Association of Colored Women

NU: Neighborhood Union

RRC: Reynoldstown Revitalization Corporation

SRC: Southern Regional Council

WCTU: Woman's Christian Temperance Union

WSIC: Women's Social Improvement Committee

YMCA: Young Men's Christian Association

INTRODUCTION

O N SATURDAY, 22 SEPTEMBER 1906, thousands of white men initiated a brutal attack against African Americans in downtown Atlanta. By dawn, at least twenty blacks lay dead and hundreds more had been seriously injured. When violence returned to Atlanta on Sunday and Monday, what began as a racial massacre escalated into a racial war. On both nights, armed blacks successfully defended their neighborhoods from attacks by whites—first in Dark Town, a working-class neighborhood near the city's center, and then in Brownsville, a middle-class settlement south of the city. On Tuesday, whites, reinforced by three state militia companies, reentered Brownsville, beating, threatening, and arresting many of its male residents. Both white and black elites feared an escalating spiral of white attacks and black counterattacks.

Successful defensive measures by blacks and international condemnation persuaded leading whites that interracial dialogue offered the only way out of a bloody impasse and public relations fiasco. Previous southern racial massacres had provoked relatively little soul searching among powerful whites. In 1898, for example, many white North Carolina Democrats had gloried in their success at killing at least twenty African Americans in Wilmington as part of a larger campaign to crush an insurgent Republican-Populist coalition. But in Atlanta, white business and religious leaders enlisted the aid of black collaborators in hopes of resolving a short-term crisis and permanently increasing their power over a divided city. White elites sought to establish controls not simply over "disorderly" blacks but also over the city's rapidly growing white working-class population, which was widely blamed for the eruption of the riot.[1]

The riot's destructiveness and these white overtures prompted a rising generation of self-styled New Black Men to reassess their racial loyalties and masculine identities. In the years leading up to 1906, this close-knit group of college educators and other professionals had increasingly lionized fellow Atlantan W. E. B. Du Bois. Their elitist ideals, much like his, equated black manliness with intellectual achievement and a courageous willingness to speak out against racial injustice, even in the face of white threats. The heroic roles of working-class black men in shielding black residential areas during the riot led some New Black Men to question their class prejudices. But white-imposed conditions for interracial negotiation included black denunciations of defensive violence. Black elites could seize the enhanced physical safety and public influence promised by biracial cooperation only if they forswore direct protest and turned their backs on their newly found working-class allies.

The responses of New Black Men to these dilemmas varied widely. Led by Henry Hugh Proctor of First Congregational Church of Atlanta (First Church), many shunned public militancy and outwardly embraced visions of order articulated by the white elite. In turn, white civic and business leaders promised to prevent renewed white racial violence, they selectively funded the institution-building efforts of accommodative blacks, and they offered a small group of black elites a nominal influence over municipal affairs. Other blacks, most notably the women-led Neighborhood Union (NU), struggled to preserve black visions of full racial equality and to reactivate the sense of collective black unity so evident during the four days of rioting. A new social and racial order gradually emerged from these postriot developments. Memories of the riot haunted Atlanta's politics and public life throughout the twentieth century, influencing everything from Leo Frank's famous 1913 trial to the distinctive twentieth-century evolution of the city's civil rights movements.

These local struggles quickly became entangled with America's broader political and racial debates. Published reports of the riot jolted black and white national audiences. The white mob's brutality aroused black fears of racial genocide. The successful black counterattacks fueled disputes among African Americans over the wisdom of defensive violence. Among many northern whites, newspaper descriptions of "uncivilized" white mobs battling "savage" black criminals conjured up the specter of a coming race war engulfing the entire South.[2]

No individual had more to lose from these national riot stories than did Booker T. Washington, the era's most powerful African American. Washington immediately grasped that the mob's violence against middle-class, clearly law-abiding African Americans called into question many of his public declarations. Particularly untenable became his argument that white southerners recognized their financial and moral stake in rewarding black progress and protecting African Americans from racial violence. Protests and federal intervention, he maintained, were therefore unnecessary and even counterproductive. Washington harnessed Atlanta's interracial movements in defense of his besieged racial program. Du Bois, the leading black critic of Washington's accommodative stance, braved local white threats in hopes of exposing his city's lingering racial injustices and confirming the need for continuing civil rights agitation. But white intimidation and promises of interracial cooperation silenced many of his local black allies.[3]

In the long term, Washington's refusal to rework his philosophy in the riot's aftermath further isolated him from both national white racial progressives and all but his most loyal black supporters. The growing radicalization of these groups facilitated the birth of the National Association for the Advancement of Colored People (NAACP) in 1909 as a national civil rights organization. While these national debates helped spawn the NAACP, Atlanta's interracial movements ultimately served as a model for the far more conservative Commission on Interracial Cooperation (CIC), described by one historian as "just about the only Southern organization with any influence or effectiveness at all in opposing racial violence" during the 1920s.[4]

Echoes of the Atlanta riot reverberated in the writings and racial programs of countless other national figures who continue to influence American conceptions of race and the South. National Progressive commentators, including leading white muckraker Ray Stannard Baker, studied Atlanta's interracial experiments in hopes of discovering lessons for other cities attempting to sort out similar urban problems. Baker's findings laid the basis for his 1908 *Following the Color Line*, one of the early twentieth century's most influential studies of race relations. Black Atlantan Walter White, dubbed "Mr. NAACP" for his role in guiding the civil rights organization between the 1930s and 1950s, traced his own racial awakening at age thirteen to the riot and grounded his civil rights program on lessons learned in Atlanta. Margaret Mitchell's childhood fears of black retaliatory attacks during the riot helped inspire *Gone with the Wind*'s vivid descriptions of black rapists and criminals. In a 1980 autobiography, Martin Luther King Sr. recounted the riot and the tradition of interracial cooperation that it had helped spark. King's famous namesake son announced, just prior to his 1968 assassination, the possibility of protests against the unseemly underside of Atlanta's riot-influenced framework for addressing racial conflict.[5]

THIS BOOK, LIKE many other studies of southern racial violence, examines the origins of the Atlanta massacre and the dramatic clashes between blacks and whites during its unfolding. Influenced by scholars' growing interest in historical memory and racial reconciliation, this book also offers the first comprehensive analysis of the local and national repercussions of the 1906 riot. Atlanta's protracted struggles allow us to pinpoint the concrete ways in which the memories and representations of an individual race riot helped reshape a city and a nation—culturally, politically, and socially. So, too, do Atlanta's experiences offer an unparalleled opportunity to heed scholars' clamor for historical studies that analyze the political and social interplay among a broad spectrum of black and white groups—businesspersons and workers, men and women, civic leaders and social outcasts—whose interactions are only beginning to be interwoven into a synthetic narrative.[6] Approached from this perspective, Atlanta's history underscores the potential instability of Jim Crow social identities, the multiplicity of *intraracial* divisions among both blacks and whites, the potentially far-reaching consequences of highly localized struggles, and the numerous opportunities for social change, even at the nadir of American race relations.

To understand the riot and its repercussions, we must also recognize that local and national developments are not distinct phenomena that intersect only intermittently. In Atlanta, these levels crisscrossed and overlapped one another at so many points that they became nearly indistinguishable. Many historical actors recognized that their words and deeds had both local and national ramifications. By touting the city's interracial movements in the national press, for example, black minister Henry Hugh Proctor was simultaneously cementing his relationship with local whites, drumming up northern donations for his Atlanta church, inventing what became the most influential national interpretation of the riot, and defending Booker T. Washington's racial program. Examining these connections allows us to recover the national significance of "local" individuals such as Proctor. This approach also helps us uncover rationales for seemingly incongruous behaviors and utterances. Thus, threats by local whites temporarily forced Du

Bois to exercise rhetorical restraint at the very moment that national developments were bolstering his confidence in the long-term viability of racial agitation.[7]

Any attempt to examine a single riot and its significance risks exaggerating the historical importance of individual events, trivializing other turning points in American history, or slighting what Thomas Holt has characterized as the "global levels" of experience—that is, the cultural, political, discursive, and social frameworks that structure human activity and social relations.[8] My goal, however, is not to turn our attention away from the historical influences of slowly evolving social and political structures, or even other incidents. For the ultimate significance of the riot derived as much from its interactions with other events and broader social forces as from its own internal processes.

ALONG WITH TELLING the riot's interrelated local and national stories, *Veiled Visions* addresses theoretical issues relating to the evolution of Jim Crow Era racial ideologies. In particular, I draw upon both my own research findings and those of a growing corps of historians to emphasize the potential instability of southerners' social identities and their ideas regarding social differences. Social distinctions exercised a particularly powerful hold over American imaginations during the late nineteenth and early twentieth centuries. In Atlanta as elsewhere, individuals and social groups defined themselves and others in terms of race, class, and gender differences—categories accented, in turn, by cultural distinctions based on factors such as education, religion, and behavior. Scholars now broadly agree that these social categories do not represent unchanging, innate divisions but are made and reshaped by political and cultural conflicts as well as broader social and economic relations. The meanings and implications of these categories vary over time and place and shift from social group to social group.[9]

A historiographical tradition, pioneered by black activists and then made famous by C. Vann Woodward, maintains that, because racial ideologies and identities are mutable, the late nineteenth-century emergence of Jim Crow segregation and vicious white racism was never foreordained. These phenomena were not even the offspring of broad and immutable historical forces. Instead, white decision makers who were driven by political and economic considerations consciously steered white southerners away from more racially progressive alternatives into a wasteland of reflexive racist prejudices and hatreds. White Populist Thomas Watson, perhaps Woodward's most dramatic illustration of ideological discontinuity, battled lynching and promoted black political rights in the 1890s, for example, only to champion black disfranchisement and white supremacy in the early 1900s.[10]

In a highly influential 1982 essay, historian Barbara J. Fields extends Woodward's ideas even further, arguing that "race" is not a "physical fact" but a "notion that is profoundly and in its very essence ideological." Racist ideologies, even the most constricting, are sufficiently fluid that they can simultaneously carry different meanings among different white groups and mutate over time within a given group. Like many others studying this period, these two historians trace relatively gradual shifts in white racial ideas. Woodward posits a "gray decade" of transition separating Watson's broad-minded "Jekyll" from his intolerant "Hyde." Fields examines ideological continuities and discontinuities spanning three continents and four centuries.[11]

In riot-era Atlanta, by way of contrast, individual black and white elites issued seemingly inconsistent statements and contrary behaviors within days and even hours of one another. Social and racial notions were expansive enough both to sanction seemingly contradictory public actions and to permit a wide range of claims regarding social affiliations and divisions. White newspaper editors who advocated violence on the eve of the riot counseled peace in its immediate aftermath. Black elites joined working-class blacks in defending their neighborhoods one day, only to excoriate their newly found black allies as public enemies on the next. Some white businessmen participated in Saturday night's rioting before denouncing the white mob's savagery three days later.

These apparently inconsistent statements and behaviors have long puzzled historians, including Joel Williamson, who has described riot-era Atlanta as "at once radical and reactionary, forward and backward, progressive and regressive." Williamson's brilliantly imaginative paradigm of discrete, broadly shared white southern racial "mentalities"—influenced primarily by collective experiences and psychological conflicts rather than social differences—never fully resolves these apparent dualities. "Atlanta" voluntarily abandoned racist hatreds following the riot, he concludes, simply "because it could not see itself in its ideal image and continue in violence." Mark Bauerlein's portrayal of the riot's outbreak as the product of relatively stable and universal white "Negrophobic" attitudes similarly fails to account fully for the dramatic shifts in white behavior before, during, and after the riot.[12]

In order for whites' and blacks' seemingly contradictory words and actions to become comprehensible, we must recognize the role that social and power arrangements play in structuring and shaping the articulation of identity claims and racial notions. In Atlanta, public words imperfectly reflected underlying ideologies partly because enormous social and economic disparities dramatically influenced both what blacks and whites could say and how they could say it. As the drama unfolded, for example, white elites purposefully isolated or physically threatened blacks who publicly criticized white civic leaders. Thus, when Jesse Max Barber wrote a newspaper article pointing to white civic leaders' complicity in the riot's outbreak, white elites threatened to lynch the black journalist before they forced him from the city. At the same time, white businessmen's fears of negative national publicity moderated their antiblack rhetoric. As far removed as black elites were from the official levers of public power, their academic training and urbane manners facilitated their communication with influential whites. Asymmetrical power relations, then, constrained and distorted the types of public identity claims that social actors could utter and act on.[13]

The varied ways in which public and private institutions configured social and discursive relationships further influenced how residents defined their own identities and positioned themselves in relation to other groups. Diverse white groups, such as newspaper editors and politicians, used threats and intimidation to prevent both blacks and whites from openly challenging exaggerated public stereotypes of black criminality, particularly about the alleged threats black rapists posed to white women. Such restrictions on public discourse discouraged black elites from forming visible alliances with working-class African Americans, a group portrayed by whites as inherently disorderly. Black elites could not openly challenge white definitions and stereotypes of African American criminality. Yet these white concerns and predispositions regarding black behavior simultaneously provided "respectable" blacks an entrée into public debates, so long as they depicted themselves and their proposed reforms as promoting white notions of law and order.[14]

These distortions in the public discourse were further magnified by the dual role of utterances as both conveyors of meaning and tools for manipulating others. Blacks and whites who made statements regarding social identities balanced a desire to broadcast "authentic" or "genuine" beliefs with the self-conscious aim of enhancing their access to social power and influence. In particular, various social groups articulated their similarities with and differences from other groups as a means of claiming social authority and cementing loyalties and alliances. Thus, decades after the riot, the fair-skinned and blue-eyed Walter White countered black nationalists' criticisms of racial disloyalty by recounting exaggerated stories of his affiliations with other armed black resisters during the riot.[15]

Identity claims made by one group regarding its relationship with a second entity usually represented simultaneous claims regarding still other groups. Thus, white rioters, by flaunting their supremacy over blacks, were also consciously claiming a shared status with all whites, even their putative social superiors. Before and after the riot, black elites claimed a shared authority with their white counterparts by arguing that both groups possessed common class and cultural identities, distinguishing them from white mobs as well as disorderly blacks.[16]

Claims of affiliation and difference jelled but never solidified. Many black elites sought safety in the midst of the riot by highlighting their shared racial affiliations with working-class blacks only to publicly emphasize intraracial divisions during its aftermath. Once more, the compositions and goals of what we heuristically label "groups" also evolved over time as members seceded either to form their own groups or to establish affiliations with others. Thus white newspaper editors and other commercial leaders could agitate white hatreds and even participate in rioting one day, only to distance themselves from their "disorderly" white counterparts the next.

Events and experiences also affected the construction and reconstruction of social identities and identity claims. We can speculate, for example, that black elites would have been less willing to cooperate with their white counterparts had the state militia not moved into Brownsville—killing, beating, and arresting alleged black resisters. Indeed, the very articulation of claims to identity and authority via words and deeds invariably affected how groups and individuals defined themselves and others. After the riot, white ministers and businessmen repeatedly acknowledged how their racial assumptions were affected by the very act of sitting down and discussing social issues for the first time with their highly educated black counterparts. Lawyer Charles Hopkins admitted to a northern journalist regarding the postriot interracial negotiations, "I didn't know that there were such Negroes in Atlanta."[17]

As southern historians have long recognized, cultural and class notions played a crucial role in shaping both the ideological assumptions and organizational frameworks of regional black and white social institutions. Most recently, for example, both Evelyn Brooks Higginbotham and Kevin Gaines have traced the development of exclusivist notions of propriety among black elites in the late nineteenth and early twentieth centuries. This "politics of respectability," as Higginbotham characterizes it, sought to undermine white assertions that African Americans were inherently morally inferior to whites. This strategy drove a wedge between its black practitioners and those African Americans whose social circumstances and cultural values made them unable or unwilling to meet the rigid behavioral and sexual standards mandated by their elite counterparts. Higginbotham arrived at her sophisticated insights by closely examining the evolution of southern black women's activism in the black Baptist church. Gaines's study represents a cultural analysis of the writings of leading early twentieth-century black thinkers, poets, and novelists. Subsequent histories of black elite notions of propriety have often focused on the common attitudes shared either within individual social groups or among a broad spectrum of social and cultural leaders.[18]

A study of Atlanta's postriot developments allows us to delineate variations in the politics of respectability both over time and among diverse black groups. This approach underscores how the structures that institutions and social relations imposed on human interactions could alternately strengthen, redirect, or weaken a priori cultural assumptions. As was the case with First Church and the NU, marked differences could emerge among groups that initially shared relatively similar moral values. Both of these organizations originally offered stopgap social assistance to a black population almost utterly ignored by municipal social service providers, including the police and sanitation departments. First Church minister Henry Hugh Proctor's postriot alliance with whites and his congregation's growing isolation from other blacks reinforced Proctor's exclusivist leanings, ultimately alienating him from many of his former black associates. In contrast, the NU's grassroots organizational structure and its focus on community organizing attenuated its members' elitism and facilitated the development of social ties that transcended traditional class and denominational divisions.[19]

The NU's and First Church's widening ideological divergence corroborates social scientists' findings that there is a direct correlation between the quality of informal face-to-face communications and peoples' levels of cooperation and trust. The evolution of Atlanta's interracial efforts further confirms these insights. Segregation practices prevented black and white participants from forming close personal relationships and communicating informally across the color line. These restrictions dramatically reduced the effectiveness of interracial organizations in fostering white awareness of black concerns, visions, and capabilities.

My research, then, sensitized me to the potential pitfalls of either over-emphasizing the primacy and permanence of voiced ideas or accepting articulated "beliefs" regarding race, class, and gender as mirrorlike reflections of interior thoughts. Underlying cultural beliefs and values dramatically influenced black and white Georgians' thoughts and decisions. The vast majority of whites, for example, rarely questioned their underlying certainty that most, if not all, African Americans were inherently morally and intellectually inferior to whites. Long-standing racial loyalties tugged powerfully at the hearts and minds of many African Americans, as did a shared commitment to resisting white racism. Many New Black Men, for example, gloried in the pride that came with courageous acts of resistance during the riot; others experienced profound feelings of self-doubt after making ideological compromises in its aftermath.

Yet, just as striking as the power of ideas in Atlanta is the wide array of identity claims that emerged and evolved within races and even particular individuals. Social and racial notions were expansive enough to sanction seemingly contradictory public actions and to permit a wide range of assertions regarding affiliations and divisions. Conscious and unconscious rhetorical manipulations heavily influenced human utterances just as experiences and institutional structures constantly refashioned basic assumptions. To understand Atlanta and the riot, then, we must, as have so many other New South historians, trace broad, gradual changes over time. Yet we must also underscore the divergent and even contradictory actions, expressions, and outcomes that can result from what otherwise appear to be static racial ideologies and inexorable social and political processes. As Higginbotham argues, we must acknowledge that a shared "racialized cultural identity has clearly served blacks in the struggle against discrimination" while "fully recognizing race as an unstable, shifting, and strategic reconstruction."[20]

IN ADDITION TO highlighting the potential flexibility of southern racial and class ideologies, Atlanta's experiences also reveal the potential costs of interracial cooperation.[21] Postriot interracial arrangements helped shape the contours of the city's social struggles for nearly a century. Equating commercial progress with racial peace, white elites successfully sought to discourage the naked expression of white racist hatreds and brutalities. Elite cooperation across racial lines suppressed the sorts of verbal and physical conflicts that often precipitated racial violence in other southern cities and towns. The resulting environment offered black Atlantans a thin opening for political activism that was generally closed to African Americans facing more brutally repressive local regimes. Against overwhelming odds, black voters took advantage of this opportunity, successfully rallying to win new concessions from white elites, first between 1919 and 1921 and then in the post–World War II era.

Yet Atlanta's postriot arrangements also spawned intense black jealousies and repeatedly crowded out alternative black visions seeking to promote interracial cooperation but refusing to compromise fundamental principles or abandon grassroots organizing. During the early twentieth century, for example, New Black Men sought unsuccessfully to pursue biracial dialogue without sacrificing their civil rights and free speech ideals. During the 1910s and early 1920s, the NU successfully enlisted interracial cooperation to address common white-black public health concerns, to increase black access to basic social services, and to strengthen the black community politically. White powerbrokers ultimately weakened these movements and others by extending financial resources, seats at the negotiating table, promises of protection, and other plums almost exclusively to accommodative black elites. Between the 1950s and 1970s, oppositional black protest movements in other southern cities generally secured higher levels of residential and public school integration. Even more than in other southern urban areas, Atlanta's unbroken tradition of biracial compromises—rooted in long-standing interracial relationships dating back to 1906—primarily benefited their white and black negotiators while only cosmetically addressing the city's glaring racial and class inequalities.[22]

Atlanta's elites and their national allies have successfully obscured the shortcomings of this interracial tradition, tainted at its core by the city's vast social inequalities and by whites' subtle deployment of intimidation to prevent true reconciliation. Atlanta's long-standing axiom that racial progress hinges on elite biracial cooperation was born of the riot. Since then, the city's public relations machinery has played a crucial role in keeping this formula for racial understanding lodged in American minds. In this way, Atlanta's dominant local myths have become many Americans' racial "truths."

CHAPTER ONE

Atlanta: Junction of Everything Finest and Most Foul

T HE RISE OF Atlanta as a regional rail hub laid the foundation for the city's breathtaking postbellum commercial expansion. By 1906, twelve rail lines radiated out of Atlanta, linking this "Gate City" with a broad hinterland of cotton fields and pine forests and annihilating the geographic and psychological spaces separating it from the world's financial capitals. Between 1895 and 1905, annual bank clearings nearly tripled to approximately $186 million. Business leaders, largely southern in origin, enthusiastically embraced this expansion and tirelessly trumpeted their city's advantages.[1]

Outside the business community, many early twentieth-century residents openly acknowledged that the city's rapid commercial growth had created new economic inequalities and undermined old cultural and social sureties. Whether longtime residents or recent migrants, many black and white Atlantans were struck by the growing sense of social anonymity that they experienced in a city whose population more than doubled between 1890 and 1910, to nearly 155,000 residents. As was the case in rapidly growing cities across America, the sheer scope and swiftness of Atlanta's transformations overwhelmed traditional mechanisms for maintaining order and triggered fears of moral and social chaos. For local white commentators, two distinctive anxieties particularly stood out. As black migrants streamed into the city and black social progress grew more visible, many whites became uncertain of traditional racial identities and boundaries. Concurrently, growing wage work among once independent yeoman farmers and their female dependents appeared to threaten white fathers' and husbands' social status and patriarchal authority. For many whites, these twin images of white women and "strange" black men adrift became powerful metaphors for the social disruptions and cultural dislocations wrought by Atlanta's growth. The visible commingling of the two groups in public spaces throughout the city stirred up many white men's most profound fears of racial and gender disorder.

BY THE EARLY 1900s, Atlanta had emerged as both a commercial and a manufacturing center. The city's thriving wholesale trade distributed consumer and agricultural goods throughout the Southeast. Atlanta's role as a nexus between southern cotton plantations and northern factories facilitated the S. M. Inman Company's emergence as the world's largest cotton-trading firm. Banks, law partnerships, and national insurance firms directed the city's surging number of financial transactions. The city's rail connections also encouraged national corporations to establish regional offices there. Although industry lagged behind commerce, the city's manufacturing production was valued at approximately $33 million by 1910. Cotton remained king in manufacturing and commerce. Increasingly, however, lumber mills, furniture companies, metal foundries, machine shops, and fertilizer plants arose both to process the raw materials pouring into the city and to service the railroads. This city of Coca-Cola was also a laboratory for still other elixirs, concocting more than $1 million worth of patent medicines in 1900.[2]

Atlanta's business leaders understood that the railroad and their city's economic expansion were increasingly pulling them into the broader currents of world commerce. In keeping with this cosmopolitan vision, Chamber of Commerce leaders issued a stream of reports, relentlessly trumpeting the city's possibilities in western and northern journals as well as in view books and city guides. They touted their white population as principally composed of the "best elements of the Southern States, with an admixture of the enterprising and progressive from the North and West." More than any other asset, local boosters advertised the "Atlanta Spirit"—"a spirit of transcendent energy, which surmounts all obstacles and builds even on disaster the fabric of success," a spirit of orderliness and unselfishness that purportedly encouraged citizens to transcend conflicts and disagreements in service of their metropolis's long-term growth.[3] Atlanta's unique public

Broad and Peachtree Streets as seen looking southward from the Candler Building's seventeenth floor, ca. 1906. Peachtree is on the left and Broad is on the right. (Kenan Research Center at the Atlanta History Center)

spirit, so business leaders had boasted since Reconstruction, rendered the city godly and safe from the labor and racial strife associated with its competitors. In 1902, Thomas Martin ignored an 1889 Atlanta lynching and countless similar incidents in neighboring counties to brag that the city had never witnessed mob violence or any of the other "bloody scenes which have saddened the history of other communities." Local residents also described Atlanta as a "city of churches," and, so one white minister claimed, never in history had there existed a metropolis "where the Church of God has a more potent and acknowledged influence upon the population."[4]

Chamber officials, in addition to pursuing investors and new businesses through their bold advertising campaign, also courted tourists. In 1906 alone, Atlanta secured more than twenty-five national conventions and attracted close to 80,000 visitors who spent approximately $200,000 in the city. In advertising their metropolis, chamber officials were enriching Atlanta's fortunes as well as their own. With outside firms and wealthy newcomers competing for commercial and residential property, real estate schemes substantially augmented the wealth of the city's richest families. Writer Thornwell Jacobs later recalled how "thousands of dollars were made on vacant lots over-night. Everybody was in the real estate business." At the

Peachtree Street business district above Five Points as seen looking northward, ca. 1907. The Candler Building, the tall white structure to the right, constituted the northern boundary of the downtown business district. (Library of Congress)

same time that Atlanta businessmen were courting northern and western money, their own financial investments were simultaneously spreading outward. After completing the seventeen-story Candler Building on Peachtree Street in June 1906, Coca-Cola tycoon Asa Candler turned his attention to constructing similarly impressive skyscrapers in Kansas City, Baltimore, and Manhattan. With Coca-Cola factories stretching across the country and advertisements touting the drink in national magazines, Candler recognized that the railroad (and his own financial interests) inseparably joined Atlanta with a larger national and global economy. Many chamber officials shared Candler's assumption that their city could convince others that it was a truly modern metropolis only if its businesspersons erected mansions and skyscrapers and embraced the outlook and mannerisms of their New York and Chicago counterparts.[5]

DESPITE ITS ECONOMIC expansion, Atlanta remained a metropolitan oasis surrounded by a desert of farms, woods, and small towns. Less than a mile beyond the city's streetcar lines lay piney forests interrupted only occasionally by isolated farms. The very railroads transforming Atlanta were also linking the state's overwhelmingly rural population with an international economy and serving as the advance guard of a radically new culture and social fabric. Night and day, trains thundered through Appalachian passes just to the north, rumbled by one-mule farms and 10,000-acre plantations in the cotton belt, and probed the monotonous piney woods and sugarcane fields in the state's southwest corner. Rail travel obliterated the cycles of work and rest that had long given rural and agricultural life its peculiar rhythms, and it deposited in country stores and post offices novelties from the world economy—copies of the *Atlanta Constitution*, bottles of Coca-Cola, packs of Lucky Strike cigarettes, and cartons of ready-made clothing.[6]

Both black scholar W. E. B. Du Bois and white journalist Ray Stannard Baker, traveling through the cotton belt in the early 1900s, noted occasional signs of vitality and prosperity. The two men admired the accomplishments of a small minority of black Georgian landowners (approximately 12 percent of a population numbering more than 1 million in 1900) who together possessed approximately 1.4 million acres assessed at more than $28 million. In Dougherty County, Du Bois was especially heartened by his introduction to Jack Nelson, "a great broad-shouldered, handsome black man, intelligent and jovial," who owned 650 acres, a small store, and "a neat and tidy home nestled in a flower garden." Despite such occasional indications of economic health and black progress, what ultimately struck both men was the "forlorn and forsaken" appearance of mansions now deserted by once proud plantation owners and the sullenness and gloom of the region's propertyless majority. They also recounted stories of whites beating and lynching black tenant farmers, threatening them with imprisonment, and chasing them down with bloodhounds.[7]

These signs of stagnation and social conflict were symptomatic of still broader transformations that had for more than four decades been sweeping agricultural regions throughout the state. The financial disruptions initiated by the Confederacy's collapse posed immediate challenges to cotton belt slaveholders, who reeled under the financial and social turmoil associated with emancipation as well as the economic crises resulting from invasion and defeat. In the Civil War's aftermath, they faced growing difficulties obtaining favorable loans and controlling a free black labor force that was determined, despite being landless, to wring out as much freedom and income as possible. To the north of the cotton belt, once proudly independent white yeomen similarly suffered the economic devastations associated with the war and the constriction of credit. In the 1870s and 1880s, these cash-strapped farmers devoted ever greater acreage to readily marketable cotton in order to reap the cash returns necessary to secure loans. Thus compelled by financial desperation and seduced by the new consumer products transported by the railroads, Georgia's farmers became increasingly enmeshed within a global economy. Each year they gambled their farms and futures on the fluctuating world price of cotton. With precipitous declines in the price of the commodity during the 1890s, growing numbers lost their property to creditors, as did many former slaves who had acquired land following emancipation. Indeed, between 1880 and 1910, the number of Georgia's tenant farmers more than doubled. Even those who retained title to their land gradually saw their incomes decline before cotton prices rebounded at the turn of the century.[8]

Whether payments were made in cash or cotton, the fraction of a tenant's crop or income that went to the landholder or furnishing agent rose in direct proportion to declining cotton prices. Landholders typically skimmed still more money from powerless black tenants by charging their borrowers exorbitant interest rates or selling them staples at grossly inflated prices. Consequently, even in years of high cotton prices, the majority of tenants barely broke even or finished the year in debt. Wage laborers, the lowest class of agricultural workers, received subsistence wages without the potential of accumulating a windfall in a year of high yields and favorable cotton prices.[9]

Discord infused the landlord-tenant relationship. The relative mobility and independence of black tenants frustrated white landowners, who continued to view slavery as their lodestar. In the early 1900s, state legislators from the region secured passage of a series of loosely worded vagrancy and peonage laws that compelled African Americans to accept employment or face jail. These laws also provided landholders with a claim on the labor of debtors so absolute that they could literally force tenants to remain on plantations or even sell indebted tenants to other farmers. In the tense cotton belt, the ever present threats of lynching and white violence both diminished black challenges to the authority of white landowners and discouraged black protests against mistreatment. Between 1880 and 1930, mobs killed at least 202 victims in this region of the state. Blacks also chafed under a system that provided dishonest proprietors with unlimited opportunities to fleece their tenants. Du Bois was shocked at the rage that he encountered among many black tenants, particularly a "big red-eyed black" mired in debt, "beginning with nothing, and still having nothing." This tenant, hearing of a neighbor's lynching, told his interviewer, "Let a white man touch me and he dies. . . . I've seen them whip my father and my old mother in them cotton-rows till the blood ran."[10]

THE ILL TREATMENT that blacks encountered in the violent cotton belt, the inadequacies of schooling for blacks there, and the tenants' distrust of their white landlords—all combined to encourage black migration to cities and villages. At the turn of the century, growing numbers of black migrants chose to pursue their new lives in Atlanta. According to census figures that probably undercounted a sizable black floating population, the number of African Americans in the city increased by more than 27 percent between 1890 and 1900—from fewer than 28,117 to 35,727. Most of these migrants were young single men and women between eighteen and twenty-five years old.[11]

When they arrived in Atlanta, black men and women confronted a discriminatory job market that generally reserved factory and clerical positions for whites. Since white employers almost completely excluded black women from mill and office work, by 1900 more than 90 percent of all black female wageworkers were employed in the domestic service sector. White prejudice consigned many black men to chronic unemployment in Atlanta and other southern cities. The majority of black men who did secure jobs worked as common laborers, as servants and waiters, and as porters, helpers, draymen, hack drivers, and teamsters. In 1900, just over 60 percent of all black male workers labored in these occupations alone—jobs often marked by low pay and extended periods of unemployment and underemployment. Sizable numbers of blacks also worked as carpenters, masons, machinists, and construction workers. These relatively skilled workers were marginalized in white-dominated industries that usually hired whites first and relegated African Americans to only the least desirable jobs. To the consternation of white competitors, black men dominated the barber profession, outnumbering whites by a two-to-one margin and often serving a white clientele. Black men also accounted for nearly 38 percent of the city's 166 bartenders.[12]

Black workers engaged in myriad strategies to raise money and protect their families. Both single mothers and extended families often pooled their resources by sharing houses and child care responsibilities. Domestic workers and other laborers established both formal and informal labor unions in search of better wages and working conditions. Many African Americans sought economic security and advancement through secret societies, fraternal orders, benevolent societies, and other cooperative organizations that raised capital for institution building and life insurance benefits. Men and women secured supplemental income by opening lunchrooms and illegal juke joints, by peddling eggs or flowers, and by laboring in cotton fields on the city's outskirts.[13]

Despite African Americans' hard work and ingenuity, Georgia's labor economy often split black families and prevented black men from permanently settling in one place. Underemployment led many black men either to hustle for day jobs on downtown street corners or to leave their wives and children for extended periods in search of employment in other locales. Saloons and poolrooms offered convivial meeting places for men with nothing else to occupy their time, while craps games and gambling dens offered hopes (often dashed) for fast money. There was a demand for black male workers on itinerant railroad crews and in rural lumber mills and turpentine camps, particularly in southwest Georgia. These sites provided neither job opportunities for women nor environments conducive to child raising. Ironically, then, the "vagrant" and "strange" black men that whites saw "loafing" downtown or "roaming" the countryside were often seeking work or returning to their families.[14]

A select group of elite African Americans achieved a measure of respectability and wealth as educators in Atlanta's prestigious black colleges and as ministers, teachers, and journalists. In addition, a small group of black business owners and aspiring capitalists were as much on the individual make as their white counterparts. No black individual better embodied the city's rags-to-riches possibilities than formerly enslaved Alonzo Herndon, who by 1904 had become the proud owner of three downtown barbershops. His flagship operation on Peachtree Street near Five Points employed an all-black workforce to groom an all-white clientele that included the city's movers and shakers. Like his white customers, Herndon recognized that real estate investments offered the quickest and surest path to wealth. Between the 1880s and his death in 1927, he constructed a veritable real estate empire that stretched all the way to Florida and included more than 100 houses as well as substantial commercial holdings along Auburn Avenue. Many black Atlantans of more modest means participated in their city's land craze, whether by purchasing their own homes or by creating small realty investment trusts. By 1905, aggregate black property values in greater Fulton County approached $1 million.[15]

Many of Atlanta's most respected black families resided in established black neighborhoods in the Fourth Ward, just east of the central city along Auburn and Houston Streets. Both Dark Town, just east of the city's central business district, and Pittsburg, on the city's southwest periphery, were black working-class enclaves. Many striving African Americans joined whites in fearing the crime and vice associated with these neighborhoods. The city's prestigious collection of black colleges on the West Side made this district the cultural center of the black South. By 1906, however, even this area's previously "low hum of restful life" was rapidly quickening as working-class African Americans poured in. This new presence proved unsettling for an elite cadre of black professors and other professionals disturbed by the dives and occasional gunshots that they associated with their rambunctious new neighbors.[16]

MANY WHITE AGRICULTURAL workers from the piedmont and mountains similarly sought escape from the economic bondage of low cotton prices and tenant farming by searching for urban employment opportunities in Atlanta as railroad workers, factory operatives, cotton mill laborers, office workers, and service providers. The population of whites soared by approximately 175 percent between 1890 and 1910, from 37,416 to 102,861. Many working-class whites shared their black counterparts' struggles with poverty, inadequate housing, and squalid environmental conditions. One-third of the city's residents, including many whites, lacked access to modern toilets and running water. Cotton mill workers generally endured sixty-six-hour workweeks and grappled with one of the nation's highest costs of living on wages that were less than 65 percent of the national average. These financial pressures forced many families to put their children to work simply for subsistence. The combination of low wages and high living costs left as many as 50 percent of all white children malnourished and chronically ill.[17]

The most dramatic and visible transformation in city employment patterns was perhaps among white women, whose participation in the labor force nearly doubled between 1890 and 1900, from 2,381 to 4,381, and then more than doubled again between 1900 and 1910, from 4,381 to 9,352. By 1910, just over 18 percent of all white women worked outside the home. Approximately 24 percent of white women workers were between ages ten and nineteen, and many still lived with their parents. Approximately 20 percent of white women workers were married. By 1920, roughly 20 percent of all white female workers were single and living away from their parents. At the same time that women's participation in the workforce was rising, a small, yet highly visible, coterie of middle-class suffragists and Woman's Christian Temperance Union (WCTU) members was publicly challenging men's traditional monopoly on voting rights and civic participation.[18]

The employment of growing numbers of wives and daughters challenged both the patriarchal authority of men and their social role as their families' principal wage earners. The claims of white male Georgians to manhood and social status derived largely from their roles as protectors and guardians of their dependents, especially their wives and daughters. In a society shaped by kin networks and family relationships, the primary duty of white men as husbands and fathers was to safeguard their families' financial independence and honor from outside threats. Any failure along these lines was a sign of weakness and dependency, a sign that a man was less of a man than his counterparts. No point of honor was more sacred among men than the integrity of their households and their female dependents' sexual and moral purity. In a society that linked the honor of men with the chastity of their female relatives, men interpreted the sexual violation of their wives and daughters, whether coerced or voluntary, as an act of aggression against their own claims to manhood. Those too weak to protect their wives and children from sexual assault and seduction risked both social ostracism and loss of the status they enjoyed among other whites. As a 1906 commentator noted, "There is no cost too dear to pay for the protection of our dear wives and daughters."[19]

In rural Georgia, a wide range of social institutions aided men in narrowly limiting women's social power and controlling their wives' and daughters' sexual impulses. Informal contact between men and women was circumscribed by fears of gossip and social exclusion in rural areas, where neighbors and extended family members might observe any untoward behavior. Fellow church members kept close tabs on one another, and threats of expulsion and other forms of discipline prevented women from violating standards of sexual purity. In rural societies without commercialized forms of leisure, the dominant social institutions of church and home were tightly segregated along sexual lines. When heterosexual mixing did occur, it was usually highly structured.[20]

As Nancy MacLean has pointed out, wage work and the relative anonymity of city life decreased daughters' and wives' dependence on fathers and husbands and offered women countless opportunities to escape their families' supervision. A working daughter, for example, could pursue romantic relationships and even marriage without her father's approval. She might claim for herself all or part of her pay. Newspaper commentators and city residents often bemoaned the dramatic new freedoms that urban life provided women of a rising generation—women who had never experienced the gender restrictions associated with smaller communities or with life in an earlier Atlanta. For example, Eva Mauck, after visiting the city from Clarkston, revealingly noted the "growth of carelessness upon the part of our [white] women in their new found independence." Having seen "many women out as late as 10 and 11 o'clock, unattended, except by another woman," she reminded readers that "ten years ago those women would have been ostracized." Many white men in the city were particularly disturbed by Atlanta's downtown area, where "fallen women" lived in bordellos and cheap houses of assignation, where visibly drunk women walked the streets, and where unescorted daughters and wives might appear and disappear among large crowds. As in cities across America, the visible presence of unattached women in Atlanta's public spaces came to represent the broader threats to male authority and traditional morality triggered by the city's rapid modernization and growth.[21]

THE SPECTER OF white women adrift took on a special meaning in early twentieth-century Atlanta when white men of all classes coupled this powerful image with their growing fears of black men freed from the traditional restraints of white supervision and dominance. Whether in comic portrayals of the lassitude of petty black thieves or in pornographically detailed depictions of black-on-white sexual assaults, Atlanta newspapers and magazines offered their readers a veritable orgy of exaggerated images of black criminals unrestrained by white influence and unregulated by traditional social institutions. White journalists focused on "strange" or "vagrant" black men who reputedly hid in saloons and flophouses, far from the gaze of white eyes, to prey upon society before quickly disappearing into secret garrets. These local depictions drew from a larger national discourse that flooded northern and southern publications with images of black male brutishness and moral retrogression. This rhetorical onslaught, which reached its high point in the 1890s and early 1900s, wedded traditional white southern proslavery notions with late nineteenth-century Social Darwinist ideas that located social groups along a continuum from civilization to savagery. This line of reasoning placed European Americans at civilization's pinnacle. Africans and their descendants, in contrast, represented the depths of savagery. Postbellum African Americans, many of whom had been born after slavery and never "benefited" from direct white discipline, were allegedly retrogressing morally and physically back toward their natural "savage" state.[22]

Whatever their class or background, African Americans purportedly breached every Victorian expectation regarding manhood and womanhood, thereby endangering not merely themselves but whites as well. As early as the 1880s, for example, Virginia planter Philip Bruce characterized African Americans of all backgrounds as "unable to resist the solicitations of their physical instincts" and possessing "the same insensibility to whatever is elevated in life and beautiful in the universe." Black women's "sexual laxness" and black men's "vile, brutal, and depraved" nature made them utterly insensitive to the crime of rape. Wherever African Americans were left to themselves, Thomas Nelson Page argued, they became corrupted by "a general depravity and retrogression . . . closely resembling a reversion to barbarism."[23]

Wildly exaggerated stories of black-on-white assaults buttressed these racist beliefs. Black men's unchecked sexual savagery purportedly endangered all of southern society, particularly innocent white women. According to South Carolina senator Benjamin Tillman, black brutes, their "breasts pulsating with the desire to sate their passions upon white maidens and wives," wandered the South on the lookout for potential assault victims. Social Darwinists and white supremacists portrayed sex between black men and white women as a threat to a superior race's integrity and a challenge to whites' political and social authority.[24]

This racist agitation aggravated white men's fears that black rapists threatened their wives and daughters in Atlanta, and it reinforced their certainty that assaults on white women by black men stigmatized white men like no other crime. Any white man incapable of protecting his wife and daughters from persons of such low community standing must be feeble indeed. Any form of familiarity or physical contact between a white woman and a black man could forever ruin the reputations and claims to honor of the woman and her male relatives. In this sense, almost every white male in the city could empathize viscerally with the shame and dishonor that Knowles Kimmel continued to suffer months after newspapers reported in 1906 that an unidentified black man had assaulted his wife. Kimmel told a white journalist that the attack had "just about ruined" his life. Despite his neighbors' sympathy, Kimmel, originally from Pennsylvania, dreamed of losing himself "where people did not know his story."[25]

Such fears were compounded by whites' recognition that Atlanta's rapid modernization was undermining traditional racial hierarchies. Preserving the personalized and intrusive power that white landlords once exercised over black tenant farmers proved impossible in Atlanta, where a shifting, highly mobile black population resided in self-sustained neighborhoods. In contrast to rural areas, the city's public spaces—its thoroughfares, sidewalks, and streetcars—were filled with zones that lay beyond the reach of both Jim Crow segregation and firm white control. Ray Stannard Baker was repeatedly struck in late 1906 and early 1907 by the number of city whites recounting to him "how extremely difficult it is to get at the real feeling of a Negro, to make him tell what goes on in his clubs and churches or in his innumerable societies." Tom Watson, betraying a Populist distrust of cities, located the causes of a society ripping apart at its seams in what he perceived as African Americans' growing surliness: "There are too many idle negroes lying around our towns and cities. There are too many insolent negroes crowding white people off the streets. There are too many surly blacks elbowing white girls and ladies to one side on the sidewalk." This growing black resistance, he warned Georgians, suggested that "blindly, madly, we are drifting into social and industrial chaos."[26]

Whites tacitly acknowledged the limits of their power and influence by embracing both segregation and the elimination of African Americans from Democratic primaries. Such exclusion sought to prevent potentially open-ended conflicts between blacks and whites. These restrictions also degraded and humiliated African Americans just as they legally cordoned off from black penetration both large swaths of physical space and virtually all forms of political participation. The separate public institutions and services provided blacks were shockingly unequal. Atlanta officials would not open the first black public high school until 1924. Even after dividing black elementary students into two groups assigned to separate half-day sessions, public schools accommodated only approximately 50 percent of eligible black children.[27]

In this urban environment, police officers and judges assumed official responsibility for enforcing racial codes and discouraging black resistance against white supremacy. Law enforcement officials' patent prejudice and disregard for black lives were legendary among both black Atlantans and national journalists. Although they composed slightly less than 40 percent of the city's 1906 population, African Americans accounted for more than 62 percent of all arrests. That year, more than 88 percent of the city's 21,702 arrests resulted from charges of disorderly conduct, drunkenness, idling and loitering, or simply suspicious behavior. The prosecution of these and other petty crimes fell under the exclusive jurisdiction of the municipal court. Here, Judge Nash Broyles exercised overwhelming, often arbitrary power over suspects who were bereft of any kind of legal representation. In 1906, despite the vague accusations of victimless crimes facing most defendants, only 17 percent of all cases before the judge were dismissed. The typical sentence—five dollars and costs—condemned poor suspects to as many as fifty days on Georgia's notoriously brutal chain gangs or in Atlanta's filthy jail. In 1906, more than 37 percent of the city's court-levied fines were worked out rather than paid. Twenty-four percent of those blacks arrested were aged twelve to twenty, and many spent time in the stockade, to which Judge Broyles never sent white boys or girls. To do so, he warned, would lead to their "complete ruin."[28]

Under the state's convict lease system, which was finally abolished in 1909, most black felons (and occasionally misdemeanants) were literally sold to the highest bidders, who then exercised absolute authority over their purchases. Black and white commentators concurred that in camps throughout the state, convict laborers (more than 85 percent of whom were black in 1908) endured harsher and bleaker lives than they would have under slavery. White Atlanta civic leader James W. English, the Chattahoochee Brick Company's principal owner, controlled nearly 70 percent of the state's convict labor force at a camp infamous for its brutality. English's company worked convicts between fourteen and twenty hours daily. Guards served prisoners worm-infested salt pork, stripped and beat juveniles to death for minor infractions, turned a blind eye when their coworkers raped female convicts, and murderously whipped old or sick men unable to make their labor quotas. In an all too typical case, two women were "stripped and beaten unmercifully in plain view of the men convicts, because they stopped on the side of the road to bind a rag about their sore feet."[29]

Despite policemen's zeal in arresting unemployed blacks or those suspected of openly challenging white authority, large zones in the city remained relatively impervious to white control and dominance. Poor blacks repeatedly challenged the authority of an overwhelmingly racist criminal justice system by resisting arrest, by ambushing policemen with guns and knives, and by shouting threats and epithets. The strong sense of community in black working-class neighborhoods rendered these territories refuges from white violence and racist threats. Especially after sundown, police officers and other whites entered black working-class neighborhoods, particularly Pittsburg and Dark Town, only with reinforcements. A thinly staffed county police force provided only token protection for the vast hinterland of suburbs and isolated farms on the city's edges. African American men, usually by streetcar or on foot, freely traversed Atlanta's outlying borders as they moved from job to job, traveled homeward to visit their families, sought agricultural employment, or literally foraged for survival. Some impoverished black men pilfered vegetables from gardens or storage bins, camped in the woods bordering isolated settlements, or found overnight shelter in barns. Happenstance encounters involving these "strange" black men and unescorted white women stirred terror in the minds of many whites.[30]

ATLANTA'S CENTER CITY was the focal point of white fears of white women encountering black men adrift from traditional social controls. This district radiated outward from Five Points, the city's historic heart, the junction of its railroad network and streetcar lines, and the merging point of Atlanta's busiest thoroughfares: Edgewood Avenue and Marietta, Decatur, and Peachtree Streets. In the heart of Five Points and stretching outward rose many of the city's famous hotels and skyscrapers, whose brightness, newness, and sheer verticality, boosters proclaimed, were reminiscent of New York. Office buildings housing Atlanta's wealthiest and most powerful business leaders dotted Peachtree Street from the railroad tracks northward. The city's "self-confident, noisy, successful, energetic population" reminded one white visitor of Chicago. The "seething whirl" of streets, the "screams" of factory bells and whistles, and the "rattle and roar" of trains overwhelmed many visitors and recent immigrants. Equally oppressive as downtown's noise pollution was its air, which was saturated with a dust comprised of dried and pulverized animal excrement, spittle, and other noxious substances.[31]

Five Points's kaleidoscopic human activity swirled like a whirlwind on Saturday afternoons and evenings. For it was on these days—paydays—that black and white Atlantans descended on the downtown area to celebrate the close of their five-and-a-half-day workweeks. They were joined by tourists and conventioneers lured to Atlanta's energy and excitement as well as by nearby farmers, often derided as "hillbillies" and "rednecks," who were attracted by the city's good deals on retail merchandise and its insatiable demand for produce. Crowds of men dressed in starched or checkered collars alternately cheered and jeered the soapbox speeches of colorful politicians and infamous eccentrics. Throughout the day, bearded mountaineers rubbed shoulders with city-slicked businessmen and their wives. Jewish saloonkeepers shared the streets with Chinese laundry owners. The sounds of electric pianos and gramophones bellowed from nickelodeons and small cinemas. At virtually any hour, customers could buy a meal of chop suey or fried fish and choose among a vast collection of dresses, overcoats, watches, knickknacks, knives, and guns available in countless pawnshops. Nearby on Piedmont Avenue, Langford's White Midway offered black customers a roller skating rink, sideshows, a merry-go-round, and minstrel shows.[32]

Decatur Street, the center of Atlanta's underside, stretched eastward from

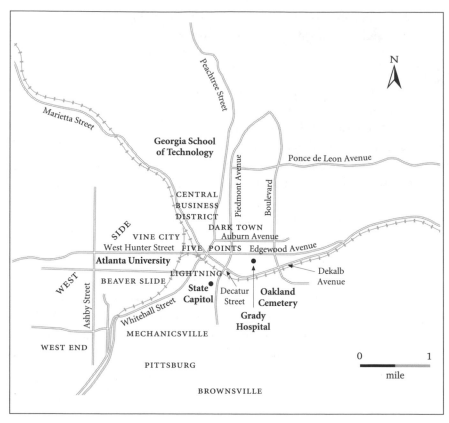

Atlanta, 1906 (adapted from map in Hunter, *To 'Joy My Freedom*)

Five Points in the shadows of towering skyscrapers and gilded hotels. Anyone with the slightest pretensions of respectability avoided (or at least pretended to shun) this thoroughfare. In one journalist's words, "The whole street stunk [from] . . . the odors of mullet, of week-old beer, of corn and rye whiskey, of frying grease, of barber shops, of humanity." Smoke from the railroad yards and manufacturing firms filled the air. At the Star, audiences could enjoy burlesque shows featuring striptease acts and vulgar comics. The cheap saloons, restaurants, and dance and billiard halls on Decatur (as well as similar establishments on Marietta and Peters), though largely segregated, were magnets for working-class men and women of both races. Unlicensed saloons, cheap lunchrooms, and black-operated ten-cents-a-night hotels serviced black patrons who poured into the area after nightfall. Both black and white journalists bemoaned the swaggering men and women crowding these streets and alleys. White women complained of the small

9400 Peach Tree St. from the east—a typical business district of a southern metropolis, Atlanta, Ga. Copyright 1907 by Underwood & Underwood. U 90961

Five Points, looking northeastward on Peachtree, ca. 1907. (Library of Congress)

groups of white men who harassed passing women with remarks that would "make his satanic majesty himself, blush with shame and indignation."[33]

Rumors circulated throughout Atlanta of a growing epidemic of cocaine use among Decatur Street's black denizens, who could allegedly purchase for a dime enough of the drug to render them utterly depraved. Whiskey retailed for a nickel a glass or fifty cents per quart. Lining the nearby streets were open-air stalls offering cheap meals. In dance halls, working-class black men and women dressed "fit to kill" in hats, suspenders, hip-hugging skirts, and patent leather shoes. Under dim lights, in air heavy with the summer's heat and beer and cigar fumes, black couples, accompanied by pianos and fiddles playing ragtime, danced the Itch, the Grind, and the Slow Drag—labels evoking the sensuous friction they encouraged.[34]

The intimate, unregulated contacts between white men and black men inside and outside the dives generated tensions that often erupted into violence. Journalists expressed particular indignation that white and black men sometimes shared cigars at integrated saloons while black customers, who gulped five-cent whiskey, were allowed to gape openly at the pictures and prints of half-nude white women plastered on their walls. Black customers also reputedly cursed white saloonkeepers, who frequently addressed their clients as "mister" and interacted with them on a basis of equality. A careless racial epitaph or a faint signal of disrespect might cast a sudden chill over even the warmest, most convivial setting. Referring to a slightly later period, one black resident recalled that it was a "tame Saturday night in the notorious Decatur Street section if there were only six razor operations performed or if only four persons were found in the morgue on Sunday morning." Police officers regularly raided the low dives, particularly targeting black patrons. The accumulation of Saturday night arrests often produced more than 100 unlucky defendants for the Monday morning police courts.[35]

FEARFUL OF BLACK mobility, whites turned to violence and threats in an attempt to cordon off whole territories from black penetration. Boys and young men in Atlanta's mill district assaulted and forced out African Americans who wandered into their neighborhoods. Judge Nash Broyles warned black defendants that the central city north and west of Decatur Street was Atlanta's "Modern Rubicon," so that their crossing into the territory after dark constituted sufficient grounds for arrest. The free movement of blacks that trolleys facilitated served as a powerful symbol of the growing black mobility associated with city life. Trolley interiors themselves illustrated what Baker described as the relative "absence of a clear demarcation" between the status of the races in the city, "the white not in a place of command, the Negro without an obligation of servitude." Disagreements and fights over seats frequently erupted as blacks and whites attempted to negotiate the trolley company's vague segregation policy that required blacks to seat themselves from the back of the car while whites seated themselves from the front.[36]

The fashionable attire, impressive homes, impeccable manners, and Ivy League educations of a small coterie of elite blacks directly challenged both white working-class claims to racial superiority and dominant racial ideologies linking blackness with economic dependency and moral inferiority. The downtown area was honeycombed with approximately fifty black businesses—including Yale alumnus William Penn's medical office, Benjamin J. Davis's *Atlanta Independent* newspaper office, and Alonzo Herndon's finely appointed barbershops—as if mocking their economically struggling white competitors. Headquartered in a downtown office, the *Voice of the Negro* distributed as many as 15,000 copies per issue by 1906, arguably making it the era's leading African American magazine. Under Jesse Max Barber's editorship, this strident publication ridiculed white racist pretensions and became, by the fall of 1906, the unofficial organ of Du Bois's radical, Georgia-based Niagara Movement, a national organization demanding full racial equality. Among strangers, the reality of race itself literally melted away as white Atlantans occasionally mistook the light-skinned descendants of slaves for "whites" on busy streets and in crowded streetcars. The ability of some blacks to pass as whites led some Caucasians to fear that they might accidentally fall in love with and marry a black man or woman.[37]

Along with such threats to traditional racial hierarchies, the central city's so-called filth and sin also embodied the fears whites had of the moral effects of urban growth and social dislocation on their own race. The pleasures associated with the saloons, dance halls, and brothels lining Decatur Street posed a direct threat to the moral authority and influence exercised by churches and patriarchal families over the sexual and moral behavior of sons, daughters, and even wives. On Decatur, even the most respectable man or woman might sin without notice or lasting disgrace. Tales circulated of unescorted white women carelessly enjoying nights on the town, of Chinese male immigrants seducing innocent white women into lives of opium addiction and prostitution, and of "respectable" men donning blackface at night to pursue "monstrous" lives of "shame and sorrow." Large numbers of black ministers, educators, and church members similarly condemned the "dancehells" and dives associated with Decatur Street. In contrast to their white counterparts, however, the black elites linked the "degradation" of young black men and women not to the new freedoms of city life but, rather, to Atlanta's "despicable discrimination," its crushing humiliations and insults, and its inadequate black schools.[38]

ATLANTA'S WHITE RESIDENTS, in summary, feared their city was perilously suspended between the certainties of timeworn traditions and the unpredictable consequences of contemporary social transformations. Individuals once embedded in a web of interlocking community relationships felt both liberated and threatened in the new urban environment. Whites and blacks alike pointed to Atlanta's contradictions. Its population and landscape were described as rural and urban, northern and southern, backward and modern. The same observers who praised Atlanta as a religious center also castigated it as a breeding ground for vice. White residents frequently voiced fears that social identities were in flux and under contestation as African Americans ceaselessly struggled to unfasten the remnants of slavery's shackles while whites almost universally sought to block blacks' advances toward full citizenship. White yeoman migrants fought to maintain their fierce pride in the face of the growing dependencies associated with financial debt and factory work. To the consternation of many fathers and husbands, white working women enjoyed new freedoms even as they encountered new forms of sexual harassment and exploitation. Black and white residents repeatedly commented that they were confronting a transitional moment in which established social hierarchies and moral boundaries were losing their hold. All that had once appeared solid now seemed to be melting away as capitalism and the railroad's transportation networks created new economic inequalities and undermined cultural and social sureties.[39]

As has often been the case among social groups in rapidly changing societies, many early twentieth-century whites represented their inchoate fears of social disruption via concrete symbols of impurity and pollution. What is striking, given the antiblack rantings of so many white social commentators, is the wide array of images marshaled by separate groups to represent different forms of perceived disorder. In pursuit of public attention, reformers deployed images of wealthy employers forcing underpaid white women into lives of prostitution and perverted Jewish capitalists despoiling innocent, young working girls. Despite the potential resonance of these alternative images, white residents repeatedly portrayed the sexual mixing of supposed racial bloodlines as the ultimate symbol of social disorder and transgression. Commentators described white Atlantans as exceptionally obsessed with maintaining racial purity. In many white men's minds, no image more viscerally embodied the nightmare of a world turned upside down—a world of black social assertion and sexual anarchy—than the image of a black man sexually assaulting a white woman, a crime defined as any form of physical contact implying sexual familiarity. This fear assumed a heightened power in early twentieth-century Atlanta as images of white women socially adrift commingled with images of black men cut loose from traditional white social and labor controls.[40]

Research suggests that a group's creation and deployment of a scapegoat representing all of society's ills is only the first phase of a multistage process. Once identified, this perceived public enemy becomes the focus for all of the frustrations and rage stemming from otherwise incomprehensibly abstract social transformations. In the process of creating scapegoats, social groups dehumanize "unclean" outsiders, thus generating the ethnic and racist hatreds that commonly underpin racial massacres and terrorist acts. The scapegoat's physical or symbolic sacrifice marks the culmination of the ritual process. This purification ritual metaphorically cleanses society of its tensions and corruptions while simultaneously providing an opportunity for diverse group members to reaffirm their shared identity as they emphasize their oneness in opposition to the sacrificial victim's moral contamination.[41] Participants often bring an intense sexualized energy to their sacrificial rites. These rituals' symbolic resolution of simmering social tensions through acts of physical violence metaphorically mirrors basic human sexual processes—that is, a highly charged sense of physical and emotional agitation followed by an orgasmic release and transition to a tension-free state. Out of the crucible of racial violence and black extermination there would emerge, many 1906 whites avowed, a new Atlanta, a city whose racial and gender boundaries were forever restored.

Black commentators, in contrast, overwhelmingly rejected white representations casting black men as the embodiments of pollution and the legitimate targets of white rage. In their minds, the social order's greatest threats were mob violence and white men's continued sexual exploitation of black women. As African Americans recognized, both of these crimes signified whites' continued refusal to recognize African Americans' free status and full citizenship. Enslavement, in its ideal form, represents a state of natal alienation—a condition in which individuals are "socially dead"—that is, utterly lacking any claims either to honor or to the legal rights and social ties that come with being a member of a family, a community, or a nation. A central marker of a woman's slave status in the antebellum South was whites' refusal to recognize the inviolability of her marriage vows and her claims to sexual virtue. African Americans thus associated freedom with the absence of white sexual aggression. There were also striking similarities between ritualistic lynching ceremonies and the enslavement process. Mob violence was reminiscent of the corporal punishments and physical degradations associated with slavery. In addition, lynching victims' utter isolation from their families' support, their community's protection, and their legal system's safeguards represented a social death similar to that inherent in slavery. These continuities explain Du Bois's characterization of slavery as "the arch-crime, and lynching and lawlessness its twin abortion."[42]

Lynching, in addition to serving as a means of labor control and a tool for the maintenance of white racial dominance, then, often assumed a ritual function. In the short term, the very transformations associated with Atlanta's modernization—including its growing national integration, its dramatic population growth, and its rapid commercialization and industrialization—aggravated racial tensions and encouraged whites to seek a sacrificial scapegoat as a means of explaining and symbolically resolving social tensions. Even in this highly combustible environment, however, whites' festering racist hatreds would explode into riot only through the determined efforts of human agitators and the blind inattention of public officials.[43]

CHAPTER TWO

Chivalry's Multiple Meanings

—⟡—

BY SEPTEMBER 1906, many whites and blacks recognized that, in one white journalist's sexually suggestive words, their city was "standing upon the crusty crater of a volcano now dangerously nearing eruptions." Throughout the summer, local newspapers, led by the *Atlanta Evening News* and the *Atlanta Georgian*, had trumpeted the social threats posed by black rapists and openly advocated torture and violence as the only solutions to this alleged crime wave. These newspapers' staffs understood that public fascination with black-on-white assaults helped boost sales in an intensely competitive market. The racist vituperations of the press tapped into broad white fears generated by the effects of Georgia's recent social transformations and Atlanta's rapid modernization. The troubled *News*, so fiscally strapped that it underwent financial reorganization in August, received hundreds of supportive letters, and its circulation reportedly doubled between August and September.[1]

Intraracial rivalry, rather than solidarity, among whites served as the riot's catalyst. Competition among white males for status and political power encouraged diverse groups to mass around this racist campaign. White agitators, far from forging a broad ideological consensus, fanned the flames of hatred to advance diverse, often conflicting goals. Their short-term political objectives ranged from disfranchisement to prohibition and from better labor conditions to enhanced public status for particular social groups.

Many struggling white farmers and workers embraced this racist crusade. By underscoring their dominance over black men and their role as patriarchal defenders of white women, these marginalized groups hoped to augment their waning social authority and reaffirm their equality with other whites.[2] Far from moving decisively to avert an escalating crisis, white elites and public officials signaled a willingness to condone racial violence. They also endorsed white agitators' inflated claims that black criminality was spiraling out of control. Meanwhile, white women and elite black men sought to transform a discourse aimed at their subordination into one that protected their interests and elevated their status.

IN 1906, VIVID portrayals of alleged black assaults in Atlanta newspapers represented an amplification of long-standing traditions. Since the 1890s, every imaginable media outlet had piped pornographic images of imperiled white womanhood into the city. Newspapers throughout the South were brimming with accounts of such crimes. During a 1905 Atlanta staging of Thomas Dixon's infamous *Clansman*, a riot almost broke out between African American and white audience members. White onlookers were captivated by the scene featuring thirteen-year-old Flora Cameron's desperate attempts to escape the clutches of a lecherous freedman named Gus. Cornered, Flora leaped from a cliff, choosing suicide to protect her virtue. At the drama's climax, the Atlanta audience screamed, "Lynch him," after the Ku Klux Klan (KKK) captured Gus. They then cheered at his ritual murder. When black audience members protested with loud hisses, the police silenced them and arrested a young black man following a violent struggle.[3]

Yet even as late as July 1906, local white newspapers carried stories of black assaults and attempted assaults without incorporating incendiary editorial comments and dire warnings of a coming crisis. Only after Annie Laurie Poole's 31 July allegation that a black man had brutally attacked her did the *News* begin portraying individual black assaults as part of an escalating local emergency. Poole identified Frank Carmichael as the man who had surprised her on an isolated road in Atlanta's Lakewood section and then choked her and forced her into the woods, where she lost consciousness. Spurred by newspaper extras describing the crime, white men from throughout the city descended on the suburb and killed Carmichael in "a roar of powder." Throughout August and September, *News* editors gleefully chronicled the putative exploits of black rapists and openly advocated lynching as a suitable punishment for their crimes.[4]

The city's other newspapers initially disregarded the *News*'s editorial campaign. Then, on 15 August, Georgia Hembree reported that while she had been walking to a trolley stop in Atlanta's northwestern suburbs, a black man had surprised her. After robbing her, the assailant allegedly threw her down and assaulted her. On 20 August, Ethel Lawrence, an English visitor in her twenties, and Mabel, her fourteen-year-old niece, electrified white Atlanta with their dramatic testimony of the violent struggle they had with an unidentified black man in a wooded area in Copenhill. Before the women could escape, their attacker had gouged out Ethel's eye and slit open the bridge of her nose. Mabel received minor facial lacerations.[5]

Newspaper stories and word-of-mouth reports of the Lawrences' awful ordeals fired white imaginations throughout the city. "No crime in Fulton county in years," the *Georgian* reported, "has so stirred up the people as the attack on Miss Lawrence and Miss Mabel Lawrence." During the week, white vigilantes had captured a number of black men and taken them to the Lawrence home, but Ethel had not identified anyone as her assailant. Rumors spread that white mobs had murdered several black suspects. In the wake of the Lawrence attack, the *Georgian* and the *Atlanta Journal* initiated their own antiblack campaigns. Newspapers joined white lynching advocates in describing as rapists black men attempting to break into white homes or merely walking near white women. On 24 August, for example, Mittie Waits accused a black man of following her and ordering her to stop in a wooded area nine miles outside Atlanta. Even though the suspect fled upon hearing Waits's screams, newspapers described the incident as an attempted assault, and white men from throughout Atlanta descended on her father's farm in eager pursuit of her attacker.[6]

Although the newspapers continued throughout September to warn of an escalating crime wave, there were, with the exception of Mrs. J. H. Gregory's testimony that a black man had grabbed and choked her, few, if any, reports of attempted assaults until Thursday, 20 September, two days before the riot. That day, a white mob surrounded Fort McPherson, located just south of the city, where police were holding a black man suspected of assaulting Etheleen Kimmel. At the sheriff's request, Governor Joseph Terrell called out two state militia companies to maintain order. Authorities released the suspect when Kimmel failed to identify him as her assailant.[7]

On Friday, 21 September, 400 white men gathered in front of the downtown police station in an unsuccessful attempt to wrest from the authorities a young black man accused of attempting to assault Orrie Bryan in her home in the city's center. The assault charge was based on Bryan's and her mother's testimony that the apparently drunk suspect, Lucius (or Luther) Frazier, had on the preceding night entered her family's house while only partially dressed, chased Orrie with a shoe in his hand, beat upon a closet door after she had locked herself in it, and professed that he loved her. As Frazier left the house, a crowd cornered him and turned him over to police. Mr. Bryan joined the men congregated at the courthouse that Friday and demanded that the judge release the suspect so that he could settle the case himself. The judge, reinforced by police, refused, and Frazier was placed in jail to await criminal trial.[8]

The next day, in the hours leading up to the riot, women and newspapers described even relatively innocuous encounters between white women and black men as attempted assaults. In the competitive war of editions, the white public rewarded editors who published first and asked questions later. On the evening of the riot, the *Journal*, the *Georgian*, and the *News* all offered city residents at least one extra edition headlining attempted black assaults against white women. The day after the riot, even the less sensationalistic *Constitution* linked the riot's outbreak to four alleged attempted rapes on 22 September. The so-called assaults and attempted assaults included an elderly woman's spying a black man peering into her window, a married woman's brief encounter with a black man "lurking in the bush," and an incident involving a man who allegedly forced a single woman to the ground before running away. Finally, Mattie Arnold informed neighbors that a black man had seized her and knocked her down while she was attempting to enter her back door. Newspapers widely described this encounter as an assault.[9]

In the absence of detailed court testimony regarding these alleged crimes, it is difficult to see through the distortions of white prejudice and the niceties of Victorian modesty to determine which, if any, of the white victims, besides Etheleen Kimmel and Georgia Hembree, were actually sexually assaulted. On city streets, whites often interpreted a black man's mere glance in a white woman's direction as evidence of malicious intent. Northern white journalist Ray Stannard Baker concluded, based on white testimony, that of the twelve assault charges against black men published in newspapers during the six months preceding the riot, only two involved actual rapes and only three were possible rape attempts. In addition to exaggerating the incidences of assaults and attempted assaults, reporters played on white prejudices to portray rape as a crime overwhelmingly perpetrated by black men against white women. While stories involving alleged black criminals were garnering headlines in 1906, white editors completely ignored or relegated to their newspapers' back pages similar incidents involving white men.[10]

In headlines and in editorial pages, these newspapers repeatedly portrayed individual crimes as part of a larger conspiracy pitting Atlanta's entire black male population against the city's white women. In the aftermath of the Lawrence assault, the *Georgian* contended, "If the negro were no longer a part of our population, the women of the South would be freed from their state of siege. . . . But under the black shadow of the fiendish passion of these ebony devils our women are as completely slaves as if they were in bondage to a conquering foe."[11] Eroticized descriptions of black criminals' exploits titillated readers and inflamed their passions. The *Georgian* and the *News* featured graphic descriptions of an "imp from hell fire" beating "a young woman almost to death in his heinous purpose of assaulting and outraging her, and destroying her honor and her hope, and her right to life, liberty, happiness and innocence." In a typical story, the *Georgian* reported how a "burly" black man had choked "a delicate, refined little woman," leaving her "almost prostrated from her terrible experience." The day before the riot, the *News* painted the "terrifying spectacle" of a partially undressed Frazier, "his yellow lips forming insulting phrases" as his "hand brushed against her [Orrie Bryan's] clothing."[12]

AS PUBLISHERS CLEARLY recognized, accounts of black men raping virginal white women yanked at the very core of the social identity of local white men, heirs as they were to a chivalric tradition that equated status and honor with the ability of men to protect and guard their female dependents from outside threats. Far from exclusive to a particular class, key tenets of this chivalric code were reiterated in letter after letter to the newspapers from a wide range of Georgians, including Protestant ministers, commercial leaders, rural farmers, owners of small businesses, and workers. This chivalric code had a long history and influenced a wide range of Georgians and other southerners. On a personal level, the determination of white male residents to prevent such crimes and apprehend black perpetrators reflected a desire to protect their own family members from possible attack. In late August, the *Georgian* bemoaned the mounting "terror" and "apprehension" experienced by men forced to leave their homes unguarded when they went to work. On a broader level, the duty of men to protect white women from outside sexual pollution extended beyond the family to their neighborhoods, their city, and, ultimately, the South at large.[13]

The *News*'s and the *Georgian*'s frequent clarion calls for men to fulfill their chivalric duties assumed a heightened immediacy in an Atlanta in which the masculine authority of husbands and fathers over their female dependents was being eroded both by women's increased public presence and by the new freedoms available in a rapidly growing city. Stories of white women's need for protection enhanced the psychological and social power of men over their female counterparts. "Citizen" joined other white male Atlantans in reaffirming his traditional role and long-standing prerogatives in a new urban context: "The most sacred interest on earth," he reminded fellow readers, is the "protection of a man's mother, wife, sister or daughter." A man, he concluded, "would not be much of a hero who would even go through fire or blood for the protection of these interests."[14] That summer women reported feeling "sick with fear and apprehension" at the terrible dangers they might encounter in the absence of their husbands whether at home or in the city's public spaces. One woman complained, "It takes away the joy of living, and no doubt, shortens ones life." This escalating sense of dread exiled many women from the city's public spaces and encouraged them to stay with family friends when their husbands left town. Upon arriving in Atlanta two months after the riot, journalist Ray Stannard Baker was surprised to find women so terrified that they "dare not leave their homes alone after dark."[15]

In white men's minds, a black man's assault on a white woman also constituted a power grab for black political and social dominance. The cultural heritage of white Georgians had long predicated claims to masculine power and independence on the ability of men to protect female dependents from sexual seduction and aggression. Both the inability of white men to safeguard white women from black assaults and their failure to avenge crimes against white women's virtue signaled their submission to blacks and their public and political emasculation. As a result, the string of alleged black assaults humiliated all white men and challenged their claims to racial supremacy. In a letter seeking to reaffirm his own and other white men's racial and gender dominance, Hugh Wallace advocated a popular solution to the alleged crime wave: "Let us meet this great question like men—and let us with the consent and cooperation of our mothers and our sisters settle this thing for now and forever—by letting the negro know that he is a 'hewer of wood and a drawer of water,' and that if he values his life or anything he has got, he must stay—now and forever—in the negro's place."[16]

From the onset of the newspapers' campaign to its conclusion, white Atlantans overwhelmingly blamed their city's crime wave on the "strange negro" cut off from the restraining influences of white employers and white social institutions. On 17 August, the *News* announced a willingness to stake its "printing press that the four brutal negroes who have . . . outraged or attempted to outrage four of the white women of this county in recent months were idlers, loafers, and vagrants on the streets of Atlanta or along the roadsides of this county." The passions of this "low, vicious, uneducated element" were first stoked in the "slums, dance halls and negro resorts at Decatur Street." After committing assaults and petty crimes, these outlaws, their identities unknown to any whites, could "make good their escape in the swamps and woods" until the "sentiment of the people" subsided, and they would "again roam the city and the county districts without fear of arrest."[17]

These anonymous African Americans, white commentators argued, posed the greatest danger in those zones of the city, such as the suburbs and the Five Points area, that were impervious to firm white control and rigid Jim Crow segregation. "Where find more horrible contact," the *News* bemoaned on 24 August, "than is witnessed every day in our own city of Atlanta, where the refinement, culture and modesty of our women is contaminated by being forced to come in bodily contact with the lowest class of dirty, repulsive negro laborers?" Given white racial assumptions interpreting any close contact between white women and black men as dishonorable, many white Atlantans probably reached the same conclusion as Clarence Jester: "It has got to where a lady cannot walk the streets of Atlanta without being insulted by a negro."[18]

In the minds of these whites, sexual intercourse between black men and white women was the ultimate signifier of black freedom from white intimidation and control. Many feared these "strange negroes" because they represented the antithesis of the dependent slave, servant, or sharecropper whose labor and freedom were constrained by white employers. Because of their profound uneasiness with black men liberated from traditional white controls, whites proposed new police efforts, exiling black men from the city to workhouses, to convict lease camps, or "into the country" to "work for some farmer who needs his labor." Whites' overriding fears of black independence are most clearly apparent in the ease and frequency with which white commentators shifted the attention of their attacks from these "strange negroes" to African Americans whose economic and educational progress might otherwise have signaled a commitment to manly self-discipline. White letter writers repeatedly censured black ministers and black educators for encouraging black assaults by teaching their parishioners and students that they were the social equals of whites.[19]

White commentators generally agreed that trials by jury and the death penalty were inadequate means of restraining black passions and stamping out other forms of black resistance. Some whites suggested the complete

Atlanta Georgian editor
John Temple Graves, 1911.
(Library of Congress)

elimination of blacks from the South through extermination or mass deportation; others advocated making "eunuchs of all the new male issues before
they are eight days old."[20] White racist agitators repeatedly linked the efficacy
of a punishment with its ability to signify graphically on their bodies the
utter subordination of black men. Only the horror of torture and physical
terror, many whites averred, could cow African Americans into submission.
Georgian editor and native southerner John Temple Graves, who had won
fame and fortune on the Chautauqua circuit by "preaching the separation of
the races from Maine to California," struggled to identify a legal replacement
for extralegal violence that would adequately awe black men. Graves advocated the invention of "some new and mysterious mode of punishment—the
passing over a slender bridge into a dark chamber where in utter darkness
and in utter mystery that assailant of woman's virtue would meet a fate which
his friends would never know and which he himself would never come back
to understand. Darkness, mystery, uncertainty have always been deterrent
influences upon the minds of this ignorant and superstitious race."[21] This
solution embodied both Graves's own subconscious fixation on phallic images of penetration and an ironic symbolic re-creation of the very crime he

sought to eradicate. Most tellingly, this sexualized vision also symbolically represented a reaffirmation of whites' utter dominance over formerly restive black men, now utterly degraded and isolated from any family or community protection.

In white minds, no mode of retribution except overpowering violence could demonstrate the marginal position of African Americans and whites' determination to punish black transgressions against the dominant social order. Indeed, many whites viewed punishments secured through the criminal justice system as both admissions of their own weakness and affirmations of black power and legal rights. Like many letter writers, the *News* protested against the formal mechanisms of the criminal justice system precisely because its rules and regulations afforded accused African Americans the opportunities, however slight, to avoid any retribution whatsoever for their alleged crimes. Trials, an editor argued, only reminded African Americans of "the ease with which they can escape punishment by securing the services of an unscrupulous lawyer, who will dilly-dally with justice . . . until, perhaps, they find an opportunity to escape from jail, secure commutation of their sentence to imprisonment instead of hanging by their necks on the gallows, as they deserve."[22]

DESPITE WHITE MEN's widely shared desires to shore up racial and patriarchal dominance, the newspapers' summonses to protect white women reverberated differently in the minds of varied groups, depending on their social position. Because the city's and the state's social transformations helped to accelerate class divisions and affected varying groups in different ways, clear divisions arose among white Georgians regarding the meaning of chivalry and which white men it empowered. A desire for the claims to manhood embodied in white chivalry must have burned fiercest in two white groups: Atlanta's emergent working class, and small farmers and tenants who continued to engage in agricultural pursuits on the city's fringes. Overwhelmingly composed of yeoman farmers and their descendants, these groups were raised to view the assertion of equality with, and independence from, other men as a rite of passage to adulthood and manliness. As tenant farmers or factory workers in Fulton County, these men daily faced humiliating reminders of their new dependence—in every payment they made to creditors, in every thought of losing their land or being fired, in every order or criticism issued by bosses or supervisors, and in every belittling glance they encountered on city streets. Threatened as they were with declining economic prospects and a loss of personal autonomy, these men could reclaim their lost social status by embracing a code that elevated all white men to a privileged position of guardianship over white women and dominance over African Americans.[23]

Despite the potential psychological benefits offered by rigid racial demarcations, a number of yeoman farmers and members of Georgia's white working class had sporadically sought the cooperation of African Americans in attempts to unite the two races around their mutual class interests. Fiery Populist leader Tom Watson, who in the 1890s had challenged the Democratic Party's dominance in state political affairs, had been the most famous advocate of interracial cooperation. Even as he supported segregation in "private" affairs, Watson focused on the political powerlessness and economic suffering endured by all farmers, black and white alike, as they confronted plummeting cotton prices, usurious interest rates, and exorbitant freight costs. Only through a biracial alliance, Watson maintained, could the producing classes challenge the political power of bankers, railroad magnates, and other moneyed interests. Yet Watson's attempts at forging a biracial coalition were repeatedly thwarted as a consequence of numerous Democratic machinations, including the appropriation of the least radical Populist proposals, the manipulation of white fears of black political participation, and the use of wealthy whites' overwhelming economic and political influence to mobilize black voters against Populist candidates.[24] In Atlanta's nascent labor movement, the 1890s brought a gradual hardening of racial divisions that mirrored trends throughout the city. Yet as historian Clifford Kuhn has demonstrated, black bricklayers held positions on an integrated union's grievance committee as late as 1897. A year later, the city's unions refused to participate in a parade when its organizers banned black workers' participation.[25]

Ironically, the very social marginality that prompted some yeoman farmers and factory workers to recognize their shared political and economic interests with blacks could also lead these same groups to view African Americans as their most threatening competitors for jobs and status. Watson, for example, disillusioned by his political defeats, abandoned his erstwhile black allies in the early 1900s. Now a perennial People's Party presidential candidate, Watson controlled the votes of approximately 23,000 white Georgian supporters. He became convinced that his party's political influence in Georgia was undermined both by the Democrats' ability to purchase and manipulate blacks' votes and by white fears that a vote against the Democrats was a vote for "Negro domination." By 1904, Watson had concluded that he could regain political influence only by trading the votes of his loyal followers for influence over Democratic politicians. As he sought enhanced power via an alliance with the Democrats, Watson characterized African Americans, not his white opponents, as democracy's despoilers. "Wherever we have been defeated at the polls," he concluded, "we have been beaten by the negro who sold his vote." Linking black political power with black men's sexual degradation of white women, Watson accused black politicos in New York City of holding white women in a "state of slavery, *to minister to their lusts.*" By the early 1900s, white supremacy was also increasingly appealing to Atlanta's white working class. The 1890s and early 1900s brought renewed attempts at white racial exclusionism within unions, culminating in a series of strikes organized by textile workers and machine operatives to prevent the hiring of blacks for jobs traditionally regarded as white. In June 1906, the Georgia Federation of Labor, fearing that the increased use of black laborers would lower white wages, petitioned the state's railroads to exclude blacks from skilled positions by arguing that black men were not smart enough to comprehend orders and signals.[26]

The increased entry of women into Atlanta's labor market inordinately affected this class of white workers and farmers. It was predominately their wives and daughters who left the household to work in factories in order to supplement their husbands' and fathers' inadequate incomes or to take advantage of the freedoms promised by wage labor. While the social status and economic security of these white farmers and workers were declining, their dominant role in the household economy was also diminishing, and their female relatives were embracing new opportunities and confronting new dangers outside the home. As much as any other whites, men from these classes discovered a special satisfaction in a white republican chivalry that proclaimed all white men to be guardians of white women's virtue. This formulation elevated all white males to a shared status above every African American, and it legitimized all white men's claims to public authority. This ideology's implicit promise to equalize the social and political status of all white men by affirming their race's permanent superiority and domination over blacks can be likened to the "herrenvolk egalitarianism" described by George Fredrickson and other scholars.[27]

This egalitarian strain of white chivalry was echoed in Atlanta newspaper articles and letters to the editor exhorting southern men to "organize a solid phalanx" against black criminals. This formulation also surfaced in proposals that "every man . . . in Fulton County . . . be made a deputy, with all the deputies' rights and authorities and with the will and power to make every suspicious negro character give an account of himself." Indeed, the defense of extralegal violence by the *News* and its allies centered on populist claims that mobs of white men embodied "the people's wish." As "A Friend" argued in a letter to the editor denouncing public officials' efforts at protecting African Americans from lynching, "Do not the people make the laws? Do not the people put the judges on the bench? . . . This being the case, why should the Atlanta police department take it upon themselves to thwart the wish of the people to whom they are indebted for their very existence[?]"[28] By the very act of joining the mobs patrolling the city and county, white Atlantans, whatever their social class, were explicitly claiming positions of community leadership and authority as upholders of public order and white supremacy.

Some supporters of this chivalric vision openly questioned white businessmen's own claims to manly leadership. "Athena," a nom de plume for female labor advocate O. Delight Smith, argued that southern white commercial leaders were providing African Americans with excessive rights and privileges in hopes of ensuring their loyalty as workers. "Has it come to pass," she wondered, "that the sons of this grand old Southland shall let their love of money and commercialism override their care and thought of womanhood?" In response to his own question regarding why white business and civic leaders were not taking effective action against black rapists, "Junius" asserted, "I can tell you—for the negro's labor—to get more wealth for the South out of him. It is commercialism willing to trade on ravished white women! Oh proud Anglo-Saxon race, chivalrous cavaliers of the South, you once were kingly men, lords of creation, but you have sold your birthright for a mess of pottage! You have fallen too low to act as protectors of your women." Their very desires to "retain cheap labor" and depress white wages, some letter writers thundered, encouraged these "arrogant aristocrats" to provide African Americans with "too many rights and too many privileges" and prevented their supporting the expulsion of African Americans from the South or the use of wide-scale violence to terrorize them. As these advocates' writings suggest, this particular construction of chivalry, one that utterly excluded blacks from claiming any social and economic rights, offered dispossessed whites both enhanced economic opportunities and a shared equality with all whites, even the wealthiest and most powerful.[29]

On 17 August, *News* editor Charles Daniel announced his offer of a $1,000 reward for the capture, conviction, or murder of those "guilty wretches who violate the sanctity of southern womanhood." Eight days later, the board of county commissioners, spurred to action by this and other calls to arms, offered a $500 reward for the capture and conviction of any black rapist. At the meeting, Sheriff John Nelms, his body shaking and voice quivering, vowed that "we will suppress these great indignities upon our fair wives and daughters if we have to kill every negro within a thousand miles of this place." "The time has come," he proclaimed, "when every man who is worthy of the name must rise in the might and power of manhood and put a stop to such crimes." Nelms's apparent endorsement of vigilante justice and the empowerment of all white men in defense of white womanhood was even more striking, given that he had repeatedly forced back white mobs in the past. On 26 August, Daniel announced his intent to organize a "News Protective League" that would be "identical" to the KKK. The following day, anonymous handbills began circulating in Atlanta announcing an organizational meeting to revive the infamous Klan itself.[30]

BUSINESS LEADERS AND lawyers generally perceived Daniel's league as a challenge both to law enforcement officials' authority and to their own informal influence over public affairs. Following Daniel's public announcement of his proposed vigilante organization, more than 300 white businessmen, lawyers, and ministers held a public meeting and signed a petition warning city residents that the Klan and similar organizations might be composed of "good" men but risked falling into the hands of the irresponsible, thereby triggering "friction, riot, and chaos." As the group's leader, W. D. Ellis reminded Atlantans that the petitioners represented the "men who pay the taxes"—that is, Atlanta's wealthiest and most respected managers and business owners, including Chamber of Commerce officials. The body appointed a twenty-five member committee to push their own anticrime proposals before the city council on 4 September. Prior to their forum, these men had largely ignored the potential dangers posed by the newspapers' incendiary campaigns.[31]

Opposition by business leaders to the News Protective League reflected not merely fears that their own authority would be challenged but also their desire to preserve the order necessary to safeguard factory production, commercial trade, and their city's national image. "Rube Hayseed" and other commentators recognized the tensions between a herrenvolk chivalry that protected white women at all costs and the business community's conservative desires to maintain order and prevent the negative national publicity that widespread white vigilantism might generate. Noting "the long list of merchants who condemn the proposed Ku-Klux Klan," "Hayseed" argued that they "by no means . . . represent the masses." "The masses are determined," he concluded, "this thing shall stop, but would indorse even Ku-Kluxism as a means of last resort."[32]

These businessmen's efforts represented a rejection of the methods and leadership of vigilantism rather than a fundamental questioning of the city's anticrime crusade. Even as their petition criticized Daniel's KKK proposal, the document never questioned his newspaper's underlying assertion that white womanhood was under siege in Atlanta, imperiled by the sexual designs of thousands of black rapists awaiting opportunities to strike. In addition to advocating additional new police hires to patrol the city's suburbs, the businessmen's meeting also called upon existing officials to arrest "tramps, vagabonds and well known criminals" and to force the closure of the cheap downtown saloons and restaurants catering to blacks. Winning the audience's applause and endorsement, Judge George Hillyer called for "radical" changes in the administration of criminal law to enhance its swiftness and certainty. Other speakers advocated the enforcement of stricter segregation measures. Daniel, perhaps in an effort to regain white civic leaders' trust, spoke at the meeting and endorsed its measures. White elites abandoned their reform efforts once the *News*'s editor canceled his vigilante plans, and the commercial leaders never sought dialogue with Atlanta's black elite or middle class. Later that September, Chamber of Commerce secretary Walter G. Cooper and other business and civic leaders reentered the public debate over mob violence only to dismiss as false a nationally syndicated news article claiming that a Klanlike organization was patrolling Atlanta. These misrepresentations, prominent elites argued, threatened to "injure the entire South" and seriously damage the city's national standing.[33]

Concerns with Atlanta's image thus motivated commercial leaders to evade rather than directly confront the gathering threat posed by white racist agitation. Their own connections with incendiary newspapers and racial demagogues reinforced this impulse. For example, Linton Hopkins, the leader of the delegation appointed to visit the city council, was the brother of Charles T. Hopkins, a member of the *News*'s board of directors. Ellis, Chamber of Commerce president Sam D. Jones, and other prominent participants in the campaign against Daniel's league were close friends and supporters of Hoke Smith, that summer's leading political advocate of disfranchisement and racial exclusionism.[34]

IN JULY 1905, Smith, a local litigator and former *Journal* owner, had entered Georgia's 1906 gubernatorial race on a broad reform plank that included support for black disfranchisement and increased railroad regulation.

1906 gubernatorial candidate Hoke Smith, ca. 1912. (Library of Congress)

Smith's disfranchisement stance secured influential Populist leader Tom Watson's support. Political opponent Clark Howell, a perennial Democratic insider who owned the *Constitution*, nevertheless remained confident that he might emerge victorious from the race. Howell countered the particulars of Smith's disfranchisement proposals with images that attempted to pre-empt Smith's racist thunder. "This is a white man's country," the editor repeatedly emphasized, "and it must be governed by white men." In speeches and editorials, Howell criticized Smith's disfranchisement provisions as undermining white supremacy. Smith's support for restricting the vote through literacy qualifications, the editor warned, would block thousands of disadvantaged whites from voting and encourage blacks to seek an academic education. Howell attempted to frighten audiences with images of African Americans "getting bow-legged with the burden of carrying their books to school" as they sought to abandon the "cotton patch" for black colleges.[35] Howell's attacks on black education and Smith's attacks on black voting rights particularly menaced African Americans' civil rights because both white men had once enjoyed reputations for relative racial moderation. By advocating disfranchisement, Smith was striking at one of the few black civil

1906 gubernatorial candidate and *Atlanta Constitution* editor Clark Howell. (Library of Congress)

rights still nominally protected by the state constitution. By linking all forms of black education with social disorder, Howell was threatening both the survival of African American public and private schools and any hopes of long-term black economic and social progress.

In the summer of 1906, Smith and his business allies purposefully took advantage of the rape scare's timing, coinciding as it did with the frantic last month of gubernatorial campaigning. On 1 August, the *Journal*, edited by Smith's campaign manager, James Gray, capitalized on the emotional atmosphere following the alleged assault against Annie Poole. Twenty days before the scheduled Democratic primary, the newspaper directly linked the crime of black-on-white rape with Clark Howell and the *Constitution*'s opposition to the passage of a disfranchisement measure. According to Smith and his political supporters, all black men were potential rapists. Voting rights emboldened and empowered African Americans to defy racial barriers and white authority throughout the city. The editorial concluded,

POLITICAL EQUALITY BEING THUS PREACHED TO THE NEGRO IN THE PA-
PERS AND ON THE STUMP, WHAT WONDER THAT HE MAKES NO DISTINC-
TION BETWEEN POLITICAL AND SOCIAL EQUALITY. HE GROWS MORE BUMP-

TIOUS ON THE STREET, MORE IMPUDENT IN HIS DEALING WITH WHITE MEN; AND THEN, WHEN HE CANNOT ACHIEVE SOCIAL EQUALITY AS HE WISHES WITH THE INSTINCT OF A BARBARIAN TO DESTROY WHAT HE CANNOT ATTAIN TO, HE LIES IN WAIT, AS THAT DASTARDLY BRUTE DID YESTERDAY NEAR THIS CITY, AND ASSAULTS THE FAIR YOUNG GIRLHOOD OF THE SOUTH.[36]

The next day, Smith's campaign organ warned that offering Georgia blacks any hope of political and social equality would inevitably result in a "blind, unreasoning revolt on the part of the negro against his destiny" and the commission of the "one crime more heinous than all others." The *Journal*'s rhetorical attacks linking black political participation with rape spoke directly to its white audience's profound chivalric fears of black equality, interracial sex, and female sexuality. On 22 August 1906, Smith rolled over his opponents in the Democratic primary, an achievement tantamount to securing elective office, while Howell placed third in the contest, securing majorities in only six counties.[37]

The 1906 campaign signaled the Populists' and Democrats' utter abandonment of any pretense that they endorsed any form of black educational or economic progress. Smith, Howell, and their supporters in the business community—despite their divisions—joined Watson in advocating the absolute submission of African Americans to whites politically, socially, and economically. Much like the champions of lynching, these men broadcast a rhetoric that equated even the slightest hint of black advancement with the commission of black sexual assaults. The 1906 election and Smith's dramatic political victory provided both radical racism and mob violence a new legitimacy, with both antiblack bludgeons now having the clear endorsement of Georgia's leading politicians and many of its white voters.

LIKE HOWELL AND Smith, Georgia's Anti-Saloon League leadership also manipulated images of the "strange negro" to gain entry into Atlanta's public debate and promote its own narrow political agenda. As late as 13 September, William D. Upshaw, superintendent of Atlanta's Anti-Saloon League and editor of the *Golden Age*, used his religious weekly to condemn both lynching and the creation of vigilante organizations. The relative racial moderation that Upshaw and other Anti-Saloon League members continued to display during much of the summer of 1906 reflected a long tradition of interracial cooperation among prohibitionists that dated back to the 1880s. During that decade, white prohibitionists—led by ministers, religious laypersons, and

WCTU members—had viewed at least some African Americans, especially religious leaders, as potential allies in their struggle against alcohol. Although many ardent black reformers never wavered in their opposition to the saloons, black politicians and the masses of black voters had proved to be fickle temperance advocates, alternately siding with "wets" and "drys" in hopes of taking political advantage of white divisions. In the 1890s, however, Democratic leaders, fearful that prohibition parties and any form of interracial alliance might undermine their influence, adopted the white primary and agreed tacitly among themselves never to amend the saloon laws enacted in 1887. By 1906, most prohibitionists had become divided and dispirited. Their faith in the possibility of an immediate dry victory flagged under the weight of repeated defeats and Democrats' intransigence.[38]

In September 1906, however, concerns with black crime turned the attention of white newspapers and white civic leaders to the cheap restaurants and saloons along Decatur Street. A night on the town reputedly prepared even the most timid blacks for an attack on white womanhood. Prohibition leaders and ministers grasped the new opportunities that heightened concerns about black crime and drinking might provide them in gaining publicity for their battle against the saloons. When white fears of black crime were at their height, J. C. Solomon, a Methodist minister and superintendent of the state Anti-Saloon League, warned white Atlantans that as long as they kept the "lust-exciting, crime-producing" saloons open, black men would continue to be "a horrible menace day and night." "Tank him up on booze and his beastial nature is aroused. Full of liquor, full of lust, and the black brute makes toward a white woman." Some of the white ministers and Christian laymen who filled the temperance movement's ranks had criticized mob violence in the past, but their protests had been sporadic and never gave shape to a sustained antilynching movement. In August and September 1906, Atlanta's white ministry largely ignored the growing threat of mob violence. Of the three white ministers who publicly expressed opinions on law-and-order issues, two openly applauded the News Protective League. Only John E. White, pastor of the exclusive Second Baptist Church, attacked the editorials in the *News* and chided his fellow whites for refusing to take a vocal stand against mob violence.[39]

WHITE WOMEN'S DIVERSE reactions to the newspapers' campaign similarly reflected the growing social and economic divisions aggravated by the city's rapid social transformations. Ironically, the very newspaper editorials seeking to elevate white men's status as guardians of their female dependents simultaneously promised white women some new powers and heightened access to the city's public discourse. Both the *Georgian* and the *News*, for example, lionized as heroines those women who successfully resisted black rapists. This journalistic practice may explain some of the false reports regarding alleged attempted assaults that summer. Some women may have falsely claimed that they had resisted black rapists as a means of winning public commendation. The *News* even advocated addressing the city's law-and-order crisis by providing every white woman with the ultimate male symbol of public power: a "firearm sufficiently effective to protect her from assault." There is little evidence that any households adopted this proposal. Had they, potential white female victims could no doubt have used these guns to protect themselves from their most likely attackers, white men, especially abusive husbands and fathers. Still, repeated criticisms of male violence and acknowledgment of women's "God-given sanctity" by white newspapers and politicians could, many white women may have hoped, become an ideological weapon to deploy against both white and black abusers.[40]

In addition, chivalry's affirmation of white women's shared nobility elevated the status of all females and provided them with forceful social weapons. White men's frenzied willingness to mutilate and brutalize alleged black rapists dramatically reinforced white women's power in relation to black men, who no doubt gave their potential accusers an increasingly wide berth in Atlanta's public spaces during the late summer of 1906. As early as 1897, working-class white women had taken advantage of honor's prerogatives in successfully battling the attempts of Atlanta's Fulton Bag and Cotton Mills and other employers to integrate some work assignments, thereby potentially lowering female workers' wages. At the turn of the century, white residents increasingly complained of the escalating resistance of black domestic workers to white authority and their growing willingness to abandon their white employers. A northern journalist described hearing in 1906 countless complaints of black women challenging white women's claims to superiority both on the job and in the streets. Even little black girls had been arrested for reportedly saying "obscene things to little white girls" and taunting whites that restive domestic workers had already "brought white Southern women to the kitchen and soon would bring them to the washtubs." In the face of these growing challenges by black females, many white women undoubtedly recognized newspaper endorsements of their exclusive claims to womanly honor as potentially empowering and reassuring.[41]

Yet chivalry was always at best a double-edged sword for women—one that ultimately sought their silence and submission. White women believed to have been sexually violated by black men (or even by white men) were so utterly disgraced and dishonored that they often fled the city in shame. A small group of women suffragists and temperance reformers were sensitized to these trade-offs by their political programs and middle- to upper-class status. They sought to reorient the public discourse on criminality and chivalry both by affirming white women's right to exercise public power and by highlighting white men's sexual and physical abuse of white women. These women rightly understood that white females were victimized almost exclusively by men of their own race and that men's chivalric claims posed a threat to women's independence and social authority. The only truly effective means of protecting white women, they argued, was the passage of laws that simultaneously restricted men's ability to arbitrarily abuse their authority and provided women with the rights necessary to defend themselves and their interests.[42]

Suffragist Vara A. Majette, for example, blamed newspapers for helping to fan the flames of fear among white women. By rejecting the assumption that all white men had the moral authority to protect all white women, she challenged the potentially egalitarian impulses underlying the *News*'s calls for the creation of a protective league. "If riot, bloodshed and extermination must come in the name of justice," she countered, then "let it be by men who are fit guardians of the South's honor." Similarly, the WCTU was one of the few white reform organizations in Atlanta that shunned racialized attacks against African Americans prior to the riot. Its leaders never wavered in their quest to discourage public drinking among all men, regardless of their race or social position. Woman suffrage advocate and WCTU leader Mary Latimer McLendon championed a "protection that does protect" and asserted that "gamblers, drunkards, libertines, and men of generally bad character should not be considered in any capacity as protectors of women."[43]

McLendon accepted the elevated status accorded to women by the chivalric code, but in a mode that attempted to empower women and allow them to participate in public affairs. White women, she realized, confronted a patriarchal society without access to the ballot and other forms of public authority. A narrow focus on the exploits of black criminals, McLendon contended, encouraged whites to ignore other "matters that concern women so vitally," especially the myriad ways in which white men endangered both women and the integrity of the family. Real protection for women and the home could come only through new laws controlling the behavior of men and forcing them to live up to their role as guardians. "As a general rule the women do not want whisky," she argued, "and those who suffer daily and hourly from the consuming outrage of the drunkard in the home would say if they could with power: 'Keep the deadly poison out of the reach of my husband, father, son or brother, and from the negro brutes whose passions are inflamed by it when they commit their dastardly outrages.'" In addition to prohibition, she maintained, protecting women and the family also required both the passage of laws securing woman suffrage and changes in a notorious state law that placed the age of sexual consent at ten years. Majette similarly advocated new controls on the sexuality of white men, stressing that men who were genuinely concerned with racial purity should acknowledge the occurrence of sexual intercourse between white men and black women—"the result is the same, outraged nature and degradation of our Southern blood."[44] Yet even as they asserted that white men had the same propensity for crime as black men, these female reformers never directly criticized lynching or white supremacy.

White male violence against black women was a problem of relatively little concern to either the *News* or other white male commentators. Rapes committed by white men against black women (or even against white women) lacked the symbolic import of black-on-white assaults, which white men perceived as a challenge to both their dominance over black men and their control over the sexuality of their white wives and daughters. Many white men must have viewed the violation of black women as a symbolic representation of their own potency, not only in regard to black women but to black men as well. Chivalric assumptions condoned sexual violence against black women, whom whites cast as inherently impure and dishonored.[45]

WHAT WAS MOST striking about the antiblack crusade during the summer of 1906, then, was the wide range of whites—including law enforcement officials, Populists, once racially progressive white Democrats, white businessmen, white ministers, and white prohibitionists—who deliberately deployed provocative racist images in pursuit of their own narrow political and economic goals. Ironically, white men massed together around the image of the black rapist and the privileges of chivalry not as a sign of growing unity but because of heightened social inequality and the rise of fierce political rivalries. Influential whites' refusal to condemn lynching and white newspapers' dehumanizing racist characterizations helped make the Atlanta riot possible. What was publicly spoken and unspoken allowed mob participants to claim that they were acting on behalf of all white citizens. Many white racists became convinced that public officials would certainly tolerate and perhaps endorse extreme violence as a means of protecting all that white southern men most treasured: their equality with (or superiority over) other whites, their role as guardians of white women's purity, and most of all, the certainty of their supremacy over African Americans.

CHAPTER THREE

Voicing Black Manliness

———

D URING THE SUMMER OF 1906, white racist agitators linked black assaults not simply with alleged black rogues but also with a rising class of black teachers, ministers, and newspaper editors. In late August, the *Georgian* initiated an editorial series that fingered black institutional leaders as direct contributors to the black rapist's crimes: "The negro mass, hearing the preacher, and heeding the teacher, takes to his heart . . . the deadly conclusion that, in the eyes of his leaders, rape is a light fault of passing moment, but that lynching is an awful crime for which his race furnishes the lamented and strangled martyrs." The newspaper cautioned ministers and educators that any resistance to the city's current anticrime crusade would only provoke destructive violence against black institutions. "The shelter from which these criminals emerge and the shelter in which they are protected or helped to escape," the *Georgian* vowed, "should be put under the same martial law that Sherman found to be so effective."[1]

The *Georgian*'s newest campaign posed in stark, life-or-death terms a central dilemma with which diverse black civil rights strategists had long wrestled. Since Reconstruction, white racists had successfully deployed characterizations of black men's moral depravity and mental inferiority to marginalize them as "unmanly" and to legitimize vicious assaults against their human rights and physical bodies. In response, many black activists had long embraced a politics of respectability that cited black men's educational, moral, and economic achievements as evidence of their fitness for equality. Tragically, however, black men's accomplishments, far from ameliorating white prejudices, often only intensified white men's determination to block further black progress. White landholders and businesspersons hoped to profit from black labor rather than welcome potential black competitors into their exclusive circle. Economically and politically marginalized whites often interpreted black elite claims to manliness as threats to their own privileged white status.[2]

The riddle presented to Atlanta's black professionals, then, was one that they had yet to answer fully: How could black elites challenge pernicious white stereotypes of black inferiority without triggering a crushing white backlash? In the past, black men had addressed this dilemma with strategies ranging from integration to black separatism, from public silence to open protests. With Atlanta's white newspapers calling for the wholesale murder of recalcitrant African Americans, black professionals desperately sought new solutions to an old puzzle. Their responses affected not only their own self-conceptions but also how they positioned themselves in relation to female and working-class blacks.

INTO THE EARLY 1900s, the most visible and influential black American was Booker T. Washington, the Tuskegee Normal School principal who was nicknamed the "Wizard" for his formidable political talents and the sheer power he derived from his near-monopoly on black access to powerful white politicians and philanthropists. It was from Atlanta that Washington broadcast his famous 1895 Atlanta Exposition address—the speech that outlined his solution to the problem of hardening white racism and catapulted him into the national spotlight. Washington argued that materialist concerns would lead whites to abandon prejudice once they recognized racism's high financial costs.[3] He maintained that, despite any differences temporarily dividing white and black southerners, they would always share a mutual interest in the economic development of their desperately poor region. Blacks should not openly agitate against segregation and disfranchisement. Direct black attacks against Jim Crow threatened to exacerbate the racial violence and white prejudice impeding black progress. Blacks would win the admiration of southern whites by quietly accumulating wealth and following an uncompromising individual moral code centered on the values of thrift, sobriety, and hard work. Once blacks established their trustworthiness and economic indispensability, Washington anticipated that white prejudice would wither away. Forward-looking, profit-seeking southern

Booker T. Washington, 1902, the year after the publication of his bestselling *Up from Slavery*. (Library of Congress)

white businessmen would inevitably link their own financial interests and desires for social stability with the eradication of mob violence and other injustices. "The Negro merchant who owns the largest store in town," Washington promised, "will not be lynched." Washington consistently supported interracial cooperation at the local level between elite whites and their black counterparts as a means of allaying racial tensions. Calls by blacks for national intervention in southern affairs, Washington asserted, only alienated white southern moderates.[4]

The Wizard opaquely refuted white Social Darwinist assertions of permanent black inferiority by claiming a "civilized" identity for black men grounded in their material success and their acquisition of the visible self-discipline and sobriety associated with middle- and working-class respectability. Washington tirelessly ridiculed the classics as inappropriate for black Americans just as he dismissed academicians as pretentious dreamers. Only practical training, he maintained, truly promised manly financial independence and self-confidence. The ideal black man, the Wizard suggested, remained in the South. He stoically and silently avoided direct conflicts with whites in service of his race while pursuing practical ambitions rather than artistic and academic distinctions. In the early 1900s, Washington occasionally spearheaded legal challenges against segregation and disfranchisement, but only covertly. He promoted white Republican support for civil rights but did so almost exclusively behind the scenes.[5]

Washington might have felt more secure in his leadership role had his ascendancy not coincided with a succession of dramatic black losses and the coming of age of a rising generation of ambitious, college-educated African Americans. Following the Supreme Court's 1896 ruling that "separate but equal" laws were constitutional, the passage of local and state segregation measures had rapidly accelerated in Georgia and the rest of the South. By 1902, of all Deep South states, Georgia alone had yet to complete the process of disfranchising African Americans. Although the incidence of lynching had gradually declined in the South after peaking in the 1890s, black southerners remained at the mercy of white mobs. Yet even in the face of this white racism, 3,880 African Americans were attending black colleges and professional schools in the South and Washington, D.C., alone. Many more were enrolled in academic high schools. As Washington recognized, his vision of black advancement through industrial rather than academic education appeared increasingly irrelevant to the South's growing black educated elite. In addition, Washington's reluctance to speak out against African Americans' mounting setbacks put him at risk for criticism that his racial program was less one of strategic compromise than of passive capitulation.[6]

Washington, a consummate politician, proactively countered potential challenges by blacks to his leadership by constructing a finely tuned political machine greased by his access to money and influence. His success as a fundraiser and political insider reflected his skill at manipulating white racist assumptions and appealing to white audiences' material interests. Many northern whites lauded Washington's program because they felt it had the potential to civilize the black masses and encourage them to resign themselves to a lasting status as obedient laborers. Following his 1895 speech, Washington rapidly won the support of northern philanthropists, particularly Andrew Carnegie, and Republican politicians, including President Theodore Roosevelt. Carnegie, who underwrote the construction of buildings on twenty-nine black college campuses, seldom donated to southern black institutions without first consulting the Wizard. Roosevelt often sought Washington's advice on political matters affecting African Americans and generally solicited his recommendations before making black or white political appointments in the South.[7]

Shrewdly dispersing money and job opportunities, the Wizard mobilized an army of black supporters indebted to his patronage and eager to win his confidence. By 1906, Washington had successfully created a public relations juggernaut by skillfully wheedling and cajoling black and white editors into publishing favorable newspaper and magazine stories. He had surreptitiously purchased an interest in both T. Thomas Fortune's *New York Age* and Boston's *Colored American Magazine*. Only the *Voice of the Negro*, the *Washington Bee*, the *Boston Guardian*, the *Chicago Broad Ax*, and Du Bois's *Moon Weekly* were consistent and effective critics of his policies. Washington was also the Wizard behind the curtains of many of America's most powerful national black organizations, including the Committee of Twelve, the Negro Business League, and the Afro-American Council. Thousands of letters annually poured into and out of Tuskegee, and Washington tirelessly toured the country in search of followers. Well-placed allies rooted out potential black critics and documented opponents' moral lapses and political mistakes.[8]

Turn-of-the-century Atlanta, on its surface, appeared to embody Washington's New South vision. If there were one place where white desires for commercial development might dissolve abiding racist hatreds, that would be the Gate City. As much as anywhere else, a small group of blacks had stockpiled an unprecedented amount of property and wealth. The city's six struggling private black colleges sought the white philanthropic monies to which Washington held the key. Influential black Republican Henry Rucker and other political appointees depended on Washington's goodwill to retain their federal positions.[9]

YET BETWEEN 1903 and 1906, the city's vibrant black intellectual community surfaced as the national center for a movement opposing Washington's racial and masculine ideals. Atlanta's black colleges offered high school and even industrial arts courses but took exceptional pride in their strong liberal arts traditions. By 1904, these institutions enrolled more than 2,000 high school and college students and employed a relatively youthful cadre of black professors and administrators who were part of a larger social network that included black entrepreneurs and ministers. These self-proclaimed "New Negro Men" ranged in age from early twenties to early fifties, and they were just beginning to come into their own as professionals. W. E. B. Du Bois, the Wizard's foremost critic, personified this group's cultural and intellectual aspirations as, in one admirer's words, the "black man who is the strongest evidence of the capabilities and possibilities of his people." After arriving in the city at age thirty in 1897, the Atlanta University professor of history and sociology forged close relationships with many of the city's leading New Black Men—Atlanta Baptist College professor John Hope, Atlanta University professor George Towns, black physician William Penn, and First Church minister Henry Hugh Proctor. Atlanta's racist realities gradually convinced Du Bois that the cure for racism was not "simply telling people the truth, it was inducing them to act on truth." Du Bois's 1903 *The Souls of Black Folk* announced the author's full awakening as a passionate propagandist. The book's unstinting defense of black intellectual capabilities and its evocative exposure of racism's palpable brutalities deeply touched and profoundly influenced a rising generation of ambitious African Americans.[10] Despite his avowed aim of speaking for all African Americans in *Souls*, Du Bois focused primarily on the individual and collective struggles of black *men* to forge authentic identities and realize their human potential.

Du Bois repeatedly employed the image of the veil as a metaphor for how racial inequality and white prejudice had estranged blacks from whites and distorted their visions of one another. Much as an opaque cloth obscures human sight, the veil of white racial hatred clouds whites' perceptions of African Americans and, when internalized by blacks, prevents African Americans from fully recognizing their innate dignity and dormant capabilities. The veil of racism also serves as a barrier that blocks the entrance of African Americans into the larger world of white privilege and opportunity. In addition to signifying racial segregation and human misperception, the metaphor of the veil highlights the latent potential of African Americans for enriching the world intellectually and culturally. In many religious traditions, including Judaism and Christianity, veils cordon off holy spaces, thereby protecting the sacred from impurity and shielding the uninitiated from the luminosity of divine truth. Henry Louis Gates Jr. and Terri Hume Oliver have noted that in many African American folk cultures, individuals born with a covering of fetal membrane on their faces were believed to possess the supernatural powers of foretelling the future and sensing otherworldly beings. By locating African Americans behind a veil, Du Bois was suggesting their access to insights and truths unavailable to others. The unique experiences of blacks had offered them a "second sight in this American world" derived from their peculiar "two-ness—an American, a Negro; two souls, two thoughts, two unreconciled strivings; two warring ideals in one dark body, whose dogged strength alone keeps it from being torn asunder."[11]

As a child born and raised in rural Massachusetts, Du Bois opted to prove his superiority over prejudiced whites by excelling athletically and intellectually. He remembered initially confronting the "veil" of white hatred and ostracism at a tender age when a white schoolgirl rejected his visiting card. A close white friend later surmised that these and other racist snubs were partially responsible for the academic's cold, gruff exterior and the "half-sneer" that produced a "cruel look" in his otherwise "sensitive, poet's face." If there were one place where Harvard University's first black Ph.D. graduate could relax his psychological defenses, it was in the crystalline world of reading and contemplation, where intellectual insight pierced racism's veil of disdain. Du Bois told readers that in his study,

> I sit with Shakespeare and he winces not. Across the color line I move arm in arm with Balzac and Dumas, where smiling men and welcoming women glide in gilded halls. From out the caves of evening that swing between the strong-limbed earth and the tracery of the stars, I summon Aristotle and Aurelius and what soul I will, and they come all graciously with no scorn nor condescension. So, wed with Truth, I dwell above the Veil. Is this the life you grudge us, O knightly America? . . . Are you so afraid lest peering from this high Pisgah . . . we sight the Promised Land?

This passage poetically encapsulates many of the major points found in *Souls*. Particularly striking is its Platonic vision of human souls ascending from the dark caves of ignorance into a transcendent realm where they can attain true reconciliation with others and full awareness of themselves.[12]

In contrast to Washington, who endorsed industrial education, Du Bois argued that black literary genius and artistic mastery represented the surest strategy for refuting the tenets of Social Darwinism, particularly its underlying assumption that African Americans were innately intellectually inferior to whites. The professor advocated the pursuit of manly black independence and self-sufficiency via a Talented Tenth who possessed the "manhood" qualities of intelligence and courage and, above all, "the broader, deeper, higher culture of gifted minds and pure hearts." Whites would recognize the civilized manliness of the African American only through "his striving . . . to be a co-worker in the kingdom of culture . . . to husband and use his best powers and his latent genius." Training the Talented Tenth would hone their mental skills, allowing them to offer the world new insights gleaned from "the rich and bitter depth of their experience," thereby winning acclaim and recognition for the entire race.[13]

White and black southerners could transcend the veil of racial division and dim perception only if New Black Men acted on their true ideals and voiced their convictions openly and forthrightly. A Washingtonian stoicism in the face of racial injustice, Du Bois argued, undermined black men's self-respect and confirmed white stereotypes of black submissiveness. Rather than "belittling and ridiculing themselves" in front of whites, he averred that "Negroes must insist continually, in season and out of season, that voting is necessary to modern manhood, that color discrimination is barbarism, and that black boys need education as well as white boys."[14] By 1905, these ideals reigned triumphant among the self-identified New Black Men affiliated with Atlanta's private colleges.

Morris Brown College professor John Henry Adams and other New Black Men shared both Du Bois's faith in the liberating power of intellectual striving and his commitment to the principled defense of black rights. Talented black men who clung to the mechanical and industrial arts rather than scaling the literary heights, Adams told readers in 1904, only confirmed white stereotypes, stunted the race's full development, and crushed their own souls. In Adams's mind, the "New Negro Man" was college trained, conversant in the liberal arts, and eager to serve his race as an editor, an artist, a businessperson, a Christian worker, or a governmental official. Though always seeking reconciliation with racially progressive whites, the New Black Man was willing to sacrifice his very life in defense of truth, justice, and racial progress: he, "like Socrates, would prefer the hemlock, or its equivalent, to all the vain pleasures outside of death than give over a single unit of right." A refusal to bend to white injustice and intimidation, even if such resistance meant certain death, exemplified black manliness and promoted long-term racial progress. Black elites' racial struggle was a corporate "fight for manhood—not man. Man dies. Manhood lives forever." The ultimate goal of this manly struggle was racial reconciliation and true racial equality. As late as 1906, Du Bois and his allies continued to hope that the best elements of the two races might shortly, in one black writer's words, "get together . . . establish righteousness and bring in the kingdom of peace and brotherhood."[15]

New Black Men put these abstract ideals into practice in diverse ways, reflecting their individual personal traits, professional circumstances, and ideological leanings. For example, Atlanta Baptist College professor John Hope, a native Georgian and an alumnus of Brown University, generally avoided rhetorical flourishes and messy public controversies. His emotional reserve and graceful bearing endowed the strikingly handsome Hope, often mistaken as white, with an uncanny charisma. Shunning the limelight, he quietly endorsed many of Du Bois's efforts. Despite his gifts as a diplomat, Hope, according to his wife, linked his own manly identity with the coura-

W. E. B. Du Bois, 1907, epitome
of the New Black Man. (Special
Collections and Archives, W. E. B.
Du Bois Library, University of
Massachusetts Amherst)

geous defense of truth and principle. John Wesley Bowen, Gammon Theological Seminary's interim president in 1906, in contrast, punctuated his
high-profile speeches against white supremacy with dramatic gestures and a
booming, melodious voice. Although Bowen publicly defended Washington's leadership and educational philosophy, even Atlanta's most militant
black elites admired both the theologian's educational achievement as one of
America's first black Ph.D. graduates and the courageousness of his salvos
against white racism. As an educator, he sought to train an elite cadre of
"pure, strong and broadly cultured" ministers who would fan out throughout the South, replace their less educated elders, and elevate the black masses
by providing them with the training necessary to improve the race's economic and political status.[16]

UNDER JESSE MAX Barber's firm editorship, the *Voice of the Negro*, first
published in 1904, emerged as the leading national advocate of the ideals of
these New Black Men. Barber was born in 1878 of "poor and respectable"
formerly enslaved parents in Blackstock, South Carolina. After primary
school, he left home for Rock Hill, South Carolina, with "$25 in his pocket"

to continue his education. Barber's ambitions eventually led him to Virginia Union University in Richmond. After graduating in 1903, he moved to Atlanta at age twenty-five to assume his position as editor. Barber aimed through the *Voice* to defend the reputation of black Americans and the ideals of free speech in the South by mercilessly lashing "the devil of prejudice and the demons of lies."[17] He quickly won a well-deserved reputation as a verbal and physical daredevil. In his first editorial, Barber announced both his elitism and his commitment to strident civil rights agitation: "There may be times when literature we publish will rip open the conventional veil of optimism and drag into view conditions that shock. But we mean to attempt to add to the sum of human knowledge by furnishing the world a journal which shall be intellectual, aesthetic and moral."[18]

Barber described his magazine's contributors as representatives of the best and brightest among African Americans. He marketed the *Voice* primarily to an emerging class of black urban professionals and ambitious strivers. The editor championed this imagined community of writers and readers as members of a black advance guard whose college (or at least high school) training had polished their manners, sharpened their minds, and purified their morals. Editorials portrayed the magazine's contributors as the "companions of nobles" who had garnered "hoards of rich thoughts." Their speeches and writings promised an "intellectual awakening" that would inevitably lead to a "golden age" among African Americans.[19] According to Barber, a Du Bois apostle, members of this black intellectual elite were uniquely positioned to address the "tremendous responsibilities of the age," to solve the "problems of a complex civilization," and to "accelerate the social betterment of mankind." Their achievements both belied white stereotypes of black inferiority and made them ideal role models for other aspiring blacks. Their cultural attainments conferred upon them a unique opportunity to reform the morals of the black masses and educate their minds.[20]

True to its readership and name, Barber's magazine focused primarily on topics of potential interest to educated blacks and offered a black perspective on politics as well as on current and local events. Almost every leading black public intellectual of the era contributed articles, with women being especially well represented. Subjects ranged from the personal lives of major black literary figures to the role of black women in their husbands' businesses. There were studies of American slavery and profiles of black colleges. As was so clearly the case with Adams's articles on topics such as the New Negro Man and the New Negro Woman, the *Voice* aimed at helping its

Jesse Max Barber in his study, which he characterized as his "Sanctum Sanctorum," or private refuge. (*Voice of the Negro*, October 1904)

readers forge a Talented Tenth identity and acquire the skills and knowledge necessary to fulfill their aspirations.[21]

Barber, characterized by defenders and critics alike as possessing a youthful egotism and a hot temper, sparred occasionally with Booker T. Washington in the early months of the *Voice*'s existence. Disagreements were probably inevitable between the two men, especially given Barber's emphasis on manly protest and Washington's jealous distrust of alternative black voices. These differences were further exacerbated by the contrasts between the magazine's elitist, academic bent and the Wizard's faith in industrial education. Between late 1904 and early 1905, Barber published a series of editorials criticizing the Wizard's educational views and his lack of courage to "speak plainly" on racial issues. The editor also broadcast Du Bois's uncharitable, though largely accurate, allegations that Washington was covertly subsidizing black periodicals as a means of squelching their criticism of his leadership. Behind the scenes, Washington and his lieutenants formulated a series of schemes to rein in Barber's editorial independence. Washington initiated a round of complaints to *Voice* advertisers as well as to the magazine's white owners and Barber's black associates. In reaction, the *Voice* published a laudatory April 1905 article on Tuskegee Institute, in which senior editor Bowen praised Washington's "grasp upon details, his comprehension of the industrial needs of his people, his faith in God and in the divinity of his mission." The Wizard applauded this apparent shift, privately expressing hope that the young editor might be "educated into something good."[22] Soon, however, Barber and Washington were again at loggerheads, their brief rapprochement splintered by black Georgians' growing determination to protest rising local and national threats to their civil rights.

As late as the fall of 1904, Barber and many other black Georgians continued to embrace Roosevelt as an apostle of "justice and civic righteousness" and remained guardedly optimistic that a new era of black-white reconciliation lay on the horizon for Georgia and the nation. In 1905, however, Hoke Smith's endorsement of disfranchisement and Clark Howell's gathering verbal assaults on black education dashed any African American hopes that local whites might voluntarily support black progress. At the same time, Roosevelt, following his successful 1904 reelection bid, signaled a declining interest in the political rights of blacks in the South. During a fall 1905 southern tour that included Georgia, the president welcomed whites into the fold of the Republican Party and made a point of affirming that the region's problems should be addressed at the local, not the federal, level.[23]

These spiraling civil rights setbacks and Roosevelt's shifting loyalties posed thorny problems for Washington's leadership. The black educator had become closely associated with the president. If he criticized Roosevelt, the Wizard would be indirectly attacking himself and cutting himself off from one of his most powerful white supporters. Both Washington's determination to prevent the expression of black dissent and his singular influence among white powerbrokers triggered additional opposition to his program. African Americans could express their fears of hardening white racism and Republican abandonment only by questioning Washington's authority and openly rejecting his accommodative stance. In the face of this mounting resistance, the Wizard clamped down further on black protest, in turn increasing the restiveness of his black antagonists. Du Bois later recalled that his decisive 1905 split with Washington was not primarily the product of their differences over individual civil rights or educational issues. More than anything else, the black professor resented the Wizard's persistence in "choking off even mild and reasonable opposition" to his leadership. "When any Negro complained or advocated a course of action, he was silenced with the remark that Mr. Washington did not agree with this."[24]

The breaking point for Du Bois was Washington's hounding of black Harvard graduate William Monroe Trotter, the *Boston Guardian* editor who was only thirty-one when his clash with the Wizard intensified in 1903. Washington, in defending himself from Trotter's often intemperate public attacks, took advantage of almost every weapon in his arsenal. That year, Trotter, aiming to confront his antagonist with a series of questions highlighting Washington's tacit acceptance of segregation, mob violence, and other southern racial injustices, created a disturbance during a speech Washington gave in Boston. Following the ensuing melee, the Wizard used his influence and resources to ensure that the editor and one of his associates served thirty days in jail. He directed spies to find compromising information on Trotter. He also attempted to purchase a controlling interest in the editor's newspaper and surreptitiously encouraged third parties to sue Trotter for slander.[25]

Washington's attempt to silence Trotter, Du Bois later wrote, was the last of many bitter disappointments provoking the Atlanta University professor to form the Niagara Movement, an organization representing, in David Levering Lewis's words, the "first collective attempt by African-Americans to demand full citizenship rights in the twentieth century." Angered at black America's recent racial setbacks and Washington's determination to extinguish all forms of internal black opposition, in 1905 Du Bois advertised his hopes for organizing a conference to "oppose firmly present methods of strangling honest criticism; to organize intelligent and honest Negroes; and to support organs of news and public opinion." Du Bois and twenty-nine other participants, including Trotter, relocated their July 1905 meeting to the Canadian side of Niagara Falls when racist hoteliers refused to provide suitable lodging on the New York side. The conference's founding Declaration of Principles embraced "persistent manly agitation" and unsparingly condemned mob violence, segregation, suffrage restriction, and other racial injustices. It also called on the federal government to protect black civil rights and demanded that African Americans unite in opposition against racial oppression. During its first year, the organization underscored its founders' confidence in the liberating powers of culture and knowledge. Its members chose as their first short-term political goal the securing of federal financial support for the South's notoriously discriminatory and underfunded public school systems.[26]

THE NIAGARA MOVEMENT, though it branched out to embrace members from thirty-four states, had deep Atlanta roots. Along with Du Bois, numerous black Georgians helped lead the organization through its first year—among them Barber, Atlanta Baptist College professor and then president John Hope, Atlanta University professor George Towns, minister Peter James Bryant, and Atlanta tycoon Alonzo Herndon. Seeking to strengthen the incipient movement's Georgia base, Du Bois and other local Niagara leaders played central roles in planning and directing the February 1906 Georgia Equal Rights Convention (GERC) in Macon. Among other black Atlantans attending this large convention were two of Barber's *Voice* co-editors (Henry Hugh Proctor and Joseph S. Flipper) as well as Baptist minister Edward R. Carter and educator William B. Matthews.[27]

The GERC was the brainchild of Henry McNeal Turner and William J. White. These septuagenarians represented a generation of activists whose experiences during slavery and Reconstruction had taught them to view racial uplift as a collective God-ordained mission linking all African Americans in a shared struggle for full citizenship rights and educational opportunity. As ministers, both Turner and White had long viewed effective political organizing and Christian revivalism as the foundations for black social salvation. After Reconstruction, disillusioned by the setbacks in the civil rights of black southerners, Turner came to believe that African Americans could escape white racism and achieve "dignity and manhood" only by emigrating to Africa. Once there, they would fulfill God's providential designs by converting its inhabitants to Christianity. Since slavery, White had devoted a substantial portion of his energy to promoting black social progress through the establishment of black-controlled churches and schools.[28]

In contrast, Du Bois and other New Black Men represented a rising elite vanguard that based its claims to authority on its members' distinctive university training and cultural and academic attainments. These black elites would elevate all African Americans by serving as living testaments to black potential, speaking out against white racism, and uplifting the black masses to their own standards. Du Bois encouraged the formation of strong local Niagara branches but purposively eschewed grassroots organizing or the creation of what he characterized as a "vast machine-like organization." The black professor and his allies believed that the open expression of words in

Some of the participants at the Niagara Movement's inaugural meeting, July 1905. First Congregational Church member and business tycoon Alonzo Herdon is standing in the third row, second from left. Jesse Max Barber and W. E. B. Du Bois are seated in the second row, third and fourth from left, respectively. (Special Collections and Archives, W. E. B. Du Bois Library, University of Massachusetts Amherst)

and of themselves would play a crucial role in strengthening black self-esteem, moderating white prejudice, and defending black civil rights. By August 1906, Barber acknowledged that the Niagara Movement had reached only a small group of black elites, but he was confident that propaganda alone promised to build a mass following. Asserting that ideas on their own "travel with amazing rapidity and gather accelerated force as they go," Barber portrayed Niagara leaders as "the tiny piece of leaven which we expect to leaven the whole lump." The New Black Men's secular orientation and elitism aroused the distrust of Turner, who, despite honorary degrees, had attended but never graduated from college. As chancellor of Morris Brown College, he encountered opposition from Adams and other faculty members when he unsuccessfully attempted to shift the college's curriculum away from the liberal arts to one combining industrial and Christian training. Turner equated classical education and what he termed "mere literary culture" with moral corruption and agnosticism.[29]

These generational differences notwithstanding, the February 1906 Macon convention's "equal rights" title and agenda signaled its participants' shared rejection of Washington's short-term willingness to accept racial inequalities with silent forbearance. In a public invitation to the conference, White portrayed the GERC as offering an opportunity for African Americans to reclaim their manliness. Recent white proscriptions, the document maintained, compelled black male Georgians to speak "as men for ourselves and thus maintain our manhood rights or not."[30] After listening to speeches and participating in debates, delegates cheered and endorsed an address that organizer White hoped to distribute to local and national audiences. The Christian and civilized pretensions of whites, the address argued, mandated that they reward black men's "growing intelligence, our ownership of property and our conservative, law-abiding tendencies" rather than stunt this progress via lynching and Jim Crow measures. Nearly one-fifth of the address was devoted to cataloging inequities in the state's criminal justice system, charging that "old and young, thug and mischief-maker and often men and women are herded together after unfair trials before juries who would rather convict ten innocent Negroes than let one guilty one escape."[31]

Highlighting participants' continued hopes that sympathetic whites might support black progress, the GERC address implored African Americans' white "brethren" to view the two races as "friends and not enemies" and to avoid stirring up the "darker, fiercer passions." Any biracial cooperation must be based not on the relationship of "master and slave" but on that of "man and man, equal in the sight of God and in the eye of the law."

Drawing on Booker T. Washington's notions of self-sufficiency, the document encouraged wealth building and property accumulation as foundations for black progress. The address's conclusion, teeming with Niagara militancy, challenged all black Georgians to join their efforts at promoting the interests and defending the rights of blacks: "We must agitate, complain, protest, and keep protesting against the invasion of our manhood rights; we must besiege the legislature, carry our cases to the courts and above all organize these million brothers of ours into one great fist which shall never cease to pound at the gates of Opportunity until they fly open."[32]

Many GERC participants viewed Turner's courageous opening day speech as the high point of the convention. Comparing the American flag to a "dirty rag," the black bishop described hell itself as an "improvement upon the United States where the Negro is concerned." He also inverted white discourses that represented black men as beasts incapable of responsible citizenship. The genuine savages were immature, morally degenerate, and physically puny white lynching advocates and racist mobs. Deriding "little ignorant and stupid" racist agitators, he challenged "any one or all of them to meet me in public discussion and I will show that the Negro is a far better man than they are." Turner's bold, black nationalist criticisms of whites reflected a long history of frustrations extending from his slavery and Reconstruction experiences to the current era of renewed racist threats. Widely quoted in white papers throughout the country, Turner's claims of black superiority enraged white supremacists. His denunciations of both America and its flag provoked northern whites to call for his lynching, and President Roosevelt briefly considered arresting the bishop for treason. Turner would, Barber approvingly wrote, "defy the thunderbolts of Jupiter" in defending black "manhood rights."[33]

In March 1906, William J. White, after recounting local reactions to Turner's utterances, gleefully wrote to Du Bois: "We have the Georgia white people in a quandary. They are afraid to talk about our Macon Meeting. It was such a great big thing that they do not know how to take it." Following the convention, White elevated Du Bois as an equal partner in his statewide equal rights movement and sought to arrange an immediate planning session with other GERC participants. Despite his proposed alliance with Du Bois and his praise for the militant Turner, White remained hopeful that his movement would encourage local interracial dialogue rather than permanent black separatism and racial confrontation. Informing Du Bois that he was now seeking an audience with a local minister and other "white folks," the aging black journalist concluded that "this is what we want to do."[34]

Into the summer of 1906, GERC delegates and their allies, drawn together by their recent meeting, appeared to be closing ranks around the vision of manly agitation endorsed by the Niagara Movement and pushed at the Macon convention. In Atlanta the Reverend Peter James Bryant goaded black Baptists to "contest and protest, strike with the battering-ram of righteousness until the door of justice shall open[,] admitting us into the temple of equality, civil and political, and to full-fledged American citizenship." In 1906 at least three more black Georgians—Republican leader Judson W. Lyons, Atlanta Baptist College professor John B. Watson, and Atlanta physician William F. Penn—officially joined the Niagara Movement.[35]

Even many avowed opponents of Du Bois now embraced protest methods, among them Benjamin Davis, a Washington disciple and *Atlanta Independent* editor, who previously had criticized "Fesser" Du Bois as being a charlatan directing "headless" Niagara and GERC meetings and possessing little mass support. By the summer, however, the feisty black journalist had turned his pen against Tom Watson, Hoke Smith, and other whites who supported disfranchisement. In July, Davis denounced these white politicians' maneuverings as an unmanly and criminal "raid to steal the Negro's vote."[36]

Between 15 and 18 August 1906, Niagara Movement members from throughout the country—including a large Georgia contingent joined by John Hope—assembled at Harpers Ferry, West Virginia, in commemoration of the fiftieth anniversary of abolitionist John Brown's famous raid. In true New Black Man fashion, they publicly championed Brown's "incarnate spirit of justice, that hatred of a lie, that willingness to sacrifice money, reputation, and life itself on the altar of right." Declaring, "We are men," participants forthrightly claimed for themselves "every single right that belongs to a freeborn American, political, civil and social; and until we get these rights we will never cease to protest and assail the ears of America!" Movement leaders publicized their organization's recent accomplishments: an increase in their national membership to 170 men, the distribution of 10,000 pamphlets nationwide, the sponsoring of local lectures in northern and southern cities, and the launching of political lobbying campaigns in Chicago, Boston, and Maryland. Between the summer of 1905 and the fall of 1906, Barber's *Voice*, now one of the nation's most popular and influential African American magazines, trumpeted Niagara ideals and hailed the movement's leaders, particularly Du Bois, in almost every issue.[37]

ATLANTA'S NIAGARA DELEGATES returned to their city just as the *Georgian*'s and the *News*'s editors were escalating their antiblack rantings. On

22 August, the *Georgian*, in an apparent response to the Harpers Ferry meeting, accused civil rights protesters of undermining white police authority, helping incite black criminals to rape white women, and shielding rapists from the law. Mincing no words, the newspaper denounced "Negro tirades" against the "lawlessness of lynching" as well as "Negro platitudes and resolutions against the injustice of the South." Demanding the racial submissiveness that New Black Men had recently spurned at the GERC and Niagara Movement meetings, the *Georgian*'s editors maintained that black assaults would end only if the "leaders of the Negro race shall give us from this time forth that co-operation which they heretofore refused." Citing Turner, Congregationalist minister Henry Hugh Proctor, and others by name, the newspaper called on black elites "to stand shoulder to shoulder with us." It dictated that each black professional "devote some part of his sermon or some portion of his editorial or some segment of his scholastic hours to preaching hell and damnation to all who are guilty of this fiendish crime" of rape.[38]

These nonnegotiable demands ensnared African American ministers and journalists in a rhetorical trap. They could publicly ignore the *Georgian*'s finger-pointing only at the risk of imperiling themselves and their institutions. Yet any defensive suggestion that whites were exaggerating the threat of sexual assault would only confirm white suspicions that black elites were in collusion with their race's criminal element. In recent years white southerners had rhetorically savaged blacks who publicly criticized similar crusades against black rapists. On 25 August, the *Georgian* slammed a veiled criticism of mob violence published in Benjamin Davis's *Independent*. Editor Graves cautioned the black journalist to "suspend for a time his denunciation against lynching, until he and his fellows have impressed upon his whole race the tremendous and thrilling purpose which is pulsing in the aroused and indignant veins of Southern manhood." Escalating his threats still further, Graves explicitly warned that, should assaults by blacks continue, the destruction of black schools, churches, and other institutions was inevitable.[39]

Between late August and 22 September, more than a dozen black religious leaders and journalists, many of whom had GERC ties, condemned black sexual assaults in conciliatory missives published in the local white newspapers. These black elites distanced their own class from the alleged rapists' crimes by depicting this disorderly element as a small minority possessing no ties whatsoever to respectable African Americans. Atlanta's Baptist Ministers Union, for example, asserted that "negro preachers, teachers and editors" were blameless for "these crimes," which had been committed, so these correspondents claimed, by the "vicious, 'rounders,' loafers and grossly ignorant, who do not read our papers, do not and have not attended our churches and schools, but instead frequent the barrooms, poolrooms, gambling dens, dives, and restaurants attached to these bars." The ministers petitioned for an expanded role in civic affairs and assured whites of their unwavering support for the capture and conviction of black rapists: "So bitter are we against the crime and the criminal, that if given an opportunity to compose the entire jury, as the evidence warranted, even if circumstantial, we would instantly bring in a verdict of death."[40]

Although the communications of Benjamin Davis and black ministers now pulled away from the rhetoric of manly protest advocated by the GERC and the Niagara Movement, black professionals continued to push for interracial relationships based on mutual respect and relative equality. Davis warned whites that "this crime and menace to the virtue of our women cannot be put down by the white man alone nor by the Negro single handed; but the united and determined action of both can put to death or expell every fiend from the community." Even as they pledged their support for white campaigns to "clean out the dives and restaurants and enforce the vagrancy laws," other African Americans joined this black journalist in simultaneously highlighting the dangers posed by disorderly white criminals and lynching mobs. Their letters to white newspapers cautiously questioned white supremacist assumptions by positing the empowerment of both white and black elites as the surest solution to the city's crisis of public order. Only interracial cooperation, these black men argued, could turn back the gathering storm of racial violence.[41]

THE REVEREND HENRY Hugh Proctor's responses to the *Georgian*'s published threats illustrate the complex dangers and opportunities posed by the entry of black elites into the discourse on the black rapist. Proctor's intellectual pedigree and record as a civil rights advocate placed him at the center of Du Bois's circle in Atlanta. Approaching age thirty-eight in the summer of 1906, Proctor was a *Voice of the Negro* coeditor and the minister of the First Congregational Church. Born in Tennessee's backwoods to formerly enslaved parents, Proctor won admission first to Fisk University and then to Yale University's Divinity School. At the turn of the century, Proctor's speeches and writings repeatedly challenged white northerners to revive the Reconstruction Era's interventionist spirit. Proctor once bluntly warned whites that, should local injustices continue, they had "better beware or they

Rev. Henry Hugh Proctor, ca.
1899. W. E. B. Du Bois included
this photograph in the American
Negro exhibit at the 1900 Paris
Exposition. (Library of
Congress)

would find firebrands under their houses and poison in the coffee." In
Georgia he joined forces with Du Bois to author a stream of petitions to the
legislature, protesting everything from the state's inadequate black schools to
a proposed 1899 state disfranchisement measure that never passed. The
Constitution criticized these two men as outside agitators when in 1905 they
sought black support for a resolution demanding black representation on
the board of a proposed Carnegie library for African Americans, which was
never constructed. In a 1905 speech Proctor publicly affirmed African Americans' full rights to racial equality, and he signed the GERC's call and attended
its session in Macon. Yet, with the hardening of white racism, the black
minister increasingly voiced his rising fears that whites might mount a
destructive antiblack massacre. As he cautiously advised his 1905 audience,
"But duties and rights go together. . . . Often the highest duty we can
perform is not [to] exercise a certain right."[42]

Long before 1906 Proctor and other First Church members had viewed
themselves as intermediaries between African Americans and Atlanta's white
elites. Northern white missionaries affiliated with Yale University and the
American Missionary Association had established the church in 1867. True

to the association's overarching vision, First Church's white founders sought to train an elite cadre of race leaders whose achievements would belie white racist stereotypes and whose leadership would spread the liberating message of Congregationalism among the black masses. Financial prosperity and cultural progress, Proctor had long argued, "shall turn prejudice away from us by making it unreasonable." Public drinking, dancing, and other forms of vice, in contrast, blocked black moral progress and confirmed white stereotypes. Though vastly outnumbered by black Baptists and Methodists, Proctor's congregation claimed the city's wealthiest and best-educated black residents. White-collar workers and college-educated professionals stood at the forefront of a church whose membership included both Alonzo Herndon, a Niagara Movement participant and the state's wealthiest African American, and Henry Rucker, Georgia's collector of revenue and one of the South's most influential black Republicans.[43]

Similar to the communications of other black ministers, Proctor's initial response to the *Georgian*'s incendiary editorials of 1906 stressed the contrasts between what he characterized as "the educated, property-holding or church-going element of the colored race" and "the worthless irresponsible vagabond." Proctor endorsed the white newspapers' war against black criminals. He encouraged city officials to clear the streets of all "idlers" and put them to work. Proctor supported the forcible closure of the downtown's "dens of vice and iniquity" because it was there that "thieves, cut throats and rapists are hatched out." In a published speech, the minister proposed the creation of black "vigilance committees whose duty it will be to point out in the community the dives and hell holes frequented by the gamblers, vagrants and women of ill repute." Proctor also argued that elite blacks could fulfill their critical role as forces for municipal order only with the explicit support of whites: "Is not this a time for all good men, white and black, to stand together?" "What have we to gain by suspicion and estrangement? Are not our interests identical?" In posing these questions, Proctor was appealing for recognition by the white elite that his class's moral probity merited its members a shared role as guardians of Atlanta's social order. The clear parallels between Proctor's proposed black vigilance committees and the *Georgian*'s demands that African Americans enforce white visions of order infuriated some African Americans. In a newspaper column appearing on 22 September, Benjamin Davis denounced Proctor for focusing his animus solely on the black victims of the dives rather than denouncing as well the white saloon owners who profited from the sale of alcohol.[44]

As Davis immediately recognized, Proctor's recent denunciations of black criminals ran the risk of reinforcing white stereotypes that both encouraged and justified the harassment, arrest, and incarceration of working-class African Americans. White racial violence and black criminal stereotypes endangered all classes of African Americans. Yet for thousands of struggling black men, the state's deadly convict lease camps and other white schemes to coerce black labor posed threats almost as grave and surely as immediate as lynching. In attempting to ward off white mob violence by endorsing the legitimacy of some of the criminal justice system's worst abuses, some black elites were now overlooking fundamental inequities that they had previously denounced at GERC and Niagara meetings. Proctor later acknowledged the criticisms among some African Americans that his public characterizations of black criminality helped provoke the riot's outbreak. That summer, he never pointed to the dramatic structural inequalities that forced many black men to hustle in the countryside or Atlanta's downtown spaces for food and employment. Nor did he acknowledge the right of black men to withhold their labor from grossly exploitative employers.[45]

LIKE PROCTOR, many New Black Men and their older GERC allies had long based their claims to civil and political rights on their moral probity and intellectual and professional achievements. Whites deployed images of black immorality and shiftlessness to condemn the entire race. Black vice and disorderliness, black elites believed, weakened their race and confirmed white Social Darwinist stereotypes of black degeneracy and laziness. So, too, did black elites often promise that the enhancement of their own public influence would augment the effectiveness of manly African Americans at improving the morals of the black masses. Many black reformers sincerely hoped to save struggling African Americans from the suffering and despair associated with both chronic unemployment and often brutal harassment by law enforcement officials. To entice young men away from saloons and dance halls, the Young Men's Christian Association (YMCA) and other black organizations offered debates, academic coursework, public lectures, and moral instruction. At its worst, however, the faith of New Black Men in the leadership of a Talented Tenth hardened their own cultural, intellectual, and class prejudices. Even Du Bois, for example, who took great pride in both his rejection of traditional white stereotypes and his commitment to scientific inquiry, cautioned aspiring black men never to forget that "a rising race must be aristocratic; the good cannot consort with the bad—not even the best with the less good."[46]

Thus, Proctor's and other black elites' calls for *punishing* and *expelling* disorderly black men rather than simply *uplifting* them represented a subtle but crucial reorientation of long-standing discursive strategies. This reworking of the uplift discourse of New Black Men boldly highlighted its inherent potential for affirming white stereotypes of working-class African Americans, for exacerbating social divisions among black men, and for pulling public attention away from the structural inequalities that limited the opportunities and choices of so-called disorderly blacks.

THE 1906 LAW-AND-ORDER discourse excluded the input of black women from a topic of vital interest to them. Black women were especially vulnerable to sexual harassment and sexual assault as domestic workers in white homes, as interlopers in the downtown's white-controlled spaces, and as residents of black neighborhoods almost completely ignored by an all-white police force. Black women's entrance into interracial public debates, especially on issues relating to sexuality, invited the very slanders and white threats against which they sought protection. If black women braved these dangers by writing letters to white newspapers that summer, their communications went unpublished. But in messages penned exclusively to audiences of African Americans and their white allies, New Black Women had long criticized the refusal of white men to offer black women the protections and claims to respectability enjoyed by their white counterparts. These black women, like their male contemporaries, had long attempted to turn white attention to the social threats posed by white mob violence. Although Niagara Movement and GERC participants shared many of their wives' and daughters' concerns regarding black women's public safety, the speeches and missives of these black men never fully captured the perspectives of New Black Women. New Black Men tended to view the issues of chivalry and female protection through the prism of their own claims to manliness.[47]

Some GERC and Niagara men deployed traditional chivalric notions to reject white men's singular claims to power. White men argued that their social authority stemmed from their ability and willingness to protect their female dependents' reputations and sexual purity. Whites deployed the image of the black rapist to justify disfranchisement, lynching, segregation, and other forms of racial domination as essential mechanisms for containing black men's alleged savagery. In countering such white aspersions, New Black Men often highlighted both white men's sexual exploitation of black women and black men's roles as protectors of their female relatives. Du Bois responded to white characterizations of black criminality with a reminder that the "rape which your gentlemen have done against helpless

black women . . . is written on the foreheads of two millions of mulattoes."
John Henry Adams, in a *Voice* article on the "New Negro Woman," argued
that black men and white men shared a chivalric duty to honor and respect
the women of both races as mothers and vessels of purity. The "final triumph of civilization," he concluded, would come only with society's recognition that black and white womanhood was a "unit in all things for good"
and that black and white manhood was "a common factor in her defense."
Shielding black women from white sexual predators on the job and in the
streets, GERC members concurred in Macon, required that black men financially support their wives and daughters, keep them inside the home
as much as possible, and spare no efforts in the defense of black wom-
en's honor. In a speech rejecting black women's claims to public leadership,
John Hope once lectured an audience of black clubwomen, "The surest way
for our men to become more manly is for our women to become more
womanly."[48]

Rather than retreating into their homes, Georgia's emerging female Talented Tenth pursued racial progress and women's safety by publicly participating in neighborhood affairs and by organizing uplift programs targeting black mothers and their children. Addie Hunton, president of the black
Atlanta Woman's Club, and many of her peers demanded that southern
whites recognize the right of black men to protect their wives and daughters
from sexual abuse. Yet, viewing the turn of the century as the Woman's Era,
Hunton and other New Black Women implicitly rebuffed black men's chivalric pretensions with arguments that the social and cultural redemption of
their race depended on women's unique talents and gifts. Exposed to the
ideals of the Young Women's Christian Association as a Spelman student,
Hattie Rutherford Watson, wife of Niagara participant John B. Watson, for
example, vowed in college to devote her life to the "uplift and protection of
colored women." Watson's commitment to public service was typical for her
generation and for Atlanta's female college graduates. Other wives of Atlanta
Niagara men assumed positions of public influence by volunteering as social
service providers, by founding parent-teacher associations, and by participating in national club activities.[49]

IN CONTRAST TO elite black men who advocated shared authority and
equality across the color line, the *Georgian* and other white racist agitators
made it clear that their visions of interracial cooperation sought to affirm
black subservience. The *Georgian* demanded that African Americans "join
with all their hearts and hands with the better element of the white race to

terrorize and to intimidate the criminals of the negro race." In late August, the *Georgian* had argued that the entire white race should stand in dominance over African Americans. The newspaper had also warned readers that black progress inevitably led to black crime and black resistance against white authority. The newspaper rejected African American pleas that it acknowledge and encourage black achievement. Its editorials instead linked racial peace with disfranchisement, increased segregation, and the willingness of African Americans to "restrain and curb" their aspirations for equality and public respect.[50]

On 19 and 21 September, at the height of racial tension in Atlanta, the *Georgian* praised Proctor and other elite blacks for their promises to aid the cause for law and order; its editors reconsidered their earlier statements that black-on-white assaults were "a crime for which we can attack the negro as a race." Thanking Proctor, Davis, and others by name for "co-operating heart and soul," the newspaper "praised the swift responses" of these black elites to its calls.[51] Ultimately, however, the *Georgian* and many whites remained suspicious of black peace offerings. Although white newspaper editors were willing to publish black criticisms of black-on-white crime, they denounced any black protests, however muted, against lynching and civil rights inequalities. Rather than real cooperation or communication with blacks, the *Georgian*'s editors demanded black institutional leaders' explicit acceptance of a chivalry that emphasized the subordination of all African Americans, regardless of their moral, intellectual, and financial attainments.

Possessing the pledges of Proctor and his fellow ministers, white newspapers could now claim that they had successfully united their residents in opposition to the "strange negro" and his crimes against white women. The rhetorical war against the black criminal dramatically influenced the actions and decisions of public officials between 5 and 22 September. Under a city council directive, local police officers spent this period vigorously enforcing the vagrancy law by arresting hundreds of black men unable to provide adequate proof of legitimate employment. On 17 September the city council passed an ordinance, publicly endorsed by Proctor, to shutter the "disorderly" saloons catering to a black clientele. On 22 September plain-clothed police entered the local saloons catering to blacks and arrested five African Americans for working in bars displaying portraits of nude white women. That same day Police Chief Henry Jennings made his first report to the city council regarding the "dives" on Decatur and Peters Streets. Jennings asked the members of the city council to refuse licenses for twenty-six restaurants owned by or catering to blacks.[52]

The explicit threats that newspapers deployed against elite blacks that summer were extreme examples of the myriad ways in which whites actively shaped discussions of the black criminal throughout the Jim Crow Era. In August white editors portrayed a series of alleged black assaults as a concerted black attack against white womanhood and white supremacy. Having set the terms of the debate early, newspaper editors exercised control not only over the coverage of events but also over the admissibility of opinions. We can never know the range of alternative ideas that were advanced in letters to the newspapers but never published. Evidence of the purposeful distortion of speeches and letters can be found in the reworking by white newspapers of Booker T. Washington's 30 August speech presented at the conference of the National Negro Business League in Atlanta. Emphasizing African Americans' economic and moral progress, Washington criticized "black vagabonds" before castigating lynching as the greatest enemy of business progress in the South. Atlanta's white press ignored both his paean to black success and his denunciations of mob violence. Newspaper editors instead summarized his speech in banner headlines reading, LAW-BREAKING NEGROES WORST MENACE TO RACE and BOOKER T. WASHINGTON'S SOUND ADVICE TO THE BLACK RACE.[53]

MUCH AS WHITE mobs twisted and maimed the bodies of black victims that summer, white newspapers employed threats of violence and utilized their control over public discourse to mangle and reshape the words of African Americans. White racist coercion and extremism were overwhelmingly responsible for black commentators' dramatic turn toward accommodation. Yet these rhetorical shifts also reflected New Black Men's ambivalence regarding tactics and social loyalties. Although black elites recognized the black men who frequented Decatur Street's saloons and dance halls as victims of social and legal injustice, they also detested "disorderly" behavior as a demeaning obstacle to racial advancement. If white racist persecution had moderated in late September, black elites would likely have refocused their energies on redeeming marginalized blacks rather than isolating them as public scapegoats. Likely, too, New Black Men and their allies would have revived their protests against their state's patently racist criminal justice system.

Even at the height of the rape scare, New Black Men and other black commentators clung to visions of chivalry that promoted their full participation in public life. They entered the public law-and-order discourse by promising to help control the criminal black brute. Once there, black elites vainly sought through letters and speeches to turn public attention to the threats posed by the white mob. They unsuccessfully claimed an equal partnership with white men in protecting Atlanta from the twin threats posed by the black and white disorderly classes. As summer turned to fall, these men could still hope that their labors had saved black Atlanta—and particularly their own schools and congregations—from wholesale massacre. So, too, could they envision building on the recent successes of the GERC and the Niagara Movement once their city's racial tensions dissipated. For good measure, black businesspersons and professionals—blocked from purchasing firearms from white businesses—secretly began importing arms into the city.[54]

CHAPTER FOUR

Testing Loyalties and Identities in

the Crucible of Riot

———

O N 22 SEPTEMBER 1906, a heightened sense of excitement and foreboding hung over Atlanta as blacks and whites from miles around descended on Five Points to enjoy their customary Saturday on the town. On the preceding evening the *News* had carried an anticrime editorial boldly concluding, "It is time to act, men; will you do your duty now?" In the morning a group of whites posted a sign advertising a "K.K.K." action for Sunday. Throughout the day, newsboys shouted out the headlines of the numerous extras published by the *News* and the *Journal*:

NEGRO ATTEMPTS TO ASSAULT MRS. MARY CHAFIN

TWO ASSAULTS

THIRD ASSAULT[1]

In the early afternoon, police fanned out through much of the downtown area, forcibly closing the "dangerous" and "disorderly" black dives and saloons. Word spread among whites that an antiblack massacre was imminent, and white businesspersons reportedly encouraged their black employees to leave work early to avoid possible danger. One unidentified black man remembered his boss's words: "We are going to kill all the niggers tonight." Yet most blacks still had little inkling of the coming storm's timing. As late as approximately 9:00 P.M., thousands of African Americans remained in the downtown area—shopping, waiting on tables, dancing, or playing pool in the saloons along Decatur and Marietta Streets or cutting the hair and shaving the whiskers of their white clients. Well after the riot erupted, other blacks continued to enter trolley cars whose routes would transport them through the city's center.[2]

In a 1948 autobiography, Walter White recalled his experiences that night as a thirteen-year-old making his way through downtown Atlanta by carriage with his father. White remembered the riot's central role in the development of his racial identity. "I am a Negro," the fair-skinned executive secretary of the NAACP stated, "[but] the traits of my race are nowhere visible upon me." Given his physical characteristics, what made White black? White recalled comprehending the depth of his racial identity only during the upheaval when he witnessed rioters kill a black acquaintance and observed a mob inch toward his family's lawn the following evening. White now understood: "I was a Negro, a human being with an invisible pigmentation which marked me a person to be hunted, hanged, abused, discriminated against. . . . I was gripped by the knowledge of my identity," he continued, "and in the depths of my soul I was vaguely aware that I was glad of it. . . . I was glad I was not one of those whose story is in the history of the world, a record of bloodshed, rapine, and pillage."[3]

The next week white newspaper editors, businesspersons, and officials would announce their own epiphany as they sought to distance themselves from mob participants. Responsibility for the violence, they argued, lay not with the city's respectable classes but, instead, with both bloodthirsty white "hoodlums" and unrepresentative newspaper editors. There was a kernel of truth in this portrayal of the disorder; even many black accounts of it described the mob as made up overwhelmingly of economically marginalized teenagers and young men.[4] Yet blacks and more honest whites would testify that middle- and upper-class whites also joined in the massacre.

Still, leading whites did not need to participate physically in the riot to share culpability for its outbreak. Recent historical scholarship emphasizes the "open ended and contingent" nature of racist attacks, suggesting that "white supremacy did not unalterably script or encode what southerners would do when confronted by racial conflict or potentially lethal racial situations." As late as 22 September, there were still numerous opportunities for white public officials and civic leaders to foil the mob or at the very least minimize its destructiveness. "Had the Police Department opposed a determined front to the mob at the inception of the riot," a postriot grand jury concluded, "all serious trouble could have been averted."[5]

The businesspersons' portrayal of the riot's origins was disingenuous in

Above: Facsimiles of Atlanta newspaper extras, 22 September 1906. (Baker, *Following the Color Line*, facing p. 7) **Below:** Walter White's graduation photograph. (Yale Collection of American Literature, Beinecke Rare Book and Manuscript Library)

still another way. The mob was clearly disorderly, and it repeatedly revealed a boisterous disregard for human life, private property, and police authority. At the same time, an emphasis on the mob's irrationality may prevent our fully understanding its members' motives. Before the riot broke out, the advocates of racial violence repeatedly stressed that they were attempting to impose their own visions of order on a rapidly changing city. Once the riot erupted, its violence was far from random, flowing instead along well-worn channels of racial strife and jealousy.

The riot experiences of Walter White and white businesspersons suggest the life-and-death choices that blacks and whites faced. Words spoken (or left unspoken) and actions taken (or left untaken) could promote violence or turn the tide against the rioters. In the process of experiencing the riot and making decisions during it, many city residents gained new insights into whom they could and could not trust. This onrush of thoughts and feelings led many to reevaluate their social identities and community loyalties. As Atlantans shaped the riot, they were reshaping themselves and one another.

BY 8:30 P.M. that Saturday night, thousands of whites had packed into the Five Points area; many congregated at the intersection of Decatur and South Pryor Streets, just outside the Kimball House, the city's most luxurious hotel and dining spot. Paperboys, still screaming the newspapers' headlines, pushed their way through the crowd. Throughout the afternoon white men animatedly discussed the newspapers' reports of rapes and attempted rapes. "What are we going to do about it?" they repeatedly asked, often answering their own question: "Something must be done." A white man peered down on the crowd from a dry goods box and challenged his audience to avenge these crimes: "Are we Southern white men going to stand for this?" he shouted. "No. Let's kill all the Negroes so our women will be safe," was the reply. For ninety minutes small groups of whites chased African Americans in and out of the mass of people crowding the area. Newsboys cornered young black men and beat them. Whites twice knocked a black messenger from his bicycle. Rumors passed through the crowd that a black man had snatched a white woman's purse. Others screamed that a black woman had insulted a white man and that a black man had cut a white man's thigh. A crowd saw a black man enter a pool hall on Decatur Street. Shouts went out that he was a "bad nigger." Whites surrounded the building to prevent his exit.[6]

Hearing of the trouble, Mayor James Woodward rushed to the area. Arriving at approximately 9:00 P.M., he pleaded with whites to go home and

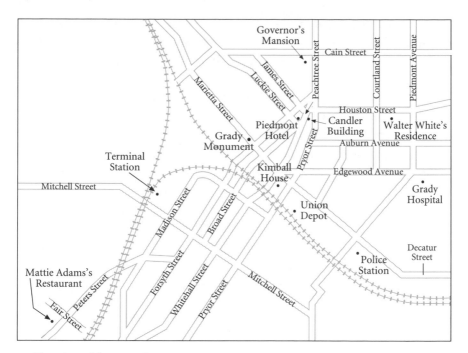

Downtown Atlanta, 1906

let law enforcement personnel address the crime wave through official channels. "I beseech you," he told the crowd, "not to cause this blot on the fair
name of our most beautiful city. . . . I implore you to leave this matter in the
hands of the law, and save the blood-shed that is sure to follow if you allow
yourselves to be governed by these reports, that are certainly exaggerated."
The crowd paid little heed to the mayor's message. Instead a large group of
whites surged down Decatur Street toward the black saloon district, but
their advance was temporarily checked by police. Enraged at the sight of a
"boisterous" black man, the crowd quickly broke through the thin barrier;
its members surrounded their prey and beat him with sticks and barrel
staves. During the next few minutes, whites pursued and struck down any
blacks they happened upon. A mass of whites pursued a number of African
Americans toward a Central Avenue skating rink serving as a temporary
sanctuary for blacks. After hearing pistol fire, a mob, thinking that the
Detroit Barbershop was sheltering the alleged black triggermen, stormed it.
At approximately 10:00 P.M., many of the local bars and theaters let out, and
even more whites and blacks spilled into the streets, adding to the confusion
and providing a fresh audience for the newsboys' incendiary shouts.[7]

The mayor pleaded with the mob a final time. Noting the crowd's inattention, he set off a nearby fire alarm and called on the fire chief to use hoses to disperse the mob. White crowd members simply retreated along side streets beyond the reach of the firemen's spray. About fifty white men began shouting "Lynch him!" "Lynch him!" as they tracked a black man accused of stabbing George C. Tomlinson. This mob, which attracted nearly a thousand additional participants as it pursued its prey north on Peachtree Street, trapped the man in front of the Piedmont Hotel, approximately 500 feet away, and broke sticks and beer bottles over his head. Repeatedly forced to the ground, he was saved only by a passing police officer who pushed the crowd back with a nightstick and carried the victim away, eventually hiding him in a store. James English, the president of Fourth National Bank, located on Peachtree just south of Five Points, positioned himself in front of the hotel and unsuccessfully attempted to subdue the crowd while whites plunged knives into the bodies of black pedestrians. William Welch—a one-eyed, one-legged Confederate veteran—later bragged, perhaps apocryphally, that he had gunned down two African Americans early in the evening before the general rioting broke out.[8]

His voice drowned out by the mob's shrieks, English rang the fire bell ten times, calling to duty every policeman in the city. For approximately four hours, whites armed with almost every weapon imaginable—shotguns, revolvers, iron bars, knives, sticks, canes, bricks, stones, or anything else that "could be wrenched off a building"—surged through Atlanta's downtown in search of their black quarry while shouting, "Kill them!" "Lynch them!" "Kill every damn nigger in sight!" Newspapers reported a thousand shots reverberating through the night air. Residents of outlying neighborhoods heard the white mob's cheers and black victims' screams. At Atlanta Baptist College, approximately a mile and a half from Five Points, Lugenia and John Hope, sensing the evening's preternatural energy and commotion from a distance, silently fidgeted, neither wanting to burden the other with their unvoiced feelings of terror. Late in the evening John heard the fire alarm and militia call and left his house to investigate. The mob's din, perhaps on nearby Peters Street, confirmed his worst suspicions.[9]

AT APPROXIMATELY 10:30 P.M., streetcar no. 207 reached the Marietta and Peachtree intersection en route to Grant Park. A nearby crowd of white men was thrown into a frenzy when a white observer excitedly pointed to the car on which white women mingled with black men. "Look at that!" he shouted. Screaming for the help of bystanders, the men surrounded the car and lifted it from its guide wires. After letting the white men and women exit the immobilized car, the crowd forced its way in by shattering the windows and prying open the doors. Two black women waved umbrellas and hatpins trying to stave off the white attackers. The mob moved past them toward the rear of the trolley where four black men and one black woman hid. One black man pleaded for his life. The white men beat the black men with sticks and clubs. Police, avoiding the use of their weapons, entered the car and pulled the white men off their victims only after the attackers had knocked them to the floor. When one of the black men lifted his head to look out the window, the crowd shouted, "He ain't dead, beat him again!" Meanwhile, the motorman had vaulted to the top of the trolley so that he could reconnect the wires and steer away from the scene. The trolley sputtered forward as the white crowd attempted to climb "like rats" up its sides while the police successfully pushed and pulled them away. The police reported that three blacks died in this trolley alone. It was perhaps during this attack that a white man stabbed James N. Reeves, a black chaplain's son, in the forehead with a dagger before a white gang trampled him.[10]

Hearing of this melee, the streetcar superintendent initially wavered regarding whether to halt streetcar service into the downtown area to protect the trolleys' drivers and occupants. Discontinuing service, he later rationalized, would have only energized the mob as it sensed the company's weakness. Many motormen aided the mob by bringing their cars to a standstill when whites pushed themselves into their trolleys' paths. Some motormen even joined in the antiblack attacks. Before the company finally halted its downtown service, the mob stopped at least nineteen additional cars and entered at least four more.[11]

When another car, this one carrying six black women and four black men, crossed the junction of Peachtree and Marietta Streets, mob members repeatedly screamed, "Take them off! Take them off!" The conductor tried to speed past the danger. Before he could, a crowd member pulled the trolley from its guide wires. Then others broke its windows with sticks and climbed aboard. Following a brief struggle, the whites overtook the black passengers, assaulting the black women and pulling other passengers through the windows. Five black passengers disappeared through the streets, but a sixth was knocked to the ground. Bloodied, he attempted to draw a knife but was chased to the side entrance of a barbershop, where he was beaten to death. A dozen whites stormed another car and bludgeoned two men to death, their blood collecting in small pools on the floor. Later, an African American

Le Petit Parisien's depiction of the 1906 Atlanta riot as a massacre of blacks. (Kenan Research Center at the Atlanta History Center)

leaped from a car at the Marietta and Forsyth intersection as it neared a white group hoping to intercept it. The mob caught and killed him. Another black man similarly escaped from a trolley car. Aiming a pistol at the crowd, he sprinted away as the mob chased him into a nearby store. The mob broke through the door and killed him. Still later that evening, eighteen-year-old messenger Frank Smith fled from a trolley car on Decatur Street only to be caught, stoned, and slashed to death on the Forsyth Street viaduct by a mob led by Walter Edmunds, a butcher who had long practiced his deadly craft. "We do not know a single person," Frank's friends later asserted, "who would or could say Frank ever did them a harm. He was the favorite child among six in the family" and his mother's sole supporter.[12]

White passengers riding on an eleven o'clock trolley overheard a strapping black man speaking angrily of the night's violence and daring anyone to attack him. Six white men jumped him and thrust knives into him. With his coat torn and his back bleeding profusely, he was pushed from the car and surrounded by whites. Remaining still for approximately thirty seconds, he pulled himself upward, his coat and shirt completely torn to shreds. A deep gash spanned his right and left shoulders, and two cuts across his abdomen exposed his ribs. Police lifted him into the patrol wagon, and he was taken to the hospital, where he reportedly died. The streetcar violence ended only after the rail company halted service late that evening.[13]

BETWEEN 10:30 P.M. and midnight the white mob fanned out from Five Points, its members separating and reuniting in countless combinations. While whites were attacking African Americans on the streetcars, another ragtag collection of whites marched up Marietta Street to a barbershop across from the post office, where black barbers and bootblacks were servicing their white customers. Armed with assorted weapons and their bare hands, the white men forced themselves through the shop windows and rushed two of the workers, including lame bootblack Henry Welch. Members of the mob fired guns at both men, killing them instantly. After vandalizing the shop and stripping the slain barber and bootblack of their clothes, the white men dragged their bodies face-first from the shop. A short distance from this ghastly scene, a mob of whites killed another black man. The three corpses were heaped together at the base of the famous Henry Grady Monument, an ironic tribute to the New South spokesperson who had argued in the 1870s and 1880s that racial conflict no longer threatened the South. A white crowd, numbering approximately 200, cornered three black draymen loading scenery for white Bijou Theater manager J. B. Belser. Belser somehow managed to pull the men back inside the theater. A white man shouted, "He's got fifteen inside!" Guarding the door with a pistol, Belser held the surging crowd at bay.[14]

At one point the crowd on Marietta Street spotted an African American and chased him toward Forsyth Street. The black man quickly disappeared. Suspecting that he was hiding inside a fruit and cigarette store, the crowd forced its way into the small structure. As the Greek proprietor and three of his white friends attempted to defend the shop, the crowd of whites tore it apart, littering the sidewalk with candy, fruit, and cigarettes. In the melee one of the white grocers was seriously wounded. Spotting another black man, this group of whites pursued him as he escaped toward the Forsyth Street viaduct. A white man emerged from the bridge's shadows and clubbed the African American to the ground. After members of the mob had kicked their victim senseless, a small group of whites emptied their revolvers into him at short range. Nearby on Peachtree, another group of whites shot and killed Will Marion at Leland's barbershop as he was polishing a white man's shoes. White witnesses testified that the bootblack was "acting in an inoffensive manner at the time." Leola Maddox, trapped with her husband downtown while shopping on Mitchell Street, was beaten and fatally stabbed.[15]

LATE INTO THE evening, large crowds of whites remained ensconced at the Kimball House. Sighted by the white mob, a black man attempted to escape into the building, but a volley of stones and clubs stopped him in his tracks. The lobby's plate glass windows were smashed, and the crashing glass forced backward a mixed crowd of whites and blacks seeking refuge from the violence on the streets. Another African American proved luckier as he successfully dodged a similar volley of stones and bricks and safely entered the hotel. The crowd's attention was diverted to another black man captured just inside the lobby. The mob passed him to the waiting horde on Wall Street. After knocking their victim unconscious, whites abandoned this African American to be trampled by others. Then, spying a fashionable restaurant nearby, the group of whites sprinted toward it, hoping to surprise its black waiters. The black men escaped, however, as some exited through a ground-level back door while others leaped from second-floor windows onto carts filled with mail sacks. From there they fled toward the unlit railroad tracks.[16]

These escapees were followed by a growing stream of African American porters and draymen—employees at the Georgia Railroad Company's Union Depot offices—who were racing along the railroad tracks to avoid the mob. Meanwhile at the depot itself, a group of whites quickly overwhelmed the futile efforts of railroad officials to protect their station from rioters. A few of the porters had failed to escape. Two of them sought refuge by locking themselves inside nearby railway coaches. After smashing the train windows, a mob stormed the coaches, dragged the porters out, and began beating them. Falling to his knees, one of the porters begged his assailants for mercy. In response, one of the white men felled this victim with a blow, after which others beat and shot him to death. Seeing no additional black targets, the crowd smashed the windows of parked railcars. Lining the streets surrounding the depot were horse-drawn cabs abandoned by their terrified black drivers. Inside the depot, white men, women, and children remained stranded and fearful into the night.[17]

With the trolleys no longer running and most African Americans having fled the riot's epicenter, the white mob began searching for new targets. Small groups of white men went from house to house and business to business throughout the downtown's white and racially mixed areas in quest of blacks in hiding. At approximately 11:45 P.M., rumors circulated that in East Point (a settlement just south of Atlanta with a tough reputation) whites had trapped a black rapist and African Americans were arming themselves to retaliate. On Forsyth Street a number of men brandishing firearms demanded that W. E. Jones provide them with horses to help them protect East Point citizens from the rumored black uprising. The white man stood his ground at the stable's entrance, pointing a pistol at the mob and daring it to cross the threshold. The mob gave in after heaving bricks and stones against the structure.[18]

Around midnight two large mobs left the Union Depot. One marched east approximately a third of a mile to the opulent Terminal Station, only to be turned back by county police. Another group, numbering approximately 100, headed southwest while shouting, "To Peters Street! To Peters Street!" The mob swelled, collecting stragglers during the quarter-mile trek to its destination, a street lined with small restaurants and saloons, many of which catered to black customers. Although African American property holders and tenants had a large presence near the railroad tracks on Peters Street's northern reaches, their numbers thinned out over a long stretch of the street as it continued southwestward. En route to Peters, the white crowd literally crashed through the Penson and McCartey hardware store and stripped the business of its guns, knives, bullets, and hammers. Three policemen joined local white residents in a vain effort to reason with the mob and convince it to turn back. Maddened by the sight of a black man, the crowd smashed the windows of restaurants it believed to be owned or frequented by African Americans.[19]

Approximately a half-mile farther down Peters, the white mob came upon Mattie Adams's residence and small restaurant, one of only two black properties on a block crowded with white residences and businesses. Adams barred her door to keep the invaders at bay. Positioned at the head of the mob, George W. Blackstock shouted threats at her and goaded the group on. Terrified, Adams braced herself against the door as Blackstock knocked out its window, stuck his hand through the opening, and slowly lifted the wooden bar. After rushing inside, Blackstock broke a wagon spoke over Mattie's head while another man struck her with a glass pitcher. A tall white man harassed her grandson by shooting bullets to his left and right. Before leaving, the mob destroyed the restaurant's furniture and glass cases. Among her white assailants, Adams recognized neighbor John Jaillette, likely the son of William Jaillette, owner of a competing establishment across the street.[20]

After leaving Adams's establishment, the mob stoned and beat against a small house owned by a black family. After one of the black occupants fired a gun through his window, white crowd members emptied their pistols into the dwelling, rearmed, and fired into the dwelling a second time. A group of whites sighted Milton Brown, a black man employed as a driver, as he made his way home after having been trapped during a downtown shopping expedition for his family. As Brown wheeled and ran, he was targeted by a forty- to fifty-bullet fusillade. Hit multiple times, Brown lurched about before reeling to the ground. Lifting the bloodied and dying man into their patrol wagon, the police could hear Brown gasping for breath through a hole in his lung. Late into the night, mobs stormed Peters and Marietta Streets, smashing poolroom and restaurant windows, battering down doors, turning rooms topsy-turvy, and wrecking entire buildings. As white commentators noted, "Furniture was destroyed, small shops were looted, windows were smashed, [and] trunks were burst open" by mobs in search of money and other valuables. By morning, downtown streets and sidewalks were strewn with shattered glass.[21]

IN A PRIVATE letter, Atlanta resident and prominent speaker of the Georgia House John Slaton admitted that "practically nothing was done to stop the mob" by the police, by law enforcement officials, or by civic leaders. Throughout the night the police proved unequal to their responsibility of maintaining order in the city. County sheriff John Nelms, who had earlier boasted that his force would curb the threat of black rape even if it required killing "every negro in a thousand miles of this place," explained his initial absence from Five Points by telling newspapers that the telephone wires to his house had been cut, blocking calls to and from his home. Police Chief Henry Jennings similarly reported that unknown persons had slashed the police station's telephone wires, disrupting departmental communications. The station itself, located within shouting distance of Five Points, disintegrated into mass confusion as African Americans poured in desperately seeking asylum. In October a Fulton County grand jury criticized some members of the county and city police for failing "signally and absolutely in their performance of duty on that fatal Saturday night," whether from "cowardice" or "active sympathy with the rioters." When the police did intervene, they generally refused to use their weapons against white mob members who ignored or challenged their authority.[22]

As the mob grew bolder, attacking property and looting white businesses, the police finally began to move against it. Just prior to midnight, Chief Jennings led a group of mounted police to the Terminal Station to prevent new conflicts from erupting between whites and blacks there. At the station the police arrested a handful of African Americans for carrying concealed weapons. At roughly the same time, three policemen attempted to force white rioters away from the Kimball House, where their frenzied pursuit of African Americans resulted in broken doors and smashed windows totaling more than $400 in damage. During the next few days, as the police turned their attention away from the threat of continued white-on-black violence, they would increasingly seek to prevent African Americans from using weapons either to protect themselves from whites or to initiate retaliatory violence. The inability of the police initially to turn back the rioters is particularly noteworthy, given the relatively small area in which the rioters confined their activity. Although witnesses reported that white mobs marched as far as one mile south of Five Points, most of the riot was confined to that main intersection and its adjacent side streets. The mob reached Peters Street only toward the end of the night and generally avoided residential areas heavily populated by blacks, perhaps fearing defensive action.[23]

At approximately 12:20 A.M., from his mansion near the Peachtree and Cain intersection, less than a third of a mile from the riot's concentrated activity, Governor Joseph Terrell summoned one artillery and eight infantry companies to the city to restore order. The governor's associates would subsequently explain Terrell's delayed response by claiming that the governor had been asleep until approximately 11:00 P.M. Given the close proximity of the governor's residence to the riot scene, it is unlikely that he could have slept through the loud noise or that his aides had no earlier knowledge of the upheaval. Terrell's decision to summon only the local militia was itself an extremely conservative response. He never declared martial law in the city, and he did not summon federal troops. The first state troops did not reach the city until approximately 2:00 A.M.[24]

By 3:00 A.M. the white rioters had tired. Blacks who had survived the mob's attack were in hiding or had fled the downtown area. Police officers' renewed determination to end the riot probably contributed to the gradual restoration of peace. A heavy rain, commencing at approximately 2:00 A.M., thinned the white crowds as all but the most enthusiastic sought cover. Late into the night, nurses and doctors at Grady Hospital dressed wounds and administered medication to many blacks and a few whites who had sustained injuries. The militia cordoned off city streets, now "sprinkled with the blood of victims that were beaten or killed" and "dotted with hats and torn clothing of Negroes who were chased by the maddened crowd." Members of the white mob, many wearing blood-soaked clothes, made their way back to their homes and farms.[25]

IN THE RIOT's immediate aftermath, local newspapers described the white rioters as the lawless element of the community or as young laboring men with a penchant for drinking and violence. W. E. B. Du Bois similarly suggested that poor, young whites were disproportionately represented among the members of the mob. Rumors spread among the city's businesspersons and manufacturers that the mob had been principally composed of cotton mill and manufacturing workers and local railroad shop laborers. In contrast, as Charles Crowe and Joel Williamson have noted, other accounts argued that the mob represented all of the city's white social classes. For example, local prohibitionists called on white Atlantans to acknowledge that at least some participants had come from the city's finest saloons. Visiting actor Arthur Hoffman suggested that well-dressed men had strenuously urged the rioters to continue their attacks. For information about the arrests on Saturday night, we must rely on the incomplete reports of newspapers and magazines. During the riot, police arrested only forty whites, or less than 1 percent of the mob's members, and they targeted the mob's most aggressive and destructive leaders. At least two of those whites later indicted for participating in the riot—George Blackstock and Herbert Talley—did indeed possess criminal records and unsavory reputations for violence. The other white men arrested by police were employed in a variety of occupations. According to magazine and newspapers accounts, those arrested included a doctor, a dentist, a carpenter, a butcher, a local business college student, a clerk, a nattily dressed white man, a wealthy Mississippian, a railway machinist, a cement worker, and a blue-collar employee of the Georgia Railway and Electric Company.[26]

Anecdotal evidence, then, does suggest that young, dispossessed white men may have composed a large portion of the mob. Yet white men from virtually every socioeconomic class contributed to the riot, either by participating in the action, by running with the mob, or by egging on its participants. In the words of one reporter, "There were thousands swept along by curiosity with no intention of crime who added by their mere presence to the ferocity of mob leaders." Support for the rioters among the police and white bystanders suggests the powerful and visceral hold that chivalric fears and desires for retribution exercised over the minds of white men in the city. Yet despite their sympathy for the white mob's desires for revenge, many white businesspersons recoiled from the momentous property damage accruing from the destruction of trolley cars, the smashing of store and hotel windows, and the looting of white hardware stores and other businesses. The *Constitution* later noted that the white mob "was at one time becoming careless of race and color in its hunger for further horrible attacks." The fact that the rioters battled police and militiamen, threatened streetcar conductors, and turned against whites, the newspaper concluded, "can not but strike apprehension into the mind of the conservative thinker."[27]

AS DAWN BROKE over the city, local militia companies were firmly encamped and patrolling the downtown area. In the early Sunday morning hours, small squads of African Americans whisked black corpses off the streets to ensure proper burials for the victims. Meanwhile, African Americans who had sought refuge from the mob in alleys and makeshift hiding places ran for the safety of black neighborhoods. Empty carriages and the corpses of horses littered the streets. The interiors of barbershops, restaurants, and hotel lobbies "bore pools of blood," while traces of "brains were still to be found in places sheltered from the rain." On Sunday, African Americans avoided the downtown area, and most hotels and restaurants had to begin operations without waiters, cooks, and other essential workers. Few domestic workers reported to work during the following days. As one white journalist noted, African Americans "did not seem to think that trolley cars were healthy places for them, and if they went out, they preferred to walk."[28]

Throughout Sunday, small groups of whites taunted and challenged the authority of the soldiers charged with maintaining order. In the afternoon a small number of white vigilantes apprehended Jack Murray, a black suspect implicated in the alleged assault attempt against Mattie Arnold. The posse hauled him into Atlanta for confinement at the jail. The buggy holding the suspect overturned, Murray escaped, and a mob of 600 white men chased the African American but failed to overtake him. Police officers frustrated another mob's attempt to lynch a second alleged suspect for the rape by transporting him into the city. In the evening a white crowd chased down another African American. The black man ran into the Marion, a fashionable hotel, where he darted for the stairs. A white man fired at him from a few feet away. The black man fell, clambered back to his feet, and ran out of the hotel, followed by a volley of bullets.[29]

Late that night in East Point a white mob lynched Zeb Long. In a general sweep of African Americans suspected of carrying concealed weapons, authorities had arrested the tall, imposing black man and charged him with possessing a cache of firearms. Around midnight a white mob of approximately fifty men broke into the flimsy jail and fastened a noose around Long's neck as the African American pleaded for his life. As Long continued begging for mercy, the mob carted him into the woods and hanged him from a pine tree limb.[30]

In Atlanta itself, the militia and the police similarly focused on harassing black residents and searching them for weapons to head off the massive retaliatory attack they now feared. As blacks noted, militia members, far from upholding the law, acted instead like "ordinary, revengeful people, pouring out their hatred for the Negro." One gang of soldiers reportedly chanted, "We are rough, we are tough, we kill niggers and never get enough!" On Sunday morning, in response to rumors that blacks were attempting to cut the water mains before torching the city, Mayor Woodward sent a squad of police to protect the local pumping stations. That night on the West Side, the area containing Atlanta's black colleges and predominantly black neighborhoods, the militia disarmed black professors who had been guarding the schools and replaced them with white officers. Militia members feared that the professors might be planning an attack; the professors were wary of relinquishing their arms to white troops. John Hope, the first black president of Morehouse College (at the time Atlanta Baptist College), defused these tensions by serving an anxious militia member refreshments inside his home and by organizing a meeting for local black residents in the college chapel. After prominent Baptist minister Peter James Bryant called upon God "to protect us, and come sooner than quick," the audience's apprehensions visibly eased.[31]

While public officials were disarming African Americans and securing white neighborhoods, white Atlantans were allowed to form vigilante groups throughout the city. Hundreds of white neighbors patrolled the areas near the Georgia School of Technology and the Third Ward after rumors spread that blacks were organizing an attack. On Sunday night in the West End, neighbors heard that hundreds of African Americans were organizing a raid on the white residential section. White men patrolled the area from Sunday morning through Monday evening.[32]

AFRICAN AMERICANS CONTINUED to organize for their defense as anger and terror pulsated throughout the black community. Blacks of all social classes were guarding their homes with rifles and guns; black neighborhoods were building their defenses just as were many white neighborhoods. In the past, many black men and women had forcibly defended themselves

Le Petit Journal's depiction of the riot underscoring black resistance to the white rioters. (Kenan Research Center at the Atlanta History Center)

from attacks by the city's racist police force, and there was a long tradition of violent resistance to any white encroachments on black neighborhoods, especially among the working class and the poor. Long after the riot, black residents recollected how African Americans had imported rifles and ammunition into their neighborhoods during the tense weeks before its outbreak.[33]

On the night of the riot, many African Americans courageously battled the white mob or struggled to silence newspaper vendors and other whites attempting to provoke the restive crowds to violence. From Saturday through Tuesday, black individuals and small groups hurled rocks and bricks at passing streetcars, and they chased down white individuals who entered their neighborhoods, whether accidentally or on purpose. Blacks vocally threatened whites with curses and epithets and fired bullets at police attempting to arrest blacks. On Tuesday a group of young black men beat a young white boy in a residential section bordering Piedmont Avenue. Although such confrontations were perhaps more numerous and intense in the immediate wake of the riot, similar racial scuffles frequently occurred in the city during the late nineteenth and early twentieth centuries.[34]

Truly extraordinary, however, was the initial success of black Atlantans in repulsing massive white assaults against two of their own neighborhoods, first in Dark Town and then in Brownsville. On Sunday evening the black residents of Dark Town, an area just down the hill from Peachtree Street in the vicinity of Houston Street and Auburn Avenue, turned out the lights of their makeshift wooden shanties and prepared for the possibility of attack by whites. The neighborhood's residents reportedly responded to white officials' promises for protection with the curt rejoinder, "Don't send the militia; we want the mob!" Though perhaps apocryphal, this urban legend reveals Dark Town's reputation among both blacks and whites as one of Atlanta's roughest neighborhoods, a tight-knit community that had always protected itself from the incursion of outsiders, especially the notoriously racist city police. As whites gathered on the hill near Peachtree Street, blacks, hearing their yells, darkened the path by putting out streetlamps. A procession of whites carrying torches and firearms moved down Houston Street toward a row of respectable black homes that divided the white neighborhoods to the west from Dark Town to the east. Before the mob could harm any person or property, a group of African Americans fired guns into its ranks. With the whites temporarily dazed, the African Americans fired again. The whites finally broke ranks and bolted back up Houston Street. As historian Carole Merritt has noted, Dark Town's defensive success blocked the further advancement of whites eastward into an area heavily populated by blacks.[35]

The residents of Brownsville first heard reports of rioting late Saturday night. The community, composed primarily of middle-class African Americans, had coalesced around Gammon Theological Seminary and Clark College, approximately three miles south of Five Points. Its residents included store owners, professors, college administrators, and postal workers, many of whom owned attractive, handsomely furnished homes nestled adjacent to the well-tended grounds of the two colleges. Through Sunday and Monday, wild rumors circulated among residents that blacks were still being massacred in downtown Atlanta and that the mob was on its way to attack their tiny settlement. Many townspeople sought safety in the chapel of Gammon Theological Seminary, where they prayed for an end to the carnage. Gammon interim president John Wesley Bowen worked feverishly, comforting residents and attempting unsuccessfully to negotiate by phone with city officials to dispatch law enforcement officials to protect Brownsville.[36]

Meanwhile rumors of a very different sort were spreading through white Atlanta—rumors that Brownsville's residents were planning a retaliatory strike against nearby white settlements. On Monday evening seven police-men joined three deputized citizens to mount an offensive against Browns-ville. At approximately 8:00 P.M., on the Jonesboro Road, just outside the settlement, the county police contingent came upon a small, open-air meet-ing of African Americans, many of whom were armed. The police arrested six of them. Continuing down Jonesboro Road with their prisoners in tow, the officers sighted approximately twenty-five additional African Americans. Upon seeing the officers, these Brownsville residents retreated back toward their village, pursued by the white posse. Now cornered, the local residents feared the white posse was bent on destroying their village. Upon entering the settlement, Officer Henry Poole ordered the residents to raise their hands in surrender. The two groups exchanged shots—each side charged the other with firing the first volley. In the ensuing melee the villagers shot and killed Officer Jim Heard and slightly injured four other posse mem-bers. Black resident Frank Fambro, a grocer, died during the encounter, while other African Americans sustained injuries. Blacks scattered into their houses.[37]

Clearly outnumbered, the white posse retreated to a white residential neighborhood at the intersection of Jonesboro and Mcdonough Roads. From there the leaders of the posse telephoned both the county sheriff and militia commander Clifford Anderson. The white contingent, still holding its Brownsville prisoners, boarded a passing streetcar and began making its way into Atlanta. At 10:30 P.M., at the intersection of Crew and Jefferson Streets, a white mob halted the trolley. Two of the suspects—Sam McGruder, a brick mason, and Wiley Brooks—escaped from the vehicle and ran up Crew Street tailed by white pursuers. Just as the two black men reached a nearby porch, the mob overtook the suspects and, in the words of a local newspaper, "literally" shot them "to pieces." Magruder died; his companion was in critical condition. A pregnant neighbor, Mary Thompson, thirty-five years old and already ailing from another health problem, was reportedly so shocked by the scene that she dropped dead of heart failure.[38]

Meanwhile militia companies hurried to Brownsville. Rather than attack the black village in the uncertainty of nighttime, the militia waited for dawn. By that time three infantry companies, the Governor's Horse Guard, a ma-chine gun, and 10,000 rounds of ammunition had been readied. By Tuesday morning's first light, the soldiers began searching village homes for am-munition and potential suspects. Still fearful of possible black resistance, the militia moved with dispatch. One of the first homes they entered belonged to L. J. Price, a local postmaster, whom they immediately arrested for the

The state militia halted on Marietta Street at Five Points, 1906. Inset is a posed photograph of a white posse surrounding a Brownsville building alleged to have been a gathering place for black resisters. (Kenan Research Center at the Atlanta History Center)

possession of weapons and ammunition. Encountering a bedridden resident, the soldiers shoved revolvers against his chest and shot him several times in front of his family members. The victim miraculously survived. When carpenter Sam Robinson refused to halt on the militiamen's orders, the soldiers opened fire and fatally wounded him. President Bowen, wrongfully blamed by white officials for Heard's death, was assaulted by soldiers and kept under house arrest throughout the morning. A seventy-year-old man was later found dead in a nearby grocery store with a knife wound across his abdomen. For two hours the military searched the houses. They arrested more than 250 African Americans, of whom approximately 70, charged with either weapons violations or Heard's murder, were marched to the county jail. Wives, daughters, and sisters wailed and prayed as their houses were searched and their husbands and fathers were assaulted and arrested.[39]

The county police, still convinced that armed African Americans threatened white Atlantans, scoured the area around Gammon Theological Seminary until early afternoon. Sheriff Nelms deputized 300 whites in case the militia proved inadequate to the task of maintaining order and protecting the city's white population. Law enforcement officials readied streetcars to transport the militia to any area of the city. In all, at least four black men were killed in Brownsville during the riot. Struggles between whites and blacks throughout the city continued through Tuesday morning. Mobs of white men shot to death a black man in the vicinity of the South Pryor Street and Ridge Avenue intersection; another crowd of white men "literally shot off" both legs of another African American male on Haygood Avenue. In gunfire exchange near Inman Park, law enforcement officials reportedly killed two more black men. While the city remained tense the rest of the day, members of the militia and the police continued to disband white mobs and search for armed blacks without a major confrontation.[40]

THE OFFICIAL ESTIMATES of the number of individuals killed during the riot grossly underreported the three days' mortalities. On 29 December 1906, Chamber of Commerce representatives published the findings of an official riot investigation suggesting that only twelve persons had died. This figure included three of the four Brownsville deaths and the two whites who died in the riot's aftermath—Officer Heard and Mary Thompson. The report concluded, "Wild rumors of a larger number killed have no foundation that we can discover." The chamber representatives had an obvious interest in minimizing the number of fatalities to protect their city's long-guarded image. Accounts of killings found in several newspapers—including the report about the three black men said to have been killed on the first trolley car attacked at the Peachtree and Marietta intersection—were never tallied in official records because the victims' bodies were never found. The county coroner decided early not to conduct an inquest into the riot's mortalities. In contrast to the official numbers, the most conservative newspaper accounts immediately following the riot suggested sixteen black deaths on Saturday night alone. But even this number is clearly an undercount. The *News* estimated on Sunday that as many as twenty or thirty blacks had been killed, and city newspapers were filled with reports of corpses reportedly seen on "good authority" mysteriously disappearing overnight. White public officials and black commentators noted that many African Americans secretly interred their dead comrades to ensure them proper burials.[41]

Prominent white Atlantan John Slaton argued that the local newspapers, far from exaggerating the white rioters' violence, left untold "one-half the things done and the outrages committed" by whites against blacks that Saturday night. Francis Jackson Garrison recounted a private conversation with Walter Hines Page in which the southern white journalist contended that there were hundreds of mortalities, perhaps 250, that night. Black Atlantans frequently stressed the undercounting of white fatalities much more than the underreporting of black fatalities. Jesse Max Barber estimated as many as six white deaths on Saturday night alone, and throughout his life prominent black undertaker David T. Howard regaled friends and relatives with stories of the large number of whites that public officials asked him to quietly bury. In addition to Monday night's two white deaths, one could reasonably estimate, at a minimum, a combined total of at least twenty black deaths on the Saturday night of the riot and during the two-day Brownsville struggle. Zeb Long's lynching and the Tuesday morning deaths of three more black men increased the riot's total mortality count to twenty-six.[42]

These aggregate figures do not include a man that Evelyn Witherspoon remembered seeing shot to death as he swung from a light pole or a black man "cut all to pieces at the corner of Richardson and Pryor Streets" or the many bodies reportedly seen but never recovered in areas throughout the city. Episcopal minister Cary Wilmer, who worked closely with white public officials following the riot, remembered that the Atlanta police department's recording secretary had estimated that fifty blacks had been killed that Saturday night alone. It is almost certain, then, that Charles Crowe's conjecture that at least twenty-five African Americans died during the four-day period between 22 and 25 September is an undercount. The chamber's report admitted that at least ten whites and at least sixty African Americans were injured during the riot. Yet African Americans hid their wounded for fear of white retribution against those injured by violence.[43]

The riot also affected Atlanta's African American population in ways that can never be measured simply by statistics enumerating the injured or dead. As the chamber's official riot report noted, "Most of the dead left small children and widows, mothers or sisters with practically no means and very small earning capacity." Many black Atlantans lost their jobs or abandoned the lives they had attempted to build in the city. All of the Western Union Telegraph Company's black messengers fearfully quit their jobs after the brutal slaying of their coworker Frank Smith. Many of the downtown restaurants, barbershops, lunchrooms, and small stores owned or patronized by blacks also sustained heavy damage or were destroyed. As many as 5,000 residents left the city, many only temporarily, so apprehensive were they of a replay of the night's grisly events.[44]

Among the permanent black émigrés were William Hunton, an internationally recognized YMCA official, and his wife, Addie, a nationally prominent clubwoman. Before the September violence, the Huntons had enjoyed a rewarding home life and close friendships with Jesse Max Barber and John and Lugenia Burns Hope. The riot, Addie painfully recalled more than thirty years later, left her family "very empty, for we knew in that hour that all for which we had labored and sacrificed belonged not to us but to a ruthless mob." Her husband, she was convinced, never fully recovered either emotionally or physically from this "stunning blow to his fine sensitive soul as well as to his physical condition." In the riot's aftermath, William "kept grimly serious" and contracted the first of many devastating illnesses that would culminate in his death in 1914. At his insistence, the family relocated to Brooklyn in December 1906. With the Huntons' departure, black Atlanta lost two of its most influential black activists.[45]

Other blacks similarly staggered in horror at the mob's destructiveness and reacted with a deep sense of betrayal at the relatively timid efforts of public officials to control the mob. In the words of one former city resident,

> How would you feel if you saw a governor, a mayor, a sheriff, whom you could not oppose at the polls, encourage by deed or word or both, a mob of "best" and worst citizens to slaughter your people in the streets and in their own homes and in their places of business? Do you think that you could resist the same wrath that caused God to slay the Philistines and the Russians to throw bombs? I can resist it, but with each new outrage I am less able to resist it. . . . I must hurry through the only life I shall live on earth, tortured by these experiences and these horrible impulses, with no hope of ever getting away from them. They are ever present, like the just God, the devil, and my conscience.[46]

THE RIOT'S VIOLENCE was singular in Atlanta's history for its excessiveness, its brutality, and its duration. Yet the riot did not mark a departure from the city's everyday racial struggles so much as an intensification of long-standing conflicts. Comparative studies of racial violence conclude that ethnic riots can be "interpreted as efforts to taunt and humiliate victims, deny them honor, demand their subservience, demonstrate their powerlessness, and redefine them as alien and illegitimate occupants of the place where the attack takes place." The riot broke out in Five Points, an area notorious for unregulated contact between the races. Throughout the city, mill workers and other laborers shared a long-established tradition of "rocking" (i.e., chasing and beating) African Americans who accidentally entered their villages and residential areas. Viewed in that context, the violence in Five Points was partly an attempt by whites to cordon off the center city as their own. For a brief period white rioters established their unquestioned dominance over an area where conflicts had previously been open-ended and where blacks had at least occasionally gained the upper hand. This display of white men's power represented the imposition of the utter white male supremacy demanded during the summer's newspaper and letter-writing campaigns. And it constituted an attempt among white men to claim the physical territory of downtown Atlanta as their own space. Between Saturday and Tuesday, white mobs also targeted both black dwellings that were situated alongside white residences and black settlements that bordered white neighborhoods. These massive downtown attacks and residential incursions are comparable to the pogrom-like efforts to rid entire towns of African Americans that took place in areas throughout the state's upper piedmont and mountain regions during the late nineteenth and early twentieth centuries. Had Atlanta's black population been smaller, the substantial postriot outmigration of African Americans would have critically affected the city's ratio of blacks to whites.[47]

As John Dittmer has suggested, the rioters' actions also reflected growing economic tensions between the races, as was so baldly evidenced during Jaillette's attack on Adams's restaurant. In particular, many whites had long voiced anger at the fact that black barbers and black-owned barbershops could service white customers, thereby snagging business from their white competitors. Such jealousies were reflected in the brutal attacks leveled by whites against barbers and bootblacks—two professions still dominated by blacks at the turn of the century. For several years after the riot, whites in many skilled occupations, especially machinists and railway firemen, would continue voicing concerns that job competition with African Americans threatened to lower their wages. The attacks against the small lunchrooms and saloons on Decatur, Marietta, and Peters Streets financially devastated marginal black owners. In the riot's aftermath, the concentration of black businesses along Auburn Avenue accelerated dramatically, while black business activity in the city's center languished before a precipitous decline after 1910.[48]

No single spectacle on Saturday night had so inflamed the white mob and spurred it forward as that of streetcars ferrying black passengers through the downtown area. The riot provided frustrated whites an opportunity to physically beat down and impose their will on black passengers, who in ordinary circumstances employed a myriad of strategies to resist Jim Crow oppression. The viciousness with which white rioters attacked black passengers had been building for more than a decade as blacks stalwartly resisted attempts by whites to force them to accept second-class treatment. In adjusting the segregated seating arrangements as the trolleys filled up, white operators often roughly handled black passengers, shouting commands such as "Heh, you nigger, get back there!" Yet tales of black impudence were as common in the white community as stories of white injustice were among the black population. For their own part, some black riders occasionally refused to pay their fares or even tussled with the conductors, who armed themselves to stave off such threats. Many more ignored or challenged white directives, as the sheer number of blacks provided an anonymity that shielded individual rule violators, particularly when protests were voiced from the back of the car or under the breath. Crowded conditions occasionally forced white females to sit near black men, which only inflamed white men's sexual jealousies. During the riot, one white motorman, perhaps betraying his own frustrations with repeated black resistance against his authority, assaulted a black passenger with a brass control lever.[49]

Saturday's attacks were centered on black businesses and the public spaces of interracial contact. In contrast, the raids against Dark Town and Brownsville were bold attempts to extend white power into the private spaces that African Americans had long defended from white incursion. After Reconstruction, local blacks had created webs of public and private relationships in their homes, neighborhoods, and churches—places that shielded them from the virulent racism of white officials and private citizens, whom they encountered in the city's public spaces. Confronted with overwhelming terror, blacks retreated into their own neighborhoods, seeking shelter in churches and private colleges. The cooperation necessary to turn back heavily armed white invaders had been forged over decades in the course of countless conversations and exchanges of favors at church services and socials, at meetings of the hundreds of mutual aid societies and neighborhood clubs dotting Atlanta, over drinks at the cheap saloons in the city's center, and at the deliberations of labor unions and secret societies. Black journalist Jesse Max Barber argued that whites sought to close black restaurants, saloons, and barbershops immediately after the riot precisely because they knew that these locations "afforded the Negroes a rendezvous for congregating and discussing the situation."[50]

BETWEEN 10:00 P.M. and approximately midnight that 22 September, the proponents of lynching succeeded in uniting a wide range of white male Atlantans around a violent vision that emphasized the shared role of all white men as guardians of white womanhood and upholders of white supremacy. For a brief moment, whites established their unequivocal dominance over downtown public spaces—the streetcars and the railroad stations, the central business district, and the cheap saloons along Decatur and

Peters Streets—spaces that had in the past been scenes of more open-ended daily racial struggles. In this context the riot revealed the powerful hold that shared gendered conceptions of white supremacy and chivalry exercised over many white males in the city. Whites representing a wide range of classes applauded the pacifying effect that the riot seemed to have on African Americans. Referring to the riot, *Georgian* editor John Temple Graves maintained, "It is common testimony of thoughtful men that not in two decades have the Negroes of this region been so accommodating, so reasonable, so polite, and so thoroughly kind and considerate in their attitude toward white persons as they are today." As many blacks recognized, the riot demonstrated the desperate and random violence that many whites were willing to deploy to shore up white dominance and discourage black resistance. In the short term at least, the white rioters partially achieved their objective, in Jesse Max Barber's words, "to 'whip and humble'" the city's black population. Blacks could hardly resist the three infantry companies and the 10,000 rounds of ammunition marshaled by the state government during the Brownsville invasion.[51]

Ironically, however, given the aims of the white mob, many African Americans, especially members of the middle class and the elite, discovered within themselves and their various communities new sources of strength and a renewed sense of unity. Throughout much of the twentieth century, blacks continued to take pride in the heroism displayed by black residents while defending themselves and fellow African Americans. In 1979 Horace Sinclair, who launched his career as an Auburn Avenue barber in the 1920s, informed an interviewer that the actions taken by Dark Town residents during the riot helped to seal the area's reputation as the place where "the bad niggers" reigned. That Sinclair punctuated his account with phrases such as "You ought to hear them talk about that" and "That's what they say" suggests how widespread these stories had become.[52]

In the past, black elites had publicly counseled against confronting white violence with counterattacks. During and immediately following the riot, however, members of this group armed themselves to protect their own families and homes. Many, like John Wesley Dobbs, would continue stashing away guns and ammunition for years following the riot, just in case the mobs returned to their neighborhoods. Du Bois, looking back on his life in an autobiography completed in 1960, confessed that he could never imagine killing a bird or a rabbit, much less another human being. Yet in the riot's immediate aftermath, he "bought a Winchester double-barreled shotgun and two dozen rounds of shells filled with buckshot. If a white mob had stepped on the campus where I lived I would without hesitation have sprayed their guts over the grass."[53]

Du Bois and others, by defending their families with arms and later recounting their bravery, were also reaffirming their manhood and their self-avowed roles as protectors and guardians of their wives and children. The white rioters' attacks had targeted both the bodies and the masculine identities of black men. African American affirmations of black manliness simultaneously marginalized the importance of black women's resistance against the white mob and almost certainly exaggerated the defenselessness of the women. Largely lost to black historical memories, for example, were newspaper accounts of black women defending themselves and others on 22 September both in trolleys and on the streets. The *Los Angeles Times* described black women as the "most warlike, urging resistance to the mob, and they themselves fighting like Amazons." Some black men, including Walter White, clearly exaggerated their role in guarding female family members, whether purposefully or unconsciously. White's mother privately disputed her son's recollection that his father and he had defended their home and female family members with firearms while the women hid in rooms far from the street. As she remembered events, there had never been any firearms in the house, and the women had peered down on the mob from an upstairs window.[54]

THE RIOT ULTIMATELY emphasized to white civic leaders and businesspersons the insupportable costs of racial violence. White elites, confronting property damage and devastating national publicity, recoiled from both the rioters' indiscriminate destructiveness and the very success of their attacks. Once more, the determination of African Americans to defend their communities prompted some whites to acknowledge the potential dangers of a racial philosophy that eagerly promoted racial division and violence. According to John Hope's wife, Lugenia, who witnessed firsthand the confrontations between black professors and the militia at Atlanta Baptist College, the possibility of continued black violence forced whites to recognize the ongoing threat posed by a black community that had united to defend its neighborhoods and institutions. Emphasizing blacks' determination to resist white encroachment, she wrote, "[African Americans] felt they had stood as much as any man could—They were prepared for every eventuality." Once blacks demonstrated an unequivocal willingness to protect their communities at any cost, Hope argued, "the white man learned . . . in this riot to get along together [with blacks,] that there must be cooperation."

Many whites discerned a new distrust among the black masses in the riot's wake. A white woman observed that black residents had "grown so glum and serious that I'm free to say I'm scared of them!"[55]

Working-class blacks drew on the common bonds that they had forged in the saloons, dance halls, and other private spaces beyond white control to force back the white mob. Professor William Crogman of Clark College noted the riot's central irony: "Here we have worked and prayed and tried to make good men and women of our colored population, and at our very doorstep the whites kill these good men. But the lawless element in our population, the element we have condemned fights back, and it is to these people that we owe our lives." Crogman's admission is remarkable considering his prior characterizations of "physical resistance" as "literal madness" and his arguments that racial progress depended on the establishment of clear distinctions among African Americans. Only such demarcations would ensure that the race would be judged not "by the criminals among them" but by those "honest hard-working men and women" of wealth and property. Similarly, in a private letter Dr. Horace Bumstead, the white president of Atlanta University, reported a black pastor's observation: "We were saved by our worst element, because they fired back."[56]

WALTER WHITE CONCLUDED his 1948 autobiography with the assertion, now widely accepted by scholars, that no essential biological difference separates "whites" from "blacks." With this insight, he looked back again on the riot and "how I felt when I stood beside my father and feared that the whites would not let me live, that I must kill them first and then be killed." According to his narrative, it was not biology but the riot and other shared historical experiences that had rendered White's "spirit" and his "heart" black. He loved this black inner self "for her patience and her sorrows, for the soft sound of her singing, and for the great dawn which is coming upon her, in which her vigor and faith will serve the world."[57] So ended White's final account of an event that his writings had repeatedly revisited over a span of more than twenty-two years.

Taken together, White's often contradictory narratives reveal the riot's powerful role in strengthening the shared racial identities and loyalties of diverse groups of African Americans. White's assertion that the riot reinforced his racial pride and fired his resolve to battle mob violence appears indisputable. In the decades following this massacre, White put his life at risk over and over again, investigating forty-nine separate incidences of racial violence for the NAACP between 1918 and 1930. Then, as NAACP executive secretary from 1931 to 1955, he worked tirelessly as a fund-raiser for the organization's legal battles, a lobbyist for antilynching legislation, and a foe of discrimination. Despite these civil rights commitments, White suffered from frequent accusations that he identified more closely with whites than with the African Americans whose interests his organization represented. These recurring criticisms were only aggravated by his light skin color and elitism, his many close white friendships, his support for racial integration at the expense of black separatism, and his 1949 decision to divorce his black wife of twenty-seven years to marry a white woman. As Kenneth Janken points out, White's portrayals of the riot affirmed his black identity for an African American audience. White addressed public doubts regarding his racial loyalties by describing his near-murder at the hands of a white mob, by emphasizing his courageous role in his neighborhood's collective defense, and by offering readers an apparently fictive story of his father's and his own heroism in saving a black cook from the white mob.[58]

Additionally, White's 1948 account traces the distinct limits of black Atlantans' incipient alliances across traditional class lines. White, in his final description of the riot, posits middle-class African Americans as his race's saviors at the cost of marginalizing the role of working-class African Americans in defending their community. White implicitly characterizes the black heroes compelling the white mob's final retreat as middle-class "friends" of his family, barricaded "just below our house."[59]

Mary White Ovington, in a 1927 essay, portrays the NAACP leader as recognizing the importance of Dark Town's repulsion of white aggression. Unlike White's 1948 version, this earlier account describes the white mob as suspending its attack on White's house not in retreat but in a rush to continue down the street toward a second group of unidentified black men "barricaded in a brick house" and firing their weapons with the aim of "tempting the invaders to come on." The "big fight" takes place only when the whites reach Dark Town, where the neighborhood's working-class black residents finally force a white retreat. By revising his public memories of the riot in 1948, White was both defending himself from charges of racial disloyalty and claiming that black elites were their race's authentic heroes and leaders.[60]

Just as the successful defense of black institutions initially reinforced feelings of intraracial strength and solidarity among most blacks, so, too, did it suggest the limited ability of whites to extend their power and influence beyond Atlanta's public spaces into the African American world behind Jim Crow's veil. Yet even after its defensive successes, the city's black population was also forced to acknowledge the overwhelming power demonstrated by the state militia during its attack on Brownsville. In the riot's immediate aftermath, white public officials and racist demagogues throughout the state clamped down on any signs of black resistance. That week in Albany and Macon, at the insistence of white politicians, police moved into the saloon districts, harassing and arresting black men in an effort to rid their cities of "worthless and criminal" African Americans. In Augusta, black journalist W. J. White received death threats in response to an editorial critical of segregation and racial prejudice.[61] Faced with these bitter lessons and new threats, middle-class and elite blacks throughout Georgia turned their attention to the long-term problem of securing their churches, colleges, neighborhoods, and businesses—indeed their very lives—from the twin threats of renewed mob violence and police incursion. Elite blacks confronted new choices. As had been the case during the riot, their decisions and words would be public declarations of who they were and where their loyalties rested.

CHAPTER FIVE

Competing National Constructions of

Manhood and Mayhem

—

WELL INTO THE SPRING OF 1907, stories on Atlanta filled national newspapers and magazines, indulging Americans' seemingly insatiable demand for details of the riot. As James Waring of Baltimore noted, African Americans empathized with black Atlantans' "misery and suffering" and "saw in their own neighborhoods more or less of the causes which led to that unfortunate affair." White northerners nervously read about the city's crisis as they sought lessons on how to cope with their own rising black populations and simmering social conflicts. Both blacks and southern whites recognized the dangers and opportunities posed by the debate that these stories triggered. White southerners had long defended lynching with arguments that it targeted black outlaws and rapists. Yet northern editors immediately fastened on the fact that Atlanta's mob had paid no attention to "good character and orderly behavior" but had instead killed African Americans without any "account of the guilt or innocence of their victims." The *New York World* railed, "Out of blind race hatred Atlanta has turned its main streets into shambles and has butchered Negroes for sheer lust of blood."[1]

To African Americans' consternation, denunciations of alleged assaults by blacks reverberated just as shrilly as did tales of brutality by whites. Beneath headlines reading "Frequent Attacks on Women Lead to Reprisal," the *San Francisco Chronicle* asserted that four assaults that Saturday had "followed two others of a similar nature within the week and at least half a dozen others within the last two months."[2] National newspapers also expressed a fascination with black defensive violence. One, for example, carried the headline REVENGE BY BLACKS. Another noted that ATLANTA NEGROES were KILLING WHITES in A WAR OF RETALIATION. After broadcasting the front-page headline NEGROES BEGIN A CAMPAIGN OF MURDER, the *Chronicle* warned, "Should race hates intensify, should the war be carried beyond Atlanta and involve Georgia and adjacent states . . . the South would be reaping a terrible harvest."[3]

These descriptions of Atlanta's black and white "savages" cast the riot-associated discourse in metaphors that exercised a powerful hold over American racial imaginations. Turn-of-the-century middle-class white men grounded their claims to moral and political authority on their "manliness" and "civilization"—that is, their self-control and respectability as well as their capacity to protect, with violence if necessary, their familial dependents and larger society from the alleged lawlessness and brutality of "savage" white working-class men and men of color. White southerners had legitimized disfranchisement, lynching, and racial inequality through a veritable outpouring of images and texts that linked black masculinity with sexual dissolution as well as aggression and intemperance.[4] Black commentators generally countered this discourse with their own representations of southern white savagery and African American manliness.

In wrestling over the riot's meaning, then, whites and African Americans were battling over which groups and ideologies might rightfully claim political and social power in the South and the nation. Many immediately sensed that the national struggle over the interpretation of Atlanta's events had the potential to reshape America's racial debate. For many African Americans, the discourse on the riot provided an opportunity to point out injustices in southern society and to seek federal protection of their civil rights and physical bodies. Through the metaphors of manliness, W. E. B. Du Bois and his allies sought to use the riot to challenge Booker T. Washington's policy of accommodation, not only among African Americans but also among Americans at large. Both Washington and his opponents understood that Atlanta's developments could dislodge the union of influential blacks and racially progressive northern whites that had coalesced around his leadership.[5]

AS MUCH AS any African American, *Voice of the Negro* editor Jesse Max Barber recognized the dangers posed by the widespread broadcasting of stories linking the riot with the sexual crimes of "depraved and brutal" black men. Having encountered this perspective even in foreign publications, Barber warned, "This wholesale misrepresentation has been sent out from the theatre of mischief and an effort is made to deceive the world that is supposed to have fathomless gullibility on this race question." Barber sought to challenge white racist stereotypes of black criminality by altering Americans' dominant interpretations of what had taken place in Atlanta. Barber's national perspective helps explain his courageous decision to telegraph to the *New York World* an anonymous dispatch refuting Atlanta whites' justification of white brutalities as a measured response aimed at controlling black sexual savagery.[6]

Barber's piece was a reply to a 24 September *World* article penned by John Temple Graves and widely circulated through the Associated Press. Graves had linked the riot's outbreak to "a horrible carnival of intolerable crime" and reiterated his long-held assertion that only the complete "separation of the races" would solve the problem of black assaults. Playing on northern fears, Graves admonished readers that they, too, would have embraced a "lawless revolution" had their women been terrorized by a wave of black-on-white assaults. Barber clearly feared the potential negative effect of Graves's article on a national audience. The *World* had a circulation of more than 300,000 readers in 1906, more than twenty times the size of the *Voice*'s readership.[7]

Barber's article refuted Graves's equation; it was not black criminals who were responsible for the riot but, rather, a white mob "as lawless and as godless as any savages." The black journalist placed responsibility for the violence squarely on the shoulders of "sensational newspapers and unscrupulous politicians." He described Hoke Smith as a "human moccasin" and castigated *News* editor Charles Daniel for his "fire-eating and reckless editorials." Once more, Barber reported a white business leader's confession that the brutal beatings and attempted assaults that had occurred just before the primary election had been the work of Smith "emissaries" who had "blacked their faces." Of the four rapes that Graves alleged had taken place on the day of the riot, three clearly represented false reports. "The remedy" for racial violence lay not with segregation but with "an impartial enforcement of the laws of the land" and the protection of "all the people." In short, Barber blamed the riot on the city's leading white journalists and the Smith campaign. There is no evidence corroborating Barber's claims that white rapists had blackened their faces that summer. Still, this image nicely encapsulated Barber's larger message that white men of all classes, not black men, represented Atlanta's arch criminals. Barber heaped respon-

sibility for the riot on wealthy white Atlantans and even fingered "a prominent banker" as a potential conspirator in the Smith organization's nefarious
attacks against white women. True peace in the city, he concluded, required
national intervention.[8]

Local civic leaders denounced the article as an insult against Atlanta and
its finest men. City newspapers called for its author's lynching. On the day
after the article was published, local telegraph office employees revealed
Barber as its sender. Fourth National Bank president James English, who
had assumed a leadership role in Atlanta's efforts to restore order, summoned Barber to his office. He castigated the black journalist for his "vile
slander" against the city. English demanded that Barber appear before a
grand jury and openly disavow the article. Then the black editor must publicly renounce the article's assertions in the local and national press, including the *World*. Otherwise, English informed Barber, "You must leave the city
within twenty-four hours or I will not be responsible for the consequences."[9]

After his Friday session with English, Barber departed immediately for
Montgomery, Alabama; he returned on Sunday only to retrieve his page
proofs and other valuables. Shadowed and accosted by suspicious whites
claiming to be special officers, he left for Chicago on the next train. His
circulation manager followed the next day. Now situated in Chicago without
any printing equipment, Barber sent out a circular pleading for donations
and subscription payments from readers. He had sunk his last dollar into the
magazine and was utterly broke. "If our people don't rally and come to our
support," he importuned, "we must go down, for we have lost all in the
Atlanta riots."[10]

Barber's exodus appears to have profoundly shamed this New Black Man.
From his new home, Barber asserted that he left Atlanta not because he
feared death but because he hoped to preserve his manhood. "A man," he
told black reporters, "has to die but once and I feel that he could die in no
better cause than that of the Negro. But if I went before the grand jury . . . I
would be . . . railroaded through the penitentiary and the chain gang," truly a
fate "worse than death." Accused of cowardice by Booker T. Washington,
Barber defensively affirmed both his manly pluck and fearless commitment
to unselfish racial service: "My little life is but a drop in the great ocean of
truth. Gladly would I give my life if it would vindicate our cause and ameliorate the conditions of my people in the South. . . . Yes! I will pledge myself to
work, if necessary, sixteen hours a day and live on crust and cold water to
serve my people in this righteous cause." Throughout the fall, Barber worked

furiously to rebuild his magazine, whose name he changed that November to simply the *Voice*, apparently in hopes of attracting more white readers.[11]

Following his brush with English, Barber abandoned any remnants of his earlier faith in interracial cooperation and his hopes that "thoroughness of work, beauty in manners, care and tact in business and an uncompromising fidelity to truth . . . will win respect" among white southerners. The manhood and striving promoted by the Niagara Movement could never survive among white southerners, those "greatest dwarf-makers of history," who were intent on tethering black men to "some dank and fetid, sub-human, super-animal world." The only hope for southern blacks, he argued, was for white northern powerbrokers to "lead us out of this wilderness of fratricidal hatred" by forcing the South to abandon its castrating oppressions. Barber thus challenged northerners to live up to their own claims of manliness and civilization by intervening in the South to control its white savages.[12]

THE ATLANTA RIOT also triggered a political and intellectual crisis for Booker T. Washington at a crucial moment in his racial leadership. Even before the riot, he had been placed on the defensive by recent developments—especially the birth of the Niagara Movement, Theodore Roosevelt's growing abandonment of African Americans, and weakening support for his own program among the white ideological heirs to the nineteenth-century abolitionist movement. The Wizard's inflexible refusal to adjust his strategy in the face of mounting racial setbacks spawned new doubts regarding his leadership capabilities among both a small group of northern white civil rights proponents and a growing number of independent-minded African Americans. As early as 1903, a band of self-proclaimed white "neoabolitionists" led by newspaper and magazine publisher Oswald Garrison Villard had begun questioning Washington's philosophy of accommodation and his emphasis on gradualism. As late as 1906, however, this group remained distrustful of the motives underlying criticisms of the Wizard made by Du Bois and his allies. At the same time, many nationally influential blacks were quietly distancing themselves from Washington and his views. Among these were Kelly Miller, Mary Church Terrell, African Methodist Episcopal (AME) Zion bishop Alexander Walters, and Francis Grimké. Yet, on the eve of the riot, they remained reluctant to break openly with Washington or to publicly endorse Du Bois's attacks.[13]

While Washington recognized the physical dangers that the riot posed to himself and other blacks, he also feared its potential for radicalizing African

Americans and alienating them from his leadership. After the riot, Washington privately expressed his apprehensions regarding the well-being of Atlanta blacks and the commitment of local whites to law and order. In a series of confidential letters to trusted friends, he described the mob as "disgraceful and discreditable" and mentioned their "unspeakably cruel acts" as well as the criminal negligence of the police authorities. In late September the Wizard learned that whites had railroaded Barber out of Atlanta after the interception of his telegram to the *World*. Washington, fearful that his own correspondence might trigger a similar white reaction, warned a northern correspondent that it was "not safe" for him (Washington) to receive any "telegrams bearing upon Atlanta conditions," even at his home in Tuskegee.[14]

Interpreting black condemnation of Atlanta as a threat to his influence, Washington carefully guarded these private concerns. Since his famous "Atlanta Compromise" speech, Washington had been closely associated with the city. During the late August meeting of the National Negro Business League held there, Washington had spoken with the editors of the major newspapers in an attempt to calm the increasingly tense situation. Although all four major dailies printed parts of Washington's speech before the league, the *Constitution* and others misrepresented his message, making it appear that he posited black criminals rather than white lynchers as the greatest dangers to law and order. After the riot broke out, many of Washington's enemies, especially the editors of the *Chicago Broad Ax*, deployed white newspaper characterizations of his speech to dismiss the Wizard as "a cringing coward, without any honest convictions . . . more than willing to do the bidding of the murderous editor of the News."[15]

Washington could initially address these concerns for leadership and public safety by advocating the immediate restoration of peace in Atlanta. On Tuesday a shaken Washington authored a letter published in the *World* and the *New York Times*. Feeling "the present situation too deeply to give an extended utterance at this time," Washington urged the "colored people in Atlanta and elsewhere to exercise self-control and not make the fatal mistake of attempting to retaliate." In an ambiguous statement that could be read as critical of both white rioters and putative black rapists, he expressed "very deep grief on account of the death of so many innocent men of both races because of the deeds of a few despicable criminals." Washington also advocated "the inflexible enforcement of the laws against all criminals" and encouraged the efforts already under way among "the best white people and the best colored people" to "come together in council and use their united efforts to stop the present disorder." In this and other letters he repeatedly portrayed Atlanta's violence as unrepresentative of the larger South by reminding blacks that "while there is disorder in one community there is peace and harmony in thousands of others."[16]

Once some semblance of peace had been reestablished in Atlanta, Washington narrowed his focus to the public defense of his long-standing racial program from potential black criticism. In a 1 October *New York Age* article Washington, already aware that Barber had moved to Chicago to avoid arrest and a possible lynching, counseled readers that no man who fled the South had any right to "spend his time in giving advice to the Negro from a long distance how he should conduct himself in the South." In thus attacking Barber, Washington was simultaneously reaffirming his preriot vision of black southern manliness. True courage, Washington maintained, required a silent, stoic acceptance of injustices as a means of preserving black institutions and ensuring black survival. According to Washington, Barber's militant criticisms of local whites did not reveal bravery so much as a suicidal immaturity. Once the black journalist had retreated from the South, the Wizard insinuated, he had abandoned any claims to speaking on behalf of black southerners. On 8 October in a second *Age* article, Washington warned a national black audience that "intemperate and wild utterances" would not "help matters in the South," especially the attempts to restore order in Atlanta. Finally, Washington's private secretary Emmett J. Scott authored an October *Age* article charging that Du Bois's genuine reason for departing Atlanta for Alabama in late September was not to complete an ongoing research project, as the professor claimed, but to calm his unmanly fears. Washington, in contrast, Scott maintained, had bravely run to Atlanta, not from it, on 28 September to promote racial peace.[17]

AS WASHINGTON SENSED, the riot had radicalized African Americans and was encouraging even many of his once trusted allies to question the key assumptions underlying his strategy of accommodation. Du Bois's "A Litany of Atlanta," penned immediately after the riot, directly refuted Washington's doctrine that black moral and economic progress might protect African Americans from white mobs. The typical riot victim, Du Bois suggested, had followed Washington's advice: "Work and Rise! He worked. Did this man sin? Nay, but someone told how someone said another did—one whom he had never seen nor known. Yet for that man's crime this man lieth maimed and murdered, his wife naked to shame, his children to poverty and evil." Du Bois thus emphasized the mob's indiscriminate murder of African Americans.[18]

For others, the fact that the mob had attacked respectable blacks demonstrated a profound flaw in Washington's hopes that whites might support black progress. Far from random, this choice of targets revealed a general jealousy among whites toward all successful African Americans as well as a desire among poor whites to prevent any African Americans from advancing economically. As early as 1903, Francis J. Grimké, a Presbyterian minister in the District of Columbia, had privately praised Du Bois as divinely chosen to voice the concerns of all African Americans. Still, Grimké remained wary of Du Bois's Niagara Movement. The formerly enslaved minister, born of a black female slave and a white master, was the nephew of the Grimké sisters, Sarah and Angelina, white reformers famous for their abolitionist and women's rights agitation. After the riot, Grimké penned a widely circulated sermon on the disturbance. Atlanta's developments, he argued, demonstrated that "the feeling among certain elements of southern society, among the poor whites . . . is more pronounced, is more virulent in its opposition to the well-to-do, the self-respecting, the aggressive elements of the colored race than against the shiftless, non-progressive, self-satisfied . . . who are without hope, without aspiration, without ambition." Other black commentators correctly maintained that selected members of the white mob had viewed attacks against the proprietors of small businesses as an opportunity to annihilate black rivals. An anonymous black contributor to the *Independent* contended that the brutal killings of barbers had been committed by "white barbers . . . unable to cope successfully in Atlanta in competition with negro barbers." These mob members, the author suggested, constituted only one of many white groups that had used the riot as a "cover to destroy their competitors."[19]

DARK TOWN'S AND Brownsville's successes in turning back the white mob resurrected long-standing debates among blacks over the use of defensive and retaliatory violence against white vigilantism. In the immediate aftermath of the riot, Washington advised blacks to shun all forms of violence. Mainstream white northern newspapers and magazines, fearing a possible race war, rejected the legitimacy of defensive violence by blacks. Even the most militant critics, black and white, of southern racial injustice remained ambivalent about the use of armed defense. Whites, after all, controlled state militias, local police forces, and federal troops. Any form of violence perpetrated by blacks threatened to bolster white claims that African Americans' savagery and uncontrolled passions demanded white political and social dominance to hold this destructive bestiality in check.[20]

Although, in his *The Souls of Black Folk*, Du Bois recognized on an intellectual level the "hopelessness of physical defence," his attitudes toward armed resistance remained contradictory and complex. For the location of the second meeting of his Niagara Movement in August 1906, a month prior to the riot, Du Bois chose Harpers Ferry, the site of John Brown's ultimately unsuccessful raid to secure guns and ammunition for a regionwide slave revolt. At the meeting, the movement's participants spurned all forms of violence while simultaneously celebrating John Brown. Participants also thanked God for Nat Turner (famous for directing a seventy-person slave revolt that ended in fifty-six white deaths) and for "all the hallowed dead who died for freedom!" Du Bois's "Litany of Atlanta" includes a confession of "a clamoring and clawing within, to whose voice we would not listen, yet shudder lest we must, and it is red, Ah! God! It is a red and awful shape." In coming years, Du Bois would increasingly embrace physical resistance as a last resort for self-protection.[21]

As scholars Dominic Capeci and Jack Knight perceptively note, the riot drove Du Bois to reconsider his Niagara faith in mobilizing a southern Talented Tenth vanguard to push for racial justice. The white rioters had targeted the black colleges and other institutions associated with Niagara Movement and GERC members. The mob's overwhelming destructiveness punctured Du Bois's hopes that locally based organizations might orchestrate effective protests against disfranchisement and other forms of southern racial injustice. Local agitation now appeared suicidal. Faced with this realization, Du Bois, Capeci and Knight argue, suffered crippling self-doubts in the riot's aftermath, as evidenced by his lackluster writing and emotional restraint in a November *World To-Day* article.[22]

When analyzed from a local rather than a national perspective, this essay, it becomes clear, represented one of Du Bois's most courageous and decisive acts. Concealed in its passionless prose are the precise arguments that had recently triggered Barber's exodus. Du Bois, holding back his anger and indignation as conditions in Atlanta so often demanded, avoided the blistering tone that had imperiled his close friend. Still, like Barber, Du Bois flatly refuted John Temple Graves's claims that black assaults had triggered the riot. He boldly suggested that none of the white accusations of black criminality had been substantiated. Mentioning Hoke Smith and Clark Howell by name, he condemned their political campaigns for stirring up whites' most vicious hatreds. Linking manliness and democratic citizenship with the "self-defense of law-abiding citizens against the lawless," he dryly praised the successes of Dark Town and Brownsville in turning back white invaders.[23]

Shorn of his hopes for regional activism, Du Bois now focused on pressing the federal government to protect black southerners' physical bodies and civil rights. His exclusive attention to federal remedies in his *World To-Day* article reflected this shifting emphasis. Du Bois portrayed black voting rights as the only means by which the black man could "peacefully defend his life and property, help the best class of whites defend theirs and put down the criminals of both races." He consequently endorsed growing calls among national civil rights advocates for the federal government to enforce the Fourteenth Amendment by reducing the apportionment of congressional representatives in states practicing disfranchisement. He also linked the twin dangers of black crime and white racial violence with southern states' refusal to fund education adequately, especially for blacks. The maintenance of law and order in the region depended on "government aid to the southern public school system to reduce illiteracy and barbarism."[24] Before the riot, the black professor, betraying his elitist bent, had sought "like-mindedness" in a Niagara Movement that he hoped to limit to 500 race leaders. After the violence, he cast his net widely. If all African Americans united to insist on their rights, he concluded in March 1907, the "nation must listen to the voice of ten millions."[25]

While both Du Bois and Barber acknowledged the presence of black criminals in Atlanta, the two men cast the white mob as the ultimate despoilers of women and homes. These white brutes were primarily "hoodlums," both agreed, but their attacks were provoked by white politicians, newspaper editors, and other white elites. Howard University professor Kelly Miller, after penning a description of the riot in October 1906, titled it "An Appeal to Reason," in an explicit attempt to emphasize the mounting extremism and irrationality among southern white demagogues and their followers. Miller similarly drew on white notions of civilization to liken the wild nature of the white mob to contemporary stereotypes of uncivilized, primitively savage Africans and American Indians: "The half-grown, half-drunk, half-savage descendents of Oglethorpe's colonists can no longer contain themselves. Like the Indian on the war-path, they must have a savage yell. 'Kill the Negro brutes!' is the tocsin. They kill and beat and bruise Negroes on sight. The air is filled with goulish yells, mingled with shrieks and groans of the mangled and dying." In characterizing southern whites as uncivilized brutes and rejecting Washington's faith that a best element existed among them, these African Americans were hoping to convince white northerners of the need for an increased federal presence in the South to control white savagery.[26]

Still other African Americans extended this logic further by contending that uncivilized and unrestrained white mobs could be controlled only by federal military intervention or black retaliatory violence. Calvin Chase of the *Washington Bee* challenged the government to "civilize the South" at gunpoint. Minister Francis Grimké encouraged southern blacks to avoid "unnecessary" dangers and confrontations that might provoke attack. But this sixty-six-year-old, who as a slave had fiercely resisted white beatings and torture, added, "There is but one way, as I have already said, to deal with a mob; and that is to shoot it to death; to riddle it with bullets or dynamite it." As early as 29 September the *Wichita Searchlight* started encouraging black male readers to save their money for the purchase of arms and ammunition. The race would secure its "God-given rights" in America, its editors concluded, only through "blood."[27]

WASHINGTON COULD SCARCELY ignore his widening isolation from the growing number of black commentators who were demanding federal intervention and white pacification. On 8 October, the day before the opening session of the National Afro-American Council, Washington telegraphed a message to Oswald Garrison Villard encouraging the white participant to ensure that "all classes who have tried to uphold law and order" be given "full recognition" and that the meeting "should not fail to condemn [the] criminal element" among African Americans. A direct descendant of the National Afro-American League founded in 1890, the Afro-American Council originated as a response to the 1898 Wilmington massacre of blacks. Unable to attract a large national constituency, the council was moribund by 1905. That year Bishop Alexander Walters called for its revival just after Du Bois announced the organization of his more radical Niagara Movement. Many of Du Bois's allies became convinced that Walters's efforts were part of a larger plot, hatched by Washington, to draw attention away from their more militant protest efforts. In the past Walters had occasionally expressed ambivalence toward Washington's silence in the face of undeniable injustices; but the two men nevertheless worked closely with each other, and Walters was careful to avoid potentially embarrassing challenges to the Wizard's leadership. Fearful of a shift in Walters's rhetoric, Washington called on Villard "to counsel bishop Walters and others in the direction of careful and conservative utterance in resolutions and addresses" at the meeting.[28]

As Washington had feared, the riot took center stage at the Afro-American Council gathering, held in New York between 9 and 11 October. After years of relative inactivity within the organization, this 1906 meeting attracted the largest audience and the most militant speakers to date. The delegates repeatedly rejected Washington's racial program, albeit without directly mentioning the Wizard by name. Referring to the riot throughout his opening presidential address, Walters encouraged his audience to "dedicate themselves anew to the work of securing our rights, with a resolve to continue until we die." Demanding nothing less than "equal rights," Walters portrayed in naked terms the central struggle between the "enemy" who "is trying to keep us down" and those among the race "determined to rise or die in the attempt." Moving far beyond the most radical calls for armed defense, Walters hinted that, should southern whites continue denying the ballot to "intelligent virtuous and property holding Negroes," a race war was inevitable. "If they persist in their foolish course," he warned, "a conflict is sure to come in which the Negro will not be the only to suffer, as was the case in Atlanta; business will be paralyzed, credit destroyed, desolation and ruin will surely follow."[29]

Vice-President Mary Church Terrell followed with a speech countering the Wizard's focus on reforming a black criminal class. Washington had supported the 1901 presidential appointment of Terrell's husband, Robert, as a Washington, D.C., judge. An outspoken feminist and leader of the National Association of Colored Women (NACW), Terrell was strongly committed to civil rights agitation but in the past had taken care not to alienate her husband's powerful backer. In her speech Terrell emphasized that "80 percent of negroes who are lynched are not accused of the crime generally supposed to be responsible for the unlawful murders." She did not portray lynching as a southern issue best addressed through local interracial cooperation in keeping with Washington's recent statements. Instead, she argued that it was precisely the "better class of Southern white people" who were ultimately responsible for mob violence. She rejected Washington's argument that African Americans themselves might through their own actions and moral conduct gain southern whites' sympathy. It was, she countered, using a politically charged metaphor, "as impossible for the Negroes in this country to prevent mob violence by . . . any course of conduct which they may pursue as it is for a straw dam to stop Niagara's flow." Referring directly to events in Atlanta, she argued that lynching was a national issue, and "if the American people wish to throttle mob violence they must demand an enforcement of the law both North and South."[30]

Spurred on by Terrell's speech and by Walters's utterances, the council

Afro-American Council vice-president Mary Church Terrell. (Library of Congress)

passed a resolution calling on Roosevelt to appoint a nonpartisan commission that would "visit the states wherein these outrages and barbarities have been perpetrated." This organization would collect information and sponsor national legislation to remedy the "evils which threaten the civilization, peace and integrity of the republic." The next day Joseph Smith, editor of the *Boston Pilot*, not only called on Roosevelt to intervene directly in southern affairs but also warned that he and fellow Massachusetts veterans were willing to return to the South to "do the job over again if it becomes necessary."[31] Many black commentators welcomed a northern military intercession in southern affairs so reminiscent of Reconstruction. Still, Smith's speech marked a subtle shift from the emphasis on collective black defense espoused by Grimké and others, for it explicitly authorized northern white men, not southern black men, to use violence to reestablish law and order in an uncivilized South.

As reported in the *Brooklyn Standard Union*, the emotional zenith of the council meeting occurred on Wednesday afternoon during a speech by Villard, the very man Washington had enlisted to counsel conservatism among the organization's speakers. Frequently referring to the riot throughout his speech, Villard told audience members that "since the news of that barbaric slaughter reached the North," it had "not been out of my mind many hours." Villard argued that Washington's racial strategies had made sense during "the first three decades after freedom" when blacks had been "absorbed in obtaining an industrial foothold." Yet 1903 had witnessed the publication of Du Bois's *The Souls of Black Folk*, which represented an "awakening of a race to its powers, duties and dangers, and of its readiness to think and feel as a whole." Noting the increasing threat posed by mob violence and antiblack legislation, Villard challenged council members to "organize to agitate, organize to demand your rights under the Constitution, organize to fight back for yourselves by every legitimate means—by the strike, by the boycott, but best of all by argument and by reason."[32]

Villard praised Atlanta blacks for standing firm in a series of interracial meetings with whites and for announcing that they "would be satisfied with nothing in the way of injustice." But in a clear departure from Washington's emphasis on local cooperation, Villard suggested that "splendid as the work of the colored men was and is in Atlanta," it would have been "a thousand times more effective had a great and rich national organization like this Afro-American Council stood behind them, to endorse their views and give them publication." Such an organization, he argued, could have mobilized an independent commission to publish the truth about the riot. It could have funded a "corps of able lawyers" to pressure the local government into punishing members of the white mob and prosecuting those municipal officers who allowed "the vicious dives, black and white, to flourish in Atlanta." And it could exert pressure on Atlanta's business community by demanding "justice for the Negro under penalty of withdrawing from Atlanta all Negro trade possible, and of spreading through the whole world the story of Atlanta's shame."[33]

Villard—the grandson of abolitionist William Lloyd Garrison, a celebrated advocate of nonviolent resistance—was clearly frightened by the black armed defense of Brownsville and Dark Town and by black intellectuals' growing advocacy of defensive violence. The white speaker emphasized that the battle against racial injustice must be "fought in every possible way save with arms." Violence, Villard warned, would only lead "back to barbarism by way of anarchy." Though radical in its support of civil rights and equality for blacks, Villard's proposed organization was conservative in its goal of channeling black resistance away from all forms of violence, especially given black commentators' growing acceptance of armed defense. "The colored editor or preacher who advocates a resort to arms is a false

Oswald Garrison Villard, the wealthy white publisher and NAACP cofounder who spoke at the 1906 Afro-American Council meeting. (Special Collections and Archives, W. E. B. Du Bois Library, University of Massachusetts Amherst)

guide who cannot be dispossessed of his leadership a minute too soon," the white editor asserted.[34]

Washington's oration on the conference's final day went largely unnoticed in the press. He cautioned "the members of my race who reside in the Northern States" that, "in your enthusiastic desire to be of service to your brethren in the South, you do not make their path more thorny and difficult by rash and intemperate utterances." Washington encouraged council members to avoid departing from their past moderation lest they "assist in lighting a fire which you will have no ability to put out." Equating manhood with stoic forbearance, Washington added that "any child can cry and fret, but it requires a full grown man to create—to construct." "We must frankly face the fact," he warned, "that the great body of our people are to dwell in the South, and any policy that does not seek to harmonize the two races and cement them is unwise and dangerous."[35]

The October meeting of the Afro-American Council thus marked a dramatic shift in Washington's influence among a group of moderate black leaders once wary of openly breaking with the Wizard. The council's calls for federal intervention directly contradicted Booker T. Washington's unwavering faith in the benefits of cooperation between southern black and white elites. Though echoing Washington's confidence in material progress and reminding southern blacks to "preserve a manly spirit and sober judgment," the conference's published declaration of principles echoed the Niagara platform. It linked manhood with agitation and called on African Americans to embrace "a manly, sensible and unceasing insistence upon every right guaranteed by the Federal Constitution." "Liberty loving Americans," it contended, "can have little respect for a people who would allow their rights to lapse by default."[36]

BETWEEN SEPTEMBER AND OCTOBER, T. Thomas Fortune's *New York Age* had served as the primary mouthpiece for Washington's attacks against Barber and Du Bois. Immediately after the riot, the *Age* also trumpeted Washington's heroism in rushing to Atlanta to provide "succor" for his race. Despite the close ties between Fortune and Washington and Washington's financial support for the newspaper, the relationship between the two men had grown increasingly strained in the years preceding the riot. The *Age's* publication of Washington's postriot communiqués initially appeared to signal a growing rapprochement. Yet even while the paper's front pages served as a soapbox for Washington, the *Age's* editorials implicitly challenged key tenets of Washington's philosophy, repeatedly concluding that, in the South, "the future holds much of hell" for all African Americans. Fortune noted white northerners' repeated refusal to enforce the Reconstruction amendments by intervening in the South to protect the civil rights or even the physical bodies of southern blacks. Abandoned by the federal government, the African American's only option was to "hold wide his hands like a man and fight for what he has by all honorable means." In the past Fortune had recognized the narrow restrictions placed on Washington's expressions by his twin roles as a southern race leader and the principal of an institution dependent on both northern white philanthropy and southern white toleration. On 1 November, Fortune openly rejected the Wizard's calls for African Americans to lay down their arms. Noting that "to err is human," the black journalist editorialized: "Dr. Washington is a man whom we delight to honor . . . but we reserve the right of dissenting from any position he may take which we regard as erroneous. . . . We believe that Afro-Americans guiltless of crime and outraged by the mob who defend themselves to the death will inspire the respect of white hoodlums." In a private letter to Washington's chief lieutenant Emmett J. Scott, Fortune went further: "The trouble will go on in Atlanta until the Negro retaliates—until, driven to bay, the Negro slays his assailant. What an awful condition we have at Atlanta. . . . I would like to be there with a good force of armed men to help make Rome howl."[37]

As the vital center of black thought drifted ever further from Washington's racial verities, the unrepentant Wizard clung resolutely to spells and incantations that had lost their magic, especially among blacks. Between the riot and early November, correspondents repeatedly warned Washington publicly and privately that his old policies and deeply held instincts no longer made sense, given the increasing radicalization of many of his former allies, the growing intransigence of many white southerners, and Theodore Roosevelt's disaffection from the black cause. In the face of growing criticism, the Wizard refused to reconsider his public faith in the power of black moral and material progress to alleviate southern racial tensions. Nor was he willing to rethink his public preference for local interracial cooperation over national intervention. Washington's unwillingness to reevaluate his public stance is clearest in his correspondence with black novelist Charles Chesnutt. In a private letter written in early October, Chesnutt acknowledged the delicacy of Washington's position and the need for exercising discretion in words and actions, especially given the fierce hatreds displayed by whites during the riot. Yet he counseled the Wizard to avoid endorsing or appearing to endorse anything less than African Americans' unfettered right to vote. Washington responded by agreeing that African Americans must never surrender their voting rights, but he chastised Chesnutt for placing "too much reliance upon the ballot to cure evils that we are at present suffering." Ignoring the fact that the riot had come on the heels of a strident white campaign for black disfranchisement, Washington asked Chesnutt how he and other voting advocates could "account for the Atlanta riot, the worst that we have had in forty years?" "That," Washington argued, "occurred in practically the only Southern state where the Negro has not been disfranchised by reason of constitutional enactment."[38]

EXCEPT FOR A handful of civil rights advocates, northern whites seldom linked Atlanta's violence with the erosion of black civil rights in the South or with the federal government's capitulation to white racism. Much like Miller and Du Bois, mainstream white northern journalists did highlight the savagery of Atlanta's rioters. So lacking in civilization did the *San Francisco Chronicle* find the riot's mob that the editors compared its actions to how "a black mob would act in the interior of Africa, in the presence of an inferior population of whites." Yet these white editors implicitly isolated Atlanta's events and conflicts from the larger South's crimson record of lynching and racial oppression. The *Outlook*, citing Atlanta's rapid industrialization and dramatic population growth, informed readers that "Atlanta is not a typical Southern city," and "this outbreak ought not to be regarded as typical of the South." The *World's Work* described Atlanta as "one of the very worst of American cities," a considerable part of whose population was "made up of the adventurous riff-raff that the mining towns of the West used to relieve us of."[39] This emphasis on Atlanta's uniqueness had the potential to discourage white readers from supporting black demands for federal intervention in the South or national agitation for racial equality. If Atlanta were unrepresentative of the larger South, there was little need for national civil rights organizations, regional reform, or federal intervention.

Instead, mainstream publications, many of which were headquartered in cities with rapidly growing black populations, tended to portray the riot as illustrating the national urban problem of controlling black criminals, especially black rapists. The *Outlook* blamed the riot on the unmanly black race, "a race isolated and untrained in self-restraint," which invariably infected with anarchy any city in which it settled in large numbers. The magazine argued that mobs had proved singularly ineffective in controlling "lawless" blacks and that "assimilation" was unthinkable and deportation impossible. An "entirely new and immensely forcible and practical" strategy, other white journalists agreed, was necessary to wipe out this deadly pathogen.[40]

The only solution was a highly localized one. A first step would be the deploying of black elites to maintain white visions of order among their own people. "That community," the *Outlook* contended, "which succeeds in utilizing the force for law and order existing within the Negro race in controlling the vicious and lawless elements of that race will put an end to at least one of the conditions which made such a race war as that in Atlanta possible." As had white Atlanta newspapers prior to the riot, the *Outlook* sought to force white-identified black civic leaders to accept responsibility for the crimes of their race's "lawless" element. Quoting southern white novelist Thomas Nelson Page, its editors continued: "The negroes might be given, within their province, powers sufficiently full to enable them to keep order among their people, and they might on the other hand be held to a certain accountability for such good order." If Atlanta's best white men could find a permanent means of both controlling black criminals and easing racial tensions, the *Outlook* and other national publications maintained, civic leaders could "erase the shame that has stained their city."[41]

Immediately after the riot, Atlanta's white business leaders initiated interracial campaigns to restore order and counteract these national images of savagery and mayhem. White boosters bristled at the outpouring of newspaper and magazine accounts comparing their denizens with Europe's least civilized outlaws—the "brigands of Sicily, malcontents from Poland, terrorists from Russia, anarchists from France, disturbers from Britain and Germany." On 26 September the *Atlanta Journal* reminded readers that their city's prosperity depended on both Atlanta's fair name and its burgeoning commercial relations with northern and eastern cities. The newspaper then decried the possible negative effects of "cruel and unjust comments upon the situation here" in national publications. In early November the city council passed a resolution denouncing as "false, slanderous and libelous" the *World's Work* article describing Atlanta as one of "the worst of American cities" and its government as "an encouragement to crime."[42]

ATLANTA'S POSTRIOT PUBLIC relations campaign entwined with the efforts of Booker T. Washington to stave off the rising challenges to his racial leadership. Atlanta's interracial law-and-order movements seemed the perfect test for Washington's hypothesis that racial tensions were best ameliorated through local dialogue among the better elements of both races. Washington, increasingly isolated from black critics and former allies alike, gambled his future influence on both the outcome of the law-and-order efforts in Atlanta and Roosevelt's commitment to protecting African Americans. On 5 October, in reaction to a *Philadelphia Tribune* editorial criticizing Roosevelt for not intervening in Atlanta's affairs, Washington pointed out the near-impossibility of the federal government's military intervention in local jurisdictions, given recent judicial precedents and widely shared legal assumptions among whites. Washington added that federal intervention was both unconstitutional and impolitic: "In proportion as we can get the leading classes of Southern white people to shoulder the responsibility of the protection of the Negro, we shall go further in securing protection than by depending upon some outside force." He noted the "awakening of the local public conscience has brought a security to the Negro and a closeness of relations between the whites and the best class of colored in that city [Atlanta] to an extent that hardly prevails in any other part of the South today." "Our good President has spoken out so often and so bravely against lynching and rioting," Washington maintained, "that no one can question where his heart is in all such matters, and no one can question his disposition to speak and act whenever speech and action are wise."[43]

To most African Americans and a small group of white civil rights advocates, Washington's faith in Roosevelt and southern white fair-mindedness rang untrue. Yet it remained unclear whether white Atlantans would succeed in restoring their now blemished reputation among the members of a national white audience. Simultaneously, an ever resourceful Washington, long fearful of any black or white opposition to his program, was searching for a strategy that could somehow rehabilitate his credibility among racially progressive whites. He was also on the lookout for new evidence that he might marshal to draw black thought away from the growing pull of the manly ideals and principles associated with Du Bois and Atlanta's New Black Men.

CHAPTER SIX

Interracial Cooperation's Profits and Costs

————

WHITE CIVIC AND business leaders in Atlanta initially responded to Saturday night's violence with silence and hesitation. A national correspondent captured the spirit of prominent citizens as late as Sunday evening: "Among the people generally there is regret because of the city's disgrace in the eyes of the world, but there is little or no regret over the deaths of half a score of Negroes, while some even rejoice that the whites have taken vengeance." That evening, Mayor James Woodward openly asserted that "as long as black brutes attempt rape upon our white women, just so long will they be unceremoniously dealt with."[1]

Only the threats of economic devastation and continued black retaliation convinced white elites to move decisively against mob violence. By Tuesday, the high costs of continued white and black counterattacks became increasingly apparent. Factories remained closed and laborers refused to report to work. Unloaded railcars sat idle in train depots, banking activity came to a standstill, and real estate sales ground to a halt. Rumors of imminent raids by blacks terrified whites in neighborhoods throughout the city. These unsettled conditions eventually cost local businesses more than $200,000 in lost revenue and threatened Atlanta's long-standing public relations campaign for tourists and investors. After a summer of inaction, some white elites were finally willing to condemn racist agitators, promote interracial dialogue, and acknowledge some of the city's most glaring racial inequities.[2]

The ensuing law-and-order movements of influential whites simultaneously promised new avenues for racial progress and highlighted the wide array of social forces discouraging fundamental change. Their postriot search for order led white elites to reevaluate long-standing social certainties and improvise new forms of racial interaction. Even the simple act of publicly consulting with black ministers and college graduates, for example, represented a dramatic departure from past Jim Crow practices. Yet there was always a contradiction between white civic leaders' avowed promises of color-blind justice and their fundamental commitment to white supremacy. So, too, was there an underlying tension between pledges of racial equity by white elites and their realization that any racial reform effort risked triggering the violent white backlash they now so desperately feared. Another barrier to change was the city's Byzantine governmental structure, over which even the most powerful white reformers exercised only limited influence. Ward-based city council members controlled the legislative process. Elected judges and notoriously racist police officers enjoyed far-reaching discretionary powers while administering the law. Despite these obstacles, both black and white elites sensed that postriot reform efforts might lay the foundations for a new racial order.[3]

These overtures by whites forced leading African Americans to make hard choices regarding their competing social allegiances and identities. After years of exclusion, black elites finally had an opportunity to participate in civic affairs and directly enter their city's public discourse. Yet white reformers insisted that interracial cooperation was possible only if black participants abandoned their recent protest activities and renounced the "lawless element" that had defended black neighborhoods and institutions during the riot. Black elites could embrace biracialism only by forsaking their newly discovered bonds with working-class and socially marginalized African Americans. New Black Men and their elderly allies could claim the enhanced civic powers proffered by whites only by publicly distancing themselves from the manly ideals and civil rights demands associated with the 1906 GERC. Thus, black elites could contribute to Atlanta's rebuilding only if they were willing to redefine the public meanings of black manliness and respectability.

BLACK AND WHITE elites' initial attempts at interracial cooperation highlighted the wide gulf separating the goals and intentions of the two groups. At private and public meetings, white business and civic leaders revealed their overriding concerns with restoring Atlanta's sullied reputation, controlling a "disorderly" black element, and preventing continued black defensive violence. In contrast, black elites repeatedly conditioned their support for interracial cooperation on color-blind justice and the immediate termination of white violence. During the first white-initiated meeting at city hall that Tuesday morning, white Baptist minister John E. White and white factory owner H. Y. McCord blamed the riot on the saloons, clubrooms, and pool halls catering to the city's black population, and they advocated the permanent closure of such businesses. The proposal was endorsed by the African American ministers and journalists in attendance, but only after John Rush and others countered that "those dives which the worst element of white people frequent should also be closed." Though white audience members expressed their abstract support for these sentiments, white business leaders forwarded their original proposal to the city council without amendment.[4]

When the meeting turned to broader law-and-order issues, black physician Thomas Slater informed the white audience that he and other black elites wanted to join the crusade against black criminality but could not do so because the militia and police were "not our friends or . . . with us in the fullest protection of our lives." After additional black participants voiced similar concerns, white banker Robert Maddox guaranteed protection for those African Americans who "forced their own to obey law and order." And he asked African Americans to go "among their people" and convince "them to return to their homes and work." Only after mayor-elect Walthal Joyner and others endorsed Maddox's promises did the black audience agree "to use every effort to prevent any more trouble." Despite the promises of white civic leaders, the police chief specifically targeted African Americans in issuing an order closing every barbershop, restaurant, and other public place where blacks were likely to congregate.[5]

That afternoon, the *Georgian* announced a public meeting open to the city's "best citizens" and organized by the Chamber of Commerce. By four o'clock, 1,000 black and white Atlanta residents had packed into the county courthouse. Quieting the crowd, chamber president Sam D. Jones barred "inflammatory speeches" from the meeting. He encouraged all blacks and whites to return to their jobs and reopen their stores and factories. At his request, the cheering crowd endorsed the appointment of a committee composed of chamber officials and white civic leaders, charged with drafting a set of resolutions calling on "all good men to lift their voices for law and order and use their influence to check the riotous spirit that is abroad in the community."[6]

Charles T. Hopkins, a chamber member and white lawyer, shifted the meeting's focus away from Jones's narrow business concerns. Hopkins was the first white speaker to focus on the human suffering of the riot's black victims. His message categorically condemned the calls for racial exclusionism and black extermination that had filled the newspapers in the weeks preceding the riot. "I do not think we ought to do anything rash," he began, "but in God's name let us be MEN!" He continued with a discussion of the riot's financial costs: "Saturday evening at eight o'clock the credit of Atlanta was good for any number of millions of dollars in New York or Boston or any financial centre; to-day we couldn't borrow fifty cents." As he pointed out, "No one has yet objected to this lawlessness and the mob has spent itself without obstruction. Innocent Negro men have been struck down for no crime whatever, while peacefully enjoying the life and liberty guaranteed to every American citizen." He then stressed white civic leaders' paternalistic obligations to African Americans: "The Negro race is a child race. We are a strong race, their guardians. We have boasted of our superiority and we have now sunk to this level—we have shed the blood of our helpless wards. Christianity and humanity demand that we treat the Negro fairly." At Hopkins's prodding, white audience members eventually pledged $4,277 to compensate the riot's white and black victims, and they elected a committee to oversee distribution of the payments.[7]

Toward the end of the session, Yale graduate and black physician William F. Penn, a solidly built giant of a man and Niagara Movement member, pleaded for adequate police protection. He informed the audience that white mobs had invaded and plotted to dynamite his palatial home. It was located near Brownsville, on Ridge Avenue, in the midst of a small group of black dwellings that were surrounded by white residences and businesses. He then asked,

> What shall we do? We have been disarmed: how shall we protect our lives and property? If living a sober industrious, upright life, accumulating property and educating his children as best he knows how, is not the standard by which a coloured man can live and be protected in the South, what is to become of him? If the kind of life I have lived isn't the kind you want, shall I leave and go North? When we aspire to be decent and industrious we are told that we are bad examples to other coloured men. Tell us what your standards are for coloured men. What are the requirements under which we may live and be protected? What shall we do?[8]

At that moment, Confederate veteran and real estate dealer Col. A. J. McBride jumped from his chair, pledging that "if necessary, I will go out and sit on his porch with a rifle." Following additional assurances from whites, Penn promised that he and other blacks would aid in "suppressing disorder" and "protecting white women from the crimes committed against them by the criminal classes." Whites in the audience interpreted Penn's response as representing his absolute confidence in Hopkins's and McBride's paternalistic guarantees. Yet the black doctor clearly viewed the pledges of white men with suspicion and embraced their offers as only one of many vehicles for self-protection. On Sunday night, he had armed himself with two guns and vowed to shoot any white attacker.[9]

Before adjournment, the body appointed a Committee of Safety, charged with encouraging local government officials to curb any further threats to the public order. James English's designation as its chair signaled the importance and potential influence of the committee. A former mayor and police commissioner, English was so closely associated with the city and its postbellum growth that he was affectionately known as "Atlanta's Grand Old Man." The Confederate veteran had amassed one of the city's largest fortunes as the president of the Fourth National Bank and the proprietor of a local brick factory infamous for abusing its black convict laborers. The other Committee of Safety members, though they were younger than English and had come of age after the Civil War, were also wealthy and well connected. Virginia-born, fifty-year-old Sam D. Jones presided over both the Chamber of Commerce and the Atlanta Stove Works. Charles T. Hopkins had, at forty-two, secured a reputation as one of the city's leading corporate lawyers. The remaining committee members included two lawyers, a real estate tycoon, and an assortment of powerful businessmen and stockbrokers. The business connections of these men must have made some blacks uneasy. Not only did English's son serve as president of the infamous *News*, but Hopkins was one of its directors.[10]

Hopkins and other committee spokespersons based their claims to municipal authority on the threat posed to the city by continued violence. These men embraced a chivalry that elevated Atlanta's "best" white men to privileged positions of influence and authority over both the "disorderly" element responsible for the riot and the public officials who had failed to shield Atlanta from its outbreak. According to Hopkins, the mob that "swept away" the city's reputation had been composed not of men who "represent the character and strength of our city, but by hoodlums, understrappers and white criminals." The white lawyer added, "If that night had been properly handled by the proper authorities there would have been no murders." In addition to safeguarding white womanhood and the city's reputation from savage violation, the committee also assumed the paternalistic role of protecting innocent African Americans.[11]

Those African Americans who cooperated with whites following the riot also numbered among their community's wealthiest and best-educated members; some of the black participants had won national reputations as authors and church leaders. At a time when many blacks endured lives of desperate poverty, some of these men had graduated from leading academic institutions such as Yale and Harvard. The educational and professional status of these elite African Americans helped them capture the attention of white civic leaders. Of the African Americans mentioned in accounts of meetings between blacks and whites in the autumn of 1906, there were six ministers, three college administrators, three journalists, two physicians, two business tycoons, and one lawyer.

These black elites represented two distinct generations. A small minority had been born in the southern United States or the Caribbean islands during the 1840s and 1850s. Their reform activities and professional duties had brought many of them into intermittent contact with whites during the era of more flexible race relations preceding Jim Crow separation during the 1890s. A second generation, primarily southern-born during or after the Civil War, represented a rising generation of New Black Men. As a group, these black men also had numerous interracial experiences as students at northern colleges, as members of the integrated staffs of black colleges, or professionally as journalists or Republican politicians. With the notable exception of Benjamin Davis, dismissed by many as a contentious outsider, both generations had formed a close social clique, drawn together all the more tightly by their shared status and by the white racism that they daily encountered.[12]

The professional positions of these men afforded them unique incentives for cooperating with white business leaders. Their personal and financial investments made it particularly costly for them to abandon the city and rebuild their lives elsewhere. The churches, the businesses, and the colleges for which they had sacrificed so much of their lives had been among the rioters' prime targets. Both William F. Penn's and Thomas Slater's medical practices were located in the central downtown, as were the offices of Jesse Max Barber's *Voice of the Negro* and Davis's *Atlanta Independent*. Although Alonzo Herndon's barbershop was not physically harmed by violence, he could hardly ignore the mob's destructiveness against other barbers. The Brownsville confrontation had occurred right at the doorsteps of Gammon

Theological Seminary and Clark College, and the white militia had threatened Atlanta Baptist College and its faculty.[13]

On 25 September, these men found themselves at a racial crossroads. Henry Hugh Proctor and other GERC participants had responded to the threats of the *Georgian* and the *News* by suppressing their strident protests, by attempting to distance themselves from the "lawless element," and by begging whites to control white vigilantes. While the riot had underscored the threats that white violence posed to all African Americans, it had also highlighted the potential collective strength of a united black community. Whites were finally seeking the cooperation of these black men at the very moment that the possibility of renewed violence threatened their lives and the survival of their institutions.

WITH WHITES' ASSURANCES of protection in hand, black ministers and educators agreed to go house to house in their communities and urge African Americans to stay inside and avoid publicly congregating in large groups. The letters they published in white newspapers, though nominally addressed to blacks, primarily represented an attempt to affirm publicly their opposition to black crime and retaliatory violence. Clark College president William Crogman privately thanked "lawless" blacks for repeatedly turning back white mob members. Yet in white newspapers, Crogman joined John Wesley Bowen in his efforts to allay any lingering white suspicions prompted by the violent racial confrontations bordering the black colleges. On Wednesday, 26 September, the two men published a joint letter in the *Georgian* describing the "infamous negro dives" as "the hell-bottom of our race." They also condemned "these black men who have stirred up hatred of the races by their crimes against the white women," and they pledged their willingness to "cooperate with the proper authorities in ferreting out" the man who gunned down Officer Jim Heard.[14]

Bowen's other postriot actions similarly highlighted the powerful role that fears of renewed violence and institutional concerns played in minimizing direct criticisms of white civic leaders in the riot's aftermath. The targeting of Brownsville during the riot underscored Gammon's vulnerability. Bowen, mounting an ultimately successful campaign to win his governing board's approval for his permanent presidential appointment, feared that white anger at the armed resistance of Brownsville's citizens might force his institution to close. Convinced that he "must secure the confidence and good will of the conservative white man down here," Bowen invited Governor Joseph Terrell and Baptist minister John E. White to visit Gammon and planned sermons by other local white ministers for the upcoming year. "They are extending the hand with the olive leaf," he confided to trusted friends, "and I believe in reaching forth and grasping it."[15] Bowen also feared the effect the riot would have on enrollment, coming as it did just before the opening of classes. Via letters and newspaper advertisements, Bowen assured his students that all was now safe, and they gradually returned to their alma mater. Nonetheless, Bowen remained concerned about both the long-term image of his school and continued white threats of another invasion. He pleaded with friends not to publicize his private communications lest outsiders misinterpret his message.[16]

On 30 September, Bowen published in the *New York World* a letter that far surpassed the efforts of other black civic leaders at allaying white suspicions. Only three days earlier, white newspaper editors and Committee of Safety chair James English had issued death threats against Jesse Max Barber for publishing the *World* article so critical of white elites. Bowen's letter avoided any mention of the recent violence. Southern society's "worst enemies" were instead a "small brood of lustful, besotted, worthless and dangerous black harpies," who "attack white women and . . . pluck continuously and mercilessly at the vitals of their own race." Bowen called upon Atlanta officials to allow African Americans to help protect the city as police officers and jury members. Bowen's insinuations that black criminals were responsible for the riot generated criticisms from Du Bois and other Niagara Movement members.[17]

John Hope, Atlanta Baptist College's first black president, had received student queries similar to Bowen's and was negotiating his first year in a previously white-held position. He likewise avoided publicly discussing the riot. Hope's success at both holding back his anger and reassuring his students, many of whom trickled in late, won the admiration of northern friends and powerful philanthropists. From 1906 until his death in 1936, Hope struggled mightily and sometimes unsuccessfully to maintain his militant ideals in the face of the inevitable compromises demanded by his administrative position and his dependence on powerful whites. His wife, Lugenia, later remembered that the riot profoundly changed her husband, who viewed its violence as a test of his manly courage—a test to which, he later believed, he had not fully measured up. She deeply regretted her husband's inability to appreciate fully his heroic persistence. John's postriot strategy of achieving gradual racial progress via compromise with northern and southern whites, Du Bois later asserted, "did not make for the strong, bold and spectacular; but it did make for accomplishment; it did make for slow, sure advance, and in a world so torn by hate and difference and misunderstanding as that in which John Hope lived, it was perhaps the only sure way."[18]

ON 29 SEPTEMBER, the day after Barber was forced to leave the city for publicly criticizing white civic leaders, the white committee of ten assembled with a committee of twenty black men in a YMCA office. Given the naked intimidation already displayed by English in his dealings with Barber, Hopkins should not have been surprised at the black committee's "intelligence and diplomacy" during the two-hour interracial meeting that Saturday. "They never referred to the riot," he recalled; instead they were "looking to the future." Despite the care with which they chose their words, however, the black participants remained steadfast in their commitment to the principles of racial equity. As an outsider reported, "The colored representatives told the whites plainly that they would be satisfied with nothing in the way of injustice, but if the white people were to have saloons the colored people must have saloons, that if the colored people were disarmed the white people must be disarmed, and so on through." White businessmen and public officials successfully pressured the managers of Thomas Dixon's incendiary *Clansman* into not staging the play in Atlanta later that October. By the first week in October, white fears of renewed violence had gradually subsided, and national publications were increasingly praising the city's law-and-order efforts. As powerful whites turned their attention away from biracial cooperation, the courts finished adjudicating a series of riot-related legal cases while local religious and business leaders struggled over temperance reform.[19]

On Tuesday, 25 September, Chamber of Commerce president Sam Jones personally asked city council members to revoke the saloon licenses of all drinking places catering to blacks. On the advice of Committee of Safety representatives, the city council eventually decided that a wholesale targeting of black saloons might appear arbitrary. Consequently, both races resolved to close every saloon until early October, at which time a special committee would launch hearings to investigate each operation to determine whether it was orderly and deserved to retain its license. Although Mayor Woodward, himself an ardent imbiber, termed both measures "radical," he realized that a veto was futile, given their overwhelming council support. Like many other professional politicians since the late 1880s, Woodward had publicly pledged to ban from politics the potentially divisive and destabilizing issue of liquor regulation. Both white politicians and businesspersons recognized the saloons' importance to the city's prosperity. With annual whisky licenses set at $1,000 and beer licenses at $100, saloonkeepers' 1906 license payments surpassed $100,000. White businesspersons, even those not directly involved in the liquor trade, also profited from public drinking. Saloon rents helped stabilize downtown real estate prices, while the alcohol trade pulled conventioneers and tourists into the city, boosting the profits of major hotels such as the Kimball House. The Chamber of Commerce supported the new antidive measures not only to promote public order but also to pursue its members' financial interests. The chamber's roster included factory proprietors as well as hotel and "first-class" saloon owners. Many business leaders embraced temperance as a means of promoting discipline among white and black workers while simultaneously battling worker absenteeism. White hotel and restaurant owners similarly endorsed the elimination of dives as a way of reducing potential competition and widespread perceptions that public drinking inherently promoted crime and disorder.[20]

Between 1 and 15 October, the city council adopted a series of resolutions clearly aimed at both more tightly controlling African American drinking and more actively discouraging heterosexual and interracial mixing in saloons. The council segregated every saloon in the city. To restrict the sale of inexpensive whisky to "disorderly" blacks (and perhaps whites), the body passed ordinances setting the price of drinks at ten cents or more. To discourage loitering and the whiling away of long hours in saloons, the council barred establishments from having chairs or seats, forcing customers to "drink and leave" rather than sit. The investigating committee's dealings similarly revealed the council's overriding goals of discouraging interracial contact, limiting the availability of alcohol to African Americans, and restricting the sale of inexpensive whisky to potentially disorderly clienteles. Virtually every saloon whose license was permanently suspended was located on Peters, Decatur, and Marietta Streets—epicenters of riot activity and areas heavily frequented by poor and working-class blacks. Prior to the riot, African Americans could obtain alcohol in as many as sixty saloons, many of which were integrated. By the end of the investigation, only twenty saloons remained open to blacks, and every bar in Atlanta was segregated.[21]

The white owners of black saloons (many of whom were Jewish or Greek) and Charles Mosely, the sole black applicant for a new license, faced disadvantages from the very outset of the committee's hearings. The council openly targeted "negro dives," and, thanks to the white primary, blacks were unable to exert direct political pressure on the council. In addition, ethnic

Decatur Street saloon designated "Colored Only" following riot-associated temperance reforms. (Baker, *Following the Color Line*, facing p. 35)

and black proprietors, particularly Mosely, lacked the political and social connections crucial for success before a patently corrupt committee. Prior to the council proceedings, Mosely, described in newspapers as an African American of "considerable intelligence," owned and operated, under a white man's name, the Vendome Lounge, which catered to middle-class and elite black Atlantans. During the initial 22 September crackdown on the dives, police arrested Mosely on obscenity charges after they found a poster of a white woman in his saloon. Appealing to the committee for a license under his own name, Mosely garnered endorsements from seven police officers and from "prominent negroes" testifying that his saloon was the only place of its kind serving the black community's "better class." The committee summarily dismissed the black applicant's petition. Henry Hugh Proctor, Peter James Bryant, and other black ministers had long been prohibition proponents; before the riot, they had endorsed the antidive campaign. Yet, in their initial postriot meetings with whites, Bryant and other African Americans emphasized the absolute necessity of color-blind enforcement of the liquor laws. Black journalist Benjamin J. Davis noted the failure of white civic leaders to fulfill such black demands during the city council proceedings: "A Negro is permitted to drink whiskey, provided he buys it from a white man. This is enough to drive the Negro into open violation of the whiskey law. The government and state both may license a Negro to sell liquor, but Atlanta steps in and vetoes this authority," saying, "white men shall have the exclusive right to sell Negroes liquor."[22]

The postriot saloon measures convinced white temperance leaders that "bone-dry" prohibition was at last within reach. As early as 26 September, statewide WCTU representatives wired Mayor Woodward their appreciation for his decision to close all saloons, black and white, and implored him to keep them permanently shuttered. On 5 October, following a divisive debate, Anti-Saloon League members agreed to marshal their forces to assure a prohibition referendum in the spring of 1907. This new agenda prompted William Upshaw and fellow reformers to shift their focus away from the racist images that had dominated their preriot rhetoric. Male temperance advocates joined the WCTU's attempts to turn public attention to the "drunken mob of low down white men and boys." Upshaw plaintively queried, "In heaven's name, by what kind of argument should we stop the sale of hellhell [sic] raising liquor as you call it, to Negroes because it excites them to crime and continue its sale to white men who rush from the 'respectable saloon' to the brothel, to murder and hell!"[23]

In December, Chamber of Commerce leaders, fearing a divisive prohibition referendum, forged a consensus between highly capitalized saloon owners and those members who advocated bone-dry prohibition. President Sam Jones and others endorsed a proposed measure seeking to raise the cost of retail whiskey licenses from $1,000 to $2,000 and the cost of beer saloon licenses from $100 to $400. Joined by white ministers and the editors of major white newspapers, the business leaders helped ensure the ordinance's overwhelming passage on 6 January. The chamber's leadership eagerly supported a measure that promised to weed out at least some of the "disorderly" white saloons that had survived the city council's initial investigation. In addition, raising the price of licenses would augment government revenues, and many proponents, including the *Journal*, agreed that the measure might divide moderate and radical temperance advocates, thereby ensuring that the legitimacy of the city's liquor business "will be on a better basis than it ever has been." Jones and other white business leaders had helped to generate a vision of temperance reform that met the desires of Bryant and other black ministers for regulations establishing new controls over public drinking—regulations affecting not just working-class black Atlantans but poor working-class whites as well. This congruence between black and white visions was inadvertent. The chamber did not endorse the new measure with the goal of promoting racial equity. Its leadership sought instead to balance white manufacturers' desires for controlling laborers with commercial leaders' quest to protect their downtown financial interests.[24]

IMMEDIATELY FOLLOWING THEIR appointment, English and other Committee of Safety members called on law enforcement officials to arrest blacks and "disorderly" whites who continued to carry weapons or commit violence. John Pendleton, a Fulton County superior court judge, and city court judge Nash Broyles publicly endorsed the business leaders' avowed goals of fully prosecuting both whites implicated in the riot's violence and black men accused of assaulting white women. Like white businesspersons, Broyles and Pendleton recognized the threat that the mob's actions posed both to the authority of law enforcement officials and to public faith in the fairness of the criminal courts. On the Monday morning following the riot, Broyles opened his docket of cases arising from arrests within the city limits. Broyles generally retained jurisdiction over less serious misdemeanant cases, but he transferred to the county superior court those cases where the evidence and charges suggested grounds for felony indictments. Upon convening his first postriot city court session, Broyles pledged that "any person guilty of inciting a riot and brought before me for trial may expect to receive the limit of the law." After meeting with members of the Committee of Safety, Judge Pendleton reminded grand jurors of their solemn obligations while considering felony cases: it was their "duty to be in session for weeks, and possibly for a month, and investigate this matter and find all who are responsible for this state of affairs."[25]

Although these local judges voiced their commitment to the ideals of color-blind justice, their courts adhered to the normal practice of openly discriminating against black defendants. Indeed, in the postriot upheaval, these courts proved more biased than ever. Judges and prosecutors were particularly sensitive to allegations that the criminal courts were inefficient and unreliable vehicles for punishing assaults by blacks and other challenges to white racial dominance. Because such contentions provided justification for further mob violence, judges and prosecutors were united in seeking guilty verdicts and maximum sentences for African Americans charged with any form of black-on-white aggression (whether physical or verbal, defensive or offensive). This rigid stance contrasted with the relative flexibility of the preriot period, when lynching parties had occasionally exonerated black suspects once the mob had become convinced of their innocence.

The ingrained racial biases of white Atlanta officials and their heightened sensitivity to any signs of black resistance repeatedly compromised evenhanded justice in the postriot court proceedings. Reflecting the single-minded determination of police officers and judges to stamp out black defiance, the courts convicted approximately fifty-four African Americans on concealed weapons charges and eight more for verbally threatening whites, insulting white women, or engaging in riotous speech. Broyles, for example, fined Will Mobley $10 for attacking a white man selling newspapers on the night of the riot, and he incarcerated for thirty days another black man convicted of knocking off a white man's hat. Three African Americans paid fines ranging from $15 to $50 for hurling bricks and rocks at passing streetcars in the riot's aftermath. As a rule, whites were hauled before the court for only the most serious offenses. Broyles convicted ten white men for incitement to riot and four others for vandalism. He fined one white man $100 for dropping an iron weight on an African American's head and forced another to pay approximately $15 for attempting to shoot an African American at close range. Broyles dismissed charges against six whites for firing guns at policemen during the riot, citing the suspects' testimony that, after being deputized by police officers, they had mistaken their targets as a crowd of menacing blacks. The courts punished only approximately four whites for weapons violations.[26]

In cases stemming directly from Saturday night's violence, a grand jury indicted twenty-two whites on attempted murder and assault charges. Only two such cases before the superior court ended in convictions. Based on the testimony of a police officer and five black witnesses, a jury convicted notorious career criminal George Blackstock of brutally assaulting blacks on the night of the riot. Had county judge Leonard Roan based Blackstock's sentence on the original felony charges of assault with intent to murder, the defendant might have faced ten to twenty years of hard labor.[27] At the jury's recommendation, however, Roan sentenced Blackstock as a misdemeanant, allowing the convicted man the option of a $300 fine or a year on the county chain gang. Blackstock's conviction and that of T. F. Clements, who was sentenced to pay a $300 fine or spend six months in jail after pleading guilty to assault charges, proved to be the only criminal court convictions of alleged white rioters. Three separate suspects were pronounced not guilty, following witness tampering on the part of the police and the recantation of earlier eyewitness testimonies by whites. Even after three police eyewitnesses fingered J. H. Carr as a member of the Saturday night mob and a jury convicted him for general rioting, Judge Roan inexplicably acquitted the defendant, citing insufficient evidence. The court dropped eight other cases on similar grounds. Clearly, then, white defendants benefited from strict evidentiary standards and the presumption of innocence.[28]

In contrast, superior court judges and carefully screened white juries were predisposed to reach guilty verdicts against black assault defendants. Such persons were further disadvantaged by the desperate postriot desire of judges and white civic leaders to demonstrate the efficacy of the criminal courts in punishing black rapists as a means of discouraging mob violence. These discriminatory factors came into play in the cases of black assault defendants Lucius (or Luther) Frazier and Robert Branham. Branham stood accused of assaulting and attempting to murder both Ethel and Mabel Lawrence on 20 August. Approximately a month after the attack, Ethel positively identified Branham, but only after noting a "facial difference" between the suspect and her assailant. Following a brief trial, Branham received the maximum sentence possible for two counts of assault with murderous intent: forty years in prison.[29]

Prosecutors relied on highly speculative circumstantial evidence to charge the second defendant, Frazier, with attempted rape. His alleged crime against Orrie Bryan had taken place two days before the riot. Bryan had been inside her home in the central city with her mother and two siblings. Frazier, drunk and wearing no trousers, sneaked through Bryan's window and moved toward her while brandishing a shoe. According to Bryan's and her mother's testimony, Frazier chased her into a closet and beat upon the door with his shoe. He then moved toward Bryan's mother. According to Orrie, Frazier told her that he loved her and would never hurt her. Despite the fact that Frazier's weapon had been only a shoe and he had never touched either woman, he received a fifteen-year sentence at the conclusion of a brief trial. By custom, judges and juries could exercise broad discretion when considering cases against African Americans.[30]

In contrast to Branham's and Frazier's draconian punishments, county courts accorded marked leniency to white men convicted of attempted sexual assault in the wake of the riot. Juries composed solely of white males voiced sympathy toward these white defendants, and their recommendations helped moderate judges' sentences. In December 1906, white defendant George Cann received only a $200 fine upon his conviction for a crime that was markedly similar to Frazier's, though arguably more egregious. Cornelia Hunt testified that Cann, after entering her home to deliver groceries, had forcibly embraced her and attempted to drag her into a bedroom, tearing her blouse in the process. Despite an original indictment for attempted criminal assault, the judge permitted the jury to convict the defendant on the lesser charge of simple assault. In a second trial that December, Judge Roan characterized white defendant Robert Turnadge's attempted sexual assault of Carrie Comstock as "one of the most brutal crimes I have known of." While struggling with Comstock, the defendant broke a water pitcher over her head and struck her face, breaking her nose. Upon receiving a petition for mercy from the jury, Roan swallowed his disgust and ultimately sentenced Turnadge to fifteen years at hard labor rather than the maximum twenty-year penalty. These striking disparities in the punishments of black and white defendants represented a defeat for both African Americans' hopes for color-blind justice and preriot female reformers' hopes for public action to rein in white men's sexual and physical abuse of white women.[31]

IN NOVEMBER, REPORTS of an additional black assault and rumors of another outbreak of mob violence galvanized Charles Hopkins to revive the biracial efforts that had languished since late September. The new assault case came to light on 13 November, when Annie Camp identified fifty-year-old Joe Glenn as the armed black man who earlier that day had entered her home and brutally beaten and twice sexually assaulted her while her husband was at work. Hopkins, seeking a prompt trial to avert a possible lynching, contacted Judge Roan. This white lawyer agreed to serve as Glenn's attorney and enlisted the aid of two white colleagues. Hopkins's connivance with the judge also ensured the appointment of a jury composed of men who numbered among Atlanta's "most prominent" families. After apprising Benjamin Davis and black minister Edward R. Carter of the coming trial, Hopkins asked them to interview the suspect's friends and neighbors. Davis and Carter rounded up twenty-five white men willing to speak on Glenn's behalf. In the four days between Glenn's arrest and the opening of his criminal trial, white mobs twice came within a hairsbreadth of lynching him before being turned back by law enforcement officials. At the trial, white victim Annie Camp initially failed to identify Glenn as her attacker. Prompted by the prosecutor, Camp realized her mistake and pointed to the defendant as her assailant. Despite the victim's contradictory testimony and an energetic defense, the handpicked white jury reportedly vowed to "lynch him ourselves!"[32]

Finally, near the conclusion of the trial, messengers burst into the courtroom announcing the apprehension of Will Johnson for the crime. A police expert had confirmed Johnson's guilt based on Camp's initial description of her assailant. The investigator reported that Johnson's shoe size matched footprints found near Camp's home and that his gun's cartridges matched those discovered near the crime scene. Confronted with this evidence, the jury finally exonerated the defendant that they had earlier been so determined to punish. Subsequent juries convicted Will Johnson of both the Camp assault and the August 1906 assault on Georgia Hembree. In June 1907, the state executed Johnson.[33]

The Glenn and Johnson cases demonstrate how white civic leaders' and law enforcement officials' postriot endeavors to replace extralegal violence with state-administered punishments had the effect of undermining the relative public authority of white women. In the weeks preceding the riot, mobs had routinely empowered alleged white assault victims to make the final determination regarding a suspect's guilt or innocence. A white woman's positive identification of a black man as the perpetrator of the crime meant his certain death, while her exoneration triggered his probable discharge. That summer, white mobs occasionally released suspects after verifying their innocence in this manner. For example, following Georgia Hembree's alleged assault, Justice of the Peace William Wood condoned the lynching of a black suspect with the stipulation that Hembree first identify him as her assailant. When she informed the crowd that he was not the guilty party, the white mob reportedly released their captive.[34]

In contrast to this extralegal route, the trial process transferred the decision-making power from white women to male judges and juries. As Camp became aware following her initial confusion over Glenn's identity, this crucial change diminished a female victim's influence over the punishment of her alleged assailant. It could also endanger her honor and reputation, particularly if a judge or jury questioned her testimony. Sensing her reduced power and apparently humiliated by her loss of credibility, Camp reportedly became hysterical under questioning and begged for the jury's sympathy. She then taunted Glenn, informing the court that she would like to kill this "low down rascal" herself. Earlier that October, Hembree, frustrated by the failure of law enforcement officials to arrest and charge a suspect in her case, had publicly attacked the police for negligence. Now, infuriated at the original suspect's release as the consequence of her own extralegal testimony, Hembree explicitly endorsed the *News*'s continuing campaign for summary justice.[35]

These legal cases also suggest that the courts demanded as certain a punishment as did the lynching mob. Despite Camp's questionable testimony regarding Joe Glenn, her honor demanded retribution for the crime.

The white mob encircling the jail insisted on the slaughter of a sacrificial lamb. And many white newspaper readers thirsted for the symbolic restoration of white supremacy. Jurors had publicly vowed to convict Glenn until police offered up Will Johnson as an alternative scapegoat. Once formally charged with the rape, Johnson faced certain conviction, in spite of Camp's confusion regarding her assailant's identity, the highly speculative nature of the state's circumstantial evidence, and an alibi offered by a black person who claimed that Johnson was at home at the time of Camp's assault. Following Hembree's positive identification of Will Johnson as her attacker, a jury handed him a second conviction on rape charges. During the trial, Judge Roan had rejected the request of defense attorneys that he remind jurors of their solemn duty to set aside any prejudices and focus only on the evidence at hand. In April, Georgia's supreme court turned down Johnson's petition for a retrial by a three-to-two majority. During the proceedings, Johnson's attorneys announced that they had uncovered two highly credible white witnesses who placed Johnson at a construction site far from the crime scene at the approximate time of Hembree's assault. This testimony and a corroborating timecard convinced the two dissenting judges that it exceeded "all human probability" that Johnson was guilty of the crime. In June, the county sheriff reported that Johnson, who had theretofore maintained his innocence, had privately confessed on the execution stand, not only to the Camp and Hembree assaults but also to the attack against the Lawrence women. The *Constitution* informed its readers that this "devil incarnate" bore sole responsibility for the outbreak of the riot. As surely as any mob, the strong arm of the law had ritualistically affirmed the overwhelming racial dominance of whites and defended both Camp's and Hembree's honor. Despite Johnson's purported confession, Branham remained behind bars for his alleged crimes against the Lawrences.[36]

WITH STORIES CIRCULATING throughout Atlanta that whites were planning a second massacre during the upcoming Christmas holidays, Hopkins announced on 29 November the creation of a permanent biracial civic league aimed at organizing 3,000 of Atlanta's best white citizens along with 3,000 to 5,000 African Americans. Like the original Committee of Safety, the civic league's white leadership was predominantly comprised of elite businessmen. Noticeably absent were James English and chamber president Sam Jones. Industrialist John J. Eagan, Episcopal minister Cary B. Wilmer, and other religious leaders inspired by Social Gospel ideals also joined the league. Although Hopkins avowed that the civic league welcomed white volunteers,

At left, alleged rapist Will Johnson, fingered by Atlanta newspapers as the man responsible for the 1906 riot. At right, Lucius (or Luther) Frazier, convicted of attempted assault against Orrie Bryan. (Baker, *Following the Color Line*, facing p. 179)

there is no evidence that he ever achieved his stated plan of convening a mass meeting of the entire white membership. At Hopkins's direction, Henry Hugh Proctor assembled a black civic league with a membership of 1,500, directed by a small cadre of leaders. The black executive committee included Du Bois, college administrator Richard Stinson, William F. Penn, Richard T. Weatherby (secretary of the black YMCA), and black Baptist ministers E. R. Carter and Peter James Bryant. The black and white executive committees met separately, with Hopkins serving as their intermediary.[37]

Hopkins's announcement about the civic league represented a fundamental concession that Proctor and other black elites had publicly sought before the riot. In Hopkins's words, influential whites were finally acknowledging that "there are two classes of Negroes—the intelligent and the ignorant, the criminal and the non-criminal," and after separating "the lawless from the law-abiding . . . the white man and the Negro should work together toward a common end." Hopkins also promised to alleviate the city's worst sources of racial "irritation" and to address at least some long-standing black complaints. He relayed to police officials and streetcar company representatives black grievances regarding discrimination and rough handling. The white lawyer also promised to use his influence to help secure black police officers to patrol African American neighborhoods. African Americans had long pursued this reform in hopes of opening up expanded job opportunities for blacks and better protecting African Americans from crime and from brutality at the hands of white police officers. The white lawyer convinced fellow white civic league members to fund a defense attorney for "innocent" or "deserving" black defendants selected upon the "recommendation" of a black pastor or some other "reliable person."[38]

In December, Hopkins's civic leagues headed off a second riot and ensured fair trials for fifty-nine black defendants charged in a riot-associated criminal case. These successes highlighted the potential of interracial cooperation as a mechanism for calming racial tensions and promoting color-blind justice. In early December, white civic leaguer George Muse served as the jury foreman in the trial of four Brownsville defendants charged with murdering police officer Jim Heard. On 31 October, a jury had already sentenced Alex Walker to life in prison for Heard's murder, despite technical irregularities in the proceedings and doubts regarding the veracity of police witnesses. At this second trial, white defense attorney James D. Kilpatrick cast additional suspicions on the state's case against Walker and the other defendants. Breaking ranks with his fellow police officers, one of the prosecution's three chief witnesses refuted testimony placing them at the front of the posse where they could have clearly seen the black defenders. Kilpatrick established 7:50 P.M. as the time of the first shots and fifty feet as the distance between the posse and the black residents. A federal weather observer testified that the witnesses would not have been able to accurately identify anyone on that cloudy evening. After considering these startling revelations, the jury returned a verdict of not guilty. Moreover, foreman Muse shared with reporters the jurors' conclusion that "the Negroes were gathered together just as white people were in other parts of the town, for the purpose of defending their homes." Muse also noted that he and others were "shocked by the conduct which the evidence showed some of the county police had been guilty of." After experiencing such a resounding defeat, the solicitor dropped all of the charges against the fifty-five remaining Brownsville defendants. Alex Walker was nevertheless required to serve out his own sentence.[39]

White civic league participants also focused their energies that December on preventing a rumored second white riotous attack over the Christmas holidays. Hopkins met quietly with public officials early that month and worked closely with former governor William J. Northen in planning Law and Order Sunday, scheduled for 9 December. In hopes of discouraging black crime and white mob violence, more than 200 white and black ministers throughout the city delivered morning sermons on the Christian's obligation to obey the law. In the afternoon, Northen and Booker T. Washington spoke before an audience of more than 1,000 blacks and whites assembled at Friendship Baptist Church. The two men encouraged blacks and whites to embrace the law-and-order principles embodied in Hopkins's civic league. Washington implored his interracial audience to "frown down" upon "the element of agitators among both races that is continually stirring up strife with no end in view to bettering of present conditions." Upon Hopkins's suggestions, Judge Broyles and Judge Roan vowed to punish any riot inciters with the full force of the law. White committee members convinced newspaper editors to refrain from publishing any "sensational" extras. Members of the black committee discouraged African Americans from walking in the downtown area during the holidays. For good measure, the city council temporarily added 100 men to the police force, and Mayor Woodward ordered the closing of all the saloons at 4:00 P.M. on Christmas Eve.[40]

While Christmas passed peaceably in downtown Atlanta, renewed racial violence threatened to erupt in Brownsville. There, two drunken county police officers harassed Priscilla Frambo, the wife of a slain Brownsville resident and a defense witness who had contradicted the testimony of white police during the recent trial. White civic league members met privately with both county sheriff John Nelms and the commander of a local militia regiment. Nelms ordered the arrests of the offending police officers. White representatives then traveled to Brownsville to confer with black civic league members, who assured their counterparts that they could patrol their own neighborhoods. White civic league members, in turn, quelled rumors that Brownsville residents were secretly organizing an attack against whites.[41]

DESPITE THESE TRIUMPHS and civic leaguers' shared commitment to racial peace, conflicts continuously roiled below the organization's surface, both between blacks and whites and within the two races. Much like white public officials, Hopkins and his white counterparts generally pursued the appearance rather than the substance of justice. They focused the bulk of their concerns on controlling black crime and enlisting black support for this endeavor. To discourage extralegal violence, Hopkins argued that trials involving suspected black rapists must be "swift and uninterfered with by quibbles and technicalities argued by unscrupulous lawyers," who were "forever finding flaws in 'procedure,' thus delaying and defeating the ends of law." Hopkins and other whites voiced fears that lynching encouraged black crime and secrecy by alienating the entire race from the criminal justice system. Hopkins and other white civic league participants argued (as had preriot white newspaper editors) that black elites could play a crucial role in restraining disorderly blacks and ferreting out African American outlaws.[42]

Many black ministers and civic leaders, cognizant as they were of widespread white support for extralegal violence, enthusiastically embraced the white civic league's support for jury trials and the league's attempts to undermine the legitimacy of mob justice. Black commentators throughout the city reiterated that the central lesson of the Glenn case was, in the words of black executive committee member Richard Weatherby, "that under indescribable circumstances there is a bare possibility of 'mistaken identity' and a sacrifice of innocent blood which a fair though speedy trial would avoid." So, too, did they embrace Hopkins's central arguments, that "the courts can and will give a fair and impartial trial to the accused" and that "the officers of the law are equal to any possible emergency."[43]

Black elites shuddered at continuing white demands that all African Americans shoulder responsibility for the crimes of individual blacks. Proctor asked whites, "Is there not some quality of injustice in calling upon a law-abiding, home-owning, self-respecting Negro to apprehend and deliver a Negro criminal? . . . If the white race, with its police and detective powers, cannot arrest criminals, why should the law-abiding Negro . . . be expected to do what the white race . . . confesses itself unable to do?" This inherent conflict between black and white perspectives surfaced during Hopkins's first meeting with the black executive committee. According to Du Bois, the white lawyer became "angry" and "impatient," even threatening to "throw up the whole thing," when the black committee expressed doubts about its ability to organize and monitor Atlanta's entire black population. Yet, even while attempting to isolate themselves from their race's disorderly element, Proctor and his black allies manipulated white fears of black crime in hopes of winning additional concessions. Black civic leaguers repeatedly conditioned their willingness to speak out against black crime on white guarantees of color-blind justice. Proctor and other black elites similarly tried to advance Hopkins's ultimately unfulfilled proposal of hiring black police officers by suggesting that such officers were best suited to uphold white visions of law and order in black neighborhoods. Following Glenn's trial, black civic league participants publicly requested the opportunity to serve on the jury that would hear Will Johnson's case so that they could "go on record as opposing such crimes."[44]

This implicit endorsement of Johnson's conviction demonstrates the central flaw in a civil rights strategy predicated on drawing impassable boundaries between respectable and criminal blacks. Proctor and other black civic leaguers sought to undermine the legitimacy of extralegal violence by highlighting the coercive possibilities of Atlanta's criminal justice system and affirming its fundamental fairness. They battled white racist depictions of black criminality by drawing ironclad distinctions between "orderly" and "disorderly" blacks. These tactics ensured black civic leaguers an entrée into Atlanta's public discourse and an audience with influential whites. Yet these devices also reinforced white stereotypes linking all marginalized and working-class blacks with crime and disorder while deflecting public attention away from the criminal justice system's deeply entrenched inequities and brutalities.

IT IS NOT clear why Hopkins failed to fulfill Proctor's hopes for the hiring of black police officers and for blacks' symbolic participation on juries. Given his ingrained paternalism and his narrow focus on averting racial disturbances, Hopkins was probably uncomfortable with the enhanced authority that such reforms would provide for blacks as well as their likelihood for antagonizing prejudiced whites. If Hopkins did approach white politicians with such demands, elected officials would have had little incentive to enact reforms guaranteeing jobs for a nonvoting constituency. During the white civic league's initial meeting, Hopkins decoupled his movement from the issue of black voting rights in Georgia because of its divisiveness. Still other white committee members favored disfranchisement as a cure for the crime, racial strife, and conflict that Hopkins was attempting to alleviate. Episcopal minister Cary Wilmer, described by Ray Stannard Baker as unusually tolerant on racial issues, told the white journalist that enfranchisement was "one of the most demoralizing, and therefore, crime producing things that have been imposed upon the Negro."[45]

Both Hopkins and fellow white civic leaguer Cary Wilmer openly embraced segregation as a means of reducing conflict and preventing the violent white backlash that they associated with the enforced integration of the city's public spaces. Tellingly, Hopkins's instinctive response to black complaints regarding the streetcars was not to lessen racial separation but, rather, to institutionalize it more firmly by providing African Americans "their definite seats in every car." Wilmer questioned Du Bois's assertion that segregation was wrong. If it were immoral, the white minister advised, the best solution was a gradualist approach, redressing such ills through moral and religious persuasion, rather than via legislation. Given white prejudices, he argued, any other course threatened to unleash renewed racial violence. Cognizant of these fears, Proctor silenced his once strident criticisms of segregation even as he trumpeted the potential benefits of biracial cooperation.[46]

Still, as Du Bois and Proctor clearly recognized, the issues of black voting rights and integration were central to Atlanta's law-and-order problems. Both Proctor and black journalist Benjamin Davis hoped the civic leagues' cooperative efforts might evolve so as, in Davis's words, to "educate our white neighbors to see that there are some Negro men just as fit to vote as white men." Blacks, disfranchised by the white primary, exercised little influence over city council members, judges, and law enforcement officials. Even after the riot, in the glare of national scrutiny, white public officials repeatedly targeted African Americans for weapons violations or for defending themselves from attacks by whites. Policemen sought to influence the outcome of trials by intimidating witnesses. Ironically, the very trials by which judges hoped to showcase the courts' commitment to color-blind justice only highlighted the consequences of blacks' grossly unequal access to political and civic power. Pleas by black elites for black police, jury representation, and political participation revealed their abiding conviction that true justice was possible only if African Americans could directly influence the criminal justice system.[47]

While Hopkins and other white civic league members helped to represent the interests of blacks in high-profile legal cases, their de facto monopoly on political influence and their overwhelming wealth and power constrained black-white interactions and limited genuine dialogue. Hopkins's behavior during private interracial meetings, Du Bois believed, invariably reflected the same paternalism that the white lawyer had evinced immediately following the riot. According to Du Bois, at the first meeting Hopkins acted "as though he was talking to school children, not appreciating at all the fact that he was talking to a body of men. . . . The depression that settled upon that mass of people there—I could not help but feel it."[48]

Segregation further undermined honest interracial communication by preventing off-the-cuff interactions. Traditional white notions of racial etiquette discouraged the two groups from engaging in open discussions or meeting informally away from the bargaining table. As Du Bois recognized, the civic leagues' heavily scripted interactions limited participants' ability to build a sense of trust and discouraged powerful whites from reevaluating their preconceived racial assumptions. At the end of meetings, Du Bois noted, "everybody went away with the idea that, after all, they did not know each other." Wilmer agreed with Du Bois: "If two sets of people come together and determine what they are going to say, they are steeled against the very thing which you are trying to effect, which is the very modification brought about by contact." Despite this insight, Wilmer himself openly sought to silence black criticisms of white people, "to reform whom is hardly their task, and certainly is beyond their power." This absence of honest dialogue and Hopkins's conservative fears prevented the achievement of enduring reforms beyond the hiring of a white lawyer to represent a select group of "deserving" black defendants.[49]

Some black elites partially embraced their new contacts with influential whites as an avenue for expanding their public influence and obtaining white donations for their own churches and educational institutions. Proctor's preriot civil rights activism had prompted many whites, including the *Constitution*'s editors, to view the black minister as a potentially dangerous northern outsider. Proctor emerged from his cooperation with Hopkins with a sterling reputation for "intelligence and diplomacy," and his church won high regard for representing "the dignity and refinement of the best religious thought and progress."[50] Proctor's skillful handling of white law-and-order fears provided him with a unique opportunity to achieve his ambitious vision of creating an institutional church. In 1907, when Proctor initiated a citywide fund-raising campaign for his new church building, he raised $5,000 from white businessmen in less than a week. Governor Hoke Smith and local white ministers endorsed his drive. Fred L. Seely's and John Temple Graves's *Georgian* supported his project, as did Clark Howell's *Constitution*. At the 1908 groundbreaking ceremony for the Institutional Church, Chamber of Commerce president and Coca-Cola magnate Asa G. Candler spoke, as did Mayor Walthal R. Joyner. Contributions by local whites to Proctor's campaign accounted for approximately 19 percent of the minister's total capital fund.[51] Proctor later outlined the law-and-order pitch that he employed to win the support of white businessmen and politicians:

> God gave me a message for my people. It was only natural that they [blacks] should want to leave. I tried to assure them that out of this would come a better Atlanta, that now was the time to settle down and build anew. . . . But in order to make this appeal effective I had to produce some tangible evidence to my people that the good will of them [the whites] was genuine. In that hour a vision came to me. . . . I asked myself why it was that the people passed my church and went to the dive. The answer was simple. My church was locked and barred and dark, while the dive was wide open, illuminated and attractive. Then I said: "God helping me, I will open my church and make it as attractive as the dive."[52]

In December 1906 and January 1907, college administrators Henry Mc-Neal Turner and Richard Stinson similarly played on the law-and-order concerns of whites in preparation for seeking their financial contributions for Morris Brown College. Though not officially affiliated with Hopkins's movement, Turner's and Stinson's independent black organization—the Vigilant Reform Band—promised to support white civic leaders' goals for social control both by separating black "people of questionable character from those of unquestionable character" and by discouraging all forms of vice in black communities. White participants at a Morris Brown fund-raising ceremony sponsored by the reform organization in January 1907 included many white civic leaguers and former members of the now defunct Committee of Safety. During the ceremony, Richard Stinson lauded James English, who had recently forced Barber's departure from Atlanta, for encouraging "the race in its moral, financial, spiritual, and intellectual betterment." English donated $10, and the interracial gathering raised approximately $500, making it the college's "most successful" fund drive in memory. Stinson continued to organize similar interracial fund-raising meetings well into the 1910s. Yet the Vigilant Reform Band itself was a paper organization that sought to encourage powerful whites' financial support for Morris Brown College rather than impose white civic leaders' vision of order on African Americans.[53]

Du Bois refused on principle to accept Stinson's invitation to attend the fund-raising kickoff that January. "There is no use," he concluded, "of my going over there and saying what I really believe, and I will not go over there and say what I do not believe." The narrow constraints that white reformers imposed on postriot interracial activities had disheartened Du Bois, as had Barber's banishment from the city. As Du Bois recognized, elite black Georgians had in the riot's aftermath largely distanced themselves from their militant 1906 protest activities and New Black Man ideals. The black professor continued his national activism following the riot but permanently abandoned his local civil rights activities and severed his ties with the GERC. In exchange for symbolic court victories and the resolution of temporary crises, whites demanded blacks' silent acceptance of the numerous injustices associated with segregation and municipal neglect. Absent from the interracial discourse were the strident calls for full equality that had so dominated black speeches and writings in late 1905 and early 1906. Du Bois, writing from Atlanta in the immediate aftermath of Hopkins's movement, asserted the necessity of national black agitation. African Americans must, he stated, "protest strongly, even wildly, of the evil and the wrong of the universe." We must tell whites, he continued, that "we want those who stand on the threshold and within the veil of crime to be treated not as beasts, but as men who can be reformed."[54]

IN THE WAKE of the riot, many white business elites and public officials sought to discredit extralegal violence by demonstrating the courts' efficacy in controlling and punishing black criminals, a remedy antithetical to the fundamental principle of color-blind justice. This emphasis on the coercive possibilities of Atlanta's criminal justice machinery diverted attention away from the legal system's inherent racial injustices. White Committee of Safety and civic league participants also battled disorder through interracial dialogue. By embracing the law-and-order visions of whites, Proctor and other African Americans gained new promises of financial support from white elites, and they built a framework for interracial dialogue that helped protect black homes, businesses, neighborhoods, churches, and schools from destructive violence. Elite blacks rejected racial warfare not simply because they had so much to gain from interracial cooperation but also because they had so much to lose from continued white violence.

Despite these payoffs, this postriot interracial cooperation exacted long-term costs. By isolating black participants from other African Americans, the civic league movement bolstered black elites' dependence on, and identification with, their white counterparts. Interracial cooperation thus stymied the forging of the sorts of intraracial alliances that might have strengthened the position of the entire black population in relation to whites. In January 1907, black journalist Benjamin Davis challenged Proctor and other black civic leaguers to abandon their "selfish leadership" by bringing their movement "to the people." Davis pointed to the central weakness of the movement's inherent exclusivity by noting that if a larger segment of the black population "were organized into a civic league we could present our claims to our white neighbors with such effect and force we would be heard." Far from attempting to mobilize African Americans, black civic leaguers sought to establish clear demarcations between the race's "law abiding" and "criminal" elements. Their focus on the vices of black criminals rather than the courts' shortcomings helps to explain why, as Proctor himself admitted, some blacks outside the movement felt he "was giving away their case by seeking the cooperation with the whites." Black elites had briefly lionized working-class blacks as heroes immediately after the riot. White reformers now successfully demanded that black elites publicly condemn these resisters as criminals and threats to public order. Continued white threats of violence and a white-dominated mechanism for interracial cooperation splintered the nascent *intraracial* alliance forged among blacks during the riot.[55]

A wide gulf separated the postriot experiences of a small group of black elites from those of the vast black majority. Little more than a handful of black Atlantans were privy to the behind-the-scenes negotiations associated with the Committee of Safety and the civic league. Atlanta's experiment with interracial cooperation had little lasting significance for most African Americans and scant effect on their interactions with a racially biased legal system. This divergence helps account for the dramatic differences in blacks' memories of the riot. Proctor rejected throughout his life the black consensus that defensive violence had checked the white mob's advances. He later claimed regarding the riot, "It was the unanimous opinion that the city was better afterwards than before." Yet with the exceptions of First Church members and a small group of elites, Atlanta's black population largely forgot the city's interracial experiment. Most blacks clung instead to memories of the shared savagery of all whites and the shared success of all blacks in protecting black neighborhoods and property from white incursion.[56]

CHAPTER SEVEN

God, Give Us Men!

⟿

IN THE RIOT'S AFTERMATH, William J. Northen, an ex-governor and Confederate veteran, happened upon a series of letters authored by white ministers and Christian laypersons. Published in the *Constitution*, the correspondence stressed the potential role of Christianity and white ministerial oversight in alleviating Georgia's racial problems. This message struck a deep chord in Northen, who was already profoundly troubled by the riot's violence. In response, the ex-governor initiated an unprecedented campaign to establish a state network of antilynching leagues. Between 1906 and 1907 he visited approximately ninety counties, where he pushed his antilynching leagues and proposals for interracial cooperation before white audiences. "With tears streaming down his cheeks," Northen reportedly told black minister Henry Hugh Proctor that he "would be willing to die, if need be, if he thought that thereby he could bring the races together in harmony and goodwill."[1]

Northen's movement wedded a humanistic concern for black welfare to the goal of strengthening the power of white elites over both the black and white masses. At seventy-one, his once auburn hair now gray, Northen looked back fondly on the antebellum South's rigid social order. He remembered this lost world as featuring impenetrable racial barriers and clear class boundaries distinguishing a slaveholding elite from the white masses. Northen associated Georgia's rapidly changing order and his generation's declining public authority with sexual pollution and social decay. He viewed his state as dangerously close to descending into "anarchy and governmental hell," as the consequence of the growing threats posed by black rapists, violent white retribution, and miscegenation. Northen's locally based anti-lynching leagues sought to boost the power and authority of an elite group of "sun-crowned, God-given" white businessmen, planters, and ministers. Only such elites, he argued, possessed the moral strength necessary to protect the South from the threats simultaneously posed by black outlaws and white mobs.[2]

Northen's movement was only one of many social reform campaigns embraced by whites seeking to permanently alleviate the racial tensions that had triggered the 1906 riot. Governor-elect Hoke Smith and his political allies continued to maintain that disfranchisement offered the surest path to social peace and prosperity. White temperance reformers, energized by civic and religious leaders' law-and-order concerns, pushed a platform for state-wide prohibition, even when this campaign risked derailing efforts to quash black voting rights. Baptist minister John E. White advocated the creation of a racial commission, directed by white elites and charged with forging and enforcing a coherent regional race relations policy.

The interplay among these diverse groups, which alternately portrayed one another as allies and antagonists, underscores the complexities of Progressive Era reform in Georgia. Postriot reformers' struggles illustrate that disfranchisement was only one of many schemes through which early twentieth-century whites sought to reassert their mastery over southern society. This frantic period of social reform activity confirms historians' growing recognition that conflicts among whites over race relations in the Jim Crow South were simultaneously struggles over power relations among members of their own race. Northen's movement reveals that white racist characterizations, in this case of black rapists, could be used to challenge as well as to support mob violence. So, too, was Northen's own program open to diverse interpretations and manipulations. The ex-governor conceived of his effort as a backward-looking attempt to restore the slave South's lost social hierarchy. Black Georgians, in contrast, hoped to deploy his calls for mutual cooperation to advance their own forward-looking civil rights agendas. Ironically, Northen's efforts to eradicate racial violence provoked white fears of unrelenting social turmoil, while disfranchisement, touted as elevating all white men's status and promising social peace, ultimately diminished the public influence of nonelite whites.

NORTHEN PROUDLY EMBODIED the genteel traditions of Georgia's landed elite. Throughout his life, he fondly remembered his intimate prewar ties with slaves, including the "old negro Mammy" who nursed him as a baby. At nineteen, Northen dedicated himself to God, and he remained active in the church for the rest of his life, ultimately winning appointment as president of the Georgia Baptist and Southern Baptist conventions. After serving in the Confederate army and working as a Confederate hospital attendant, Northen returned to Hancock County, where his farming operations eventually encompassed more than 800 acres. His service as a state representative and president of the State Agricultural Society helped ensure his election as governor in 1890, with the support of the Farmers' Alliance. Northen became a sworn enemy of many of his erstwhile alliance friends, however, when they bolted the Democratic Party to become Populists. Overheard calling for the assassination of Populist congressional candidate Tom Watson in 1892, Northen flatly rejected Populists' attempts to unite black and white voters around their shared interests as farmers. He won reelection in 1892 with the backing of many elite black ministers and Republicans who were impressed with the governor's support for black education and anti-lynching legislation.[3]

Northen's wistful nostalgia for the antebellum Georgia of his youth reveals his profound misgivings about the rapid social changes transforming his state. After the Civil War, his once prosperous native cotton belt stagnated economically. By the early 1900s, the previously intimate ties between white landholders and black tenants were dissolving as growing numbers of both groups abandoned the region's plantations for the state's burgeoning towns and cities. The sea of strange black and white faces that he regularly encountered as an Atlanta investment banker must have disturbed Northen, a man who had spent much of his life in rural Georgia, where an individual's character could be quickly determined by reputation or surname. News of the catastrophic Atlanta riot led the ex-governor to fear that these social transformations might trigger the "disintegration and death of our civilization."[4]

Atlanta's white business community viewed the riot primarily as an isolated, local affair, but to Northen it heralded the coming of Armageddon. The deep racial antagonisms manifested during its violence provided telling evidence that similar scenes "can be repeated in almost any section of Georgia, where there are large numbers of people like those who made the mobs in this city." The mob's actions raised Northen's fears of a disorderly white

Ex-governor William J. Northen, the postriot anticrime and antilynching crusader, ca. 1907. (Baker, *Following the Color Line*, facing p. 252)

element. Black defensive violence and newspaper stories of black sexual assaults revived old worries that crime and disorder among blacks were escalating out of control. Fearing these dual threats, Northen was willing to focus his energies exclusively on easing Georgia's racial tensions.[5]

His imagination sparked by the *Constitution*'s editorials on the role of religion in addressing Georgia's racial crisis, Northen initiated his antilynching efforts by working closely with Hopkins and other white businessmen in the city. During November and December, Northen used his contacts among businessmen and ministers to help organize Law and Order Sunday in Atlanta on 9 December. That day, ministers around the city gave sermons on the Christian's duty to obey the laws of the state. In the afternoon, more than a thousand white and black Atlantans crowded into Friendship Baptist Church to hear Booker T. Washington speak to the twin evils of black crime and white mob justice. In addition to these local efforts, Northen also sought to expand the businessmen's movement, not only by extending it beyond Atlanta but also by transforming it into a permanent movement based on the "principles and the preaching of the gospels." Should he succeed in developing a state antilynching network, the ex-governor, weakened by age and poor health, hoped that his campaign would "take the entire South," even if doing so meant "wearing the end of my life."[6] In keeping with the postriot public relations efforts of Atlanta business leaders, Northen's favorable national press attention originally advanced a vision of Georgia as stable and progressive. In January 1907, the *Georgian* praised Northen's movement for establishing "in the minds of our neighbors to the North . . . a confidence and respect which are not to be despised" and for rendering "more stable and secure the foundations of our civilization." Throughout the ex-governor's campaign, this newspaper (which became the *Atlanta Georgian and News* in early February after purchasing its rival the *Evening News*) joined the *Constitution* in faithfully publishing Northen's dispatches and writing editorials praising his efforts.[7]

BETWEEN DECEMBER 1906 and April 1907, Northen conducted a whirlwind tour of his state, speaking in more than ninety counties and successfully establishing branches of his law-and-order league in almost every one he visited. Before his arrival at a particular location, the ex-governor would contact a public official, a pastor, a civic leader, or a prominent planter familiar to him. This individual, in turn, invited a small coterie of "conservative, law-abiding, good citizens" to a private meeting where they would plan their own antilynching initiative.[8]

The ex-governor opened each meeting by asking, "What can we do to save the fair women of Georgia from outrage and shame brought upon them by fiends from hell?" He frequently went on to depict a rape scare of his own, involving "a thrilling story from real life about a strange or tramp negro who came dangerously nigh [to] making an assault." Northen reminded audiences that similar attacks took place almost every day. Northen's fascination with black assaults was intensified by his growing conviction that the masses of postemancipation blacks, undisciplined by white supervision, were retrogressing, morally and physically. In a 1911 speech, for example, he quoted a Macon doctor who described the "appalling" nature of black males' "degeneration, physically, mentally, and morally" as well as their "almost universal infection from venereal diseases." Northen closed these meetings to white women. Just as his paternalism attempted to shield them from sexual assaults by blacks, it also aimed to protect women from the rough-and-tumble public realm of civic debate, especially explicit discussions of rape and interracial sex.[9]

Linking Georgia's social order with a woman's body, Northen modeled his "legions of honor" on the patriarch's role as the guardian of the sexual purity of his wife and daughters. Just as an individual man protected the bodies of his dependent women from outside pollution, "first-class whites" must defend "the purity of our state" from the threats of black rapists. The violation of white women by these black criminals, Northen clearly believed, challenged the authority and racial dominance of the state's white male elite. "First-class whites" were simultaneously charged with protecting the purity of Georgia's social order from a second threat—that posed by white men "easily savage enough to lynch and burn human beings." While Northen sought to empower a small elite, the communal nature of mob violence minimized social distinctions among white men even when businessmen and landholders participated in the violence, as they often did.[10]

As Northen also understood, extralegal violence had the potential to undermine the authority and legitimacy of the state's legal system, which was controlled by the very landowning and commercial elite that he exalted as Georgia's natural leaders. Large armed mobs initially organized to threaten African Americans might also destroy private property and utilize violence to wrest power from civic authorities. "Once give the mob the right-of-way for any offense whatever," Northen warned, "and the way will be open, wide open, for all defiance of the law," perhaps ultimately leading to a bloody battle between the members of mobs and the upholders of law for control of the state. Apparently unsure of the outcome of this violent male contest, Northen sought to bolster the authority of elite whites. He justified their enhanced powers on the basis of their unique masculine role in shielding an otherwise defenseless state from the ravages of this "law-abiding" element's polar opposites: the savagely violent whites who participated in mobs and the physically diseased, wholly undisciplined black "tramp" rapists.[11]

Northen's legions of honor also sought to enroll and empower a select group of "law-abiding negro ministers and negro laymen" who were "fully and heartily ready and anxious to help solve the awful conditions which confront us." Working together, the white and black "first classes" would classify the populations of each county so that they could know, "definitely and fully, the character of all the people among whom we live." Only "law-abiding" blacks had access to the requisite information to compile a complete and accurate list of the "vicious and villainous negroes," who "lounge around dives and dens and clubs during the day and commit burglaries and assaults at night."[12]

At the same time that Northen sought to elevate "first-class" blacks to positions of partial authority in his organizations, the ex-governor also tried to provide black women with some of the sexual protections previously limited to white women. "Law-abiding" black men had the special assignment of unearthing "a large body of low down, filthy, morally corrupt and physically rotten white men who have negro concubines." Once brought out into the open, every "last one of such white men" was to be dispatched to the penitentiary or a convict lease camp for twenty-five years. Punishing such men was absolutely vital, Northen stressed. He was convinced that "we can never settle the problem of the races as long as we allow corrupt white men to ruin the homes of negroes and make for them a lot of strumpets and wenches instead of pure, clean women." While Northen's choice of "strumpets" and "wenches" drew on a traditional, racist vocabulary, he clearly empathized with the victims of this "gross and cruel" abuse.[13]

Northen was also a determined opponent of miscegenation. He associated racial intermixture with the blurring of racial lines, which, he believed, violated God's law and would result in racial equality and a weakening of the social fabric. The very strategies designed to protect black women from sexual exploitation would also prevent consensual interracial relationships. By suggesting that these "third-class" white mob participants were guilty of miscegenation and sexual abuse, Northen was making arguments strikingly similar to those previously developed during the 1890s by Ida B. Wells, one of the most eloquent and passionate black critics of mob violence. Wells, like Northen, used the crimes of lynching and licentiousness to discredit the "manly" claims of white mob participants to social and political authority. Unlike the ex-governor, however, she implicated a wide range of white southerners, including members of the elite classes, in the commission of these crimes.[14]

To support the efforts of his local law-and-order organizations, Northen hoped to appoint a twenty-lawyer commission that would propose new statutes reinforcing his goals for social control. Because Northen associated black and white "idleness" with rapists and mobs, he wanted legislation loosely defining vagrancy so that white leaders might sentence individual blacks and whites to "the work house for fifteen years, or as long as may be necessary to get them in the habit of perspiring a little under moderate exercise." By reforming the characters of "strange," "idle blacks," Northen hoped to prevent assaults from occurring in the first place. In case crimes were committed, local committees needed legislation that would reduce the opportunities for suspected rapists to escape the death penalty through "delays in the courts" and "trifling technicalities." The black criminal was best handled "discretely" by the state and by "first class whites," Northen argued, who would punish him by "breaking his neck by law and not by murderous mobs." Northen sought to ensure trials by jury for defendants but not necessarily substantive justice. His desire to "patch up" Georgia's notoriously punitive and racially biased criminal justice system risked further eroding the flimsy rights of criminal suspects and encouraging executions that constituted little more than legal lynchings.[15]

Northen also feared a "second class" within both the white and black communities that threatened the state's social order by encouraging the criminal activities of these "third-class" lawbreakers. Among blacks, he identified a group of "preachers and a good lot of so-called Christian laymen and quite a number of newspaper editors" who never committed assaults or robberies but who nevertheless "hold secret meetings and plot and plan" or who "swear they will not work for white people, except upon very limited conditions." This second class of blacks allegedly encouraged resistance against white authority and white employers. Their equivalents among whites included a few editors, some ministers, and "a very large number of politicians" who never joined mobs but who nevertheless publicly supported extralegal violence and stirred racial strife through their intemperate remarks. Although Northen underscored the similarities among each corresponding class of blacks and whites, he emphasized that "only the first class of white people" would direct the local law-and-order committees and that only they would be allowed "to pursue and capture and bring to trial and conviction the alleged criminal."[16]

Once their classifications were complete, the local committees would assemble their surrounding populations monthly to hear speeches on law and order from a prominent "first-class" white businessman, judge, or other civic leader. Northen hoped that these rallies would marshal public sentiment against extralegal vengeance and exert pressure on local officials to enforce an existing antilynching law adopted by the general assembly during his governorship. This law required sheriffs to organize posses to prevent potential lynchings and made mob members criminally liable for the injury or death of their victims. Yet, as with comparable legislation passed in several other southern states, the Georgia measure proved unenforceable. Law enforcement officials refused to prosecute the members of white mobs and frequently participated in lynchings themselves. In the spring of 1907, the ex-governor dispatched a series of circulars urging sheriffs to enforce existing criminal statutes and to support the efforts of the local law-and-order leagues he was sponsoring.[17]

IN CONTRAST TO Northen's elaborate crusade, Baptist minister John E. White's schemes to create a Southern Commission on the Race Problem never advanced far beyond the planning stages. White, born just after the Civil War, was, at age thirty-eight, thirty-three years younger than Northen, but like the ex-governor he could boast a distinguished southern heritage. His grandfather had been a respected Baptist minister, his father had served as a Confederate officer, and White himself was pastor of Second Baptist Church, one of Atlanta's wealthiest and most exclusive congregations.[18]

White's proposals shared Northen's central assumption that Christian leaders must play a pivotal role in alleviating racial enmity. Echoing Northen, White complained that control of the race issue was increasingly drifting out of the hands of the region's white elite. White advocated the creation of an elite-controlled southern commission that would formulate a coherent set of racial principles to guide the publications and speeches of all white ministers, teachers, and journalists. Such a program, which had the potential to unite all white southerners, would help to restrain the "lawlessness of irresponsible white people" and to preempt any federal attempts to dictate southern racial policies. In addition to reining in the passions of white racists, the Baptist minister sought to stiffen white resolve in the face of black resistance. Commissioners would articulate once and for all the unimpeachable moral underpinnings of both segregation and the elimination of the black vote. In addition to these social controls, White also sought reforms long advocated by African Americans, including improved educational opportunities for blacks, the eradication of lynching, the encouragement of black "thrift and industry," and the creation of a more just legal system.[19]

Like Northen, White viewed slavery as his movement's lodestar. He supported renewed efforts at both limiting black freedom and expanding white influence over independent black institutions. "Everywhere a white preacher or teacher can get a negro audience," White argued, "he ought to preach Christianity, though the heavens fall." White compared Georgia's current social conditions to those of Reconstruction and suggested that the black codes enacted by postwar southerners exemplified the basic approach underlying his own regional program. Had the Reconstruction amendments not nullified those laws—which had aimed to maintain freedpeople's dependence on plantation labor and to discourage black civic participation—"there would," so White argued, "have been no Atlanta Massacre of September 22, 1906."[20]

White toyed with the idea of enlisting the presidents of white colleges in his crusade. Their apathy turned White's attention to the white business and religious leaders associated with Atlanta's civic leagues. After establishing an Atlanta headquarters, this commission would compile a bibliography on various racial topics and issue pamphlets outlining its key conclusions about how southerners could best address their region's burgeoning social tensions. These publications were to be disseminated throughout the entire South.[21]

Atlanta's white ministry generally shared White's and Northen's assumptions that their region's myths of paternalistic masters and docile slaves accurately depicted the "natural" or "essential" relationship between whites and blacks. Such perceptions among whites ignored the roles that masters' overwhelming power and the use of corporal punishment had played in limiting slaves' open resistance to authority and in silencing the honest vocalization of black discontent. Consequently, as did Northen and White, many ministers traced more recent black protests, like the Niagara Movement and the GERC, to Reconstruction—a time when "northern teachers and preachers began to teach and practice social equality, when carpetbaggers organized and led negro voters to lay burdens on the prostrate and impoverished south."[22]

Like Northen and White, the *Constitution* and its religious contributors equated racial progress with a revival of the black dependency and elite white mastery that they associated with slavery. The enmities fostered by outside agitators had, Atlanta's white ministry argued, encouraged blacks to separate themselves into voluntary religious and educational institutions that lay beyond the purview of whites. It was these autonomous spaces that allegedly provided black ministers and newspaper editors with the opportunity to encourage resistance against white supremacy. Much as Northen sought to augment the influence of "first-class" blacks, Atlanta's white ministry generally believed that once whites had properly indoctrinated African Americans to accept white religious ideals, these black elites could be entrusted with the task of training their own people. According to Presbyterian minister George H. Mack, "No greater boon could come to the interests of higher education among the negroes than that southern white people of the christian type should be in charge of their institutions." Congregationalist minister Frank E. Jenkins similarly contended that the South "must do for the negro in America what it is doing for the negro in Africa—evangelize and educate him in Christianity and civilized life."[23]

The apprehensions of White, Northen, and other white religious leaders regarding the influence black ministers exercised over their congregations reflected a distrust of independent black institutions similar to that expressed by whites during slavery and Reconstruction. White masters and ministers had viewed religion as a potential source of social control over slaves, encouraging their obeisance. To the chagrin of these whites, slaves and free blacks had drawn on their own diverse cultural heritages and social experiences to fashion a Christianity that affirmed their humanity, bolstered their sense of community, and held out the promise of their race's eventual liberation as God's chosen people. Throughout the antebellum era, black slaves nourished their religious self-determination by secretly conducting their own unsupervised religious services and by privately questioning the racist doctrines proffered by whites. Upon emancipation, one of the first ways that blacks had attempted to give meaning to their freedom was to form their own churches. Although blacks had by the early 1900s devised a wide variety of ways to express their religious beliefs and although secular organizations were increasingly influencing African Americans, black religious organizations throughout the South continued to play a dominant role in the social and political lives of blacks. Time after time, Georgia's black ministers and their congregations rejected attempts by whites to exert greater controls over their churches and civic organizations.[24]

DESPITE THE INHERENT distrust of white paternalism expressed by black elites, they recognized in Northen's movement a rejection of those chivalric ideals that both glorified white participation in lynchings and condoned the brutal sexual abuse of black women. Booker T. Washington donated $100 to help fund the ex-governor's travels. Even though Du Bois later voiced serious misgivings about the sincerity of the efforts of Hopkins and other white businessmen, the black professor praised Northen's sincerity and "good work." Northen's recognition of the potential role of "first-class" blacks as promoters of law and order dovetailed with GERC participants' self-proclaimed leadership role as the moral guides of the black masses and the chivalric guardians of black women.[25]

As much as any black leader, William J. White of Augusta, Georgia, recognized both the benevolent possibilities of Northen's movement and the potential pitfalls of refusing to cooperate with the ex-governor. The black minister and newspaper editor had cooperated during the 1890s with local and national white Baptists, including Northen himself, in hopes of securing white financial support for the establishment of black denominational and missionary schools. In contrast to Northen, who nursed fond memories of slavery, the black religious leader looked back on Reconstruction as a period of hope and promise for black Georgians. W. J. White devoted his life to establishing the black-controlled churches and schools so feared by Northen and other white religious leaders. His 1906 equal rights convention had borrowed both its name and its protest emphasis from similar meetings held in Georgia during Reconstruction.[26]

White, who had come within a hairsbreadth of being lynched in 1901, experienced his second brush with a threatening white mob in the riot's immediate aftermath. On 22 September, the black journalist published an editorial attacking Jim Crow laws and defending black domestic workers as equal or superior to their white counterparts. After the editorial was published, White received an anonymous letter and a communication from the mayor warning him to leave Augusta or face a probable lynching. White fled to South Carolina. After returning to the city in October, the editor re-affirmed his good will toward whites and his commitment to racial peace: "I have not at any time been a breaker of the peace. . . . I have urged on a thousand occasions the maintenance of friendly relations between the white and colored races in my section and the whole country."[27]

Later that winter, a chastened White commended Northen's antilynching efforts and his attempts to promote interracial cooperation. "With each race the true friend of the other," the black editor agreed, "the white and colored people of Georgia can by themselves, develop Georgia in all of her various resources" as never before. But White added a caveat: "To do this, there must be mutual confidence and mutual friendship. . . . This friendship must not be racial but mutual between all races composing the community." Other black ministers and journalists reacted to Northen's message with similar ambivalence. While generally endorsing Northen's attacks on extralegal violence, they diplomatically repudiated his goals for racial control and his vicious exaggerations of the dangers posed by black rapists.[28]

White invited the ex-governor to Macon to attend the second annual meeting of the GERC in February 1907. Citing a prior engagement, Northen missed this opportunity to counsel blacks to speak out against crime in their communities. Du Bois and Georgia's other militant Niagara men, many of whom had been embittered by the riot and intimidated by the threat of renewed violence, likewise avoided the Macon meeting. In contrast to the strident civil rights demands of the participants in 1906, W. J. White and his allies now counseled conciliation. The delegates offered to "join hands with all men of whatever race, class or condition who stand and plead for the majesty of the law, for its strict enforcement, for its complete supremacy, acting alike upon white and black, without favor of any kind whatever or to any class whatever." Delegates endorsed White's commitment to thrust aside "every other matter" of interest to them in order to promote "better relations between the races" and cooperation among elites across the color line. Participants also changed the name of their organization from the Georgia Equal Rights Association to the Colored Convention of Georgia.[29]

Although W. J. White and other participants supported Northen's stand against racial violence and enmity, they, unlike Northen, viewed the eradication of lynching and the moral progress of black men as precursors to achieving their "manhood rights" of full citizenship and equality. Despite the diplomatic overtures of convention participants in 1907, they endorsed many of their 1906 appeals for full civil rights. Criticizing disfranchisement, they argued that "it is un-American, it is unjust to deprive improperly, any American citizen of this great privilege" of voting. In dramatic contrast to Northen's support for forced-labor schemes, the black delegates denounced their state's notorious debt peonage laws, which shackled many workers to plantations and labor camps. Conventioneers called for an end to the convict lease system and described Jim Crow regulations as "degrading and unjust" as well as "revolting . . . to one's sense of justice." They highlighted the inherent contradictions between Northen's expressed aims of chivalrously protecting black women and his implicit support for segregated railcars: "The present system is so operated that our people may be, and are frequently, subjected to many indignities, such as smoking, drinking whisky, etc., in the presence of our mothers, wives and daughters."[30] GERC cofounder Henry M. Turner raised the hackles of white newspaper editors by characterizing America as a "contemptible nation," asserting that the Supreme Court "had dragged the negro and his rights to citizenship down to hell."[31]

IN CONTRAST TO such qualified black support for Northen's program, hundreds of white men, the ex-governor noted, utterly condemned his antilynching movement. In March he admitted that most white newspapers outside Atlanta refused to publish supportive articles, and that many of his "old-time friends" avoided his meetings. He received his coldest reception among "prominent politicians," nearly every one of whom "expects to be governor some day and . . . wants to be careful with his record." Such politicians recognized the unpopularity of Northen's criticism of a chivalric code that elevated all white men to privileged positions of guardianship over white women and dominance over African Americans.[32]

Journalist Larry Gauth, for example, joined other white critics in repudiating the ex-governor's attempts to augment the power of a small clique of elite whites who would organize each county's law-and-order leagues and discipline potential white lawbreakers. Convinced that "our white people do not need missionaries," Gauth argued that Northen should focus his attention exclusively on convincing blacks to turn over their own criminals rather than "trying to direct the intelligent white men of our state." Far from acknowledging a "law-abiding" element among blacks, Gauth portrayed all black men as potential rapists and linked the commission of sexual assaults to integration and black progress. "When the blacks hear a leading white man counseling and pleading with his own people to bear with these black-hearter [*sic*] criminals, and see then societies organizing in the towns to apprehend and punish white men who take vengeance in their own hands," he admonished, "it simply puts the devil in the heads of those negroes . . . and makes mob violence only the more necessary."[33]

While Northen anticipated the criticism of white politicians and journalists, he was wholly unprepared for the defection of the white elites in whom he had initially placed so much faith. In linking black assaults to idleness and the "strange negro," Northen spoke to the long-standing fears shared by many white planters, especially those in the cotton belt, the large swath of territory in central Georgia where Northen focused much of his reform energy. Looking back fondly on the labor discipline imposed under slavery, these landowners were constantly frustrated by the relative independence and recalcitrance of their black tenants. Like Northen, white planters associated "strange and tramp negroes" with labor agitation and resistance against white directives. The morning after the ex-governor's speech in Hawkinsville, J. Pope Brown, one of the state's wealthiest planters and chairman of the local law-and-order committee, advised Northen, "Everywhere you go, press the danger to come from the strange or tramp negro. I never allow one to stop on my place."[34]

Brown and other whites shared Northen's suspicions that some black ministers and other black civic leaders encouraged labor resistance and shielded insubordinate blacks from white authorities. White mobs often targeted the region's black schools and churches. In the early 1900s, state legislators representing the cotton belt secured passage of a series of loosely worded vagrancy measures and contract labor laws that compelled black laborers to remain on plantations, especially during the harvest season. Given their fears of black resistance and potential labor disruptions, many planters were comforted by Northen's avowed goal of reestablishing the mythically humane and trouble-free white dominance that they associated with slavery. Nevertheless, most whites in the region remained unwilling to relinquish their most powerful tool of labor control: physical and psychological coercion through violence and lynching.[35]

Although white businessmen initially supported Northen's law-and-order efforts, they came to view his movement as a threat to continued commercial expansion. Northen's dire predictions of an impending race war contradicted the long-standing convictions of New South advocates that economic prosperity would magically calm their region's simmering racial conflicts. Northen continued to argue that Georgia was facing a profound racial crisis even after the northern press began lauding Atlanta's business community for restoring order following the riot and ameliorating the city's racial tensions. In small cities outside Atlanta, white businesspersons struggling to promote industrial growth and outside investment warned that an appearance by the ex-governor might prompt outsiders to associate their communities with racial strife and instability. In response to a letter from the ex-governor, the editors of a Dalton newspaper argued that "it was better to leave well enough alone and not invite Mr. Northen to come, for by his coming, he might stir up a feeling of antagonism between the races that doesn't now exist." Although Northen did eventually visit Dalton, city fathers remained cool to his movement and feared public criticism of their community or any potential disturbance in it.[36]

The *Manufacturers' Record*, published in Baltimore by New South apostle Richard Edmonds, voiced similar criticisms of Northen's movement and called on newspapers to suppress the "agitation" of the ex-governor and other racial reformers by refusing to publicize their "discussions of the negro problem."[37] Even John White's relatively modest proposal for a regional race commission, Edmonds warned, promised to open "a veritable Pandora's box of negro social, economic and political agitation directed against the south, but affecting with its virus the whole country." According to one white editor, conservative white businessmen were overwhelmingly convinced that "in the race problem, silence is golden."[38]

In March and April the *Atlanta Journal* crafted a series of blistering editorials that drew on these multiple white apprehensions regarding Northen's movement. During the 1906 election, this newspaper had served as Hoke Smith's campaign organ; in promoting Smith's gubernatorial campaign, its editor, James Gray, had repeatedly trumpeted the disfranchisement cause. In contrast, Northen dismissed the issue of black voting rights as inconsequential, and he avoided issuing public statements either endorsing or criticizing disfranchisement. Gray suspected that Northen's reform efforts would deflect Georgians' attentions away from this issue. Like Gray and many white businessmen, a growing number of white reformers—including Tom Watson—argued that the passage of disfranchisement legislation might finally free white Georgians to move beyond racial issues and "proceed to the settlement of other vital questions" that concerned them.[39] On 17 March the *Journal* criticized Northen's movement as antidemocratic by accusing the ex-governor of attempting to "defeat the will of the people" through advocacy of his own solution to the state's racial problems. Broadening his attack a week later, Gray played on the fears of white businesspersons by reminding readers that the *American Magazine*, "a periodical of wide circulation," had recently published a quotation from Northen declaring that " 'Georgia's injustice to the negro lies at the foundation of this question.' " Warning that a national audience would be reading Northen's allegation, the *Journal* argued, "Therein we find an exact illustration of the harm which comes of this agitation."[40]

Although Northen defended himself from the *Journal*'s attacks, he never regained his earlier optimism that white businessmen and white religious leaders might bring salvation to his state. By June he had become convinced that many of his most trusted business associates "were in sympathy with the attack made on me by the Atlanta Journal." Atlanta's white ministry, even as it was rejecting mob violence in the abstract and was supporting increased controls over African Americans, remained deeply divided over the best means of promoting law and order. At its early April meeting, the Evangelical Ministers' Association (EMA), for example, was unable to achieve a unified stand on the race question, especially regarding black assaults and white mob violence.[41]

BY THAT TIME, much of Atlanta's religious community was joining the state chapters of both the Anti-Saloon League and the WCTU in anticipation of a legislative battle to enact a state prohibition law. According to the *Constitution*, the riot and Atlanta's ensuing temperance controversies had "brought on the conflagaration that lit the campfires of prohibition" throughout Georgia. In this context, state Anti-Saloon League president J. C. Solomon, much like disfranchisement supporters, came to view Northen's movement as potentially divisive and distracting. In April he published an editorial praising his friend Northen as "a humble Christian"—"loving and brave, kind and true, good and great." Nonetheless, Solomon openly doubted the wisdom of Northen's methods and criticized his movement for having "missed the mark" by ignoring the liquor question. "If Georgia would lift this midnight shadow which hangs as a horrible nightmare over our fair but almost defenceless women—if she would stop the hellish crime," he emphasized, "then destroy the saloon."[42]

The issues of prohibition and disfranchisement were inextricably intertwined. Former Populist Seaborn Wright and other white prohibition leaders sought to eradicate drinking among whites as well as blacks. But many of these white reformers openly supported black disfranchisement as a means of heading off potential black political opposition to their reform agenda. Once more, because fears of black political influence discouraged whites from addressing issues that might divide the white electorate, Wright and other white prohibitionists hoped that disfranchisement might create a political environment more conducive to temperance reform. In his 29 June inaugural address at the state capitol in Atlanta, Governor Hoke Smith voiced a desire to sidestep the controversial temperance issue by affirming his support for local option measures. State representatives became locked in a battle pitting urban "wets" against rural "drys," while prohibitionists vowed to continue their fight to its end. Smith and his legislative allies were forced to call for a vote on the measure. On 30 July, the house passed the bill, which had already cleared the senate, banning the manufacture and sale of alcohol in the state. Smith immediately signed it into law so that the legislature could move on to consider the governor's disfranchisement bill.[43]

Prohibition advocates often cast their struggle as a confrontation between their own moral vision, which valued individuals and their spiritual welfare, and a commercial vision, which was wedded primarily to wealth and economic profit. Although the prohibition issue deeply divided Chamber of Commerce members, Atlanta's business community saw temperance reform primarily as an economic issue. Some manufacturers endorsed prohibition as a means of ensuring a sober workforce and promoting law and order, while many merchants and saloon owners feared its effects on their own businesses and downtown property values. Unlike businesspersons who tended to focus on encouraging temperance among working-class whites and "disorderly" blacks, white female and religious temperance leaders underscored the dangers that liquor and its dealers posed to the physical and spiritual health of all imbibers whatever their race or class. WCTU President Mary Harris Armour, for example, explained her profound personal reasons for supporting prohibition by recounting her prayers the night before her appearance before the House Committee on Temperance: "As I looked at my dead father's face, who was killed by liquor, I said 'Thank God,' I have avenged you once more . . . and as I saw the face of little Mary Harris, the little girl, I said, 'I have avenged you once more.' "[44] Armour's poignant words reflected the WCTU's larger vision of temperance reform as a way to expand the public and private authority of white women in relation to that of men. While traditional chivalric notions stressed the elevated status of men as protectors of women, Armour was explicitly claiming a public and private role not only as her own guardian but as that of her father and family as well.

Prohibitionists shared Northen's concerns that blind materialism and unbridled economic expansion could threaten the South's spiritual health and stability. Many of them similarly touted prohibition as a means of controlling black laborers and the disorderly classes of blacks and whites whose interracial antagonisms, they feared, might provoke another riot. In early July the *Georgian* reminded readers that liquor had unleashed both African Americans' "most venal appetites before the riot" and whites' most violent hatreds during it. Although white cotton belt planters proved skeptical of Northen's endeavors, an overwhelming majority of their legislative representatives supported prohibition largely as a means of eliminating liquor's "demoralizing effect on the labor element" in their region.[45] While most African Americans remained silent on the prohibition issue, Henry Hugh Proctor—described by temperance leaders as cultured, noble, and wise—advised state legislators, for the sake of the "white women of Georgia and my own race . . . pass this Prohibition bill and you will have sober servants, less crime, and greater peace between the races."[46] The black minister clothed his arguments for prohibition in rhetoric reminiscent of Northen's expressed desires to control black rapists and laborers.

AT THE SAME time, the strident opposition of Proctor and other elite blacks to disfranchisement legislation demonstrated their unequivocal rejection of the efforts of whites to consign African Americans to a permanent subordinate status. Given Smith's dramatic gubernatorial victory that fall and white conservative fears that divisive racial debates might threaten stability and order, disfranchisement appeared a foregone conclusion when the legislature convened in the summer of 1907. White cotton belt representatives overwhelmingly supported disfranchisement. William H. Rogers of McIntosh County—the lone black member of either chamber at the time—was the sole legislator who openly defended African American voting rights. White opposition to voting restrictions centered instead on republican apprehensions that the measure would concentrate power in the hands of a small number of registrars who would determine whether white voters met any one of a series of new voting qualifications, many of which had an elitist bent. Those not qualifying as war veterans or their descendants could still vote provided they met one of four other conditions: being deemed a person of "good character" by a registrar, passing a registrar-administered "understanding" test, holding forty acres of land, or possessing $500 in property. Representative Joseph Hill Hall, whose apprehensions were shared by a few other house members, spoke primarily for small-scale white farmers, especially those living in Georgia's mountainous regions, which were populated almost exclusively by whites: "Nowhere in this bill," he noted, "is the word 'nigger' written."[47]

Such oppositional legislators feared that measures empowering white registrars to prevent blacks from voting might also be turned against their own white constituents. They successfully amended the disfranchisement bill in a number of ways. They extended by five years the cutoff date for registering under the bill's grandfather clause. Male citizens could automatically qualify to vote by claiming a veteran's exception as late as 1 January 1915. Other amendments permanently extended the "good character" and "understanding" provisions, ensuring potential white voters an additional opportunity to register even if they did not meet any of the other requirements. With these changes in place, the bill passed the house on 14 August by a wide margin (159 to 16) after an unamended version had already passed the senate by a vote of 37 to 6. In contrast to Northen's elitist vision of a society controlled by a select class of whites with elite blacks as their obsequious partners, the amended disfranchisement bill appeared to embody the vision of herrenvolk democracy supported by Larry Gauth and many of Northen's other white opponents.[48]

Proctor and other black Atlantans who participated in the postriot interracial law-and-order movements—among them Henry R. Butler, Alonzo Herndon, Richard Weatherby, and John A. Rush—joined the state's black Republican leadership in petitioning against the passage of this new assault on black civil rights. As white legislators had freely admitted, the measure's clear goal was to "shut out all Negroes" from voting while providing loopholes enabling all whites, even many members of those groups Northen associated with criminality, to qualify. In addition, the black petitioners noted how the bill posed new threats to free speech and the future of the Republican Party, especially via its stipulation that no person disqualified from voting could participate in a political primary or party convention.[49]

Rather than demand equal rights as they had prior to the weeks leading up to the riot, these black petitioners played on the underlying fears of

Northen and white businessmen by equating disfranchisement with racial conflict. White religious and business leaders, they asserted, had accurately recognized that the "ultimate solution of the troubles between the races must be settled, as has been illustrated recently in Georgia, through the cooperation of the best elements of both races." But, the black petitioners cautioned, the passage of a disfranchisement bill would generate "racial friction" and black labor unrest by forcing respectable African Americans to mount potentially divisive legal and political challenges against this new assault on their civil rights. Such tensions would, in turn, sabotage the efforts of Georgia's black elites at reforming the black masses.[50]

White elites, these black petitioners contended, could legitimately claim chivalric honor and paternalistic authority only if they protected the voting rights of "first-class" blacks. As Proctor and his coauthors understood, Northen and other white paternalists grounded their claims to social and political authority on their vaunted moral superiority and their ability to simultaneously advance the best interests of all Georgians. The disfranchisement debate provided Georgia's white lawmakers, religious leaders, and businessmen a clear opportunity to fulfill their paternalistic promises. "For forty years," the petitioners concluded, "your people have contended that they ought to be left alone to regulate the affairs between the races, and you have . . . pledged to the Negroes, to the nation and to the whole world that if this was allowed, you would deal with absolute fairness between your white and black citizens." With the nation and many of the black community's "ablest leaders" having "acted on this advice," the black petitioners issued this challenge to their white counterparts: "Will you now disregard your solemn vows and trample your honor in the dust by passing this bill?" White religious reformers, at worst openly supportive of disfranchisement and at best wholly apathetic to these concerns of blacks, never responded to the pleas of Proctor and his allies.[51]

Once the disfranchisement bill passed the legislature, the adoption of its provisions as an amendment to the state's constitution still required the endorsement of a majority of Georgia voters in a 1908 referendum. In hopes of defeating the proposal, Atlanta's black EMA advocated using members' pulpits to launch a black voter registration campaign in early June. Peter James Bryant, William F. Penn, Benjamin Davis, and William Fountain—all associated with the postriot interracial law-and-order movements—worked closely with white Republican C. P. Goree to create the Georgia Suffrage League. This organization promoted black voter registration for the upcoming referendum by organizing every major voting district in the state.[52] In late July 1907, William J. White and Bishop Henry M. Turner—the GERC's founding leaders—attended the inaugural meeting of the Republican State League, organized by white Republican Thomas Blodgett. This new organization, Blodgett argued, would be loyal to the enduring civil rights principles established by Abraham Lincoln and Reconstruction Era Republicans. In Blodgett, W. J. White and Turner finally found a white champion of interracial cooperation who both based his vision on mutuality and supported black men "who are not afraid to express their views." In the end, however, Blodgett's campaign further aggravated a struggle between Georgia's current black Republican leaders and a group of outside challengers. Lasting well into the summer of 1908, this intraracial conflict divided the party rather than uniting black Georgians to rally against the disfranchisement amendment.[53]

Abandoned by white religious leaders and the national Republican Party, potential black voters confronted terrorist violence, openly fraudulent voting procedures, and bills for back poll taxes in their quest to defeat a constitutional amendment whose passage was widely considered unstoppable. With the outcome of the upcoming gubernatorial election already settled by the white primary, the disfranchisement amendment passed by a margin of approximately 2 to 1 in an October 1908 referendum noteworthy for the thin participation of both blacks and whites. This antidemocratic victory marked the death knell for black political participation in Georgia, slashing the percentage of blacks who were registered voters from greater than 28 percent in 1904 to approximately 4.3 percent in 1910. Far from elevating the public influence of dispossessed whites, the new voting regulations dramatically curbed the political participation of white nonelites. Ironically, the new restrictions generally enhanced the political hands of cotton belt and rural white elites, which in turn only further entrenched social inequalities among whites and further marginalized social and economic reform efforts.[54]

After prohibition and disfranchisement became law, almost all white reformers, including John E. White, joined *Journal* editor James Gray in attempting to squash continued agitation on the race issue. Even before passage of the disfranchisement bill, Gray had criticized Northen's movement on the grounds that Georgians no longer had the time or energy "to thresh out the same question over and over again."[55] By April 1908, White also appeared content that black racial agitation and white extremism no longer imperiled Georgia. "At their hearts," he asserted, "the intelligent white people of the South are sick of the race issue as a menace to social peace." Ignoring the voices and visions of Proctor and W. J. White, this white minister portrayed disfranchisement as representing the desire of "thousands of the best men—the justest men—to ensure the true welfare of the negro race, their thought being that through such limitation only could the discipline of citizenship become possible." Prohibition, he argued, was also playing a crucial role in controlling both "the depraved and criminal Negro" and the thousands, perhaps millions, of "our own Anglo-Saxon stock, not yet raised to a safe level of civilization . . . to resist the elemental impulse of lawlessness, when racial antipathies are aroused." The best white men, he averred, had finally reasserted their mastery over southern society.[56]

NORTHEN, IN CONTRAST, continued intermittently to seek racial reform well into the 1910s, periodically addressing the Georgia Baptist Convention and other secular and religious organizations. Nobody comprehended better than the ex-governor himself the extremely small gains that his movement had achieved. Indeed, the number of recorded lynchings actually increased in Georgia from 99 between 1900 and 1909 to 137 between 1910 and 1918. Georgia's percentage of the total number of lynching incidents nationwide also rose. Although Northen continued to seek donations for his movement as late as June 1907, he had, by the beginning of April, already discontinued his county visitations.[57]

In 1911, two years before his death, Northen reflected on his long battle against mob violence and black crime in response to an invitation from the Southern Baptist Convention to contribute articles on race relations. Recalling the abuse heaped on him by whites ever since his initial denunciation of lynching in the 1890s, Northen vowed to avoid public discussions of the race issue. Noting his "sensitive" nature and the "burdens" he had carried for so many years during his solitary efforts, he contended that he had done his "duty" and his conscience was clear. In his 1911 letter, Northen recalled his disgust at the shamelessness of white lynching advocates, some of whom had, during his tenure as governor, sent him photographs of dismembered black victims.[58] During his 1906–7 effort, these white Georgians had rejected Northen's attempts to empower a small group of elite whites in hopes of eradicating a barbaric practice that symbolically reaffirmed the shared status of all white men. At the same time, he was also disappointed at the ultimate refusal of elite whites to fulfill their destinies as leaders of his campaign. The threat that the riot had posed to the city's social stability and its commercial livelihood had stirred local businessmen to restore order in its aftermath. But it was their fear of negative publicity and potentially disruptive social change that ultimately alienated white businessmen from Northen's movement. White planters overwhelmingly shared Northen's concerns about black labor resistance but proved unwilling to abandon a powerful tool of labor control. Similarly, white religious leaders, who originally shared Northen's view that Christianity had a special role to play in resolving their region's vexing racial problems, came to advocate temperance reform and disfranchisement as the most effective weapons against disorder.

Northen linked his public battle against lynching with both his racialized and gendered Christian identity and his personal struggle "to make my life, by the grace of God, pure and simple and good."[59] No matter how strenuous his efforts to distance his own soul from the sins of white mobs and black rapists and no matter how much he struggled to sacrifice his own concerns with "social position" in service of God, Northen could scarcely contain his own passions and rage as he attempted to defend his honor from the fierce attacks his movement endured. Confident in his own righteousness and moral superiority, Northen maligned critics and denounced the enemies of good order with a viciousness that spoke to his own fascination with vengeance and violent domination. In an early dispatch, the ex-governor publicly advocated the hanging of lawyers who helped guilty criminals escape punishment. Following the *Journal*'s attacks against his movement, he considered leading another statewide campaign seeking to "crush" the newspaper "into eternal forgetfulness." Black audiences bristled at Northen's explicit appropriation of imagery associated with lynching when he spoke of "breaking the criminal's neck" and employing bloodhounds to track down black lawbreakers.[60]

AFTER READING ABOUT Northen's movement, William J. White underscored the distinct limits of the ex-governor's goals, particularly his refusal to support "the political equality of white and colored Georgians." Despite this criticism, however, the black journalist had been careful to avoid discrediting Northen's movement or alienating its supporters. As White concluded, "The colored Georgian must hold himself ready to cooperate with the white Georgian for law and order and if there is a failure in the movement let the failure be wholly at the door of the whites."[61] Rather than completely rejecting the movements of Northen and other religious leaders, black Georgians grasped at the unique opportunities for racial progress embedded in visions otherwise saturated with racist imagery and desires to bolster white racial dominance. They endorsed Northen's denunciations of lynching and his goal of protecting black women from white sexual exploitation. As they knew all too well, his movement's failure would mean the continuing murder, abuse, and intimidation of untold numbers of African Americans. William J. White and William J. Northen, despite their shared opposition to lynching and their mutual desires for interracial cooperation, remained deeply divided. Northen sought to recover the lost antebellum world of his youth, particularly the lost paternalistic authority of white elites over African Americans. Elite black males, in keeping with their GERC pledges of 1906, hoped to create a new racial order—one that would nurture their goals of self-determination and full equality. Though Northen expressed a willingness to sacrifice his life in pursuit of his antilynching program, his vision for Georgia's future, much like the visions of Atlanta's white ministry, never transcended his nostalgic memories of the state's past.

CHAPTER EIGHT

Atlanta's Reconstruction and America's

Racial Transformations

⬤

NATIONAL MAGAZINES AND NEWSPAPERS applauded Atlanta's law-and-order efforts from their inception. White civic leaders' highly publicized intervention in municipal affairs spoke to middle-class Progressives' faith in the ability of a "civilized," "manly" elite to control the destructive "savagery" of the nation's criminal element. In early October, the *Outlook* lauded "the grasp which the law-abiding spirit has now upon the city of Atlanta" as "a sign of the real soundness of American democracy." In June 1907, native North Carolinian Walter Hines Page, who had privately estimated that 250 blacks had been killed in the riot, similarly praised Atlanta as home to "the most beneficial movements for improving the relation of the races that have been started anywhere." The "very worst of American cities" had become a shining model of righteousness and racial progressivism. Yet the roles of local white elites in forging the dominant national interpretation of the riot proved secondary to those of Henry Hugh Proctor, Booker T. Washington, and white northern journalist Ray Stannard Baker.[1]

In addition to boosting Atlanta's reputation, the efforts of these three commentators helped persuade influential national observers that interracial cooperation among local elites offered the surest avenue for racial progress. Proctor, eager to secure the support of northern whites for his proposed institutional church, touted Georgia's law-and-order movements in churches and publications throughout the country. Washington came to embrace Proctor's portrayal of local events as a confirmation of his long-standing civil rights strategy. Baker, borrowing heavily from Proctor's and Washington's portrayals, hoped that an article on Atlanta might help boost the circulation of his fledgling *American Magazine*. Grounding many of his assumptions and conclusions in his Atlanta-based research, Baker compiled his findings into *Following the Color Line*—arguably, the most influential book on early twentieth-century southern race relations until C. Vann Woodward's 1955 *Strange Career of Jim Crow*. Drawing on Proctor's and Washington's ideas, Baker refashioned a central Progressive assumption that linked social harmony and prosperity with the empowerment of a rising white professional class. Atlanta's civic leagues, Baker argued, proved that the South's "best colored men" and interracial cooperation were also vital to ensuring the region's progress.

Nationally, a small group of white and black commentators struggled to discredit Atlanta's resurrection of its public image and continued to demand national intervention to protect black civil rights. In January 1907, Oswald Garrison Villard's *Nation* argued that old racial injustices and antipathies continued to disgrace a city that, "thanks to the weakness and incapacity of her police and officials . . . must be ranked as a place where . . . innocent men and women may be done to death by reason merely of race prejudice." Proctor's and Washington's postriot words and actions initially crowded out this and other alternative interpretations of the riot. Yet the Wizard's short-term victory contributed to a long-term loss. Ironically, Washington's unwillingness to reconsider any of his basic strategic assumptions in the riot's aftermath helped fracture the coalition of racially progressive northern whites and conservative black commentators that he had devoted his career to building.[2]

PROCTOR, AS HEAD of the black civic league, sketched the essential outlines of what became the dominant interpretation of the Atlanta riot. Having in the fall of 1906 forwarded to Washington evidence of the "better city" that was about to "spring forth," Proctor delivered a speech at Tuskegee Institute in early December and an address at Hampton Institute in June. At Tuskegee, he characterized Hopkins's movement as a "moral revolution" or "re-construction" that ultimately promised to "extend over the whole South." To black audience members, the term "reconstruction" evoked all of the lost promises of emancipation, full political participation, and federal protection. Proctor's use of it signaled a shift in his public strategy for civil rights progress. He had largely abandoned his public backing of protest and federal intervention in southern affairs and instead advocated local inter-racial dialogue. At Hampton, Proctor similarly praised Georgia's law-and-order movements. He linked the riot's outbreak to the sensationalism of white newspapers, segregation's solidification, and Hoke Smith's disfran-chisement campaign. Despite these criticisms of preriot Atlanta, the black minister remained mute regarding some white civic leaguers' ties to Hoke Smith and the race-baiting *News*. Nor did he mention white members' continued support for new segregation and disfranchisement measures as solvents for racial tension.[3]

The national reputations of both Proctor and his congregation rose with his success in promoting Atlanta's pioneering efforts. After garnering finan-cial support and personal endorsements for his institutional church build-ing campaign from local white elites, Proctor turned his attention to north-ern fund-raising efforts. He spent two years traveling throughout the North, where he persuaded many former abolitionists and powerful white Congre-gationalists to support his new "reconstruction" vision. Outside the South, Proctor continued trumpeting Atlanta's unique spirit of cooperation, but he focused primarily on the role of his proposed institutional church in foster-ing "interracial good will." At Brooklyn's exclusive Plymouth Church in December 1907, Proctor assured wealthy white parishioners that a contribu-tion to his church represented an investment in the South's future: "For the first time the point of harmonious co-operation in an effort for the better-ment of the blacks has been struck. I ask the people of the North to join in this co-operative movement which is destined to spread" throughout the entire South. So closely did the minister become associated with Atlanta's postriot movements that Proctor credited his appointment as assistant mod-erator of the National Council of Congregational Churches to his fame as Atlanta's leading "peace-maker." Northern white journalist Bruce Barton titled an article on Proctor and his congregation "The Church That Saved a City."[4]

After canvassing more than thirty-five cities in twelve states in the South, North, and Midwest, Proctor successfully reached his goal of raising $10,000 in less than two years. While traveling outside Atlanta, the minister suffered "scars in my heart of which I have never told anyone"; nevertheless, he pressed on. The imposing, six-foot-four minister humored potential white Yankee widows and other donors, occasionally closing deals by singing slave spirituals. Proctor subsequently linked his ultimate fund-raising success to Washington's support. The Wizard supplied Proctor with the names of in-fluential white northerners and introduced him before Boston's Brahmanic

Twentieth Century Club. Washington's endorsement also ensured Andrew Carnegie's donation of an organ. It was Washington, not Du Bois, whom Proctor chose to turn the first shovel of earth at the church's ceremonial groundbreaking.[5]

In the riot's immediate aftermath, Washington embraced Proctor's depiction of Atlanta events and publicized the city's law-and-order efforts. He offered the story of the civic league as compelling evidence that southern white elites were supporting the racial advancement of blacks and working with them to prevent mob violence. In early December 1906, Washington voiced new hopes that the movements sponsored by Hopkins and Northen represented "the sanest, wisest and most helpful undertaking that has been put on foot by Southern white people to change present conditions." Their only "discouraging feature" was an absence of publicity: "The fact that notwithstanding the work is going on almost daily in Atlanta, the press outside of Atlanta, especially in the North, gives no attention to it." To remedy this, Washington forwarded newspaper clippings, furnished by Proctor, to Oswald Garrison Villard in hopes that they might form the basis of a *New York Evening Post* article. The black educator also penned personal testimonies describing the movements to white southerners and northerners.[6]

WASHINGTON'S PUBLIC RELATIONS offensive assumed a heightened significance following Theodore Roosevelt's fateful decision on 6 November to dishonorably discharge an entire battalion of 167 black soldiers stationed in Brownsville, Texas. The president acted in response to unconfirmed reports that a small number of those soldiers might have been responsible for a volley of gunfire that caused the death of a white man and the injury of a white police officer on 13 August. A series of confrontations between some of those black soldiers and racist white local residents had preceded the violence. Since none of the soldiers confessed to the crime or implicated comrades, Roosevelt summarily punished the entire, highly decorated First Battalion of the 25th Infantry Regiment stationed in Brownsville. Washington immediately understood how Roosevelt's wholesale dismissal had generated "deep feeling" among blacks at the very moment "when the race was much disheartened and sore on the account of the Atlanta Riot."[7]

On the eve of the administration's momentous announcement, Washington attempted to delay the president's decision, privately characterizing Roosevelt's refusal to accept his advice as a "great blunder." Writing from New York in early November, Washington's close ally Charles William Anderson warned that both "friendly and unfriendly newspapers hereabout" were "criticizing Roosevelt severely." A *New York World* editorial characterized the cashiering as "executive lynch law," aimed as it was at the guilty and innocent alike. Once more, Anderson argued, Washington's white and black opponents were capitalizing on the timing of the decision's announcement, delayed as it was until the day after closely fought northern congressional elections that African Americans had helped deliver to the Republicans. In a late November letter advising Roosevelt on how to deal with blacks seeking meetings regarding the Brownsville affair, Washington gently cautioned the president that he should keep in mind the antagonisms exacerbated by the timing of the announcement so close to both the race riot and the recent elections. Washington pleaded with Roosevelt to credit Washington and his allies for any change of heart on the issue. Above all, the executive office must not allow Washington's radical opponents to claim responsibility should the president retract the dismissal.[8]

Because of growing national interest in both the riot and the Brownsville debacle, well-connected whites and African Americans anticipated that soon Roosevelt might publicly address the problem of race relations in the South. That prospect was confirmed in the weeks preceding the president's upcoming annual message to Congress, scheduled for early December. Rumors circulated that the president had privately consulted with Washington and select white southerners regarding the message's content. Discussion of the race issue ultimately comprised only a small fraction of Roosevelt's rambling congressional address. Much like the radical participants at the recent Afro-American Council meeting, the president railed against the crimes committed by white mobs. In an apparent reference to Atlanta's recent troubles, Roosevelt condemned the roles of race-baiting politicians and journalists in sowing racial conflict. He suggested that all citizens, irrespective of race, deserved "even-handed justice" and acknowledgment of their individual merits.[9]

Yet, as noted in Jesse Max Barber's *Voice*, other passages in the speech signaled an abandonment of any pretense that the Republican Party was committed to protecting black rights. The president opened his discussion by emphasizing that racial tensions were best addressed at the local rather than the national level: "Next to the negro himself, the man who can do most to help the negro is his white neighbor who lives near him; and our steady effort should be to better the relations between the two." Accordingly, each section, rather than spending "its time jeering at the faults of another section," "should be busy trying to amend its own shortcomings." It was only after criminal assaults had already awakened the mob spirit that whites turned to lynching to avenge other crimes.[10]

In an indirect reference to the Brownsville incident that was eerily similar to the editorials published in Atlanta's white newspapers before the riot, Roosevelt castigated black southerners for having yet to learn "not to harbor their criminals, but to assist the officers in bringing them to justice." This alleged black shortcoming, not white lawlessness, constituted "the larger crime" and provoked "such atrocious offenses as the one at Atlanta." Like the *News*'s editors, Roosevelt argued that lynchings could be prevented only if local citizens were certain of immediate trials and subsequent punishments for persons suspected of criminal assault. Toward this end, the president was not content with merely recommending the death penalty for all men convicted of rape. He also advocated swiftness: "Provision should be made by which the punishment may follow immediately upon the heels of the offense." Given the realities of the southern judicial system, Roosevelt's advice came perilously close to encouraging legal lynchings. Specifically pointing to the successes of Tuskegee and Hampton Institutes, Roosevelt concluded his race relations discussion by suggesting that manual training along the lines outlined by Booker T. Washington was the type of education best suited for blacks.[11]

In the minds of T. Thomas Fortune and Barber, Roosevelt's speech was particularly pernicious precisely because it represented a broader capitulation among northern thinkers to traditional white southern defenses of lynching, in this instance with the endorsement of the nation's highest official. Roosevelt omitted any direct reference to Atlanta's lawless white rioters or the threat posed to the voting rights of black Republicans in the wake of Hoke Smith's infamous gubernatorial campaign. As Fortune editorialized in the *Age*, "The President's word on the subject of lynching is one of the most mischievous deliverances which he has yet succeeded in getting off on the race question . . . and will prove one of the most mischievous ever made by an American in high office." Barber found Roosevelt's rhetoric so reminiscent of the words of many white southerners that he accused the president of having "plagerized [*sic*] from John Temple Graves"—the man whose racist, prosegregationist *World* dispatch had provoked the postriot rebuttal that triggered Barber's expulsion from Atlanta.[12]

Roosevelt's speech signified the rapprochement between the federal government and white southern leaders that many blacks, including Barber and Fortune, had so apprehensively anticipated in the riot's immediate after-

The Modern Cyrenian's Cross, or the Black Man's Burden

Editorial cartoon of Theodore Roosevelt. The *Voice of the Negro* initially embraced the president as one of the black race's protective spirits (or Dii Penates). Between 1906 and 1907, however, the magazine (renamed the *Voice* in November 1906) increasingly portrayed the president as among the black man's heaviest burdens. (*Voice*, July 1907) math. Before delivering his speech, Roosevelt had actively solicited advice from Virginia governor Andrew Montague and from Clark Howell, editor of the *Constitution*. In private correspondence, Roosevelt acknowledged his debt to Howell. The *Constitution*, in turn, applauded the president for highlighting black criminality and praising black industrial education. The newspaper characterized Roosevelt's remarks as "a platform upon which any law-abiding, peace-loving, conservative citizen—north, east, south or west—can stand, irrespective of party, creed or what not."[13] With Roosevelt's words, reunion became real.

Even before Roosevelt delivered the speech, the basic themes of his message had been leaked to a small group of blacks and whites, as had news of Washington's secret discussions regarding its contents. These revelations triggered stern warnings from the Wizard's black associates. Prior to the president's address, Afro-American Council member Kelly Miller warned the black educator that he faced an irrevocable turning point in his career. Miller held Washington accountable for Roosevelt's depiction of blacks as a "lecherous race." Since the president's Brownsville order had already "evoked the universal condemnation of the race," the speech, Miller warned, "will be the most serious official blow that the race has ever received." If Roosevelt failed to amend the speech, Miller cautioned Washington, "as the acknowledged spokesman for the race, you will be held responsible for the President's utterances in these matters." In early December, T. Thomas Fortune similarly underscored the special dangers that Roosevelt's speech posed for Washington, given both the widespread knowledge of the black educator's meetings with Roosevelt prior to its presentation and the fact that the president employed phrases and themes that Washington had made famous. The choices and consequences were clear: "He has two years more as President, and you have the remainder of your life as the controlling genius of the Tuskegee Institute and leader of the Afro-American people, and your future will depend largely on how far you allow it to be understood that you are sponsor for what he says and does as far as the Afro-American people are concerned."[14]

Washington clearly recognized the dangers of his growing isolation from all but his most loyal supporters among a black population increasingly radicalized by the Atlanta race riot, the Brownsville decision, and Roosevelt's speech. The president's use of the black rapist stereotype, his suggestion that African Americans sometimes harbored black criminals, and his support for legal lynchings all clearly disturbed Washington. Washington discussed these objections with the president himself; Roosevelt agreed to "modify most of the objectionable expressions" but "gritted his teeth and absolutely refused to budge a single inch" on the rest. Since Roosevelt had thus dug in his heels, Washington capitulated to the president and reassured him that "what you are trying to say regarding crime and education is going to accomplish a great deal of good." From that moment on, Washington never publicly questioned either the speech or the Brownsville dismissal. In response to Anderson's warnings regarding black reactions to the recent presidential order, Washington wrote of his disadvantage in having to keep his "lips closed": "They can talk; I cannot, without being disloyal to our friend, who I mean to stand by throughout his administration."[15]

Washington, rather than reevaluate his earlier policies or his close ties with the president, attempted instead to head off the rising black criticism by deflecting public attention to Atlanta's interracial reform efforts. Six days after Roosevelt's December address, Washington quoted from Proctor's Tuskegee speech before his black and white audience at Atlanta's Friendship Baptist Church. Washington expressed renewed hope that Atlanta's "recon-struction" or "regeneration" movement might fulfill its potential as "one of the most helpful, sane and promising efforts that have been made in any portion of the South to improve the relations of the races since the war." On 15 December, Washington published a story in the *Outlook* in which he once again described the "reconstruction" of the city and noted that, al-though knowledge of the riot was widespread, "the story of what Atlanta is doing in the direction of reconstructing the relations of mutual helpful-ness between the races is probably only imperfectly known even in the city of Atlanta itself." Joe Glenn's acquittal, Hopkins's interracial movement, Northen's Christian leagues—all of these developments proved "that the efforts now being made represent the most radical, far-reaching, and hope-ful solution of the race problem that has ever been undertaken by Southern white people."[16]

In his rush to endorse Atlanta's local law-and-order efforts, Washington ignored the profound challenges that they posed to his more fundamental assumption that elite whites and interracial cooperation at the local level might ultimately help foster black economic, social, and political advance-ment. In his December article, Washington made no mention of Barber's forced exile from the city. Now viewed by Washington as an implacable enemy, Barber presumably exemplified what Washington had described in Atlanta on 9 December as the "element of agitators among both races" who "stir up strife simply for the purpose of attracting attention to themselves or for the purpose of securing some recognition or position." Washington delicately avoided mentioning segregation or disfranchisement in his *Out-look* story for a national audience. In his speech before the mixed-race audience on Atlanta's Law and Order Sunday, he promised that the African American had "no ambition to mingle socially with the white race, neither has he any ambition to dominate the white man in political matters." Instead, tacitly accepting Northen's and Hopkins's attempts to limit their movements to the narrow law-and-order issue, Washington could "see no reason why we cannot co-operate on the platform laid down by the league[s]."[17]

Now under fire from black critics, the Wizard was willing to place his faith in movements that detached law-and-order issues from the racial advancement and ultimate equality that he had previously espoused. As early as his 1895 Atlanta Exposition address, Washington had suggested that the long-term goals of local interracial cooperation and regional economic development were racial tolerance and "absolute justice." In Atlanta the efforts of white businessmen had demonstrated how conservative fears of instability could encourage seemingly progressive whites to work at solidifying the racial status quo or even to embrace segregation and disfranchisement as a means of discouraging disorder.[18] Similarly, the very religious leaders whom Washington praised in his December speech and article had never linked interracial cooperation with black progress but, rather, with a reestablishment of the controls, restrictions, and white compulsions associated with slavery. Washington, in contrast, had always argued that black economic and political advancement was just as necessary as the protection of African Americans from white mobs.

In contrast to Proctor, who, after cooperating with Washington, was so dazzlingly successful in achieving his vision of an institutional church, Fortune and Barber suffered numerous career setbacks following their estrangement from the Wizard. Already radicalized by the Atlanta massacre, Fortune's *Age* writings became still more militant following Roosevelt's Brownsville decision. Just as Fortune's and Washington's public stances were diverging, Washington gradually started purchasing shares of the *Age*. By the fall of 1907, Washington, using Fred R. Moore as a proxy, had secretly taken complete control of the paper. As editor, Moore altered its editorial policies, most notably reversing its denunciations of the Brownsville affair. Upset by Washington's machinations, Fortune moved to Chicago and purchased shares in Barber's *Voice*. In late 1907, Barber and Fortune found themselves sharing the responsibilities for a magazine always plagued by financial problems—problems that had only multiplied since Barber's banishment to Chicago. In desperate straits, Fortune requested monetary assistance from Washington, who ignored his former ally. Except for the period between 1919 and 1928, during which Fortune worked as a newspaper editor, the journalist, who had long battled alcoholism, found only intermittent employment.[19]

Barber, his signature magazine finally bankrupt, found a job in early 1908 editing the *Chicago Conservator*. But the black journalist's anti-Washington editorials alienated the newspaper's controlling owner, Sandy Trice, a man closely tied to the Wizard. By late March, Barber had lost his position on the paper. Barber then moved to Philadelphia, where he briefly taught at Berean Manual Training and Industrial School. Responding to a Berean trustee's request for information on Barber, Washington described the journalist as utterly "unfitted for the job." Barber lost that position as well. Forever embittered against the Wizard, the former journalist was now, ironically and all too tragically, forced to pursue a Washingtonian program for self-advancement. For "four long years," Barber endured desperate poverty and a series of menial jobs while he put himself through dental school. Though white Georgians and Washington had silenced his strident editorial voice, Barber continued to participate in NAACP-organized local and national activities from his new home in Philadelphia. Into the 1920s, he spoke stirringly to fellow African Americans about his New Black Man's faith in the value of ideas and the potential power of civil rights agitation.[20]

ULTIMATELY, PROCTOR'S AND Washington's interpretation of Atlanta's law-and-order movements achieved their widest circulation as a consequence of their inclusion in Ray Stannard Baker's highly influential "A Race Riot, and After," the first in a series of twelve articles on racial issues Baker published in the *American Magazine* between April 1907 and September 1908. The wild popularity of the series led to its eventual compilation into *Following the Color Line: An Account of Negro Citizenship in the American Democracy* (1908). As one traveler through the South noted, the issue containing the article on the riot was completely sold out. President Roosevelt personally thanked the journalist for providing him with a "clearer understanding" of the conflict's significance. Baker's magazine articles elicited the keen praise of northerners and southerners as well as African Americans and whites. As historian Dewey Grantham has pointed out, over the ensuing four decades, *Following the Color Line* remained the standard account of Progressive Era race relations.[21]

Baker committed himself to exploring American race relations just as the first great era of twentieth-century American investigative reporting was reaching its apogee. Earlier in 1906, Roosevelt had publicly attacked the growing influence of the "muck-rakes," journalists who fixed their pens "only on that which is vile and debasing" in government and society. Beginning in 1902, *McClure's Magazine* pioneered this journalistic form. In addition to *McClure's*, muckraking was also closely associated with other turn-of-the-century general monthlies. Offering readers a broad range of highly readable survey articles and formulaic fiction pieces in an inexpensive package, these periodicals targeted a new readership representing what historian Richard Ohmann has characterized as a new urban "professional-managerial class"—one composed primarily of lawyers, writers, corporate executives, and other highly skilled and specialized workers. The muck-rakers' stories repeatedly depicted the members of this new professional-managerial class as the saviors of contemporary society. Only their leadership could effectively defend "the people" from corrupt politicians, avaricious labor unions, hardened criminals, selfish monopolists, and other public enemies. This marketing strategy proved such a winning formula that by 1906 *Collier's* claimed an annual circulation of 568,000 and *McClure's* a circulation of 375,000.[22]

In May 1906, growing dissatisfaction with their publisher prompted Baker and other writers to leave their employer in the hope of reinvigorating the *American Magazine*, which they had jointly purchased. In July this publication's new editor, John S. Phillips, emphasized for Baker the importance of making "every effort possible to render the early numbers of the Magazine notable" for their readers. Baker and Phillips ultimately agreed that a study of the "Atlanta situation" might provide an ideal topic for attracting new subscribers. Baker spent much of November and part of January in Atlanta and other southern locations in his efforts at "driving our new magazine to assured success." Baker's weak background on racial issues reflected the general inattention among monthlies to topics relating to African Americans and race relations. Though Baker had researched two 1904 *McClure's* articles on lynching, he brought precious little knowledge of the South or African Americans to his investigation. Tracing his initial exposure to African Americans to his years at Harvard, he, at thirty-six in 1906, had yet to cultivate any friendships across the color line.[23]

Influenced by recent events in Atlanta, Baker began his investigation under the assumption that the race issue threatened to "furnish an opportunity for bloodshed" and was becoming increasingly national in scope. While the journalist was convinced of the public service his work might

Ray Stannard Baker, author of the highly influential *Following the Color Line*, as he appeared in 1914. (Library of Congress)

accomplish, Baker's correspondence with his editor suggests the two agreed that "for the sake of effect we must keep the interest and friendliness of Southern readers." "You are right," the editor wrote Baker, "about the importance of working as long as possible with the Southerner of the best type and being fair to the limit." The smashing success among white southerners of the article about the Atlanta riot prompted Phillips to thank the journalist for going over the final draft of the article precisely "from this standpoint."[24]

During his research, Baker repeatedly received hints and advice from blacks and whites spanning a wide range of viewpoints. Washington, Du Bois, and Oswald Garrison Villard numbered among his sources. Taking pride in his journalistic objectivity and circumspection, Baker noted at the outset of his investigation the vast gulf separating the assumptions and perspectives of his informants. White journalist and Du Bois advocate Mary White Ovington, who had just returned from Atlanta in August, warned Baker to carefully weigh the words of his black and white sources: "Any men [whom Washington] introduces you to are likely to give you one-sided information. They will tell you of progress, but they will not show you in many ways the real situation."[25] Apprehensive regarding the safety of her

Atlanta friends, Ovington told Baker, "The colored men who know most do not dare or do not think it expedient to tell what they know, and there are numbers of colored people who like to be interviewed who will give only such facts as will help them to get further money from the north." Nor should he blindly accept white stories of black assaults. "You'll keep back in your brain, won't you," she pleaded, "the ghastly truth that any unscrupulous white woman has the life of any Negro, no matter how virtuous he may be."[26] In both personal conversations and correspondence before and after the Atlanta article, Du Bois advised Baker that "the great trouble with anyone coming from the outside to study the Negro problem is that they do not know the Negro as a human being, as a feeling thinking man." Consequently, there was always the tendency among journalists "that while they speak of the Southerner in the second person, they continually regard the Negro in the third."[27]

Despite admonitions that he carefully evaluate the assertions of his sources, Baker repeatedly privileged the thoughts and opinions of elites, particularly whites. Though he recognized that "the Negro cannot speak his mind" in the South, Baker never fully considered the role of violence and intimidation in limiting what most African Americans believed they could and could not say in his presence. Baker did acknowledge that northern publications had grossly overestimated the number of preriot black assaults and had mistakenly portrayed Brownsville as a neighborhood of black outlaws rather than a middle-class enclave.[28] Despite Baker's recognition that whites had exaggerated the incidence of black rapes in Atlanta, he clung to his initial assumption that, in the absence of valid white fears of black assaults, the riot would not have taken place and "lynching in the South would immediately be wiped out."[29] Baker never fully acknowledged the overriding function of lynching as a method of labor and race control, nor did he recognize the ways that southern whites employed accusations of rape to defend lynching. Du Bois and other African Americans worried that the journalist's prominent discussion of the alleged rapes preceding the riot would reaffirm white stereotypes of black crime. In reaction to the Atlanta article and a subsequent piece on the black belt, Du Bois chided Baker: "That there is a general fear of the negroes, not only in the Black Belt but everywhere is certain but it is the fear the oppressor has of the oppressed; the fear of the man who is always looking for insurrection from beneath because he knows that the lower class has been wronged, that same fear existed during slavery time . . . but it is not the fear of the crime of rape."[30]

According to Baker, the "uneducated white" posed as great a threat to public order as the "ignorant Negro." The Saturday night of the riot, "once blood was shed," this white "brute, which is none too well controlled in the best city, came out and gorged itself. Once permit the shackles of law and order to be cast off, and men, white or black, Christian or pagan, revert to primordial savagery." Baker's narration of the riot employed standard Progressive tropes of civilization threatened by uncivilized masculine brutishness, of order imperiled by savage outside forces. Atlanta's captivity to the savagery of black rapists and white murderers represented Baker's worst nightmare of a social order turned upside down. Drawing on a stock theme, to which he repeatedly returned, in analyses of everything from labor strife to political corruption, Baker concluded that the outbreak of disorder had been possible in Atlanta because its best citizens had not accepted their social responsibilities. "The best people of Atlanta were like the citizens of prosperous northern cities, too busy with money-making to pay attention to public affairs." While "the riot brought out all that was worst in human nature," Baker, drawing directly from the vocabulary of Proctor and Washington, concluded that the "reconstruction has brought all that is best and finest." Never questioning the subordination of black elites, Baker endorsed Northen's and Hopkins's shared assumption: "What we must do is to get the good white folks to leaven the bad white folks and the good Negroes to leaven the bad Negroes." The urban professionals and managers that included Baker and his black and white readership became the heroes of his narrative.[31]

Throughout his series—as Baker shifted his focus from the southern city to the southern plantation, from the South to the North, from black activists to white reformers—he approached each story separately. Consequently, inconsistencies fill his articles, reflecting the divergent opinions of his sources as well as his own ambivalent sentiments. Baker's praise for Du Bois and his occasional depiction of mob violence as a backlash against black economic progress caused Washington to worry that "the other crowd" had "gotten pretty thoroughly hold of him." The Wizard's initial anxieties regarding Baker's interpretations ultimately proved premature. Baker dismissed as foolhardy Du Bois's support for the federal government's legal and political intervention in southern affairs. The history of Reconstruction taught a clear lesson: "Mankind is reconstructed not by proclamations or legislation or military occupation, but by time, growth, education, religion, thought." Disfranchisement remained the wisest policy for the "vast majority" of African Americans, who "are still densely ignorant, and have little or no appreciation of the duties of citizenship." As for Jim Crow laws, Baker's concern with order and his fears of a disorderly element among blacks and whites prompted him to side with Cary Wilmer and other white elites affiliated with Atlanta's civic leagues. Many such laws, he suggested, "are at present necessary to avoid the danger of clashes between the ignorant of both race[s]."[32]

Washington's rhetoric "emphasising duties and responsibilities, [and] urging the Negro to prepare himself for his rights" dovetailed with Baker's own deeply held convictions regarding responsible citizenship. The journalist consistently sided with the Wizard, concluding, for example, that "at the present time it would seem that the thing most needed was the teaching of such men as Dr. Washington." Yet solving the race problem also required that whites themselves accept their duties and responsibilities, which Baker believed had substantially transpired in Atlanta: "We cannot elevate ourselves by driving" the blacks "back either with hatred or violence or neglect; but only by bringing them forward: by service." There was, moreover, an additional ray of hope. Particularly promising to Baker was a new generation of white "industrial and educational leaders," "too busy with fine new enterprises to be bothered with ancient and unprofitable issues" like the "discussion of the Negro problem." Baker's confidence in the salutary effects of white southerners' forsaking racial agitation for commercialism marked a dramatic departure from his initial postriot conclusion—that the overriding concern of white businesspersons with "money-making" had helped make the violence possible by diverting their attention from public affairs.[33]

GIVEN HIS GOAL of winning the sympathy of southern whites, Baker must have been heartened that, in the massive correspondence his magazine received from white southerners, he found few letters that were "condemnatory." Although "some of the Southern newspapers give me the anticipated fits," "others are unexpectedly appreciative." Many African Americans, he discovered, had "criticized certain details" in his series "as severely as many of the white correspondents."[34] As Atlanta's newspaper editors understood, Baker had contributed much toward restoring the city's reputation. He portrayed the white mob as a small, unrepresentative minority and suggested that Atlanta's leading white citizens had successfully eased their city's deadly racial tensions. Overall, the *Georgian* found "many things in the article, which, coming from a northern man and stated to a northern audience, must be helpful to this city in the public opinion which the author reaches and helps to create."[35]

Baker's uncompromising descriptions of mob violence and other southern injustices and his detailed portrayals of successful southern blacks prompted widespread admiration among African Americans; at least two correspondents were convinced that Baker himself must be black. Once Baker's project was complete, even Jesse Max Barber praised the white journalist as "the fairest white writer on the Race Question that we have in America." Yet the black journalist also concluded, "I think you made Booker Washington a far more popular man among his own people than the facts warrant."[36] In a 1909 letter to Baker, Du Bois perhaps best captured the strengths and weaknesses of a journalistic approach that sympathized with widely varying white southern views, even the most racist, without closely analyzing their misrepresentations. Noting his "appreciation" of Baker's "good work," Du Bois informed the white journalist that "if we had men like you I could see the proper solution of the problem; but we have men to whom you talk who take the side of your talk which is least fair and justify unfair deeds." Du Bois also remained convinced that Baker was "thoroughly mistaken in the so-called Reconstruction Movement in Atlanta. It was gotten up primarily for advertising purposes and it served its purpose and died."[37] In January 1907, prior to completing his initial article, Baker had conducted a joint interview with Du Bois and white minister Cary Wilmer. During the discussion, Du Bois voiced concerns regarding the motives of white civic league participants as well as the narrow limits of their reform visions. Baker repeatedly promised Du Bois that he would incorporate significant portions of that interview into his magazine series, thereby introducing the articulation of alternative visions regarding Atlanta's recent events. Despite such promises, Baker never published Du Bois's interview, and in 1908 the *American Magazine* rejected an unsolicited essay from the black college professor.[38]

Disseminated in Baker's influential series, Proctor's portrayal of the riot and its aftermath had become the most influential national interpretation of the Atlanta massacre. The media no longer described Atlanta as one of America's most disorderly cities. Instead, white civic and business leaders came to represent Progressive ideals of an engaged citizenry committed to promoting order and social harmony. Atlanta's victory was Washington's victory; in the end, the dominant portrayal of the riot and its aftermath affirmed this black educator's vision that racial progress was best pursued via dialogue at the local level between blacks and whites.

This consensus among white northern journalists together with the enormously high circulations of their newspapers and magazines veiled less favorable evaluations of the postriot interracial movements. Baker's Atlanta story reached an audience surpassing 250,000, as did many later installments of his series. By 1907 the *World's Work* attracted as many as 90,000 readers; the *Outlook*, more than 100,000. On the other hand, the *Nation*, one of the few northern white periodicals that remained critical of Atlanta, claimed a readership of only approximately 7,250. The *Voice*'s circulation rates, after peaking at 15,000, declined precipitously as a consequence of Barber's postriot struggles; between 1905 and 1907, Fortune's *New York Age* reported a circulation of only 4,076. Fortune's and Barber's perspectives had been effectively crowded out of the national discourse even before Washington's machinations forced the two men from their editorial soapboxes.[39]

SINCE THE INCEPTION of Atlanta's law-and-order movements, Du Bois had distrusted both Hopkins's underlying paternalism and his civic leagues' tacit capitulation to disfranchisement and segregation. Du Bois's cynicism also reflected the profound losses that he experienced because of a riot he later described as "perhaps the greatest disillusionment which ever faced the Atlanta Negroes."[40] In September 1906 the threats of James W. English and other white businessmen had exiled his close friend Barber from Atlanta; still another ally, black journalist William J. White, had temporarily fled Augusta following similar lynching threats. By the fall of 1907, the riot's violence had destroyed the spirit and life of the GERC, and Georgia's assembly had just passed a disfranchisement bill. At that time, Du Bois's Niagara Movement was suffering from growing personality strains within a small national leadership that had failed to build vital local organizations and now faced mounting pressures from Booker T. Washington. Angered and disappointed at escalating intraracial infighting, Du Bois authored a letter of resignation from his executive secretary post that fall, before ultimately rescinding it. Family and personal problems further dispirited Du Bois. In 1907 he secured a psychiatric appointment at a Massachusetts insane hospital, apparently with the hope of alleviating his wife's mental stress. A sparsely attended 1908 meeting in Oberlin, Ohio, failed to attract many of Du Bois's closest allies. Forced to swallow his "mounting indignation against injustice and misrepresentation," he later recalled how he finally emerged from his Atlanta years as a "man scarred, partially disillusioned, and yet, grim with determination." Despite his grave disappointments in the pettiness he perceived in some of his allies, Du Bois became convinced more than ever that "we simply had doggedly to insist, explain, fight and fight again until, at last, slowly, grudgingly we saw the world turn slightly to listen."[41]

Washington proved the ultimate victor in the mainstream press's battle over the interpretation of the riot. But his refusal to temper either his public loyalty toward the Republican Party or his avowed faith in the compassion of southern whites helped to distance him forever from all but a handful of his most loyal black supporters. Washington also faced increasing estrangement from Villard and other racially progressive northern whites. Delegates at the June 1907 Baltimore meeting of the Afro-American Council, once dominated by Washington, reportedly condemned the Wizard as a "Judas to his race." Further breaking with Washington, the delegates also solicited lawyers to defend the discharged Brownsville soldiers. Within a year, council president Bishop Alexander Walters had openly endorsed a union of the council and the Niagara Movement and had joined Du Bois's campaign against Republican William Howard Taft's election bid. During his presidency, Taft continued the Republican Party's lily-white policy initiated by Roosevelt by refusing to reappoint black officeholders in the South and by vastly reducing such appointments in the North. In July 1908, Du Bois noted a growing concordance in the goals of the Niagara Movement and Afro-American Council that would have been unimaginable prior to 1907.[42]

In August 1908, three months before Taft was elected, white mobs in Springfield, Illinois, launched a two-day rampage in which at least eight blacks were killed, fifty were injured, and the city's black district was destroyed. Since it occurred in a northern state—indeed in the very town that Abraham Lincoln had called home—the riot shocked many racially progressive white northerners, particularly Villard and the *Independent*'s editors, all of whom described the massacre as the culmination of a groundswell of racial violence engulfing the United States. An initial *Independent* article, recalling the events of September 1906, concluded, "Springfield will have to carry a heavier burden of shame than does Atlanta, for Illinois was never a slave state."[43]

In September the magazine published a second article by white editor William Walling, a socialist and native Kentuckian, decrying the complicity of leading citizens and local newspapers in provoking the riot's violence. Walling also castigated white northerners for ignoring the possibility that the massacre might prove a harbinger of similar outbreaks in cities throughout their region. "What large and powerful body of citizens is ready to come to the Negro's aid?" he wondered. At Mary White Ovington's insistence, Walling joined Dr. Henry Muscowitz and herself to create an organization that would give concrete form to the journalist's inchoate ideas. Gradually enlarged, the circle included Alexander Walters, black minister William Henry Brooks, Lillian Wald, Florence Kelley, and Villard.[44]

Villard eagerly participated in an organization that metamorphosed, first, into the Committee on the Status of the Negro, then into the National Negro Conference, and ultimately into the National Association for the Advancement of Colored People. Both Villard and Ovington must have recognized the similarities between Walling's ideas and Villard's proposed Committee for the Advancement of the Negro Race, first announced at the Afro-American Council meeting immediately after the Atlanta riot. Villard quickly became "the engine" behind the new organization, placing the finishing touches on a "Call" for the National Negro Conference. The manifesto hearkened back to the campaigns of his grandfather William Lloyd Garrison, first against slavery and then against northern capitulation to white southern racism in the 1870s. Villard, whose admiration for Du Bois's emphasis on civil rights agitation was clearly growing, challenged "all the believers in democracy to join . . . for the discussion of present evils, the voicing of protests, and the renewal of the struggle for civil and political liberty."[45]

After 1906, however, Villard's and Du Bois's views regarding black violence and crime increasingly diverged. In the riot's aftermath, Du Bois's public stance shifted from ambivalence regarding defensive violence to unequivocal support for it. Representative of this sea change was the 1908 Niagara Movement's command that African Americans "arm yourselves, and when the mob invades your home, shoot, and shoot to kill." In contrast, Villard, much as he had in 1906, viewed his new reform organization as an alternative to black aggression and disorder. One of the most bitter conflicts between the two men would arise in 1913. Du Bois fumed at Villard's demand that he supplement his descriptions of lynchings in the NAACP's *Crisis: A Record of the Darker Races* with an enumeration of the crimes and violent acts perpetrated by African Americans.[46]

Villard invited Booker T. Washington to the 1909 National Negro Conference, only to be rebuffed by the assertion that it was still "through progressive constructive work that we are to succeed rather than by depending too largely upon agitation or criticism." Washington could scarcely find comfort in reports from Charles Anderson regarding the late spring conference. With the NAACP's emergence, Du Bois had become part of a formidable coalition that included not only Washington's erstwhile northern white allies—represented by Villard and *Independent* editor William Ward—but also such onetime black Washingtonians or independents as Mary Church Terrell, Bishop Walters, Archibald Grimké, and Kelly Miller. In 1910, Du Bois permanently left Atlanta for New York to direct the NAACP's publicity and research efforts and to edit its monthly publication, the *Crisis*. Within four years of the inauguration of the magazine in November 1911, its circulation averaged 30,000 per issue. By the time Washington died in December 1915, Du Bois had already usurped the Wizard's mantle as his race's most influential spokesperson.[47]

BOTH BAKER AND Washington continued well into the 1910s to cite Atlanta's postriot accomplishments as evidence of their shared beliefs that southern racial tensions were gradually easing and that the NAACP's confrontational civil rights tactics of litigation and federal legislation were misguided and counterproductive. In 1911, Washington linked Atlanta's 1906 interracial meetings with the evolution locally of a "better feeling, a feeling on the part of all for the common good." This outcome, he maintained, made the riot a "blessed visitation." Baker, in a 1910 *Atlantic Monthly* article, dismissed as foolhardy any hopes that black emigration, federal court mandates, or northern agitation might ultimately pressure white southerners into revoking disfranchisement measures. Instead of seeking quick fixes through legislation and protest, southern civil rights activists should pursue "association, the spirit of common effort"—a strategy whose origin he linked with postriot Atlanta. "Such points of contact . . . encouraged by such wise leaders as Booker T. Washington," Baker concluded, would promote an "ever finer and finer spirit of association" between the races that would eventually lead southern whites to recognize the validity of African Americans' civil rights claims.[48] Baker, occasionally expressing doubts about Washington's accommodationist strategy, did attend NAACP meetings during the 1910s, and in 1914 he privately questioned his *Following the Color Line* conclusion that the race problem could be solved without addressing the "problem of social equality." Yet, after his final meeting with Washington in 1915, Baker once again reiterated his admiration "toward those who teach duty and service." "It is so easy," he concluded, "to clamor for rights & so hard to earn or deserve rights."[49]

The dramatic rise of Du Bois and the *Crisis* after the riot affirmed Jesse Max Barber's prophetic contention to Baker in 1908: "Washington is the leader of the Negro race, not because he is the ideal of the race, not because he said strong manly things for his people, but because he said what the white man wanted the Negro leaders to say. And when the day comes when he is robbed of white praise and money, he will fall flat. . . . WE feel that Washington has been on the side of our enemies on every great issue that has come before the country pertaining to the Negro in the last twenty years."

Barber's assessment of Washington was uncharitably negative, and it ignored the Wizard's abiding popularity as late as 1906 among a southern black constituency representing farmers, small businessmen, craftsmen, and entrepreneurs. Yet, particularly among black thinkers and cultural leaders, Niagara criticisms that would have rung false before the 1906 riot and the Brownsville incident rang true less than a decade later. Utterly ignored in Baker's articles and with his prize magazine now defunct, Barber no longer influenced the national racial debate, but his protest spirit lived on through Du Bois's *Crisis*. Historian Louis Harlan has portrayed Barber as a tragic figure, a "would-be giant killer," crushed by a "giant" Washington. Yet, reflecting on his glory days, perhaps this black journalist came to view his years as the *Voice*'s editor, his confrontation with James English, and his postriot rhetorical campaign as making a vital contribution to the Wizard's dethronement.[50]

CHAPTER NINE

Disfranchisement, Disunity, and Division

T HE 1906 ATLANTA RIOT and the shortcomings of the city's ensuing interracial movements shattered black Georgians' hopes that they might successfully fight racial injustice through massive political mobilization and open protests. By 1910, disfranchisement and the national party's determination to purge southern blacks from patronage positions had crippled Georgia's Republican Party. Despite these setbacks, black Atlantans continued to pursue their visions of racial progress through a dizzying potpourri of clubs, churches, fraternal organizations, medical associations, private charity groups, unions, business leagues, kindergarten associations, and private colleges. Black Georgians' success at institution building in the face of violence and Jim Crow oppression was truly phenomenal.

These long-standing efforts by African Americans assumed a new meaning at the turn of the century—a period of intense private institution building throughout the South and the nation known as the Progressive Era. As in other urban areas, whites and blacks in Atlanta developed new types of volunteer organizations seeking to alleviate the increasing social problems associated with rapid industrialization and population growth. White reformers came to recognize what many blacks had long known: all citizens were threatened by the general failure of urban governments to address such public health and welfare dangers as the spread of disease throughout highly concentrated populations, the contamination of metropolitan water supplies and human environments, and the dramatic social dislocations generated by modernization. Whether inspired by a Social Gospel desire to apply Christian ideals to human problems or a growing faith in the utilization of social science methods and bureaucratic structures to solve human problems, private citizens stepped in to heal the breach resulting from municipal inaction. As Glenda Gilmore's scholarship has demonstrated, while southern whites were shunting black men from the public realm of office holding and voting, Progressive reformers were opening up new opportunities for exerting political influence. Private white organizations, similar to those that African Americans had so long employed in their own quest for racial advancement, were assuming the public powers of resource allocation, priority setting, and social regulation.[1]

Between 1908 and 1919, two Progressive black institutions—First Church and the Neighborhood Union—emerged as key players in Atlanta's social service affairs. These organizations built interracial alliances with white Progressives so as to enhance African Americans' access to public influence and power. Both Proctor's institutional church and the NU, a women's organization founded on Atlanta's West Side and led by Lugenia Burns Hope, traced their origins to the riot, and both sought to promote what Evelyn Brooks Higginbotham has characterized as a "politics of respectability," linking the progress of all African Americans with the moral reformation of the black working classes.[2] In addition to addressing the urban problems of black poverty and social dislocation, Proctor and Hope sought to promote African Americans' public safety by discouraging public drinking, dancing, loitering, and other "disorderly" behaviors. Black immorality, they also feared, bolstered racial inequality by affirming white stereotypes of black moral degeneracy and irresponsibility.

Despite these broad ideological similarities and a shared goal of enhancing blacks' access to public authority and resources, the two organizations espoused conflicting visions regarding racial identity and power relations among African Americans. The NU sought to revive the sense of black mutualism and intraracial cooperation that its members associated with the 1906 riot. Proctor, in contrast, focused his energies on strengthening the relationships that he had established with white elites following the riot. While Hope posited women as natural race leaders and social organizers, Proctor succeeded in using his private organization to boost the civic presence of elite black men at a time when black men across the South were losing public influence in relation both to white men and to black and white women. Over time, the divisions between the guiding assumptions of the two organizations widened still further as the consequence of their differing organizational structures. The NU's focus on building grassroots networks fostered face-to-face dialogue and the development of an inclusive leadership configuration. These structures, in turn, facilitated relatively high levels of commitment, trust, and empathy between NU members and other black women. First Church, in contrast, was comparatively hierarchical and oriented primarily toward forging relationships among elites across the color line. The simmering rage church members felt toward racism fueled their civil rights activism. Their civic power ensured them a central role in the struggle against racial inequality. Yet First Church members' elitism also repeatedly isolated them from working-class blacks and fellow activists.

BY THE 1910S, First Church had garnered widespread national acclaim as a pioneering social service institution. President William Howard Taft visited the church in 1909, as did former president Theodore Roosevelt in the 1910s. Just outside its doors, First Church maintained Conally Water Fountain, touted as the city's only integrated fountain and promoted as a dry alternative to saloons. Hoping to compete with the lures of the street and the alley, the church also offered young men a gymnasium and a black Boy Scout troop. It provided the downtown area's only black public restroom and, in summer months, a public bath for black men at one penny per visit. African Americans, shut out of the white public library, could choose among the 3,000 books housed in the church's reading rooms, which were open twelve hours daily. For children there was a kindergarten; for young women, there were cooking and sewing classes. In the 1,000-seat auditorium, church members staged pageants and dramas, including the morality play *Everyman*, with Proctor and Du Bois in leading roles. Spearheaded by Proctor, the Atlanta Colored Music Festival Association attracted audiences numbering in the thousands to annual concerts headlined by nationally recognized black soloists and famous ensembles.[3]

Social services, which touched more than 15,000 individuals in 1916 and more than 30,000 by 1918, considerably augmented the visibility and power of Proctor and First Church among African Americans. Avery Congregational Working Girls' Home charged "any girl of good moral character" approximately a dollar per week for membership in the "family of the home." A prison mission provided monthly religious services, pastoral comfort, and free Bibles for black convicts. An employment bureau served as a clearinghouse for black job applicants, providing referrals for nearly 7,000 laborers and domestic workers in 1916 alone. The employment bureau's sheer scope and Proctor's influence among whites made the financial futures of thousands of African Americans dependent on First Church's good graces. A "trouble department," which was open daily, annually dispensed advice and resources to as many as 1,000 individuals. The church offered Sunday school classes at four missions throughout the city and at the Carrie Steele Orphanage.[4]

Proctor, who only occasionally referred to women's domestic role in economic and social advancement, filled his writings and many of his sermons with advice aimed at steering ambitious young black men toward physical excellence, financial wealth, and intellectual accomplishment. Proctor envisioned First Church as shaping an elite cadre of male race leaders who, in turn, would guide all African Americans along a stream of racial peace and progress. First Church's ultimate goal, he reiterated, was to redeem the black *man* and reclaim *his* body, mind, and soul from the white racist aspersions and the legacies of slavery that had left his "manhood broken." He advised audiences, "Save the body alone, and you have a Jack Johnson; save the mind alone, and you have a Robert Ingersoll; save the soul alone, and you have an Uncle Tom; but save body, mind, and soul, and you have an Apostle Paul—a Jesus Christ!"[5]

In other southern cities, disfranchisement generally prevented black men from exercising influence in the interracial public sphere and blocked them from meaningful participation in city governance. Proctor, on the other hand, expanded his power in Atlanta by renouncing open protest and by appropriating and professionalizing many of the social services pioneered by women's organizations, such as First Church's Women's Missionary Society. His wife, Adeline, and other members of the Women's Missionary Society posited women's activism as the "key to the Negro problem" and reproached their minister for allowing his fund-raising efforts and institutional activities to divert attention from their own organization. Overshadowed by activities associated with the institutional church, the society almost disbanded in 1916. At a time when black women throughout the South were seeking, and often securing, a larger voice in church and community affairs, the women affiliated with the missionary society experienced declining authority in areas of church leadership that they once dominated.[6]

While they differed over the relative leadership claims of men and women, both Proctor and his wife agreed that an elite black vanguard had a role to play in battling white stereotypes by serving as a living "prophecy of the possibilities within the race." "We are not a race of criminals," Henry informed a northern white Congregationalist audience, "and we refuse to be

First Congregational Church, ca. 1925. Its creation was the supreme achievement of Henry Proctor's 1894–1919 pastorate. (Proctor, *Between Black and White*, facing p. 107)

judged by the vagabonds of the race who commit outlandish crimes inconsistent with the character of the race as a whole. We insist on being judged[,] as are other races, by their best and not by their worst."[7] Wealth accumulation, business probity, moral discipline, and intellectual excellence all proved that blacks were inherently capable of rising to the level of the best whites. According to the black minister, an "upper class" constituted the legitimate leaders of their race, their claims to power and authority being justified by their property ownership and superior characters and education. Proctor viewed individual economic success and the creation of comfortable, orderly homes as rewards for individual lives of hard work and self-discipline that advanced the prospects of all African Americans. Even in the face of white prejudice and black disempowerment, Proctor, borrowing from Richard Conwell's famous speech, assured black audiences that there were "acres of diamonds" just waiting to be plucked by enterprising and ambitious young black men. The accumulation of financial resources, Proctor believed, would help the black community become independent and self-supporting.[8]

Despite widespread evidence of excellence within the African American community, Proctor acknowledged that white racist assumptions of black moral inferiority continued to hinder the progress of blacks. In a southern city that segregated blacks from whites, Proctor and his parishioners could prove their moral capabilities only by publicly broadcasting their cultural and intellectual achievements. Yet, as Proctor's wife recognized, newspapers focused almost exclusively on black criminals and only rarely acknowledged achievements within the black community. Cultured and educated blacks, she noted, "rarely come in contact with the whites, and, consequently, are not much known." First Church's annual Colored Music Festival, highlighting African Americans' postslavery progress, was partially an attempt to showcase the "culture, beauty and refinement of the race" for both black and white audiences. "By organizing this music festival," Proctor asserted, "we wish to show that there is another class [among African Americans] that is eager to follow the good and not the bad in striving for the better things of life." The festival's directors encouraged whites to purchase tickets for themselves and for their black employees. Proctor and the Music Festival Association so successfully conveyed their message of black progress that white newspaper articles gushed with enthusiasm over the congregation's cultural attainments. A 1910 *Constitution* editorial, for example, reminded readers that the "membership of the church includes some of the very best and most substantial colored people of the city. They are known as a quiet, property-owning, home-loving people."[9]

PROCTOR DESCRIBED BOTH his congregation and his class as occupying a position "between black and white." This self-styled designation signaled

Rev. Henry Hugh Proctor, ca. 1925. (Proctor, *Between Black and White*, frontispiece)

Adeline Proctor, who regarded women as central to the project of
racial advancement, with her daughter Lillian, who as she matured
became increasingly embittered toward racial discrimination.
(Proctor, *Between Black and White*, facing p. 35)

the black minister's claim that he and his church were predestined to fulfill a special mission as intermediaries between white elites and the larger
black community. Looking back on his Atlanta pastorate, Proctor concluded
that First Church's primary social contribution to Atlanta was fostering a
spirit of cooperation across racial lines. In addition to inviting prominent
whites to church services and annual music festivals, Proctor almost single-
handedly reawakened the postriot tradition of interracial cooperation initially abandoned by white business and religious leaders after 1907. At every
opportunity, he effusively praised whites who were willing to cooperate with
African Americans or donate money to their causes.[10]

In action and words, Proctor constantly reminded white civic leaders of
their own postriot revelation: "The secret of the solution of the problem of

the races in the South" was interracial cooperation between white elites and "progressive blacks," working "together for the good of both." In 1910, for example, Proctor worked closely with white public defender William Smith to prevent Roger Merritt from being lynched after he was acquitted on charges of raping a white woman. With Proctor underwriting the costs, a heavily armed contingent of county police led Merritt to the city's downtown train station, where, under the cover of night, he departed Atlanta for an undisclosed place. That July, black boxing legend Jack Johnson's defeat of Jim Jeffries, "the Great White Hope," in Reno, Nevada, precipitated racial violence in cities throughout America. In October 1910, as fears of renewed racial violence pressed on white minds, Proctor made a presentation at an EMA meeting titled "Some Things the White Ministers of Atlanta Can Do." Lauded by that body as "admirable and helpful," his address initiated a series of presentations by John E. White, Cary Wilmer, and William J. Northen on the role that white ministers and laymen might play in ameliorating racial tensions. Six years later, white and black ministers, led by Henry Hugh Proctor and the members of the white EMA, formed a subcommittee on racial relationships in conjunction with the Committee on Church Cooperation. The committee itself was a direct descendant of the Men and Religion Forward Movement, an organization whose first meeting had been directed by William J. Northen and was later led by industrialist John J. Eagan as president.[11]

By 1919 these efforts had flowered into the creation of black and white Church Cooperative Committees seeking to facilitate interracial communication in Atlanta. Under the leadership of Proctor and white Baptist minister Meredith Ashby Jones, this Atlanta Plan of Inter-racial Cooperation aimed to alleviate the "racial unrest" facing post–World War I southerners. Between 1917 and 1924, nearly 250,000 African Americans migrated out of Georgia in pursuit of new freedoms and enhanced economic opportunities. Sensing blacks' restiveness, whites were further troubled by their knowledge that black men had received weapons training during the war and had enjoyed unprecedented freedoms in Europe, including romantic relationships with white women. Forward-looking white planters and commercial leaders throughout Georgia increasingly feared that rising white violence and black migration would trigger economic stagnation and a shortage of black workers.[12]

The Church Cooperative Committees sought to protect Atlanta from the kinds of racial tensions that white ministers feared might provoke a reprisal of the 1906 riot. "No sane man," participant Meredith Ashby Jones asserted, "wishes to repeat that tragic mistake." Proctor and many white leaders—including Eagan and Episcopal minister Cary B. Wilmer—had participated in the law-and-order movements immediately following the riot. True to the principles of Northen's Business Men's Gospel Union, Eagan repeatedly argued that "the teachings of Jesus Christ are sufficient for the solution of all human problems," especially racial troubles.[13] Wilmer, in a history of his city's early interracial efforts, argued that Atlanta's postriot "reconstructive work" had laid the foundation for this new interracial program. Drawing on the structural frameworks pioneered by Hopkins and Northen, the ministers created separate twenty-five-member committees of blacks and whites. After convening independently each week, the committees held monthly joint meetings in secret. Neither the black nor the white committee took any action without first consulting its counterpart.[14]

The committees' white leadership shared many of the paternalistic impulses and fears of black resistance that had informed earlier white interracial efforts. White spokesperson Meredith Ashby Jones, for example, argued that whites had a "high and holy responsibility" as members of a "maturer civilization" to help guide the "child" black race. Interracial committees, Jones contended, should enlist only the "best people among our Negro citizens." This black leadership must avoid any inclination "to sympathize with or protect the Negro criminal just because he is a Negro," and it must forswear all forms of violence and disorder. Much like Hopkins's civic leagues, Jones circumspectly sidestepped the more controversial subjects of voting rights and segregation.[15]

Despite the connections between these new interracial committees and the postriot movements, both Proctor and many white members viewed their inchoate organization as representing a marked departure from past white practices and assumptions. After the failure of white violence and condescension to ensure racial peace, Proctor argued, southerners had finally sought a third option, led "not by the black man or the white man alone, but by both working together." Ashby Jones, inching away from Hopkins and Northen's overwhelming focus on the threat of the black rapist, categorically condemned mob violence under any circumstances. Jones challenged white elites to extend their sights far beyond the narrow issue of preserving order. Just as important, he added, was ensuring "full justice" for African Americans in court and enhancing black access to proper housing and educational opportunities.[16]

After the riot, Proctor increasingly advocated a civil rights program that concealed his New Black Man demands for full racial equality within a

Washingtonian rhetoric embracing practical compromise, interracial dialogue, and material uplift. Proctor's pursuit of biracial cooperation led him to renounce publicly what he characterized as a "false" kind of "agitation"—one that unnecessarily "foments strife, suspicion, envy and ill-well." Unofficial First Church historian and Atlanta University alumna Kathleen Redding Adams noted the minister's exceptional abilities as a racial diplomat and interracial consensus builder. Adams suggested in 1980 that Proctor's ability to uncover a vein of hope in a city stained by bloodshed rendered the riot a "Godsend" that ultimately produced a new "coalition" of whites and blacks, led by Proctor and other church members.[17]

ALTHOUGH PROCTOR AND some other militant parishioners—Niagara Movement participants George Towns and Alonzo Herndon, for example—pulled back from vocal, visible protests in the riot's aftermath, many of those who came of age in First Church, including Proctor's own children, imbibed their parents' publicly veiled rage at the daily indignities of Jim Crow practices. Many congregants' sons and daughters never forgot their parents' personal resistance to segregation or their insistence that, despite white racism, a rising generation could achieve limitless goals. Henry Rucker's daughters—Lucy, Neddy, and Hazel—remembered their father's steadfast policy that "any place where it was segregated, we didn't go." One of Walter White's lasting memories was the decision of his otherwise frugal father to buy a horse and carriage rather than have his daughters endure "insults and other indignities from white male passengers" on Atlanta's trolleys.[18]

Walter White's generation had been disciplined since birth to conform to the highest moral and ethical standards; their manners and demeanor were as refined as any white person's. Parishioner John Wesley Dobbs constantly affirmed that his daughters were "*equal to anyone*" and was adamant that they "outperform, outdress and outclass their peers in Atlanta." Taught like Dobbs's children to believe that no goal was unreachable, this rising generation invariably confronted the impassable hurdles erected by white racism. Walter White and other young congregants were taught from an early age that personal merit was a prerequisite for respect and authority, and their exposure to " 'the ways of white folks' " invariably led them to question the "white man's boast of the superiority of his morals over those of the Negro." The biographer of Proctor's daughter, Lillian, similarly noted that the young woman's early training had made her "especially sensitive to that kind of discrimination that takes no account of culture and personal status but centers on color alone."[19]

By publicly shunning vice and disorder, Proctor and his congregation were not simply cultivating white allies and battling white stereotypes of innate black inferiority. They were also claiming authority and power within the black community as its moral guardians. In an article on the 1913 Colored Music Festival, the *Journal*, for example, praised First Church as being "instrumental in fostering thrift, love of law and greater efficiency among the Negroes of this community." The institutional church, having a professional staff and serving clients in an institutional setting, possessed a structure that emphasized the boundaries between social service providers and what Proctor described as a "lower element." In contrast, the tradition of friendly visitation practiced by other churches encouraged congregations to tend to the needy in their own homes and neighborhoods. First Church offered little in the way of charity; it focused instead on offering recreational alternatives to saloons and dance halls, providing employment and counseling services, and maintaining a home that protected young women from urban vices. One of First Church's central missions, Proctor argued, lay in "Congregationalizing" the race—that is, in so remaking disadvantaged African Americans that they shunned both the forms of public vice that confirmed white racist assumptions and the kinds of interracial crimes that triggered white retaliation.[20]

This focus on reforming the "criminal element" reinforced the rigidity of class distinctions between the congregation and its potential clients. Early in his reform career, Proctor publicly expressed sympathy toward black elites who feared that promiscuous contact between the race's "upper class" and its "lower element" might lead others to "presume upon our social reserve" or result in reformers' being "dragged down." As long as black elites established clear distinctions between their "kindly interest" in the poor and "an invitation to our private social functions," they need not worry, Proctor concluded. After all, even "the immaculate swan comes unspotted from the vilest sewer."[21]

Proctor cultivated white perceptions that his vision of remaking the black working class dovetailed with the goals of white elites to heighten their control over black laborers, especially the city's domestic workforce. In 1912, for example, mayoral candidate George Brown announced his campaign to create a license system that would track the employment and health records of all black domestic workers. This system would support white efforts to root out and blacklist "incompetents, thieves, and diseased persons" as well as those who frequented dance halls, abandoned their white employers, or refused to work for particular bosses.[22] Brown's portrayal of Proctor as supporting this social control plan reveals the inherent weaknesses of a racial politics that battled white stereotypes by marshaling evidence of black moral and material achievement. Following the riot, Proctor's speeches and writings seldom mentioned the role of broader structural and environmental inequities in degrading domestic workers and their families. The city's black masses endured low wages, unequal schools, and neighborhoods bereft of public sanitation services. These glaring racial inequalities prevented many blacks from securing the material accoutrements, educational training, and leisure opportunities that whites associated with middle-class propriety.

The black minister's politics of respectability also promulgated moral values deployed by whites to buttress their own cultural power over black employees. Discriminatory employment practices made domestic work the sole option for all but a small minority of black women. Forced into such labor by economic necessity, black domestic workers seldom earned a living wage and often encountered brutal sexual and racial harassment from their employers, whose power was reinforced by racist public officials. Given these gross injustices and inequalities, many black women viewed "pan-toting" (i.e., absconding with small amounts of food or household objects) and quitting their jobs (a fundamental economic right under the free enterprise system) as legitimate weapons against raw exploitation.[23]

Proctor's apparent refusal to openly criticize George Brown's proposal evidenced a growing disparity between his vision of Atlanta's black working poor and the vision held by the city's black Baptist Ministers Union—a group that claimed to represent 15,000 congregants and included Peter James Bryant and A. D. Williams. While the Baptist Ministers Union avoided directly challenging dominant white definitions of theft, it openly refuted Brown's charges regarding the honesty of domestic workers, highlighting instead this group's high moral standards. Although these Baptists expressed sympathy for the concerns Brown and other whites expressed about public health and criminal activity, they refused to "remain passive or stand silently by and allow . . . working people to be subjected to such humiliation, discrimination, hardship and inconvenience in order to reach and control a very few unsatisfactory or dishonest servants." Rejecting portrayals of working-class women as criminals and germ carriers, the Baptist ministers challenged white politicians to fight disease and filth by promoting ample sanitation services for blacks and whites. They also advocated battling theft through the adoption of careful hiring practices and the maintenance of records enumerating the items sent out for laundering.[24]

Proctor's visibility in the white community and his insistence that his church had single-handedly "saved" Atlanta must have rankled other black ministers, whose churches provided similar social services on a smaller scale. Proctor himself publicly admitted that white financial and newspaper support "aroused jealousy among some of my own people" and triggered accusations of "possible disloyalty to my own race." Proctor's reply to these accusations revealed his close identification with his white partners: "None knew better the falsity of this charge than the white people themselves with whom I always dealt in a frank and courteous manner." The relative wealth of his congregants and Proctor's confidence in their moral and social superiority only exacerbated this bitterness. Church member Walter White remembered his Atlanta years as a time of constant wariness for his parents as they attempted to guide their family between the "Scylla of white hostility and the Charybdis of some Negroes' resentment against us because we occupied a slightly more comfortable and better-kept home and were less dark than they."[25]

Proctor's overwhelming dependence on white financial and political support both facilitated and widened his isolation from fellow black ministers and civic leaders. His close ties to white civic leaders magnified his power in relationship to other blacks. Proctor did not directly battle white racist stereotypes of black criminality; instead, his claims to public influence depended on his success in distancing himself and fellow black elites from a so-called black lower element. Prior to the riot, in contrast, Proctor had cooperated with a wide range of African Americans as a participant in the GERC and numerous other campaigns against racial injustice. In 1897 he had called on Atlanta's black churches to "unite" across interdenominational lines to "rescue and reform" the black "lower classes" and support worthy charities. Yet after the riot his attention narrowed to his institutional church and its supposed role as the sole provider of black community social services. He now absented himself from other interdenominational activities, including the formation of the Southern Negro Anti-Saloon Congress, which attracted earlier ministerial allies. Proctor also isolated himself from the campaign to build a new YMCA building. Although in 1914 he gave a lecture at the YMCA titled "Lessons from the European War for Our Young Men," he rarely participated in any of the organization's other activities. Despite its parishioners' relative wealth, Proctor's church raised only $1.50 during the 1913–14 YMCA "Round Up" campaign, less than all but three of the other participating churches.[26]

BETWEEN 1906 AND 1916, black newspaper editor Benjamin Davis repeatedly ridiculed First Church's exclusivity and attacked Proctor as an inauthentic, "selfish" leader, thrust to the fore by whites rather than African Americans. The sermons that Proctor published in the *Constitution*, Davis claimed, were "not intended for the edification of your congregation, but for consumption in the white press." Davis, whose energy and forcefulness were legendary, had come of age on a rural Georgia farm before he attended secondary school at Atlanta University. Forced from a patronage job after he was accused but not convicted of selling impounded liquor, Davis never forgave Collector of Internal Revenue Henry Rucker, whom he blamed for the indictment. In 1904 Davis founded the *Atlanta Independent* as the official organ of Georgia's United Order of the Odd Fellows, a black fraternal organization that offered members life and disability insurance and pooled their resources to fund black institution building. A master of political intrigue, Davis rose to the highest ranks of the Odd Fellows, a state organization that claimed 40,000 black members by 1917.[27]

Davis realized that his advancement within the state Republican Party depended on his unseating the ruling black Republican triumvirate of Rucker, customs collector John H. Deveaux, and treasury official Judson Lyons. Georgia's Republican Party—cowed by white violence, discriminatory poll taxes, and the white primary—had turned from local elections to the securing of patronage positions and national convention seats. In newspaper articles and public speeches, Davis portrayed himself as a political reformer attempting to free Georgia Republicans from "boss rule" in order to create "a party of the masses."[28] Far from helping unite black Republicans, Davis eagerly embraced factionalism and political division to emerge as one of the state's most influential black Republicans after Deveaux died in 1909 and William Howard Taft dismissed Rucker and Lyons. Davis, dancing on the graves of his old nemeses, informed readers that "Rucker's friends ought to be contented that the community has stomached" for thirteen years a man who "has simply been a figure sitting behind the powers, while a white man of ability conducted and directed the affairs of the place." In the 1912 election, the old divisions between the two politicians surfaced again, with Davis supporting Taft's reelection while Rucker understandably sided with Roosevelt and his insurgent Progressive Party.[29]

Davis shared Proctor's sensitivity to white stereotypes of black immorality, but he dismissed the minister's vision of elite leadership. Davis linked the race's future with a rising, self-made middle class whose members were morally upright, hardworking, and committed to patronizing black businesses as a means to promote black prosperity, create black jobs, and build separate black institutions. The premium that Davis placed on black economic nationalism and middle-class propriety reflected the status of his black readership as well as his enthusiastic participation in the Odd Fellows, whose fraternal activities linked black manhood with economic mutualism and financial striving. The black journalist, according to his son, was "a bitter foe of every type of social exclusiveness," and his "most vitriolic public adversaries were to be found among the light-complexioned aristocrats." For more than a decade, Davis continued to mock Atlanta's black upper class while reserving his greatest derision for First Church, whose congregants, he maintained, identified themselves as "mulattoes," thus drawing their own color line. Davis's disdain for elitist pretensions and his bitter opposition to Rucker, a First Church member, partially explain his distrust of Proctor, Rucker's associate.[30]

Jealousies over Proctor's role in the postriot civic leagues only further angered Benjamin Davis. In December 1906, the black journalist accused the minister of purposefully ignoring Davis's early contributions to the city's interracial efforts. A month later, Davis attacked the entire black committee, calling on "our preachers who seem to be keeping the movement among themselves" to "bring it to the people." "Let selfish leadership take a backseat," he continued, "and success is assured." Perceptively noting Proctor's abandonment of an earlier vision of interdenominational unity and community outreach, in May 1908 Davis uncharitably described the proposed institutional church as a "waste of money that might be spent by improving the conditions of the unreached in the slums and alleys of the city."[31] Four years later, Davis castigated Proctor for his refusal to join "a single movement in the city outside of his own church." He further berated the minister for failing to "connect himself with some of the Negro organizations that are doing so much to furnish employment to and promote the material progress of his people." Far from a true race "evangel," Proctor had assumed public power within the black community through the "artificial means" of white newspaper publicity and elite white support. That summer, the *Independent* accused Proctor of mocking Big Bethel AME Church as unable to provide social services rivaling First Church's.[32]

Davis's scoldings targeted what must have been the most divisive and controversial aspects of Proctor's postriot program. Proctor's exclusive faith in an elite black leadership implicitly challenged the capacities of other ministers and aspiring middle-class comers. His promotion of First Church as the city's most progressive black institution trivialized other efforts to empower blacks. Finally, Proctor's avowed desire to become the city's sole intermediary "between black and white" dictated that he cultivate sympathy among white civic leaders while discouraging the formation of competitive interracial alliances. Davis's rhetorical stabs aggravated the raw sores and acute sensitivities that Proctor's "politics of respectability" must have engendered among many blacks outside his church.

IN 1912 AND 1913, Davis, as district grand secretary of the United Order of Odd Fellows, helped oversee the completion of the new Odd Fellows Headquarters and Auditorium at the intersection of Auburn and Butler. Davis portrayed what he lauded as this "quarter of a million [dollar] block" as a demonstration of his leadership abilities and the physical embodiment of his vision of black economic development and institution building. The twin structures housed six lodge rooms, sixty offices, more than a dozen stores, and a theater seating more than 1,500. The facility, which served as a meeting place for the Odd Fellows and other black groups, hosted conventions and musical concerts, screened movies in its Paramount theater, and housed black businesses. In June 1915, Davis announced the grand opening of the Odd Fellows Roof Garden, the "finest, most modern and up-to-date" such facility in the city. Pledging "there will be no dancing or any amusement or exercise to offend the most religious," Davis extended a welcome to "only those of respectability and decency."[33]

Soon after the Roof Garden was unveiled, Henry Proctor came out with a series of sermons on the evils of public dancing. Proctor had long opposed dance halls and linked them with other vices, such as drinking, that, in his mind, affirmed damaging white stereotypes of black depravity while distracting African Americans from the wholesome pursuits associated with his institutional church. Davis recognized the dangers that Proctor's sermons posed to the Odd Fellows' efforts to obtain a license for the Roof Garden. The journalist portrayed Proctor's campaign as a personal attack motivated by the minister's desire to monopolize black cultural activities. During his campaign against dance halls, Proctor played on whites' fears of black-on-white assaults and renewed racial violence. He also highlighted the social distance between a small, "responsible" black elite and an allegedly disruptive black lower element. Referring explicitly to the summer of 1906, he characterized black dance halls as cesspools that invariably inflamed the "animal instincts of those not able to control themselves." "The young men who frequent these places are in danger of yielding to the temptation to attack women regardless of race." "In a city like ours," he intoned, "where

Benjamin J. Davis's prized edifice, the Odd Fellows Building and Auditorium, located on Auburn Avenue and photographed in 1979. (Library of Congress)

the relation between the races is such a delicate one, such a place sows the seed that may ripen into riot."[34]

Davis, in turn, defended the Roof Garden by impugning both Proctor's riot-associated activities and his public representations of the riot's causes. Belittling Proctor's claims to manhood, Davis dismissed the minister as a coward who had delayed his return to Atlanta from Tennessee after the riot, thereby failing to protect his own family from the white mob. Proctor's most recent statements in the white press, Davis suggested, confirmed white stereotypes of black sexual depravity and verified white Social Darwinist beliefs that "we are still little above the animal, and despite education and all that have been done for us by the school and Christian church, we are still savages." The journalist accused the minister of justifying the 1906 white massacre of blacks, endorsing white supremacist arguments, and supporting white efforts to limit black social freedoms. Far from promoting racial reconciliation, Proctor's words threatened to aggravate white racist hatreds and fears of black rapists.[35]

In confronting Proctor, Davis was not questioning class and social distinctions among African Americans in the abstract. Rather, he was establishing his own authority as a secular representative of the respectable black middle-class strivers who attended lodge meetings and read his newspaper. Davis had long criticized black ministers for their attempts to meddle in politics and dictate community affairs. Yet Davis also denounced an "irresponsible class" of blacks with "no home, no property," and he castigated other dance halls and vaudeville shows for encouraging "all kinds of buck dancing, balling the jack and turkey trotting." Linking racial service and progress with economic development, he praised the Odd Fellows as conscientious exemplars of black manliness. Owning nearly $800,000 in property, the organization's members, he noted, employed 100 people, providing respectable African Americans the "opportunity to make bread, buy homes and to contribute to the wealth and character of the community and State Life." Characterizing Proctor and most other black ministers as "religious fanatics" and "peanut politicians," he criticized this traditional leadership as parasitic "Negroes who contribute nothing to the community but mouth."[36]

Rucker and Proctor headed a black delegation that testified against black dancing at the Roof Garden before a police board meeting that fall. The *Independent* informed black readers that during the meeting Rucker had called for the immediate closing of the Roof Garden and insinuated that it illegally sold alcohol. Despite Proctor's and Rucker's efforts, the police committee wrote a favorable response to Davis's license request. The city council quickly reversed that decision. Davis accused Proctor's allies of prejudicing the council by slipping its members an *Independent* editorial protesting residential segregation. Unbowed by the decision, the black journalist vowed that the Odd Fellows would "keep their Roof Garden open so long as the authorities permit dancing to go on for Negroes and white people at a dozen other places in the city."[37]

The next day, Proctor praised as a model of racial harmony a settlement he helped engineer to calm racial tensions that arose when African Americans purchased property in a Fourth Ward neighborhood. Whites accused their new neighbors of encroaching on a "white" residential area. A white mob threatened violence to force the black property owners from their new homes. Fearing a race riot, a small group of black elites reached a private understanding with white civic leaders. As part of the compromise, the black negotiators agreed to accept the eviction of black homeowners from the neighborhood. They also agreed not to challenge the adoption of a local segregation ordinance similar to those the Supreme Court had already rejected as unconstitutional. As Proctor predicted, these negotiations would lay the groundwork for a tradition of compromises between blacks and whites on the issue of residential segregation in coming decades.[38]

THE BITTER CONFLICTS between Davis and Proctor boldly highlighted an institution-building dilemma that black Georgians had yet to fully resolve. In the face of white racist antipathies and political disempowerment, black residents succeeded masterfully in creating and operating an array of social, fraternal, and religious organizations. Yet denominational divisions and personal rivalries limited the success of African Americans at merging their organizations into a solid front against racial discrimination and injustice. From 1904 to 1916, the ambitious Davis pursued bitter rivalries with numerous black ministers, educators, doctors, and civic leaders. In rhetorical battles with Proctor and the Republican Party leadership, he repeatedly denounced opponents as insular elites unconcerned with promoting the political and social interests of black Georgians.[39] Proctor's attempts to elevate First Church above competing black organizations also proved divisive.

The problems African Americans encountered in their attempts at coalition building and mass mobilization, black commentator H. B. Watson argued in 1906, were far from unique to Atlanta. Many national black organizations, he noted, were "organized at the top only" and "kept away from the people." Du Bois himself acknowledged that the Niagara Movement's singular weakness had been its leaders' initial disinterest in mobilizing a mass following. Davis, even while battling everyone from black doctors to Atlanta's black ministry, also recognized the importance of linking African American institutions together under a common banner of racial progress and civil rights agitation. What was ultimately striking about early twentieth-century black Atlantans, then, was not their divisions so much as their shared hopes for reawakening the sense of collectivism that many associated with the riot's immediate aftermath.[40]

In 1908 a small group of black women on Atlanta's West Side began experimenting with a new approach to promoting black solidarity by addressing African Americans' perennial institution-building dilemma. Lugenia Burns Hope's increasingly ambitious vision for uniting Atlanta's and ultimately America's diverse black protest strands originated in a private conference among a handful of black women hoping to cultivate a stronger sense of neighborliness among the residents of their small district.

CHAPTER TEN

Building a Nation of Neighbors

N 1923, BLACK SOCIOLOGIST E. Franklin Frazier perceptively described the 1908 founding of the NU as an attempt to restore the "temporary" black sense of collective bonds briefly forged during the 1906
riot. Under Lugenia Burns Hope's leadership, this women's organization
sought to resolve the problem of black disunity and fragmentation, first in a
single neighborhood, then throughout Atlanta, and finally, so Hope
dreamed, across America. As the scope and goals of the NU evolved, its
democratic structure fostered the development of an exceptionally
egalitarian and inclusive womanist philosophy. Hope increasingly came to
view black women as uniquely situated to unite African Americans' diverse
protest strands. Men's lives, she noted, centered on their careers and on
social institutions far removed from their residences. But the lives of black
women, especially mothers, Hope argued, were deeply embedded in the
inherently mutualistic worlds of home and neighborhood.[1]

According to Hope, the organic, symbiotic relationship between families and neighborhoods mandated the cultivation of strong bonds among
all black women—teachers, housekeepers, domestic workers, and common
laborers—"organized for their own development and the improvements of
the race."[2] Hope reasoned that mothers could protect their own children and
households only by extending their authority and influence outward to
encompass their neighborhoods and all of the children inhabiting them. A

neighborhood's social and physical environment and the fate of its youth impinged directly on all of its families. Hope feared that despite the common interests of mothers as women, they might be tempted to adopt the attitude of so many men: "What does it matter to me what is going on in the next house on the street to my neighbor?" The distractions of maintaining homes, paying debts, and rearing their young might tempt women to ignore "street and all[e]y children." Class prejudices and personal concerns might prompt the attitude, "I don't want my children to mix with them either." "Woe," Hope warned, unto any mothers who proved "so thoughtless—so narrow[,] so self centered."[3]

Hope's organization, which in time became increasingly sensitive to the divisiveness of denominationalism and other social distinctions, ultimately brought under its umbrella diverse groups ranging from Atlanta's most elite black families to poor single mothers, from First Church members to Holy Rollers, and from black neighbors on the West Side to downtown residents. The NU's neighborhood-centered approach laid the foundations for its unique success in mobilizing large numbers of African Americans. The aims of its women leaders to listen to and care for impoverished black children and mothers gradually attenuated the cultural and class prejudices of many members. The NU's ever increasing inclusiveness reveals the potential elasticity of black elite and middle-class notions of respectability. So, too, does a history of this organization's victories and defeats delineate the limits and possibilities of cooperation between blacks and whites in the city.

LUGENIA BURNS HOPE arrived in Atlanta in 1898 at age twenty-six to join her husband, John Hope, after he accepted a classics professorship at Atlanta Baptist College (renamed Morehouse College in 1913). Gunshot blasts and drunken shouts repeatedly interrupted her sleep during her first night on Atlanta Baptist's campus. Over the next decade, Hope grew accustomed to the symptoms of social dislocation and municipal neglect that had initially repulsed her. At the turn of the century, the neighborhoods just to the north of Spelman and Atlanta Baptist College and just to the west of Atlanta University were undergoing rapid transition. Bordering all three colleges was Beaver Slide, perceived by many as a center of vice and a safe haven for black criminals. To the east ran Peters Street, which was lined with saloons, cheap restaurants, and blind tigers (i.e., illegal or unlicensed saloons). According to one area resident, it was nearly impossible to walk along many of these streets without "seeing some low brawl going on, or hearing some coarse remark."[4]

These areas often frightened and intimidated individuals associated with the nearby colleges. In 1908 city police and judges largely ignored black-on-black and white-on-black crimes. Black social institutions and neighborhood networks informally policed individual neighborhoods. Yet the fragmentation and relative social anonymity of black Atlanta triggered by its rapid population growth made neighborhoods vulnerable to the crimes of both outsiders and disaffected community members. Hope believed that the relative absence of police and streetlights on the West Side made all women particularly vulnerable to potential sexual and physical assaults. In the 1910s a series of at least seventeen "Jack the Ripper" murders of black women terrorized the city's black community.[5]

Black poverty and municipal neglect only exacerbated such law-and-order problems. Economic necessity forced many West Side mothers to labor long hours as domestics in the homes of whites or as laundresses in their own dwellings. In their parents' absence, neighborhood youth confronted an often frightening and physically dangerous environment. The alleys that coursed through the West Side reportedly offered "inviting nests for questionable characters." White city officials redlined the area and refused to provide basic sanitation services routinely available in white residential areas. Empty fields served as municipal dumps, and garbage incinerators filled the air with noxious fumes. Outdoor latrines polluted drinking water, spread disease, and posed grave risks for children who occasionally tumbled into them. Housing, though expensive, was notoriously inadequate; rapacious landlords, many of whom were white, were infamous for failing to maintain overcrowded black dwellings. Poor ventilation facilitated the spread of tuberculosis and other diseases. The city offered no public park or playground for black youths. Throughout the 1910s, only approximately 50 percent of eligible black children attended public schools, which provided each black student only one three-hour session per day.[6]

FOUNDING MEMBERS LINKED the origins of the NU to the tragic death of a young wife who had moved into the West Side with her husband and father. Shy and withdrawn, she remained a stranger to other women. One day, so the story went, a group of women, realizing that they had not seen her, visited the home only to discover her near death from an illness that medical care might have alleviated. In the wake of her passing, these women and some of their friends vowed that "we should know our neighbors better." At this juncture, Lugenia Hope stepped in. She convened a meeting of neighbors that set about creating an organization to investigate neighborhood

Beaver Slide in the shadows of Sale Hall, Atlanta University, ca. 1935. (Charles Forrest Palmer Collection, Special Collections and Archives, Robert W. Woodruff Library, Emory University)

conditions and initiate social settlement work. With "Thy Neighbor as Thy Self" as their motto, these founding members dedicated their incipient uplift program to encouraging a sense of community, improving their neighborhood in "every way possible," and rendering the West Side a safer, more nurturing environment for youth.[7]

Familiar with the social service ideals of southern black colleges and northern social settlements, Hope brought to Atlanta an expertise and interest in community organizing. As a young woman coming of age in Chicago, she had worked for a woman's aid society and fondly remembered her introduction to American settlement house pioneer Jane Addams. With contacts throughout the country, Hope was keenly aware of the black women's club movement that was peaking during the early twentieth century. Like the NU, many of these associations sought to address the social problems stemming from black poverty, rapid urbanization, and governmental neglect. Their leaders often lobbied for a larger police presence in black neighborhoods and offered mothering classes and basic health and social services for women and children. The NACW, founded in 1895, and its state federations bound many of these local organizations together, facilitating communication and cooperation among individual clubs and leaders. On the West Side, innumerable formal and informal black women's organizations, ranging from secret societies to church mission societies, had schooled black women of all classes in the nuances of volunteer work and community organizing. The religious faith of Lugenia Hope and other members also fueled their social activism. In imitation of Christ, they viewed themselves as serving society's "friendless" women and children and helping them find God.[8]

In focusing on improving home and neighborhood life, NU members chose sites that black men and women valued highly as sanctuaries from the white violence, sexual harassment, and Jim Crow humiliations that they routinely encountered on the job and in Atlanta's public spaces. "The home," Hope argued, "is the basis of a people[']s development. Here the fundamental lessons of system, thrift, law and sacrifice were learned; and each community should try to bring its people together that they may discuss and apply these principles." For Hope and many other black women, the 1906 riot underscored the social value of black homes and neighborhoods as well as their potential vulnerability to white racist attacks. In an evocative response to Booker T. Washington's 1907 invitation to be featured in an article on black homes, First Church member and West Side resident Adrienne McNeil Herndon confided,

> The riot and the unsettled conditions here make us feel that we can never hope to have one [a home] in this ungodly section. Some times I doubt if there is anywhere a spot in this country where one with Negro blood can plant a home free from prejudice[,] scorn and molestation. The sanctity of the Negro home is to the majority (the vast majority) of the white race a thing unrecognized. I appreciate it most highly, but I have come to feel that I should like to hide from the eyes of the white man, or any rate the Southern white man the things I, as a Negro woman hold most sacred for fear they pause & look to jeer and ridicule.

Hope similarly interpreted the riot's violence as a white betrayal, forever driving a wedge between the two races, but she also cited Dark Town's success in repulsing white invaders as a lesson in the potential power of black unity.[9]

The overt goal of NU members to domesticate their neighborhoods allowed them to expand their authority beyond the household without visibly challenging either their husbands' notions of women's proper place or whites' commitment to banishing African Americans from the public realm.

John and Lugenia Burns Hope with their two sons on the veranda of the Morehouse
College president's house, ca. 1916. Lugenia convened Neighborhood Union meetings here
during the organization's early years. (Emma and Lloyd Lewis Family Papers [LLF neg. 9],
Special Collections Department, Richard J. Daley Library, University of Illinois at Chicago)

Biographers Jacqueline Rouse and Leroy Davis have perceptively chronicled
John Hope's efforts to confine his wife's activities to the household and the
nurturing of their two sons. Lugenia, in contrast, stubbornly guarded her
independence and her right to build a life outside the narrow boundaries
of her marriage and family. Although John regarded the open pursuit of
women's rights as inappropriate, he articulated a special leadership role for
women in the "distinctively feminine" endeavors of saving poor children
and struggling workingwomen.[10]

Drawing on both the black Baptist practice of friendly visitation and
modern social science survey methods, Hope created the distinctive NU
"method" during the organization's initial meeting. Women, she argued,
could transform an otherwise random collection of houses and strangers
into a neighborhood only by carefully investigating an area's social environment and familiarizing themselves with the members of each household.
During their initial meetings, NU members divided an approximately half-

A neighborhood family residing on Atlanta's West Side, undated. (Neighborhood Union Collection, box 14, folder 40, Robert W. Woodruff Library of the Atlanta University Center)

square-mile area of the West Side, with a population approaching 1,000, into ten "districts." Two district leaders assumed responsibility for reporting on and serving each subsection of the neighborhood. Between 1908 and 1914, the NU expanded into black residential areas throughout Atlanta.[11]

Over time, Hope and other activists created a democratic citywide organization that facilitated communication among black women spanning all classes. The linkage between district leaders and their neighborhood board remained the NU's basic building block. District leaders enjoyed wide latitude in addressing problems in their individual subsections, and the organization was so inclusive that it made "every person" in each district "a member by virtue of just living there." As it grew, the organization added both zone committees that coordinated the activities of multiple neighborhoods and a city board that, in turn, coordinated the activities within the zones. Decision-making powers and lines of communication ran both ways—up from the individual districts to the citywide board of managers and down from the citywide board to the districts. At all levels, members elected leaders and representatives. Hope reported that this weblike structure enabled neighborhood members to disseminate messages among as many as 42,000 African Americans within a few days.[12]

The NU was by design intensively local and personal in focus. Those qualities, Hope argued, allowed the organization to transcend traditional class and denominational lines. The organization's structure and community-building goals fostered dialogue among diverse neighbors and empowered district leaders to address their residents' specific social problems and concerns. Hope and her colleagues viewed many of the women they served not so much as clients but as potential friends and colleagues. The NU's ultimate goal, Hope once observed, was the creation of a "community, not simply a group of houses or families, but [with] those families knowing one another, assisting and ever loving another."[13] The organization's "method of relief in the neighborhood" aimed to "have each neighbor feel the responsibility of his next door neighbor." Meetings and face-to-face interactions opened up a discursive arena that promoted an unprecedented degree of egalitarianism and tolerance. Members staged money-raising showers not only to generate revenue but also to bring neighbors together socially. All of the other NU social activities—informal gatherings, monthly meetings, and social service visits—helped cultivate this larger sense of neighborliness. During the NU's early years, meetings took place in alternating private homes, including the presidential residence of Atlanta Baptist College, which had become the Hopes' quarters after John's appointment as the institution's president in 1906.[14]

The microscopically local orientation of NU activities reinforced the organization's egalitarianism and its close attention to community needs, as did the face-to-face nature of its service transactions. At the district level, NU members often donated food or small sums of money to help families weather personal emergencies such as fires and illnesses. In 1914 alone, the NU's neighborhood boards on the West Side tallied more than 500 personal visitations, enrolled 446 children in NU vacation schools, and attracted 700 attendees to neighborhood socials. The NU's slender resources and the organization's goal of promoting sympathetic, neighborly bonds demanded that members show a patient willingness to pay close attention to the wishes of clients and cultivate their support and contributions. Like Hope, other members recognized that their ultimate source of power and influence was their ability to win over neighbors through persuasion and gentle prodding.[15]

The NU contrasted dramatically with Atlanta's other black and white organizations, almost all of which constituted relatively insular groups whose members possessed a similar social status, a shared church, a common profession, or some other exclusive characteristic. "If we would do our best work," Hope asserted, "there must be no evil lines," but instead "we must reach the rich and the poor the young and the old alike." All women in a neighborhood could join the union, thereby identifying themselves as community members who believed "in good homes" and in "providing for the children an atmosphere favorable to wholesome living and good morals." One outside observer noted that among the "union directors only two or three are connected in any way with the college; the rest are ordinary neighbors." Historian Tera Hunter has discovered at least five domestic workers and laundresses who assumed leadership positions. Founding member Laura Bugg, a carpenter's wife, and Hattie Barnett, the spouse of a cook—two of the organization's most active West Side leaders during its early years—helped the NU expand its influence into working-class secret societies and private social networks.[16]

Hope still further tightened this complex social web by interweaving her unions with a wide range of municipal and national voluntary organizations. As it expanded, the NU established ties with black churchwomen representing nearly every denomination. They ranged from the lowly Holy Rollers to First Church's high-society matrons, including Adeline Proctor and other ministers' wives. Hope also linked Atlanta domestic workers' secret societies and informal communal networks with an international club movement. In the 1920s she served as director of the Department of Neighborhood Work of the NACW and chaired the social department of the International Council of Women of the Darker Races. Consciously reinforcing old community bonds and forging new ones, Hope was building a sense of loyalty, trust, and commitment among women and families throughout her city.[17]

THEIR MOTTO, "Thy Neighbor as Thy Self," spoke to the generous inclusiveness and community-building focus of NU members. But it referred as well to their goal of reshaping neighborhoods and families in keeping with their distinctive visions of respectability and order. Hope's close contacts with women of all classes and her vision of neighborhoods as social organisms encouraged her to view poverty and vice as products of environmental influences and inequalities rather than as reflections of innate character flaws. A "wayward" child was a "pitiful victim of modern life" affected by "surroundings which sear the mind by suggestions of evil." Hope urged women of all classes to acquaint themselves with the problems facing less fortunate neighbors. Just as NU members' environmentalist assumptions fostered empathy for the "fallen," those views also intensified members' efforts at eliminating behaviors they deemed dangerous or criminal. Despite the innate innocence of alley children, the "hideous ugliness" that they

Activity at a Neighborhood [Union] House, undated. (Neighborhood Union Collection, box 14, folder 48, Robert W. Woodruff Library of the Atlanta University Center)

encountered, Hope argued, "warps the soul away from ideals of truth and beauty and purity." "Think of your child coming in contact with these people and their children," she warned, to bolster her contention that "in every slum child who lives the nation has a probable consumptive and a possible criminal." This germ theory of crime and immorality led NU members to link community building with the promotion of environments "favorable to wholesome living and good morals."[18]

On the West Side, the NU's education programs coordinated its character-building activities. In early years, NU programming centered primarily on child care workshops for mothers and after-school and summer programs for the youth. In addition to forming boys' clubs, the NU offered young men physical education classes and occasional athletic competitions. In 1912 the West Side NU consolidated its expanding activities into its first headquarters building and then into a larger "Neighborhood House" located on Leonard Street. This house's programs reflected Hope's and other NU participants' environmentalist faith that reformers could morally redeem alley children by offering them "wholesome amusement" and a "good environment . . . filling every minute of their time with good things so that there will be no room for bad." NU members were ecstatic at their successes: "The same boys who were disorderly are now more gentlemanly and respectful. . . . The little girl who [originally] wanted 'to ball the Jack' [a sexually suggestive dance] as her number on the program now wants to contribute a folk dance or song." Hattie Watson hoped that these young charges might become moral agents and introduce the values of discipline and cleanliness into their families' homes. Through its new settlement house, Watson implied, the NU inspired the creation of better homes and helped save young women from "evil courses by the touch of sympathetic neighborly hands."[19]

NU members also sought to protect women's bodies and children's characters from what they perceived to be physical dangers and corrupting influences by monitoring and regulating their own neighborhoods. Just as mothers protected their homes from outside threats, so, too, did NU members serve as public guardians of the physical safety and moral purity of women and children. The organization's leadership filled press articles, minutes of meetings, and public speeches with accounts of their untiring efforts to rescue "fallen women," reform "loud" and "rough" boys, exert pressure on parents to control "bad boys," remove "vicious loafers," protect young women from being "lured" into vice, and stamp out "houses of ill repute." In September 1909 the West Side union formed an investigation committee charged with shutting down "disorderly" dance halls, poolrooms, vaudeville shows, and public musical performances.[20]

As Hope and her associates were well aware, the NU's vision of respectable black motherhood directly contradicted white characterizations of the black woman as "a breeder of all that is vile—a menace to any community." Like other southern black clubwomen, Hope and her colleagues recognized the power of this pernicious stereotype to buttress white claims of racial superiority and to legitimize a wide range of white supremacist ideologies. White portrayals of licentious black "Jezebels" utterly lacking in sexual modesty degraded all black women and undermined their claims for legal protection from sexual harassment and assault, particularly when assailants were white men. In redefining black womanhood, Hope and Watson were simultaneously rejecting white racist slurs and claiming the respect and rights traditionally reserved for their white counterparts. Hope and other NU members also regarded their notions of public propriety as personal values reflecting beliefs and moral principles central to their religious and female identities and to their mission of promoting racial progress from within the black community.[21]

Much as Henry Hugh Proctor did following the riot, the NU manipulated the law-and-order concerns of white elites to enter the city's public discourse and to win white support for programs covertly aimed at black empowerment. In private correspondence, Hattie Watson's husband, John, spoke of a

"Neighborhood Union game" that explicitly played on whites' fears of black crime and immorality to enlist law enforcement officials in its moral policing campaigns. As early as 1909, the union secured the approval of minister John E. White, who as a member of Atlanta Baptist College's Board of Trustees came into frequent contact with Lugenia and John Hope. Editorials in both the *Constitution* and the *Journal* endorsed the NU. In a December 1909 issue, the *Journal* warned that "with each succeeding year it has been complained by some that the negro grows more shiftless, more untrustworthy, more inefficient," before concluding that the white community should support the NU as an organization whose aim was to eliminate this "bad" element among blacks and increase the number of "good" African Americans.[22]

Over time, as its influence with police and judges increased, this volunteer organization enlisted public officials in its campaigns to oust individuals from neighborhoods for gambling, public drinking, and engaging in prostitution. After describing a group of Holy Rollers as one of many neighborhood "nuisances" in 1910, the NU managed to force it out of the West Side two years later. Leaders eventually devised a standard form for petitioning public officials to banish individual women whose "past reputation and present conduct" made them a threat to the community's "moral betterment." The NU's aura of authority and its governmental contacts clearly intimidated some residents. Its leadership included representatives of a small, educated elite who were married to college administrators and professors with local and national reputations as race leaders. Still further augmenting members' power was their tightly organized information network. Because of the criminal justice system's notorious reputation for railroading blacks into jail, the NU's police contacts dramatically reinforced members' informal, unofficial powers among black residents.[23]

Public health concerns of whites similarly provided the NU with opportunities to procure vital resources from public officials and to enlist the aid of Progressive white reformers in support of their goals of augmenting members' influence over their neighborhoods and Atlanta's public affairs. In 1914, for example, Hope, with the cooperation of white female reformers familiar with the NU's activities, helped found the Colored Department of the Atlanta Anti-Tuberculosis Association (ATBA), directed by an interracial committee. A volunteer organization led largely by white women, the ATBA sought to reduce Atlanta's high mortality rates by discouraging the spread of disease. ATBA members, who generally viewed black domestic workers as carriers of dangerous diseases, hoped to enlist their black counterparts in a campaign of social control aimed at sanitizing allegedly unclean African American workers. Despite the initial prejudices of these white reformers, Hope and her allies convinced their counterparts that eradication of tuberculosis was possible only if public officials and private agencies provided black neighborhoods with garbage collection and sewer services as well as enhanced access to basic health care. Uniting the ATBA's political influence with their own resources, NU members supervised annual cleanup campaigns in black neighborhoods, which public officials supported with trash collection services. Teams of black volunteers repaired private homes, sanitized ditches, improved streets, and wired streetlights. Fearful of the spread of disease from blacks to whites, the white ATBA helped fund health examinations for thousands of black families. In 1919 the white ATBA leadership, seeking to professionalize and systematize black public health efforts, underwrote an institute aimed at educating black women in modern social work methods. The institute's immediate success led to the founding in 1920 of the Atlanta School of Social Work, which offered black students, primarily women, the necessary training for obtaining employment in the burgeoning social service field. Hope self-consciously exploited these public health campaigns to create additional NU branches and to strengthen her citywide network so that "in case of any city-wide campaign we might easily call the Unions together and outline plans of work for each."[24]

AMONG AFRICAN AMERICANS, the most divisive programs of the NU were its efforts to regulate public morality and its use of white law enforcement officials to shutter illegal saloons and oust "disorderly" women from neighborhoods. Far from universally shared by African Americans, the union's notions of respectability were hotly contested. Many of the practices opposed by the NU—public dancing, loud and rough talking, and the Holy Rollers' animated church services—reflected an ever evolving expressive folk culture shared by many blacks migrating into Atlanta from rural areas. The very behaviors that NU members feared might reinforce damaging white stereotypes and prejudices were often lauded by working-class African Americans as acts of resistance against white dominance and white claims of superiority. In confrontations in their city's public spaces, poor and working-class African Americans frequently employed exaggerated gestures and rough speech as weapons to intimidate whites, to claim ownership of territory, and to voice their opposition to racist treatment. As numerous historians have pointed out, dispossessed black southerners often admired and found collective strength in the transgressive acts of men and women who, in Richard

Wright's words, "sneered at the customs and taboos, who cursed and violated the laws, who rode the Jim Crow streetcars without paying and sat where they pleased, [and] who mimicked the antics of white folks." The NU, its power reinforced by public officials, marginalized and criminalized behaviors that African Americans had long deployed to challenge whites' public power and to protect themselves from white violence, as had been the case during the riot.[25]

For many struggling African Americans, the NU's battle against "low" forms of public entertainment and public worship must have appeared comparably inappropriate or irrelevant. NU members targeted blind tigers, houses of "ill repute," and gambling dens as lairs of vice. Yet the black women who owned or found employment in these businesses sometimes viewed their participation in the underground economy as an escape from poverty and the indignities of domestic work. As demonstrated by Tera Hunter's scholarship, many black domestic workers embraced the worlds of dance halls and Holiness churches as reprieves from lives of privation and backbreaking labor. Bodies that served as sites of brutal exploitation at work became sites of personal pleasure in juke joints and of uplifting spiritual possession in storefront churches. In addition, the politics of dancing and worship challenged traditional hierarchies and status distinctions. In the dance hall, status was determined by sartorial splendor and personal skill rather than by class or color. For religious enthusiasts like the Holy Rollers, spiritual status depended less on book learning and cultivated manners than on evidence of Holy possession.[26]

The overriding concerns of Hope and other NU members with safeguarding the chastity of young black women and men similarly reflected only one of many perspectives among African Americans. In the early 1900s, growing class and cultural divisions among black southerners were magnifying their disagreements over sexual standards. Yet, based on regional census data revealing a pervasiveness of prenuptial intercourse, Herbert Gutman convincingly argues that most black southerners tolerated a brief period of premarital sexual activity among young people, especially between committed partners. Most southern black children were raised in two-parent households, and most black mothers settled into married life. Although Atlanta exceeded rural Georgia in its percentage of black families headed by single mothers, this development likely reflected the city's unique social conditions rather than changing sexual mores. Here, black women's efforts to establish and maintain marriages were undermined by black men's search for employment in other locations and by a severe gender imbalance. Early twentieth-century census returns, for example, indicate that there were approximately three black women for every two black men.[27]

Some residents—prompted perhaps by fears of NU intrusiveness or by their antipathy to the organization's moral vision—openly resisted the NU's claims to neighborhood authority. In early 1912, members expressed disappointment that one resident had refused to reveal her name to a concerned representative. That same year, settlement workers expelled a group of boys from their Neighborhood House as punishment for misbehavior. In retaliation, the youngsters hurled bricks at the structure, permanently scarring it. In the late 1920s, a sociologist sympathetic to the NU described its twenty-year efforts as having had "little effect on the boys who reside in the immediate vicinity." In the notorious Beaver Slide area, he noted, there was "an idea prevalent among the boys" that "programs sponsored by people from other communities are not for them."[28]

The organization's arsenal of weapons—ranging from gossip and ostracism to arrest and banishment—overwhelmed three impoverished women who learned in 1914 that the NU had targeted their house as a threat to public health and morals. NU members learned about this problem, involving three female-headed families living in a single dwelling, from Gary Moore, a black college professor recently hired by county officials to oversee the placement of homeless and delinquent black children in orphanages and detention centers. The women had eight children who slept together in a cramped and dank basement room—an environment conducive to the spread of tuberculosis and other diseases. When Moore revealed his plans to take the mothers to court, the NU intervened, requesting that he wait "until we had been down to the house to investigate conditions and see what we could do." Fearing the NU leaders' visit, the three women reportedly initiated such "cleaning, airing, and burning of rubbish as you had never seen before." Confronted by NU volunteers, these women promised that if the organization would "vouch for them and keep them out of court this time, they would do better." One woman claimed that she had "rescued these two other women from adulterous lives and with the little means she had was trying to help these women by letting them and their children live there with her." Convinced of this woman's good intentions and sympathetic toward her predicament, NU leaders apparently prevailed on the probation officer to keep the families out of court.[29]

Just as the NU's interactions with these women underscore the organization's potential power within black neighborhoods, this story also reveals how NU members' close contacts with local residents through face-to-face dialogue helped mediate the differences between the moral assumptions of the union and other women. Hope underscored the influence of environmental factors in perpetuating class hierarchies, and she encouraged all women to befriend and pay attention to the needs of their poorest and most isolated neighbors. Hope's alliances with domestic workers reflected her desire that the NU unite all black women around their common motherly interests. George Sale, a West Side resident and former Atlanta Baptist College president, remained uncertain as to how "the common folk" perceived the organization's activism. Yet he was certain that, because of union efforts, "our college people have been brought into deeper sympathy with their neighbors and our purpose is to make the college which is designed for the uplift of our people, a means of real help and inspiration to the common folk at its doors." Accounts of the NU's activities suggest that members had become both increasingly open-minded during the 1910s and more willing to trust women who seemed to share their Christian moralist framework or who expressed yearnings to "uplift" themselves and others. The NU's influence with police and judges allowed members in some cases to gain reprieves for black men and women whom law enforcement officials might otherwise have railroaded into jail. Union investigations exonerated women and men of criminal charges ranging from manslaughter to keeping an unclean house and public rumors of sexual immorality. In addition, the union frequently found shelter for abandoned or orphaned girls and boys by placing them in reformatories, orphanages, and private homes.[30]

In Atlanta's black neighborhoods, the NU never equivocated regarding the perceived threats from brothels, blind tigers, and gambling dens. Nor did Lugenia Hope ever demonstrate tolerance for what she deemed rough language or crude gestures. She did recognize such behaviors, particularly in her cherished memories of black defensive measures during the Atlanta riot, as constituting forms of black resistance against white racism. Yet, in black neighborhoods that lacked essential police protection, these behaviors might prove menacing, particularly to women and children. Indisputably, the owners of brothels, blind tigers, and gambling dens all contested the union's efforts at closing their businesses. Similarly, many customers of such enterprises opposed the NU's policing actions. Yet certain of these black consumers and entrepreneurs may have resisted the opening of comparable operations in their own neighborhoods.

As NU members learned from their own experiences, high levels of what criminologists now characterize as "social disorder" are strongly correlated with high incidences of more serious crimes, including violence against women and children. In residential areas, prostitution, public drinking, and violence in neighborhoods often lead to a breakdown of the day-to-day informal methods of social control as residents increasingly retreat into their private homes and shun public activities that might generate physical confrontations. Perpetrators of more serious crimes may also reason that a neighborhood unable or unwilling to curb symptoms of disorder will be less likely to defend a potential victim or help apprehend a criminal. As petty crimes and threatening behavior grow arithmetically in a neighborhood, their negative effects often rise geometrically. Consequently, given widespread police neglect of black neighborhoods and the rapid influx of rural migrants, the NU's informal methods of promoting law and order played an important role in protecting the safety of mothers, children, and whole families. In battling vice and in working to transform the West Side into a true community, the NU women *accomplished* what most men, black and white, had merely talked about.[31]

In a 1935 speech, John Hope insightfully captured how the NU's structure and activities fostered communication and helped build understanding and empathy across class lines: "When you made a survey, you found that" those being questioned "were not all evil people, just poor and couldn't do any better. . . . After you got the figures down . . . you found that the whole community was not simply a blind tiger community, but people who through the fortuities of life just got caught in the maelstrom."[32] The NU's opposition to saloons and prostitution probably reflected widespread, reasonable fears of genuine social dangers. Yet the enhanced empathy of NU members never fully bridged the chasm separating their own religious and moral concepts of purity from the cultural values of many working-class neighbors. Many residents clearly embraced the expressive culture of both town and city and perceived no pressing moral or social danger in "balling the Jack," taking part in Holy Roller services, talking rough, or perhaps even engaging in premarital sex.

AS A 1913–14 annual report observed, the initial neighborhood successes of the NU had opened its members' eyes to the political possibilities promised by its mass mobilization abilities. In 1913, NU leaders formed an auxiliary body, the Women's Social Improvement Committee (WSIC), to upgrade substandard black public education facilities. Hope's choice of school reform as her first citywide campaign provided NU members with entrée into a political struggle that did not require them to shed the protective ideological armor of womanist motherhood. As mothers, Hope argued, women bore primary responsibility for their children's education. Education reform evolved naturally out of the NU's larger goal of fostering the moral and intellectual development of youths. No issues resonated more deeply among African Americans than those relating to public education. Legally denied schooling as slaves, blacks recognized knowledge as a weapon against white manipulation. After Georgia designated literacy as a voting requirement in 1908, learning became a means for regaining a basic civil right. Even though national black leaders, including Du Bois and Washington, disagreed about the kinds of training most appropriate for African Americans, they all recognized education's liberating possibilities. Enhanced spending on black education would also translate into better salaries and improved working conditions for black teachers.[33]

The WSIC harnessed the methodologies and organizational structures that had been perfected by the NU to pursue the overtly political goal of pressuring whites into improving black schools. With Hope as its chair, the WSIC surveyed the public schools to compile data. Their findings confirmed members' worst fears regarding the effects of segregation and white inattention. Although white youth had access to modern high schools, public education for blacks terminated in the eighth grade, and student-teacher ratios in black schools were nearly double their white counterparts'. This imbalance forced black educators to divide the school day into two or even three shifts attended by different student groups. In classrooms throughout the city, vermin crawled along the walls and floors in broad daylight. One elementary school lacked a single desk. More than 100 children in South Atlanta did not have a single teacher or even a school building. NU members' varied contacts helped WSIC volunteers attract large audiences as they presented their shocking findings at churches, neighborhood gatherings, and private clubs throughout the city. The organization's publicity efforts stirred Benjamin Davis to craft *Independent* editorials demanding improved schools. NU members also enlisted their husbands, relatives, and black ministers in the cause. Inviting female parishioners from churches throughout the city to join her movement, Hope consciously fashioned the WSIC into an interdenominational organization.[34]

The WSIC petitioned the city school board to abolish multiple sessions, improve existing school facilities, and authorize a permanent school for South Atlanta. On the recommendation of Adeline Proctor, the WSIC sought the cooperation of powerful white civic leaders—including school board members, city council representatives, and members of the Ladies Visiting Board, a volunteer school oversight committee. The black women penned personal appeals and paid personal visits to numerous white civic leaders—including ministers Orme Flynn, Ashby Jones, and Cary Wilmer as well as steel industrialist John Eagan and Judge Nash Broyles. Few of those whites responded to the WSIC's letters; those who did so invariably refused to take positive action to enhance black education. The school board agreed to construct a small, temporary school in South Atlanta and promised marginal increases in black teachers' salaries. Yet, within a year, white officials purged eighth-grade classes from black schools as a draconian means of saving money without reducing white educational expenditures.[35]

The evolution of Hope's pioneering grassroots campaign pointed to both the possibilities of black political mobilization and the daunting obstacles that continued to block substantial change. Following the Democratic Party's imposition of the white primary, black civil rights activists had pursued increased funding for black public schools almost exclusively by petitioning white public officials or advocating federal intervention in southern affairs. Hope's school campaign proved that large numbers of African Americans could be mustered across traditional class lines and denominational divisions on this issue. Yet, unable to impose direct electoral pressure on city officials or civic leaders, Hope had to rely on the willingness of powerful whites to alleviate gross social injustices or initiate racially progressive reforms. Hope's disappointments proved that after the riot, whites sought increased coercive powers over black residents, but they remained uninterested in addressing African Americans' most basic social needs.

THE NAACP, WHICH in many ways had been born of the Atlanta riot, helped provide some of the missing pieces to Hope's political puzzle when it returned to the city in 1916. That December, Walter White and Harry Pace, both First Church parishioners, secured a charter for establishing an Atlanta chapter. Pace served as president and White as secretary. First Church members also comprised a substantial portion of the new organization's rank-and-file membership. White noted, however, that older members of the church distanced themselves from the NAACP's efforts, supporting instead a policy of "caution and submission to prevent angering the dominant whites." Pastor Henry Proctor, for instance, never joined the local organization but instead focused almost exclusively on interracial cooperation.[36]

In February 1917, rumors circulated that Atlanta's school board intended to purge seventh-grade classes from the black school system as a means of securing funding to construct a new white junior high. White and Pace made salvaging the black seventh grades the NAACP's first major battle, and

Officers and executive committee of the Atlanta branch of the NAACP, 1917. Back row, standing, from left to right: Peyton A. Allen, George A. Towns, Benjamin J. Davis Sr., Rev. L. H. King, Dr. William F. Penn, John Hope, David H. Sims. Front row, seated, left to right: Harry H. Pace, Dr. Charles H. Johnson, Dr. Louis T. Wright, Walter F. White. (Library of Congress)

the organization appointed a committee to negotiate with the school board. Committee members included Pace, William Penn, John and Lugenia Hope, Benjamin Davis, AME minister W. S. Cannon, and Baptist minister A. D. Williams, the maternal grandfather of Martin Luther King Jr. In addition to First Church and NU representatives, the committee also benefited from the Odd Fellows' vast organizational network, since Pace, Penn, and Davis represented the fraternity as well. At the school board session, black committee members enumerated the racial inequalities in public education that the WSIC had uncovered, and they demanded both equitable vocational training for blacks and a black high school. The school board halted its plan to eliminate seventh-grade classes from black schools, but public officials and civic leaders refused to allocate additional funds for black education.[37]

Undaunted, the NAACP and its allies pressed on. Despite frequent setbacks, First Church members and Benjamin Davis resisted the pernicious practice of letting personal rivalries trump their shared commitment to racial advancement. To the surprise of White and other NAACP leaders, Davis provided their organization with "inestimable aid" by generating supportive articles, and he pledged that despite personal differences, he was now willing to "join with all men, without regard to race, color, class or caste, to promote the general welfare and uplift of all Negroes."[38] Nevertheless, the legacies of black men's intraracial mistrust and division hindered the organization's progress, complicating even the seemingly simple decision of choosing a meeting space. NAACP leaders ruled out convening in churches because "there is so much dissension" among members from "a religious standpoint." Nor was the offer of free space in the Odd Fellows building acceptable, because of an "element antagonistic to Mr. Davis that will not attend any sort of meeting" there.[39] In 1917 a destructive fire in downtown Atlanta and America's entry into World War I temporarily turned members' attention away from the volunteer organization. Given these challenges, it is not surprising that the NAACP's membership rolls fluctuated markedly between 1917 and 1918. Following the organization's success at convincing the school board to retain the seventh grade, membership peaked at 393 African Americans in 1917 before plummeting to 49 in 1918, following White's departure to work in the NAACP's national office.[40]

Disappointed by this dramatic setback, Pace organized a membership rally in July 1918. Tendering his own resignation from the presidency, Pace oversaw new elections, which led to the appointment of a new executive committee representing "all shades of differences and local factions." The Reverend A. D. Williams, described by Pace as having been "one of our worst opponents," assumed the presidency. Despite Pace's initial misgivings, Williams's leadership ultimately fulfilled Pace's hopes that the NAACP would finally "eradicate all differences" within the organization, rendering it the "one place where all factions and all shades of opinions can unite" for the "advancement and welfare of the whole race." Aided by Davis's favorable newspaper editorials, Williams succeeded in expanding the organization's membership to 700 by September and then to approximately 1,400 by the end of the year.[41]

Finding strength in numbers, the executive committee now sought a *political* strategy for compelling whites to live up to their broken postriot promises to ensure fairness and justice for African Americans. The white primary, the requirement that citizens pay all of their back poll taxes before registering, and disfranchisement prevented African Americans from exerting direct influence on white public officials. Nevertheless, African Americans had long recognized one glaring crack in whites' otherwise solid antiblack voting apparatus. By law, new bond measures could pass only if two-thirds of all registered voters cast affirmative ballots in general elections. Bond elections bypassed the white-controlled Democratic primary process. Because many white registered voters often neglected to cast ballots, even the small number of African Americans who might qualify as voters and pay the necessary poll taxes could determine the outcome of a bond election. By blocking new bonds, blacks could force white politicians either to improve black public services or to endure a small measure of the deprivations long suffered by African Americans. In early 1919, in anticipation of upcoming tax and bond elections, the NAACP launched a voter registration campaign.[42]

To promote black voter registration, NAACP leaders reminded black residents of the inadequate roads, schools, and police protection that had long burdened their community. These black activists rallied influential black ministers and organized a house-to-house canvass, admonishing voters to pay poll taxes. By election time, this drive had successfully increased black registration by more than 70 percent, to 1,216 voters. On election eve, the NAACP packed Bethel AME Church "to the doors" with voters who unanimously agreed to reject the bonds and serve "notice upon the white people of the city that we had to be reckoned with in municipal affairs from this time forth." An ironic coalition of determined black voters and apathetic, nonparticipating whites defeated the bond measure in March. When white civic leaders refused to consider the NAACP's most minimal demands, black voters, now augmented by nearly 500 additional registrants, defeated a second bond measure in April. These victories energized the entire black community as well as NAACP leaders. As T. K. Gibson reported to the national office, "You well know that Atlanta has its full share of groups and circles, ofttimes hostile to each other, yet in this fight we have for this purpose at least welded them together and voted once, altogether."[43]

NAACP leaders acknowledged that "a large part of the praise [for our success] must be given to women who have rendered inestimable service." Lugenia Hope, drawing on the networks and organizational structures forged under NU auspices, headed the Women's Registration Committee to ensure that from the "rostrum of every service, sacred and secular, fraternal or social there is to be from now until the books close, some woman's voice calling men forth to do their duty." This committee, A. D. Williams maintained, spearheaded the registration drive: "We got our women organized and put the women in different districts and we had meetings weekly. . . . Night after night people came forward and paid their dollar. That was done largely because the women were allowed to make speeches."[44] Williams portrayed Hope as "peculiarly effective in organizations" and possessing "the happy faculty of being able to have all classes of women work together." "Whenever, we have wanted the women of our city to work as a unit," he continued, "we have always secured Mrs. Hope as a leader and . . . have never failed."[45]

After the bonds were defeated, white schools faced limited funds, and some were forced to institute double sessions. In an effort to raise the money necessary to address this growing problem, white politicians scheduled still another bond referendum in 1921. With black women empowered to vote following the adoption of the Nineteenth Amendment, black registration had more than doubled by election time. Fearing that African Americans would again vote against the proposed bonds, white mayor James Key asked white ministers associated with the local cic affiliate, a successor to Proctor's interracial committees, to investigate the reasons for blacks' opposition to the bonds. Following discussions with John Hope, white religious leaders forged a behind-the-scenes deal promising African Americans a high school and additional elementary schools if the bond measure passed. With these guarantees in hand, black voters finally rallied behind the bond proposal and ensured its passage. White politicians initially tried to renege on their promises, whereupon white religious leaders threatened court action.[46]

In the end, nearly half of the $8,850,000 raised from the new bonds was spent on black and white education, including the construction of four new black elementary schools and Booker T. Washington High School, which opened in 1924. Black demand for high school education was so great that by 1934 a school designed for only 1,500 students housed a student body of 3,600. For the first time since the riot, Atlanta's African Americans had planned a successful political strategy and secured the victory that had long been denied them despite interracial cooperation with white elites.[47]

Yet the naacp's electoral achievements underscored the limits as well as the promise of black political influence. Despite black residents' potential swing vote in bond elections, the white primary still prevented blacks from pressuring public officials on a sustained basis. Instead, mayors and city councilpersons answered to a white constituency that generally opposed improvements in black social services. As the result of continual budget shortfalls and the pressures exerted by white voters, mayors and school board members generally neglected black education after 1924. While blacks composed more than 37 percent of the school-age population, only 16 percent of the school board's budget was expended on black public education as late as 1942. Even the construction of Washington High proved bittersweet. Public officials reneged on pledges to provide black students with an auditorium and gymnasium. Classrooms for blacks were inadequately furnished, and students were provided only with textbooks discarded by whites.[48]

Lugenia Hope had hoped to capitalize on the successes of the NU's school campaign. "Our people as individuals have wrought well," she argued, "but the need is for cooperation, group consciousness and mass movements." She dreamed of expanding her movement by creating interlocking regional and national networks of rural and urban grassroots organizations modeled on the NU. "The simplicity of the method and the high degree of development that such a movement may attain make me think that here is a universal plan that may be directed through and by all classes of our people." The NU plan could mobilize black voters to defend their civil rights and secure better schools. It could facilitate national fund-raising and the creation of economic cooperatives allowing African Americans to gain "control of our labor and capital." Anticipating the power of millions of African Americans joined via a network of neighborhood unions, she believed that "one great National asso[ciation] may send its messages to the farthest corners of the rural districts and lift the most lowly." Hope continued throughout the 1930s to seek alliances with white opponents of lynching and other racial injustices, but the pervasive racism and temporizing that she repeatedly encountered only reaffirmed her core belief that true progress depended on grassroots organizing among blacks and on the mass mobilization of black voters.[49]

INTERRACIAL COOPERATION AMONG elite men, the professionalization of welfare work, and a shift in the NAACP's strategy away from grassroots organizing hindered Hope's inchoate visions of black nationalism. During the post–World War I era, the voluntary efforts of both the NU and First Church faced increased competition from a rising generation of professionally trained social workers as well as from centralized state agencies, professional welfare organizations, and citywide charity boards. In 1920 the state legislature established the Georgia Department of Public Welfare, and in 1923 white businessmen and civic leaders organized a local Community Chest (CC) aimed at coordinating the service and fund-raising activities of all black and white charitable organizations. By pooling information and resources, this umbrella organization sought to increase the "efficiency" of welfare work and prevent "dishonest" or "undeserving" clients from fleecing the welfare system. The CC also tried to replace a confusing welter of individual, ad hoc fund-raising efforts with a coordinated community drive.[50]

Henry Hugh Proctor, like so many of his white counterparts, came to believe that professional social service providers must play a crucial role in addressing municipal social problems. In 1917 he enlisted the National Urban League to establish an Atlanta chapter. Following Proctor's request, Jesse O. Thomas arrived in the city in 1919. He quickly established the league's southern headquarters in Atlanta and became a member of First Church. Thomas subscribed to Proctor's belief that the league could supplement many of First Church's elitist efforts at uniting "colored and white people of ability and means to work together for the adjustment of the masses of colored people." After Proctor departed in 1919, First Church abandoned almost all of its public outreach programs. National Urban League director Thomas, unimpressed with black Atlanta's traditional social work approach, saw his arrival in the city as an opportunity "to demonstrate a more scientific approach" to the practice of social work.[51]

Like similar chapters in other southern cities, the Atlanta Urban League (AUL) relied primarily on funding from whites and white-controlled agencies. The biracial Committee on Church Cooperation adopted the AUL as its social action agency and subsidized its operations. Local black churches and residents originally contributed precious little to the new organization so that white contributions composed the bulk of the AUL's budget. Thomas, backed by wealthy and influential whites, convinced the city council to fund the salaries of two black public school nurses and a physician for black indigents. Because of overlap between his organization and Hope's, Thomas perceived the NU as a competitor. At one point he even accused the much more established women's organization of having "encroached" on the AUL's programs. As historian Sarah Judson has shown, the interracial AUL quickly assumed a leading role in organizing neighborhood surveys and cleanup campaigns in the black community—efforts once dominated by the NU. Despite the rising influence of social work professionals in the NU, Hope and other members never wavered in their broader goal of fostering grassroots community development.[52]

This focus on nurturing neighborhood ties and encouraging community building appeared increasingly naive among some black professionals, such as Thomas, and white social workers whose training emphasized the values of program efficiency and scientific charity. The NU, its prestige undermined by the AUL's and CC's claims of professionalism, also faced growing competition from the CC's more visible fund-raising campaigns. According to corresponding secretary Louie D. Shivery, there was general agreement within the NU that it must join and "keep its place in the Chest for the prestige it gets from being listed in a recognized agency, fostered by the city government, and approved by municipal and civic organizations interested in social relief." In 1924, the first year of the ensuing alliance between the NU and the CC, Hope's organization received approximately $3,676 in funding.[53]

This grant came with the stipulation that the NU limit its agenda to the supervision of a preschool health clinic so that its social programs would not overlap with those of the AUL. NU welfare activities were to be subsumed under a larger, white-controlled citywide agency serving both whites and blacks. In 1925 the CC announced its withdrawal of financial support for any future NU activities. Breaking from the CC, the NU organized its own fundraising campaign. Despite the fact that many African Americans had already pledged money to the CC, the black community's enthusiastic support for the NU forced the CC to reverse its funding decision. Hope encouraged NU members to embrace these overtures. "The Chest is going to take care of us," she wrote in an open letter, "so let us take care of the Chest."[54]

According to Shivery, the NU's reinstatement in the CC ultimately came "with so drastic a cut" in funding that the NU never "recovered." Looking back, another member agreed that the NU's alliance with the CC ultimately proved a serious mistake. The CC provided the organization with far too few funds and robbed the NU of its autonomy. Now struggling with diminishing revenues and a narrowing mission, the NU lost much of its community influence after it abandoned the social activities and informal services that had once helped members organize black neighborhoods socially and politically. Only during the Great Depression was the NU able to regain temporarily a high-profile presence on the West Side, when, with CC approval, the organization provided small unemployment and stopgap welfare benefits to black residents.[55]

As chapter president between 1921 and 1936, Austin T. Walden, a Baptist and local lawyer, steered the Atlanta NAACP away from its previous voter registration and protest activities. Instead, Walden funneled the branch's resources almost exclusively into court battles over discrimination and racial injustice. This inattention to local organizing prevented the NAACP from building on its earlier political victories, and its membership roles dramatically declined. In the 1930s, with Walden's support, Hope spearheaded a revived NAACP voter registration campaign. With the passage of the Nineteenth Amendment, she had extended her vision of women's activism and community leadership to embrace direct political action. "When a woman begins to think directly on civic problems," Hope argued, "she will be as successful a voter as a house keeper. Then she will put on her dinner in the morning[,] take the baby in her arms, step over to the polls . . . and the world will be better for her knowledge."[56]

Between 1933 and 1935, Hope operated a series of NAACP citizenship schools that primarily attracted domestic workers and aimed at encouraging a "feeling of race consciousness with reference to the ballot." Hope's citizenship schools were the first in a series of registration drives that in 1936 culminated in the formation of the Atlanta Civic and Political League under the leadership of John Wesley Dobbs, First Church deacon during Proctor's pastorate. In July 1935 Hope resigned from the NU, the organization for which she remembered having done her "most happy and satisfactory work." Six months later, John Hope died. Later in 1936, Lugenia Hope left Atlanta. She returned permanently only after her death in 1947, when her ashes were scattered on the Morehouse grounds.[57]

IN 1925 MOREHOUSE sociology professor E. Franklin Frazier characterized Atlanta's temporarily inactive NAACP as "a very poor representation of the attitude of a so-called cultured group of colored people toward this problem facing us." "It seems," he concluded, "that many Atlanta colored people are happy to crawl into the holes (they are very fine homes to be sure) and thank God that they are living and can enjoy two or three meals a day and a dance once in a while."[58] Frazier's criticisms perceptively captured how, during the Progressive Era, dominant black notions of respectability might turn the attention of black middle-class reformers inward to a private, interior life focused on individual economic advancement and social striving. After the riot, Henry Proctor sought racial advancement by encouraging black intellectual and economic achievement and by empowering his congregation as an elite vanguard of negotiators between blacks and whites. Proctor's cultural elitism and narrow moral vision limited his ability to establish alliances across class lines. During the 1920s and 1930s, the NAACP and the AUL similarly sought racial progress primarily by empowering a black leadership cadre.

While these notions of respectability might turn the visions of elite African Americans inward, they were, however, also predicated on a radical rejection of dominant racist ideas. First Church's cultural training taught a rising generation that personal and moral attainment qualified black elites to claim full equality. Walter White's 1906 riot experiences and his bitter resentments of naked racial injustice helped fuel his radicalism and his NAACP public activism. Under White's and Pace's leadership, the membership of Atlanta's NAACP branch originally consisted almost exclusively of middle-class and elite African Americans, many of whom were affiliated with First Church. Although Proctor shunned direct protests and political confrontation, his interracial work reinforced white civic leaders' commitment to preventing renewed racial violence and avoiding open racial conflict. The commitment of white elites to maintaining law and order helped discourage an unrestrained brutality and repression that would have blocked black political mobilization, as was the case in many other southern locations.[59]

Frazier posited a rigid dichotomy between a public world of political activism and a private sphere of isolation. In contrast, the NU refused to accept traditional boundaries separating women's private household authority from men's public authority as voters, breadwinners, and civic leaders. NU members recognized the black household as one of the final refuges from white brutality and violence. Convinced of the symbiotic relationship between the home and its immediate environment, the NU continuously expanded its vision outward. Through campaigns for better schools and then via voter registration drives, Lugenia Hope sought to extend the authority of blacks beyond private neighborhoods and homes into public institutions and governmental offices traditionally controlled by whites. Under Hope's direction, the NU demonstrated that African Americans could work with whites to address shared concerns while simultaneously strengthening black institutions and organizing African Americans politically.

Hope's movement diminished the social distance between NU members and other African Americans precisely because of its radically democratic structure and its inclusive approach to political and social mobilization. Far from representing the opinions of a small minority, the NU's opposition to public drinking and illegal vice reflected widely accepted visions of community order. Yet neither Hope's profound social environmentalist bent nor her empathic neighborly concerns led the NU to tolerate forms of conduct accepted by many African Americans—including, for example, premarital sex between committed partners, public dancing, the Holy Rollers' expressive worship practices, and "disorderly" behaviors aimed at challenging white authority. Never fully bridged by the NU, this cultural gap continued to divide black residents throughout the twentieth century. The social biases of black elites constricted their visions and strategies for attaining civil rights. They never fully appreciated the many oppressions suffered by working-class African Americans or this group's unique protest traditions.[60]

Like William J. Northen and Atlanta's white ministers, both Hope and

Proctor feared the social dislocations engendered by Atlanta's rapid population growth and commercial development. White commentators often conflated these black reformers' conceptions of moral stewardship with white reformers' hopes of employing "first class" blacks to help whites crush black resistance and black criminality. The commitment of self-proclaimed white paternalists to humanitarian concerns proved as thin as their visions of law and order proved narrow. These white elites repeatedly refused to support black campaigns for better schools and improved city services. This shallowness had its profoundly tragic dimensions. Yet the defense of black neighborhoods and institutions from destructive white mobs and intrusive white paternalists simultaneously preserved liberating black visions. Beyond whites' reach, black ministers and NU members deployed a many-sided politics of respectability in pursuit of racial equality and full civil rights.

CHAPTER ELEVEN

The Ghosts of a Riot Past

⸺

THE GHOSTS OF 1906 have haunted Atlanta's politics and the imaginations of its black and white citizens for nearly a century. Walter White, Margaret Mitchell, W. E. B. Du Bois, and other residents viewed the riot as a defining moment in their lives, forever searing into their consciousnesses visceral lessons regarding race relations and the South. Black and white witnesses, interviewed as late as 1981 for radio station WRFG's Living Atlanta Project, joined Evelyn Witherspoon in recalling the "electricity in the air" on the night of the riot, as well as its horrifying sights, shrill sounds, and overpowering emotions. Local white politician Charlie Brown believed that the riot stories he heard growing up "affected the way I thought about black people for the rest of my life" and taught him "what racial hatred can do to ordinarily good people."[1]

Despite this shared intensity, a "segregation of memory" has divided riot remembrances, not simply along the lines of race but of class as well. Among blacks, E. T. Lewis warned a Living Atlanta interviewer, "You will get a whole lot of versions [of the riot]." Many black residents depicted the violence as a broad-based attempt by whites to intimidate blacks, whose collective resistance pushed back the rioters and forced whites to the bargaining table. White elites generally blamed black rapists for triggering an outbreak that allegedly ended only after civic leaders heroically intervened to restrain a mob of working-class toughs. Many black elites joined their white counterparts in seeking to shift attention away from the violence of the riot to the law-and-order movements that followed it. True to Henry Hugh Proctor's 1906 vision, black and white powerbrokers increasingly worked together after World War II to ameliorate their city's racial tensions. The city's public relations machinery and the riot memories of Atlanta's leading citizens helped ensure the national adoption of Atlanta's vision of biracial cooperation.[2]

IN A SET of highly influential articles in 1968 and 1969, professional historian Charles Crowe drew on Ray Stannard Baker's research to argue that whites had grossly exaggerated the incidence of black assaults preceding the riot. Despite Crowe's and Baker's published revelations, local white newspapers and popular histories continued, as late as the 1980s, to embrace white businessmen's 1906 depiction of events: black assaults provoked the riot, and paternalistic whites saved the city in its aftermath. In the early 1940s, Georgia's Works Projects Administration published a guidebook that, on the eve of growing black political mobilization in the city, imaginatively blamed the riot on black political participation. "Flattering appeals for the Negro vote in the state," its authors recounted, had triggered displays of "boldness and insolence by the lower Negro element," which led to "reports of attacks on white women."[3]

Franklin Garrett's seminal 1954 historical compendium, *Atlanta and Environs*, borrowing heavily from the Chamber of Commerce's official 1906 riot report, highlighted the crimes of black rapists before underscoring the roles of white civic leaders in calming "alarm" and establishing "good will between the races" after the riot. "The law-abiding majority," this Coca-Cola executive concluded, "were amazed that the small minority which constituted the 'tough element' was allowed to crucify the community in the eyes of the world and shock the moral sense of decent people." Stories of rapes by blacks and of elite whites' protection of black dependents filled accounts of the violence written by Garrett and other whites. In 1980 the *Journal* incorrectly counted three assaults by blacks on the day of the riot alone. In Living Atlanta interviews conducted between 1979 and 1981, elderly white residents who witnessed the riot firsthand repeated many of the myths embedded in these popular histories.[4]

With the publication of Margaret Mitchell's *Gone with the Wind* in 1936, Atlanta's local riot memories of black rapists invaded white America's perceptions of southern history. Mitchell's portrayals of Reconstruction borrowed heavily from widespread 1930s national myths representing the era as a disordered nightmare populated by vengeful and autocratic Yankee carpetbaggers, sexually and politically menacing emancipated slaves, and intolerably wronged former slaveholders. Yet Mitchell's imaginary vision of Reconstruction Era Atlanta also drew from her own riot experiences and whites' dominant public memories of Atlanta in 1906. Into the 1920s, Mitchell wrote of the fears she experienced as a young child during the riot when rumors circulated that black residents were planning to invade her neighborhood and torch its houses.[5]

In Mitchell's novel, stories spread throughout the city of an African American plot to battle the KKK with retaliatory house burnings and a concerted black uprising. Repeated black assaults force unescorted white women and children, with the notable exception of a stubborn Scarlett O'Hara, out of the public realm and into their homes. When Scarlett travels alone at night through an area known as Shantytown, two outlaws—one black and one white—menace her. In search of money, the black man, his face "twisted in a leering grin," rips her corset and places his hands between her breasts. Scarlett's ex-slave Sam appears and rescues her just as the black criminal is attempting to drag her away. Despite the juxtaposition of black and white roles as protector and protected in this scene, the interracial bonds of elite whites and loyal black dependents once again trump the threats posed by black rapists and disorderly whites. After Scarlett escapes, her husband and other white men are compelled to defend her honor by invading and attempting to destroy this settlement, which, much like the Decatur Street of whites' imagination, possesses the "worst reputation of any spot in or near Atlanta, filled with outcast negroes, black prostitutes, and a scattering of poor whites of the lowest order."[6]

In contrast, black residents generally preserved an oral tradition that underscored whites' shared racist antipathies while reaffirming blacks' intracial loyalties. African Americans generally rejected white portrayals blaming black criminals for provoking white violence and crediting white civic leaders with single-handedly protecting blacks. Many instead recounted stories highlighting whites' shared determination to block black progress as well as the stubborn refusal of whites to seek interracial dialogue until united black resistance compelled them to negotiate. E. T. Lewis informed an interviewer that whites attacked African Americans to reestablish their control over the population or "to frighten them, to let them know that they weren't supposed to oppose whites in any kind of an effort for anything." NU leader Lugenia Burns Hope later recalled African Americans' bitter recognition that white employers and civic leaders had moved against the violence only after blacks began fighting back: "These white people knew how they had treated the Negro all the while, now they feared retribution. The Negro man went home, sat in the door with his gun across his knees and was prepared to die protecting his home and family. Not until then did the good Christian white people care what happened to the Negro. But when they saw the Negro in sheer desperation decided to protect himself or die—did the churches open their doors—Fear."[7]

These memories recounted by blacks ultimately helped make possible Crowe's revision of the history of the riot, an analysis that served as the starting point of all subsequent academic scholarship. Explicitly thanking Atlanta University professor Clarence Bacote for his "invaluable suggestions," Crowe recognized the success achieved by blacks in preserving their own history of the violence: "The Atlanta race riot," he concluded, "was not soon forgotten by black people who remembered with particular vividness the evening of September 22 as the terror-ridden night of the white assassins."[8]

AS BLACK AND white residents of Atlanta confronted new challenges and opportunities during the twentieth century, the riot's varied lessons repeatedly influenced their choices and decisions. Fears of the potential consequences of a second violent outburst, for example, weighed heavily on Leo Frank's sensational 1913 murder trial. Atlanta's white newspapers initially played a key role in rousing readers' explosive passions with thrilling stories of white womanhood under siege, threatened this time not by black brutes but by a Jewish pencil factory co-owner and manager from the North. Newspaper headline after newspaper headline publicized prosecutor Hugh Dorsey's portrayal of Frank as a pervert who had long sexually preyed on innocent working-class gentiles before he sexually violated and then murdered fourteen-year-old Mary Phagan. As the trial progressed, both the *Journal* and the *Georgian* gradually began to question Frank's guilt as the result of mounting revelations of police misconduct and growing doubts regarding the testimony of chief state witness Jim Conley. Conley, a black janitor at the factory who was likely responsible for Phagan's death, claimed to have helped Frank conceal the body. In the end, only the *Constitution* sided with the prosecution. Crowded out of the public's consciousness by deeply ingrained anti-Semitic stereotypes, the editorial shifts of the *Journal* and the *Georgian* proved to be too little, too late.[9]

Atlanta's newspaper editors remembered their role in inciting the 1906 riot, and they eventually moderated their initial sensationalism. According to the *Augusta Chronicle*, editors vowed not to publish "flaring extras after dark," which might madden the "sanculottes of Marietta street." They also warned Judge Leonard Roan—who had overseen many of the criminal cases arising from the riot—that they feared a riot should the jury announce a not-guilty verdict on a Saturday. When the police chief and a militia commander seconded the editors' warnings, Roan delayed the proceedings so that the trial would end on a weekday. After the jury returned a guilty verdict, Roan sentenced Frank to hang and rejected defense motions for another trial.[10]

Although the judge repeatedly admitted his belief in Frank's innocence, he feared that a retrial would precipitate a riot so immense that the governor would lack "enough troops to control the mob." In a series of appeals, Frank's lawyers argued that the trial's contentious atmosphere and Roan's desire to avert a riot had produced a number of procedural irregularities, including the defendant's absence from court when the jury presented its verdict. In 1915 the U.S. Supreme Court rejected these appeals, countering that the federal government had no right to interfere with state courts when the spirit rather than the form of a trial was in question.[11]

Frank's hopes for clemency now turned to the state's prison commission and Governor John M. Slaton, a member of one of Atlanta's leading law firms and an early critic of the complicity of public officials in the outbreak of the riot. The governor and the prison commission received a flood of pro-Frank petitions bearing more than a million signatures. Newspapers from across the nation and much of the South openly criticized the jury's verdict. Slaton, convinced of Conley's guilt, commuted Frank's sentence to life imprisonment in late June, hoping the condemned man would eventually be acquitted.[12]

During and after the trial, many white men, especially marginalized factory workers, viewed the creation of this Jewish scapegoat as an opportunity to reiterate the claims they had made in 1906 of being upholders of public order and defenders of white womanhood. Throughout much of Frank's ordeal, Tom Watson repeatedly attacked both the defendant and his sympathizers, gleefully predicting "*the bloodiest riot ever known in the history of the South*" should Slaton commute the death sentence.[13] Throughout the trial, twenty guards protected the courtroom from the large, impassioned swarms of men that encircled the building, and white vigilantes issued death threats against both Judge Roan and Frank's attorneys. In the week following Slaton's decision, mobs armed with weapons ranging from rifles to heavy explosives marched through downtown Atlanta before they surrounded the governor's mansion some six miles away. Protected by Georgia's militia, Slaton completed his term in late June and promptly left the state. Less than two weeks later, a mob composed of the "best citizens" of Marietta—Phagan's hometown—kidnapped Frank from prison and publicly hanged him. An undertaker transported Frank's mutilated body to Atlanta, where it was placed on display for an audience of approximately 15,000 Georgians.[14]

In 1915, William Simmons tapped into the passions stoked by the Frank case and the stunning national success of *The Birth of a Nation*—a film that glorified the role of white vigilantes in "redeeming" the South during Reconstruction—to launch the modern KKK in a ceremony just outside Atlanta, on Stone Mountain. Headquartered in Atlanta, Simmons's organization generated large profits as a supplier of Klan paraphernalia to a membership that peaked at more than 4 million in the 1920s. By 1922, the KKK directed the votes of approximately 100,000 white Georgians, having generated widespread support among working-class Atlantans as well as small shopkeepers and low-level white-collar employees. Police Chief Herbert Jenkins, recounting the department's 1930s work environment when he arrived as a raw recruit, noted that Klan membership was "your ID card, the badge of honor with the in group, and it was unfortunately often an allegiance stronger than the policeman's oath to society."[15]

As suggested by the desperate measures undertaken by both the newspapers and Judge Roan to avert a second riot, the profound hatreds and calls for extralegal violence that emerged during Frank's two-year ordeal terrified white civic and commercial leaders. Although Frank was Jewish, his economic status was similar to that of many white elites. White civic leaders rightly interpreted the crowds' anger and violent threats as attacks against elite privilege and the authority of public officials. In commenting on the trial and the lynching, national newspapers drew on timeworn stereotypes to portray white Georgians as so savage that the federal government should intervene militarily to restore civilization. As in 1906, the initial instinct of white elites was to counter this negative publicity by organizing a series of public relations campaigns. After Frank was lynched, the Chamber of Commerce called on city residents to transcend their differences by rallying around the "Atlanta Spirit." In 1926, business leaders, envious of the real estate boom in Florida and ever fearful that Birmingham might upstage Atlanta as the South's leading commercial and distribution center, orchestrated still another advertising campaign. Titled "Forward Atlanta" and fueled by an advertising budget that exceeded $1 million, the four-year campaign blanketed national publications with messages touting Atlanta as a modern and progressive city.[16]

At first blush, one might think that Imperial Wizard Simmons's outspoken support for racial violence and his populistic disdain for America's business elite openly challenged the chamber's vision of Atlanta as a cultured city of sober white citizens. White business leaders, however, never directly opposed an organization whose brisk trade in Klan memorabilia channeled untold wealth into their city and whose annual Klanvokations attracted as many as 4,000 conventioneers. Coca-Cola, eager to supply soda to 4 million Klansmen, supported the KKK's official newspaper, the *Searchlight*, by running advertisements in it.[17]

IN ATLANTA, MANY black educators and ministers consciously avoided publicly discussing the Frank lynching. George Towns, an Atlanta University professor and member of First Church, convened a meeting of students in its aftermath and warned them not to talk about the white mob's crime under any circumstances. In a private letter, John Hope described his commitment, as Morehouse College's president, to securing racial progress. Referring both to the tense racial atmosphere following Leo Frank's lynching and to the strategy he had consistently pursued since 1906, Hope informed a friend that he would "be embarrassed any day, if I did not exercise such care as I have practised through all these years—courage and silence, silence almost absolute, for I will not speak a lie."[18]

In 1930, Hope cooperated quietly behind the scenes to calm tensions in the aftermath of a series of outrageous white racist acts that began when seven whites shot and killed Dennis Hubert, a family friend and Morehouse student, after a confrontation near campus. With memories of the 1906 riot pressing on black and white minds and with blacks arming themselves in anticipation of a second racial conflagration, Hope worked closely with prominent whites and African Americans to ensure calm during T. L. Martin's ensuing trial for Hubert's murder. When Martin was pronounced guilty and sentenced to a twelve-to-fifteen-year jail sentence, black and white civic leaders remained steadfastly calm and silent, while armed African Americans quietly guarded their homes from the potential mob attacks that never materialized.[19]

Hope and other African Americans shared a common interest with white civic leaders in defusing direct racial confrontations that might culminate in violence. Into the 1960s, both the *Journal* and the *Constitution* exercised caution in reporting potentially explosive racial stories. According to *Constitution* editor Eugene Patterson, white civic leaders never allowed journalists to forget their role in sparking the 1906 riot. As evidenced by the Chamber of Commerce's tacit acceptance of the KKK, the commitment of white business leaders to racial peace had shallow roots. Their moderation was less an end in itself than a means of promoting commerce and maintaining an image of stability and modernity. In contrast, Hope, who had once endorsed the Niagara Movement's commitment to a public life of manly protest, admitted privately that his own silence often gnawed at his insides. In his 1915 letter following the Frank lynching, he confessed, "How much I lie by remaining silent, God knows. I am doing my best to serve my folk and my country." White editor Patterson's observation that "it takes a few decades for a newspaper to get over something like" the Atlanta riot was also true for many blacks of Hope's and Proctor's generation.[20]

During World War I, Meredith Ashby Jones and John Eagan—as participants in the growing interracial reform efforts promoted by Henry Hugh Proctor—had established contact with both white northerners and southerners who envisioned the creation of a regionwide organization similar to Atlanta's local interracial church committees. Two of these contacts, Willis D. Weatherford and Methodist minister Will Alexander, who first met as Nashville residents, played a key role in shaping what became known in 1920 as the Commission on Interracial Cooperation, which was headquartered in Atlanta. Founder Will Alexander credited Cary B. Wilmer with devising the blueprint for the CIC's organizational structure—a framework that Wilmer admitted to have consciously borrowed from his own experience after the riot, namely the civic leagues developed by Charles T. Hopkins and William J. Northen. "Dr. Wilmer's already developed philosophy" and Eagan's Christian "impulse," Alexander recalled, "furnished the basis" on which the CIC was formed. Eagan, an original member of the postriot civic league and Northen's Gospel Union, chaired the CIC until his death in 1924, and he financed many of its initial programs.[21]

Like the postriot white advocates of interracial cooperation, most CIC leaders blamed racial violence on tensions involving a lower, disorderly element in both races. Under Wilmer's influence, the CIC initially focused on creating local biracial committees, which at their height spanned 604 counties and every southern state except Oklahoma. Alexander argued that local committees should be composed of the "strongest white and colored leaders"—"men of character, intelligence and good will." This emphasis on cultivating southern leaders reflected the CIC's distrust of northern solutions to what it perceived as regional problems. The aim of white participants in buttressing the power and influence of moderate black and white elites revealed their goal of marginalizing radical black voices while simultaneously reining in what many CIC participants viewed as a disorderly class of poor whites. In 1919, for example, a series of CIC-influenced meetings between white Chamber of Commerce officials and a colored businesspersons' league in Waycross, Georgia, led to the "silencing" of a black "agitator who publicly advised Negroes to open a hardware store where they could buy firearms to protect themselves and get what they wanted."[22]

The CIC, primarily a Protestant movement, appropriated the structures of these 1906 reformers but clothed them in a Social Gospel belief that Christianity required its adherents to battle social inequities, especially those that warped human souls. Most CIC members were urban dwellers influenced by Progressivism. They sought to balance Northen's and Hopkins's emphasis on social control with a countervailing push for fundamental justice. As had John E. White in 1906, regional CIC leaders often embraced a Progressive faith that research, exposés, and public relations campaigns could change human minds and sensitize Americans to social wrongs. After 1924, the organization's regional leadership shifted its focus from establishing grassroots organizations to seeking wider, regional reforms. From the CIC's Atlanta headquarters, Alexander and other whites increasingly promoted reform by publishing research on regional social problems, by publicizing the achievements of socially progressive black and white southerners, by criticizing the KKK and other enemies of racial peace, and by serving as a clearinghouse for information on mob violence and other racial and social injustices.[23]

CIC leaders were, in essence, "closet dissenters" rather than vocal reform advocates. The bulk of their publicity and research efforts occurred quietly behind the scenes; most local branches purposefully kept their meetings secret. While Will Alexander occasionally voiced his personal misgivings about segregation, neither he nor his organization ever publicly supported integration or black voting rights. Even regarding the fundamental issue of white mob violence, CIC members sought to guide white opinion rather than fundamentally challenge it. The organization's refusal to support federal antilynching legislation until 1937 highlights the underlying conservatism of an organization originally founded to reduce and manage racial conflict rather than promote change. By that time, opinion polls indicated that a majority of white southerners, though wary of federal intervention in regional affairs, already condemned mob violence. NAACP leaders perceptively recognized the role played by CIC publicity campaigns in staving off northern white outrage at continued southern racial injustices. Through the 1920s and early 1930s, for example, the CIC's relatively humane rhetoric and its advocacy of southern-sponsored initiatives discouraged some northerners from supporting federal antilynching legislation.[24]

In contrast, the NAACP, under Walter White's firm leadership, sought to eradicate lynching through congressional and presidential action. This strategy reflected the national office's long-standing traditions of confining its battles to elite-initiated legal challenges, lobbying efforts, and negotiations. As NAACP executive secretary, Walter White—true to both his First Church upbringing and his Talented Tenth Atlanta University training—promoted this elite-based approach during his 1931–55 tenure. As had Proctor, White shunned grassroots organizing, local protests, women's activism, and mass-based demonstrations. This strategy facilitated a series of stunning achievements, most notably the 1954 Supreme Court ruling that public school segregation was unconstitutional. But as historian Kenneth Janken has demonstrated, White's overwhelming elitism left the national organization ill equipped to take charge of grassroots civil rights movements inaugurated with the 1955–56 Montgomery bus boycott.[25]

The ultimate significance of the CIC lay less in its concrete achievements than in its role as a hub for wide-ranging efforts at promoting interracial cooperation and moderate racial reform throughout the South. Its public campaigns against mob violence enabled otherwise isolated white southern opponents of lynching to view themselves as part of a progressive, respectable movement. The organization partially funded or facilitated the formation of countless subsidiary organizations, including the Interracial Woman's Committee, the Southern Division of the National Student Council, and, in 1930, Jessie Daniel Ames's Association of Southern Women for the Prevention of Lynching. The programs of these organizations, particularly those aimed at college students, exposed a rising generation of southern whites to the ideals of moderate racial liberalism and provided them an opportunity to establish interracial contacts.[26]

After Alexander and other leading white members accepted positions in the Roosevelt administration, the CIC's vitality waned in the late 1930s. During the early 1940s, the CIC's remnants were absorbed into the Southern Regional Council (SRC), an entity that fulfilled former CIC president Howard Odum's vision of an academically based regional planning and research organization. While African Americans assumed key leadership positions in the organization from its inception, white conservatism prevented the SRC from publicly opposing segregation until 1951.[27]

The programs of both the CIC and the SRC gradually evolved as interracial dialogue sensitized some white participants to the frustrations of their black counterparts. Yet both organizations originally served as conservative alternatives to the destabilizing radicalism that their white membership associated with militant civil rights activists and white racist extremists. As historian David Chappell has persuasively argued, the relative racial moderation of organizations such as the CIC and the SRC demonstrated to blacks that a small group of white southerners shared a commitment to abandoning the most oppressive aspects of white supremacy. At the same time, the limited achievements of these organizations also convinced civil rights activists that lasting change was possible in the South only if blacks were willing to "seize the initiative" through more confrontational approaches.[28]

THE NEW DEAL and World War II generated new social and economic opportunities for black southerners and augmented the federal government's presence in regional affairs. In Atlanta, New Deal social programs created a new class of black professionals, hired to provide services to a segregated, all-black clientele. Works Progress Administration and Federal Emergency Relief Administration jobs often paid black teachers and other professionals far more than they had ever earned. While the New Deal's support for organized labor bypassed unskilled workers, the AUL took advantage of the New Deal's avowed commitment to organized labor to facilitate the formation of painters' and brick masons' unions affiliated with the American Federation of Labor. Attracted to Atlanta by what appeared to be insatiable wartime labor demands, approximately 30,000 black southerners streamed into the city during the 1940s. Black servicemen, particularly those from the North, literally brought the war against Aryan supremacy to city streets and other public spaces. Many of them vocally criticized segregation in train stations and other public settings. Joined by local black civilians emboldened by their heightened economic independence, black soldiers and veterans battled white racist harassment, especially on streetcars and buses, where they frequently flouted traditional Jim Crow rules and customs.[29]

Along with this mounting black resistance, a series of court decisions and white-led political reforms provided African Americans with new political opportunities. In 1942 an unlikely coalition of urban-based white commercial leaders and supporters of Franklin Roosevelt elected gubernatorial candidate Ellis Arnall, a man who had vocally supported initiatives promoting economic development and a constructive relationship between Georgia and the federal government. After he was inaugurated in 1943, Arnall employed his formidable political skills to secure the adoption of numerous state constitutional amendments, including measures to eliminate the poll tax, abolish the chain gang, and lower the voting age from twenty-one to eighteen. The governor's outspoken opposition to mob violence and vigilantism helped reduce the incidence of lynching in Georgia and undermined the KKK's influence throughout the state. Yet, like many of his antilynching predecessors, Arnall remained a committed segregationist, and he envisioned his voting amendments as applying only to whites.[30]

Black civil rights activists masterfully succeeded in making Arnall's reforms their own. A rising generation of black ministers had utilized their pulpits during the 1930s both to speak out against segregation and to endorse political mobilization as a peaceful means for blacks to address their grievances. In addition, First Church deacon John Wesley Dobbs, NAACP lawyer A. T. Walden, and Atlanta Daily World editor C. A. Scott joined these ministers in promoting black political participation. Immediately following the U.S. Supreme Court's 1944 decision declaring the Texas Democratic Party's white primary unconstitutional, Atlanta's NAACP began to organize black voters to force implementation of the ruling. Turned back from the polls, Columbus minister Primus King initiated a lawsuit against Georgia's Democratic Party for violating his civil rights. A federal district judge ruled in King's favor in a decision that the Supreme Court endorsed in 1946. Before the Supreme Court's ruling, during a special election bypassing the white primary in February 1946, Atlanta's black voters played a decisive role in electing racial moderate Helen Douglas Mankin to the House of Representatives.[31]

Seeking to capitalize on these victories, AUL leader and First Church parishioner Grace Towns Hamilton joined Clarence Bacote and others in establishing the All-Citizens Registration Committee. By May 1946, Hamilton's massive voting drive had more than tripled the number of registered black voters, from approximately 7,000 to more than 21,000. Tightly organized and initially comprising one-quarter of the electorate, black voters became a deciding factor in municipal elections. In a close mayoral campaign in 1949, overwhelming black support played a crucial role in electing William Hartsfield, who also won the backing of city business leaders and a suburban middle class.[32]

DURING ENSUING YEARS, black civic leaders would join Atlanta's highly organized white civic-commercial elite in an informal coalition or "regime" that would exercise ever greater influence in city affairs. Although both groups sought enhanced economic opportunities, they differed over larger goals. Black elites viewed their political pursuits as indelibly linked with advancing black civil rights. White business leaders, in contrast, rallied around their goals of promoting commercial growth, advertising their Atlanta as a progressive city, and securing its full integration into the national

Black Atlantans braved long lines at Fulton County Courthouse during the successful
voter registration drives of 1946. (Library of Congress)

economy. Despite these differences, both groups recognized their common
political opponents in a city once policed by the KKK and a state governed by
backward-looking, openly racist governors, including Lester Maddox, who
remained an unreconstructed segregationist during his 1967–71 tenure.[33]

This evolving coalition of white business leaders and black elites, so
reminiscent of Henry Hugh Proctor's postriot vision of interracial cooperation between the "better elements," continues to control Atlanta today. The
growing willingness of white civic leaders to cooperate with elite blacks
reflected a cold calculation of their dependence on black voters, their own
fears of disorder, and their efforts at promoting their city, first as a national
and then as an international commercial center. The raw emotions sparked
by whites' increasing massive resistance to civil rights progress deeply troubled Hartsfield and other white elites. The only way to ensure that Atlanta
economically outpaced its ambitious southern rivals, Mayor Hartsfield and
business leaders agreed, was to advertise their city nationally like a commercial product and ensure that "no business, no industry, no educational or
social organization" was "ashamed of the dateline 'Atlanta.' "[34]

Well into the 1960s, white civic leaders believed that they could achieve
these law-and-order goals only through determined resolve and concerted

effort. White newspaper editors, still smarting from their role in helping provoke the 1906 riot, continued their cautious policy of self-censorship. Although Allen and his chamber colleagues shared their predecessors' public amnesia regarding the 1906 violence and Leo Frank's lynching, the eruption of southern riots and racial conflagrations in other cities worried them throughout the 1960s. Ever protective of Atlanta's vulnerable image, white civic leaders sought to steer their city away from the displays of open racial conflict that had sullied both the reputation of Montgomery during the 1955–56 bus boycott and the image of Little Rock during that city's 1957 stand against public school integration. "Being the melting pot of the Southeast," Allen remembered, "Atlanta in the early sixties possessed all of the elements that could lead to full-scale racial bloodshed and turmoil."[35]

Between the late 1940s and late 1960s, Hartsfield, Ivan Allen, and other white elites consulted frequently (and often in secret) with numerous elite African Americans associated with the Atlanta Negro Voters League, the NAACP, and the AUL. Under the leadership of Grace Towns Hamilton, the AUL initially dominated postwar cooperative efforts, having won the confidence of white powerbrokers through a nonconfrontational approach dating back to the 1920s. Among the other black civic leaders were a small group of professionals that included Dobbs, Walden, and *Daily World* editor C. A. Scott; a coterie of black ministers led by Baptist preachers Martin Luther King Sr. and William Holmes Borders; and Morehouse University and Atlanta University presidents Benjamin Mays and Rufus Clement.[36]

These African Americans never forgot the key lessons gleaned from 1906. Throughout his life, John Wesley Dobbs recounted riot stories to his children and grandchildren. He also kept guns and ammunition tucked away at home in case of another assault by whites. Benjamin Mays recalled hearing news of the riot during his South Carolina youth. Martin Luther King Sr. included in his autobiography a brief account of his father-in-law's experiences during the riot, and he traced the city's biracial traditions to the conflagration's aftermath. The threat of renewed violence reinforced these memories throughout the twentieth century. During the 1940s, whites greeted black resistance to Jim Crow dictates with beatings and gunfire. In late 1946, a neo-Nazi group labeling itself the Columbians achieved notoriety by organizing public rallies, openly pledging its hatred for African Americans, and announcing its ambition to become "forty times worse than the Klan." Columbians harassed blacks who moved into areas bordering white neighborhoods, beating one man and bombing at least one black residence. A police crackdown and widespread white indignation led to the dissolution of this organization in 1947. Nevertheless, white groups continued to threaten bloody retaliation to restrict black encroachment on areas traditionally defined as white.[37]

GROWING BLACK POLITICAL power combined with fears of racial violence voiced by both black and white civic leaders facilitated a series of negotiated agreements that produced moderate social change while steering the city away from open interracial conflict. The shared faith of white and black participants in elite leadership further tightened this working arrangement. Black elites derived their influence with whites from their ability to mobilize black voters. Yet Hamilton, Dobbs, and other leaders saw themselves as an intelligentsia steering their nonelite supporters away from the types of direct confrontation that might trigger interracial violence or alienate white powerbrokers. Mayor Allen applauded the faith of these African Americans in biracial elite diplomacy, and he linked what he characterized as Atlanta's singular success in addressing its racial problems with the "growing understanding and respect between the moderate upper-middle classes of both races."[38]

Between the 1940s and 1970s, countless behind-the-scenes settlements steered the city away from the disruptive confrontations, negative publicity, and racial violence so feared by both white and black civic leaders. Looking back on his mayoralty, Allen noted the frequency with which he "arranged or refereed meetings of the black and white leaders in the city." From 1947 to 1960, for example, AUL director Hamilton worked closely with Hartsfield and other city officials to coordinate the peaceful transition of formerly all-white housing tracts in southern and western Atlanta into black neighborhoods. Aided by local newspapers' self-censorship, officials calmed white fears arising from this demographic transition. In exchange, Hamilton and other black civic leaders tacitly stomached informal restrictions on the areas open to black expansion, and they begrudgingly accepted the implementation of urban renewal and highway construction programs that relocated blacks and poor whites away from the downtown area. The AUL's campaign to secure new housing opportunities for blacks enriched certain black real estate developers and facilitated the construction of many of the approximately 10,500 housing units made available to blacks in the metropolitan area between 1945 and 1956. While African Americans interpreted their deals with whites as short-term compromises that might ultimately lead to ever decreasing racial restrictions, segregation in housing actually intensified between 1940 and 1970. Between 1956 and 1966 alone, governmental programs forced more than 67,000 residents out of the central city. Only one-third of these migrants, most of whom were black, received any form of relocation aid. The AUL's tacit support for residential segregation violated the National Urban League's official policies and almost triggered the local chapter's expulsion from the parent organization.[39]

The concerns of white and black elites with preventing disorder also helped guide the city peacefully through public school integration in the early 1960s. White Atlantans overwhelmingly supported segregated schools until a federal district court mandated integration in 1959. The court order recast this issue so that it centered on concerns about Atlanta's national image and apprehensions that die-hard segregationists might shut down public schools to defeat integration. An informal alliance representing white businesspersons, white ministers, and white women's clubs coalesced around their shared goal of preventing the violence and vituperation associated with the integration battles in Little Rock and New Orleans. Organized under the banner of OASIS (Organizations Assisting Schools in September), blacks and whites participated in "a law-and-order week" that preceded the first day of integrated classes in 1961. Nine twelfth graders out of a black student population of 45,000 entered white city schools on 30 August with virtually no public resistance. The *Today* show televised live footage of Atlanta's nonviolent transition to desegregated schools while business leaders and public officials shared the overwhelmingly good news with Coca-Cola-sipping northern journalists. The city won the accolades of northern newspapers and President John F. Kennedy for moving calmly, though certainly not boldly, toward racial equality. A year later, school officials permitted only 44 additional black students to transfer to "white" schools.[40]

In 1956, five years before school integration, Dobbs had warned fellow local NAACP members to shun the tactics of Montgomery's black civil rights activists. Led by Atlanta native son Martin Luther King Jr. (as well as Rosa Parks, Jo Ann Robinson, and countless others), Montgomery's activists had successfully forced the integration of municipal buses by engaging in boycotts and nonviolent protests. In Atlanta, Dobbs argued, "We don't want that. It's not the right way." Ignoring Dobbs's advice, a small group of black ministers affiliated with the city's informal biracial coalition tested state segregation laws by seating themselves at the front of a bus in January 1957. The driver contacted his supervisor, who rushed to the scene. White passengers exited the vehicle, which proceeded with its black passengers to the bus depot. Baptist minister William Borders, chagrined that his protest had failed to provoke an arrest or even confusion, broke state law a second time by exiting the bus from the front. Police Chief Jenkins privately warned Borders that public demonstrations "would only heat up an already emotional situation and do great harm"—harm avoidable through biracial cooperation followed by a court decree. Borders agreed, hoping, according to Martin Luther King Sr., that such a resolution "would be a very visible kind of evidence for the young people," who would see "something concrete that coalition politics had achieved" and perhaps recognize "the value of cooperation between antagonists." Jenkins and Borders scheduled a protest and an arrest for the following day, thereby setting the stage for the black minister to challenge in court, successfully as it turned out, the state segregation law. Looking back on the incident, Jenkins reflected, "Everybody heaved a sigh of relief. . . . The whole community had won uninterrupted transportation service, for there took place no boycott as in Montgomery. The Negroes had cooperated with our strategy and received what they desired. Everybody should have been happy."[41]

Many of the black elites who participated in these "negotiated settlements" hid their dissatisfaction with the sluggish pace of what repeatedly proved to be only token integration. Both Benjamin Mays and "Daddy King" noted the feelings of "hate" toward whites occasioned by segregation, racial violence, and white prejudice. In the 1970s, King recounted how as a child he had seen whites "beat black people up, saw 'em lynch them and hang 'em up by a tree. And I promised to hate every white face I ever saw when I got to be a man." Though the Bible and his son's faith in redemptive nonviolence gradually cooled this anger, it was only after his son's assassination that he was finally able to write "*all* hate off for anybody anyway." Daddy King, looking back on what he, like Proctor, characterized as "the Atlanta Plan," argued, "The South had to come out of a very old shell and look at itself, honestly, and with the courage to face up to what it had been. That couldn't be accomplished through polite ceremonies alone. For all the passion that was ignited in Alabama, people seemed relieved that so much of the tension could be released, so much fear among whites and blacks could be overcome."[42]

THE GLACIAL PACE of the progress achieved by 1960s civil right protesters underscores additional flaws in the Atlanta Plan. In March 1960, a year before public school integration, local black college students, energized by the Greensboro sit-ins, organized a series of nonviolent protests against segregation in Atlanta's downtown restaurants and hotels. These public demonstrations broke decisively with interracial traditions centered on unpublicized settlements brokered by elite blacks and whites. The evolution of these maverick protests reveals the powerful hold that the custom of quiet negotiations continued to exercise over race relations in Atlanta. Much like their counterparts in Greensboro and other southern cities, college students, initially led by Lonnie King and Julian Bond, planned a spontaneous, unannounced series of sit-ins at downtown lunch counters. When Atlanta University president and black city school board member Rufus Clement learned of the students' plans, he reportedly warned Bond, "You can't do what the people have done at NC A&T or these other places. You have to do something different. You have to tell people why you are sitting in." Bond later became convinced that what Clement "wanted to do was just have us put off the initial demonstration, believing that if we ever did begin we couldn't be stopped."[43]

Bowing to their elders' requests a second time, the students initially steered clear of local private white businesses and confined their protests to governmental facilities and sites directly involved in interstate commerce. Black elders warned students that "lawlessness" would never achieve what might be gained through political pressure and behind-the-scenes settlements. Throughout their protests, the students communicated closely with Police Chief Herbert Jenkins, informing him of protest locations so that he could avoid dispatching to protest scenes police who were either KKK members or likely to lash out in anger.[44]

With Chamber of Commerce officials ignoring the movement and refusing to meet with protest leaders, the students turned their attention that October to the lunch counters at private downtown department stores, including the venerable Magnolia Room at Rich's. Store owner and longtime chamber official Richard Rich called on police to arrest both the students and Martin Luther King Jr., who had joined their demonstrations. Mayor Hartsfield, working quietly behind closed doors, secured the students' release. White civic leaders immediately faced a second public relations crisis. Judge Oscar Mitchell in neighboring De Kalb County demanded King be transferred to his county's jail on the grounds that his arrest for trespassing violated the terms of a suspended twelve-month sentence, pursuant to a ruling in a misdemeanor traffic case. Hartsfield intervened a second time on King's behalf by persuading Robert Kennedy, whose brother John was nearing the end of his close 1960 presidential contest, to personally persuade Judge Mitchell to rescind his order that King serve a four-month sentence. With Rich and other white merchants digging in their heels, the larger issue of local lunchroom integration remained unresolved.[45]

Continuing protests and the initial success of a black boycott of downtown stores eventually led chamber president Ivan Allen to intervene. He and black lawyer A. T. Walden quietly arranged private meetings among white merchants, black student leaders, and a group of older black ministers and civic leaders. Held at chamber headquarters, the tense negotiations continued for five weeks. The white merchants finally agreed to integrate their lunch counters but only after stipulating that the implementation of their new policy would be delayed until after the desegregation of Atlanta's public schools in September 1961. In exchange, black negotiators agreed to halt the sit-ins. Allen secured promises from white newspaper editors that they would purposefully avoid reporting what transpired during meetings. This approach, Allen believed, would allow negotiators greater freedom during discussions and reduce racial tensions throughout the city.[46]

This compromise deeply embittered many student protesters. When student representative Lonnie King pleaded for an opportunity to consult with fellow students before the agreement became official, a white lawyer for Rich's voiced support for his request. Yet senior black ministers and black college officials pressured the black student into signing the agreement immediately. The timing of the agreement's implementation was carefully orchestrated to avoid visible conflict. African Americans, represented by Walden and Borders, accepted "control programs" establishing strict rules regarding when and how many African Americans would request service at specific lunchrooms during a cooling-off period. As the newspaper community had done so often since the 1906 riot, it voluntarily censored itself once again. At a mass meeting announcing the delayed integration compromise, black students and other audience members repeatedly heckled Walden and Borders. Martin Luther King Sr. attempted to win the confidence of doubting listeners by recounting his decades-long career as a civil rights activist. The crowd loudly seconded one audience member's retort, "And that's what's wrong!" Only Martin Luther King Jr., with a timely and emotional defense of his elders and their efforts, quieted the crowd and convinced audience members to accept the compromise.[47]

The short-term goal of the delay clause, according to Allen, was "to allow time for fever to subside in the white community," presumably to discourage violent interracial confrontations. The delay, Allen also understood, ultimately ensured that the black protesters' own "fires began to burn out," as did the momentum of their movement. With the exception of Rich's and other high-profile department stores, white businesses, according to Allen, had little reason to obey the terms of the truce once "the students were released from jail, the national spotlight swung away from Atlanta, home offices took the heat off their chain-store managers, and picketing ended." In 1963 a study noted that Atlanta had been less effective than other major southern cities in integrating its public schools and accommodations. That year, renewed black demonstrations foundered again under the weight of the black intergenerational divisions and white business resolve that had weakened the 1960–61 protests. By the time the Civil Rights Act was passed in 1964, only thirty white restaurants admitted an integrated clientele.[48]

Although slow to *act*, white civic and business leaders remained ever ready to promote their city as a beacon of racial progress. By 1963, chamber officials, sensitive to growing northern antipathy toward segregation and eager to avoid Birmingham's growing infamy, had openly accepted the inevitability of integration of public accommodations. In May the chamber called on private businesses to desegregate voluntarily in order to "maintain the city's healthy climate." In July, during testimony before a Senate committee, Mayor Allen advocated the passage of a federal bill mandating the integration of public facilities. In a letter to Allen, President John F. Kennedy praised city residents for having "been able to recognize and understand a difficult, complex problem and resolve it—at least partially—in a direct and mature fashion."[49]

AT THE INSISTENCE of his father and other black leaders, Martin Luther King Jr. distanced himself from Atlanta's civil rights struggles after the sit-ins at Rich's. Soon after he lent his support to the deal made between white civic leaders and black protesters, King noted that his hometown was "behind almost every major southern city in its progress toward desegregation." Less than two years later in Birmingham, Public Safety Commissioner Theophilus Eugene "Bull" Connor arrested the minister during the famous 1963 mobilization that King led against segregation in that city. While in solitary confinement, King penned a response to eight white ministers who had accused him of being an extremist and anarchist. In his "Letter from a Birmingham Jail," King summarized the central goal of nonviolent direct action: the creation of "such a tension that a community which has constantly refused to negotiate is forced to confront the issue." Having witnessed firsthand his father's frustrations and the effects of white civic leaders' dilatory tactics in Atlanta and Albany, Georgia, he reflected, "I have almost reached the regrettable conclusion that the Negro's great stumbling block in his stride toward freedom is not the White Citizen's Counciler or the Ku Klux Klanner, but the white moderate, who is more devoted to 'order' than to justice; who prefers a negative peace which is the absence of tension to a positive peace which is the presence of justice ... who constantly advises the Negro to wait for a 'more convenient season.' "[50]

The implications of King's insights extend far beyond Atlanta. Still, his letter speaks eloquently to many of the Atlanta Plan's seamier, long-term repercussions. Throughout the twentieth century, white business leaders possessed overwhelming financial power and influence, and they proved singularly effective in developing a coherent long-term municipal vision centered on the promotion of economic growth and outside investment. Beginning with their alliance with Proctor, commercial leaders created what Martin Luther King Sr. characterized as "a system of very real favors." This economic power and these personal favors convinced King and other black leaders that "any change that affected the city's economic, social or political atmosphere had to come through the businessmen; their point of view was always crucial."[51]

This system of favors and elite dialogue proved efficient for promoting relatively bloodless, short-term, moderate progress. As late as 1960, Atlanta's claims of relative racial progressivism reflected real, though often limited, accomplishments in discouraging antiblack violence, initiating the gradual integration of publicly (but not privately) owned facilities, and peacefully opening up new housing opportunities for African Americans. Atlanta's black elite, while promoting what they perceived as the larger interests of all African Americans, also benefited both as individuals and as a class from the Atlanta Plan. The AUL and its allies, for example, largely determined which black real estate agents and lawyers profited from the 1950s housing programs. The influence that black ministers and civic leaders could exercise over whites increased the power these elite blacks held within their own community. Their access to white politicians and commercial leaders empowered them as brokers both over the spending of public funds and the distribution of private opportunities among African Americans. This influence with white civic leaders also afforded black elites a key role in establishing and prioritizing the black community's public policy agenda. The problem with this system, Martin Luther King Sr. came to understand, was its potential for enmeshing black elites in a dependent, patron-client relationship with whites. "Like all favors," those extended by the city's civic-commercial elite could be "taken away more quickly than they had been offered, they were based in no genuine sense of mutual respect, and they had nothing to do with *rights*."[52]

In comparison with the tactics used in other southern cities, Atlanta's direct-action campaigns repeatedly failed to unite the larger black community or sustain the momentum of individual victories. The regime's efficiency in solving short-term problems and its openness to moderate change discouraged black leaders from undertaking the burdensome and uncertain work of building *intraracial* coalitions across residential and class lines. Behind-the-scenes compromises discouraged the open expressions of white racist hatred and white brutality that united blacks in other cities. The relative absence of direct racial confrontations allowed white leaders to claim that African Americans were comfortable with the status quo. The lack of law-and-order crises forestalled the intervention of federal and state courts. Their mandates would probably have secured, as they did in many other southern cities, more rapid results and higher levels of public school and residential integration.[53]

Instead, according to Martin Luther King Sr., the interracial regime aggravated intraracial generational and class cleavages during the 1960s. "Favors," he later recalled, "were now seen by young people as more evidence that Atlanta's more fortunate Negroes had a special deal going with whites that excluded the black masses in favor of a black elite." Recognizing these inherent weaknesses in the Atlanta Plan, Martin Luther King Jr. announced in September 1967 his interest in initiating a series of direct-action protests in the city whose "false image," he believed, masked gross racial and economic injustices. The assassination of King in 1968 derailed that plan.[54]

AS POLITICAL SCIENTIST Clarence Stone has demonstrated, the white business community's selective payoffs to individual African Americans and black groups increased as black political influence accelerated in the 1960s and 1970s. During this period, a highly organized and increasingly racially integrated business elite greased the wheels and mobilized the resources necessary to address short-term crises and take advantage of new commercial opportunities. The cooperative efforts of business leaders and elite African Americans played a key role in many of Atlanta's most noted triumphs between the 1970s and late 1990s, including the passage of the referendum authorizing its Metropolitan Atlanta Rapid Transit Authority subway system, the construction of Hartsfield International Airport, and the successful campaign for securing the 1996 Olympics.[55]

Together, Maynard Jackson, the grandson of First Church Deacon John Wesley Dobbs, and First Church member Andrew Young monopolized Atlanta's mayoralty for twenty years. Jackson's election in 1972 as Atlanta's first black mayor reflected growing white flight to the suburbs and a steadily climbing number of registered black voters during the late 1960s and early

1970s. The white business community originally expressed grave doubts regarding Jackson's willingness to promote its agenda. Yet Jackson's dreams of economic development and white business leaders' desire for governmental influence ultimately brought the mayor and the business community together in an uneasy alliance. The mayor's Minority Business Enterprise program primarily benefited middle- and upper-class African Americans who secured new employment and commercial opportunities as the proportion of city expenditures going to black businesses rose from 2 to 33 percent. Jackson often bragged that his affirmative action programs created approximately twenty-five new black millionaires.[56]

According to Ronald Bayor, Andrew Young cooperated more closely with white business interests than Jackson did, and Young's pursuit of business-centered goals diverted his attention away from the problems associated with inner-city poverty. In the 1980s and 1990s, the city's business and political leaders embraced the vision Young and Jackson held of Atlanta as an international city. In 1984 alone, foreign investors poured more than $3 billion into the economy. At the beginning of the 1990s, greater metropolitan Atlanta far outpaced the rest of the nation in business expansion and the creation of new jobs, but few of these opportunities benefited the black urban poor.[57]

The 1973 resolution of a school integration struggle underscores the role of the negotiated-settlement approach in limiting racial change and social justice, even after African Americans came to dominate public office. In 1973, public school officials faced the strong possibility of court-ordered busing to remedy the school system's slow progress in achieving substantive desegregation. Encouraged by a federal judge to reach an out-of-court settlement, the NAACP and the business-controlled Action Forum forged an agreement mandating increased black representation in administrative positions in lieu of requiring wide-scale involuntary student busing. Although leading black and white civic leaders endorsed this deal, representatives of the city's black working class censured black negotiators for abandoning integration ideals in exchange for economic guarantees benefiting only a small elite. The agreement so angered the NAACP's national leadership that it mandated the resignation of key black negotiator and local branch president Lonnie King. King's participation in this deal testifies to the powerful pressures exerted on blacks to cooperate with white business interests. Only thirteen years earlier, as a key architect of the 1960 sit-ins, King had blanched at the desegregation agreement reached between black ministers and chamber representatives.[58]

By the 1980s, the costs of racial peace through negotiated, biracial settlements included Atlanta's dubious distinctions of having America's highest residential segregation index and the most segregated schools of any southern city. With the city's high poverty levels exacerbated by black and white flight to the suburbs and waning federal support for social programs, Atlanta entered the 1990s with more than one-third of all black households and one-half of all black children living in poverty. Only four major U.S. cities had poverty rates exceeding Atlanta's. The fact that Atlanta is considered the "mecca of the black middle class" as well as one of the country's most impoverished and segregated cities represents what scholars often characterize as the "Atlanta Paradox."[59]

Post–World War II interracial cooperation ensured the city's relatively peaceful integration and minimized open racial conflict in an era of dramatic social change. Yet the coalition's singular success in ameliorating the worst vestiges of racial injustice and its overweening focus on maintaining order discouraged black political mobilization across class lines. Little lasting national pressure was exerted on business leaders to address Atlanta's glaring economic inequalities, and black-white compromises inordinately benefited their elite negotiators' narrow class interests. What has been missing in postwar Atlanta is a permanent public interest organization or union that might challenge the traditional business-dominated regime and prod Atlantans to confront their human problems with the same ingenuity and enthusiasm that they have applied to public relations campaigns and commercial growth initiatives.[60]

Between the 1930s and the 1980s, Atlanta lacked what the postriot NU provided before it was silenced by the machinations of the CC and the AUL— that is, an organization whose democratic vision transcends the lines of class and geographical isolation, that provides a voice for the city's marginalized and dispossessed, and that is capable of coordinating a highly fragmented city to promote lasting economic and social justice.

DURING THE 1960S, Andrew Young, like so many other Atlanta-based civil rights activists of his generation, openly criticized the claims of local white civic leaders that their city represented a beacon of racial peace and justice. Near that decade's end, Young, as executive vice-president of Martin Luther King Jr.'s Southern Christian Leadership Conference, played a leading role in organizing the Poor People's Campaign, a movement that sought to compel Americans to acknowledge and address their nation's lingering problems of poverty and economic inequality. Now was the time, King argued, for the country to come to terms with the "question of whether an edifice which produces beggars must be restructured and refurbished." During the 1970s and 1980s, however, Andrew Young and many other erstwhile protesters increasingly rejected direct confrontation, embracing instead Atlanta's lasting tradition of addressing social problems through elite biracial cooperation.[61]

In the 1990s, as the city pursued its Olympic dreams, Young touted this Atlanta Plan as a model for the entire world. In the course of selling the advantages of Atlanta as a host city to the International Olympic Committee, Young and Maynard Jackson joined white lawyer Billy Payne in publicizing this proud message: "Atlanta's global contribution is clearly in the area of human rights and the ability of people from many divergent backgrounds to live together in harmony." The Olympic Games, once snared, created a financial windfall for the real estate developers and construction firms named to complete associated building projects valued at more than $650 million. As tourists inundated the city and its property values skyrocketed, hotel interests and middle-class homeowners similarly benefited. An Olympics-related investment campaign encouraged more than eighteen national and international firms to locate operations in Atlanta, enriching the city by an estimated $130 million. The economic engine associated with the Olympics also provided Atlantans with more than 30,000 short-term, low-skilled jobs and helped the city rake in hundreds of millions of dollars in revitalization grants. Nevertheless, the impact of the games on the working class and the urban poor proved to be mixed at best. In the process of redeveloping the city, the Corporation for Olympic Development in Atlanta (CODA), a public-private partnership, privatized and downscaled many of the city's public housing units and forced thousands of impoverished residents to seek new homes. Though they were only partially compensated for their losses, more than 3,400 additional families had to abandon substandard residences targeted for destruction.[62]

In the early 1990s, the Atlanta Project, founded by former president and ex-governor Jimmy Carter, sought to unite public officials and private citizens behind a local war on poverty. Dividing the city into clusters, the organization sponsored neighborhood and community cultural programs and implemented a major public health campaign aimed primarily at poor children. The Atlanta Project also provided disadvantaged youth with educational programs ranging from music lessons to SAT preparation courses. It directed community cleanup programs and dramatically reduced the red tape and paperwork that local and federal social service agencies required. Carter's sense of mission and his national prominence lent the Atlanta Project credibility and helped it raise approximately $34 million in donations from local and national foundations as well as Atlanta-based corporations.[63]

Despite its vast resources, the organization never succeeded in establishing the communication networks, grassroots support, and neighborhood linkages that made the NU so effective. As executive director, white civic leader Dan Sweat expressed little interest in empowering existing neighborhood organizations, and he communicated infrequently with neighborhood leaders. Sweat's top-down approach and imperious leadership style alienated community organizers, triggered charges of racism, and prevented the parent organization from effectively coordinating neighborhood activities. In 1995, four of the twenty original clusters withdrew from the organization. Their departure marked the beginning of the Atlanta Project's gradual disintegration.[64]

Despite their limitations, Carter's campaign and CODA's building programs helped sustain a new generation of black-led neighborhood revitalization organizations. In 1991, Hattie Dorsey founded the Atlanta Neighborhood Development Partnership (ANDP). Backed from its inception by the United Way and local civic leaders, the ANDP has played a crucial role in coordinating and facilitating the efforts of local, grassroots redevelopment organizations. In the early 1990s, ANDP and CODA helped finance the Historic District Development Corporation (HDDC) in its efforts to redevelop a residential district that includes the Martin Luther King Jr. National Historic Site and the eastern reaches of historic Auburn Avenue. The HDDC has successfully transformed what were once decaying residential blocks into highly desirable housing tracts without displacing existing residents. The organization promotes the participation of residents in neighborhood decision making, and its districts maintain an even balance of lower-, moderate-, and middle-income homeowners. The HDDC provides disadvantaged neighbors with housing and social service assistance as well as referrals to private and public agencies. It sponsors a monthly "Coffee on the Corner" fundraiser to foster a sense of community and enhance residents' awareness of local issues.[65]

In 1974, elderly residents of Reynoldstown, located east of the city, revived the Reynoldstown Civic Improvement League, originally founded in the 1950s as a voting rights and youth development organization. In the 1970s and 1980s, the resurrected league reestablished a sense of community in the area's rapidly deteriorating neighborhoods and pressured city officials into providing the district with enhanced police protection, bus service, and street and traffic lights. In 1989, the league created a separate entity, the

Reynoldstown Revitalization Corporation (RRC), to qualify for public and private monies and attract a new generation of homeowners. Since then, the RRC has refurbished more than 270 decaying houses and built additional structures to attract new residents. Like the HDDC, both the RRC and the Reynoldstown Civic Improvement League welcome into their community families of all ethnicities, religions, and economic backgrounds. The RRC requires potential homeowners to make a commitment to participate in community meetings and redevelopment programs. Among other activities, the RRC has constructed a new park. It also arranges cleanup campaigns, sponsors educational and antidrug programs for the disadvantaged, and oversees an annual community fair that features arts and crafts and musical performances by blues and gospel artists.[66]

These and similar neighborhood initiatives simultaneously draw on many of Atlanta's finest reform legacies and elude many of the most troubling ghosts of the city's past. Admittedly, Atlanta's neighborhood redevelopment programs have targeted only a tiny portion of the city's disadvantaged residents and are by their nature limited in geographic scope. On their own, such programs cannot directly confront the structural inequalities underlying Atlanta's and America's vast social divisions. Nor can they address the needs of Atlanta's poor residents for enhanced public education opportunities, steady jobs that pay a living wage, and basic health care services. Yet the support of the United Way and corporate foundations for progressive initiatives such as the RRC and the HDDC demonstrates the vital role that commercial and civic leaders can play in promoting redevelopment programs that lessen rather than increase the segregation of races and social classes. The goal of these organizations to encourage the maximum participation of diverse groups in neighborhood decisions has the potential to help forge a new model of biracial cooperation—one that promotes inclusion and true dialogue rather than exclusion and the silencing of alternative voices. Subsidized housing programs open new avenues of wealth building among at least a sliver of the working-poor and lower-middle-class populations of both races.

AS THE OPENING day of the Olympics drew near, Young continued to turn a blind eye to the Atlanta Plan's unseemly underside. Highlighting Mayor Jackson's affirmative action programs and the city's long partnership between black elites and white businesspersons, he praised Atlanta's "fairness formula for ensuring that the benefits of development were disseminated throughout the various communities that made up the city."[67] Young predicted that Atlanta's heightened international visibility had the potential to guarantee the city "a special role in the plan of God" as the one place where people had learned to "live together in spite of their differences." "In today's world of ethnic violence and bloodshed," he insisted, "the message Atlanta could send to the multitude who will view some part of the Olympiad on television is the Olympic vision of all humankind living together in peace and prosperity with justice."[68]

This First Church parishioner's optimistic faith in his city's national and global promise hearkened back to Henry Proctor's long-held confidence in the Atlanta Plan and its potential for transforming the South into "the garden spot of the nation and the paradise of the races." "It requires," Proctor had waxed, "no prophet to stand on her hills and see the coming kingdom of interracial cooperation. The hills once red with the blood of strife will glow with a new light."[69]

True to both their Puritan predecessors and a black prophetic tradition, Proctor and Young held visions of Atlanta and America as cities upon a hill that were as much jeremiads of lost potential as they were celebrations of past accomplishments. The former mayor and United Nations ambassador decried empty materialism, laissez-faire capitalism's competitive excesses, a nation's lost faith, racism's tragic legacies, and America's mushrooming prison populations. "Everything I know," Young ultimately reassured audiences, "convinces me that the struggle to eliminate racism, war, and poverty is a burden, but in America, the most productive society in human history, it is an easy burden if we undertake it together."[70]

Yet this burden *has* proved too heavy for postriot Atlanta, a city haunted by the inescapable ghosts of its past and shortchanged by its powerbrokers' unimaginative visions for its future. In the riot's immediate aftermath and then again during the civil rights era, black and white leaders constructed a glistening facade of racial peace that veiled the city's lingering injustices. In turn, Atlanta's public relations triumph has played a crucial role in shaping the racial views of many Americans. Echoing Proctor's and white civic leaders' public interpretations of the riot and its aftermath, many national commentators have long depicted elite cooperation across the color line as the surest catalyst for social and racial justice. So, too, have they condemned marginalized blacks and whites as the ultimate despoilers of law and order. Yet, if Atlanta's twentieth-century history offers one hope, it is the potential role that highly localized movements—including the city's recent community-building efforts—can play in helping reshape the racial assumptions and social realities of a city and a nation.

CONCLUSION

The Lessons of a Riot

~

I N 1957, AT AGE EIGHTY-NINE, W. E. B. Du Bois published the first volume of the *Black Flame* trilogy, a fictional work he envisioned as completing the "cycle of history which has for a half century engaged my thought, research and action." Du Bois's sweeping narrative chronicles African American history from the end of Reconstruction to 1954, the year of the landmark Supreme Court decision in *Brown v. the Board of Education of Topeka, Kansas*. Against a sprawling tableau, the narrator traces the 1906 riot experiences and gradual political awakening of Manuel Mansart. This character comes of age in turn-of-the-century Georgia while pursuing a career in education that culminates in his thirty-three year tenure as president of the fictive Colored State College, located in Macon. Though lacking the artistry of Du Bois's best writing, this final undertaking succeeds masterfully as a profound meditation on many of the central questions regarding historical inevitability with which Du Bois grappled throughout his life. How can individuals and larger groups, particularly African Americans, preserve their humanity and achieve full self-consciousness in the face of immense historical forces such as white racism and global capitalism? Or, as Du Bois puts it, in struggles against injustice and unbridled power, "How shall Integrity face Oppression? What shall Honesty do in the face of Deception, Decency in the face of Insult, Self-Defense before Blows? . . . What shall Virtue do to meet Brute Force?"[1]

As in Du Bois's own life, the 1906 riot serves as a key turning point in the lives of his diverse historical and fictive characters. He links its violence with social tensions arising from escalating racist vituperations and the 1905 emergence of "a fight between capitalists and laborers on levels far higher . . . than ever before." White business leaders endorsed Hoke Smith's racist campaign in an attempt to deflect their opponents' attention away from larger political and economic inequalities. Even after lurid newspaper stories inflamed white anger to a fever pitch, white civic leaders might have prevented the riot's outbreak. Aware of the likelihood of violence, they nevertheless ignored "the repeated pleas of quiet Negro well-to-do communities to send police protection," and they allowed the "storm to gather and burst without protest or real action."[2]

Much as had been the case with Du Bois himself, many of his African American characters become overwhelmed with "dark clouds of doubt" following the riot and wonder how God could "permit or ignore this Atlanta horror."[3] For central character Manuel Mansart, the riot serves as a formative event that helps define his racial identity and future goals. Unwilling any longer to "cajole and coax," "crawl and beg," the black school principal travels northward seeking a job in Chicago, where he senses "a sort of free expression of manhood in the air, despite poverty and crime, which a Negro just from Atlanta could drink in like a draft of fresh air." Dismayed by the stiff job competition he finds there, Mansart returns to Atlanta, acutely conscious of his approaching middle age, and briefly contemplates a career in commerce before he recoils from the greediness of the city's leading black businessmen.[4]

Only at the end of the first volume does Mansart finally glimpse through Atlanta's "gloomy veil . . . a gleam of light, still tinged with the blood of the riot" when he senses an opportunity to secure appointment to the soon-to-be vacant position of black public school supervisor. "After all this talk of interracial cooperation," he would now "demand" a high school, additional elementary schools, and increased power for the supervisor's position.[5] Recounting the story of his baptism in the blood of his lynched father, Mansart explains to his family that the riot has helped him finally comprehend what his grandmother meant when she christened him the "Black Flame," after his birth in 1876. In the face of white oppression, Mansart admits, "The flame within me nearly died. I stooped and crawled. The prison bars bent my soul and pressed it in. . . . I was freed and yet I did not understand [I was free] until this riot, this horror of hate and death which swept over us. Now I live. Now I stand up. I am that Black Flame in which my grandmother

W. E. B. Du Bois, ca. 1950s. In 1957, at age eighty-nine, he published the first volume of the *Black Flame* trilogy. (Special Collections and Archives, W. E. B. Du Bois Library, University of Massachusetts Amherst)

believed and on whose blood-stained body she swore. I am the Black Flame, but I burn for cleaning, not destroying. Therefore, I burn slow . . . for the world needs burning." Manuel now embraces a life of dogged but careful resistance as he attempts to cleanse society of the blemish of racial injustice. First as Atlanta's top black public school administrator and then as the Colored State College president, he quietly plots to improve black public education.[6]

Much as he emphasizes the contingent nature of the outbreak of the riot, Du Bois concludes the trilogy with an affirmation of the power of both determined collective action and individual human integrity in resisting the ravages of racial violence, white prejudice, and gross economic exploitation. Throughout the trilogy, naked economic exploitation and implacable white racism ruin and destroy the lives of many of Mansart's close friends and relatives. Mansart manages to endure these and other tragedies as the embers of his life burn hotter in service to his race and larger humanity. His world travels, friendships, and second wife ultimately convince Mansart that the African American struggle against racism is deeply intertwined with broader struggles for economic and social justice both in America and abroad.

Facing east on his deathbed, Mansart broods over the fate of his grand-child and the seeming inevitability of a nuclear holocaust. His wife, Jean, ever confident of the latent possibilities of human agency, comforts her husband, who serenely passes away while dreaming of "the golden domes of Moscow," "China's millions lifting the soil of the nation," and "birds sing-ing" throughout Asia, while Ho Chi Minh celebrates "peace on earth."[7] Mansart's final vision of the world's future now seems naively romantic, just as his faith in Chinese and Soviet Communism appears misguided. Du Bois similarly simplifies the complexities of white supremacist thought by por-traying the riot as the result of a fully conscious and deliberate conspiracy among white businessmen to fan the flames of racist hatred so as to divert the attention of white farmers and white workers away from their brutal class exploitation.

YET, ON A deeper level, the ultimate questions of historical inevitability and contingency that Du Bois weaves into the *Black Flame* are the precise ques-tions ultimately posed by the riot and its repercussions. As it is in fiction, so it was for Du Bois and countless other Americans whose lives were nearly overwhelmed by the heavy burdens of southern history and the destructive forces of white racism. The sheer viciousness of Atlanta's mob, its power reinforced by an armed militia, shattered the assumptions of fundamental white rationality underlying both Booker T. Washington's trusting policy of stoic accommodation and Du Bois's militant vision of manly resistance. In the end, Charles T. Hopkins's paternalism and his conservative vision of law and order trumped any initial claims that his interracial movement sought to promote fundamental racial justice. In a similar fashion, the humani-tarian impulses of an aging William Northen ultimately sagged under the weight of his idyllic memories of slavery and his own fantasies of violent domination and chivalric virility. White demands for black submission after the riot led both to Jesse Max Barber's forced expulsion from Atlanta and to demeaning compromises for those who remained. Vicious white stereotypes of black immorality pressured even the radically egalitarian and democratic NU into narrowing the breadth of its vision of black respectability so that it excluded many working-class blacks. White financial support for more elit-ist and accommodative black institutions such as First Church and the Urban League still further undermined the NU's efforts to unite African Americans across class lines.

Yet in the context of what might otherwise appear overwhelming histori-cal and ideological forces, what is ultimately striking both in Mansart's life and in the lives of so many of the historical actors caught up in the riot's maelstrom are the potentially far-reaching effects of words, decisions, and actions—even those that initially appear trivial, insignificant, or quixotic. Far from inevitable, the riot itself might have been avoided had politicians and newspaper editors abandoned their racist summonses to arms or had police, public officials, and civic leaders mobilized quickly and forcibly to quell the initial attacks. Black resistance against attempted white incursions, first into Dark Town and then into Brownsville, forced local whites to seek dialogue with African Americans. This defensive violence also became an enduring source of black racial pride and solidarity throughout the twentieth century. These black counterattacks, rooted in long-standing neighborhood social bonds, convinced some national white leaders, including Oswald Garrison Villard, that a race war might consume the entire South unless African Americans were provided with a nonviolent means for battling racial injustice through the NAACP.

As captive to white supremacy and past traditions as the movements of Northen and Hopkins ultimately proved to be, the efforts of these men also helped lay the foundations for the more forward-looking CIC, largely, as it turned out, because of Proctor's dauntless efforts to keep the memories of interracial cooperation alive. Proctor's carefully constructed writings and speeches helped ensure the success of a fund-raising campaign aimed at enlarging his church's local influence. Revealing the symbiotic relationship between local and national struggles, Proctor's riot narrative, appropriated first by Washington and then by Ray Stannard Baker, helped shape the vision of southern race relations that attained national preeminence in the riot's wake and continues to influence America's racial discourse.

During and after the riot, the stakes of individual and collective decisions assumed a heightened drama in Atlanta. Whites and blacks recognized that actions taken or not taken might constitute the difference between an individual's life or death, a neighborhood's survival or destruction, a race's progress or retrogression, and a city's continued prosperity or its downward spiral. Many black and white commentators similarly recognized the potential impact of national struggles over the meaning of an event that took place at a seminal moment in the cultural politics of race.

In the end, however, the significance of the riot stems less from its distinctiveness than from the fact that it embodied the fears and conflicts that pulsated throughout Atlanta and the larger nation during much of the twentieth century. Reports of rapes by black men and the armed defense of black communities tapped into whites' greatest fears of a racist social order precipitously overturned. For African Americans, the destructive mob and militia attacks they confronted that weekend marked an escalation of (rather than a departure from) the brutality and racism that they encountered daily in Atlanta's public spaces. Long-standing white hatreds and economic jealousies energized both the mob's attack on black businesses and the white agitators' vicious 1906 antiblack crusade. The horror and terror that blacks experienced that night—as innocent victims were slaughtered, bodies maimed, and lives destroyed—were experienced by countless blacks throughout Jim Crow America.

This riot's ultimate lesson, then, is not that history is the product of dramatic individual events but, rather, that history results from the accumulation of an infinite number of interconnected local and national decisions made by a welter of individuals and groups. During and after the riot, ideologies and social identities faced constant modification and renegotiation—their gradual evolution punctuated by a series of dramatic and unpredictable ruptures. In riot-associated struggles, microscopic neighborhood decisions and local utterances assumed an unforeseeable national significance. The riot haunted the imaginations of whites and blacks for nearly a century. Still, its meanings and legacies were reshaped by countless other social transformations: rising black radicalism during World Wars I and II, growing black political power after 1946, and a heightened desire among white businessmen to create a "progressive" and "orderly" city whose racial mores flowed with a national and international mainstream. The riot is ultimately significant not because it stood outside history but precisely because its events were intricately intertwined with the everyday struggles and fears of so many early twentieth-century blacks and whites.

The riot's legacies cast a long shadow over local and national race relations throughout the American Century. The violence of the massacre, postriot white intimidation, and white elite offers of selective incentives to particular black groups worked together between 1906 and 1907 to squelch New Black Men's rising militancy and to crush Georgia's burgeoning black civil rights movements. Public remembrances positing black and white elites as Atlanta's sole saviors undermined city-based movements aimed at mobilizing African Americans across class lines. White and black civic leaders' shared fears of disorder helped bolster segregation locally during the Progressive Era before severely limiting the pace and degree of integration following World War II. Atlanta's biracial traditions hushed the white racist hatreds of the city's past, but only at the cost of veiling promising black visions of America's future.

NOTES

LAC: Living Atlanta Collection, Library and Archives, James G. Kenan Research Center, Atlanta History Center, Atlanta, Ga.

LC: Manuscript Division, Library of Congress, Washington, D.C.

NAACP: *Papers of the NAACP* (Frederick, Md.: University Publications of America, 1981)

NU: Neighborhood Union Collection, Archives and Special Collections, Robert W. Woodruff Library, Atlanta University Center, Atlanta, Ga.

NYA: *New York Age*

NYT: *New York Times*

NYW: *New York World*

OCB: Office of Church Building of the United Church Board for Homeland Ministries Archives (Atlanta, Georgia, First), Amistad Research Center, Tilton Hall, Tulane University, New Orleans, La.

OGV: Oswald Garrison Villard Papers, Houghton Library, Harvard University, Cambridge, Mass.

Papers of BTW: *Papers of Booker T. Washington* (Washington, D.C.: Library of Congress, Photoduplication Service, 1981)

Proctor Papers: Henry Hugh and Adeline L. Proctor (Davis) Papers, Amistad Research Center, Tilton Hall, Tulane University, New Orleans, La.

RSB: Ray Stannard Baker Papers (microfilm), Manuscript Division, Library of Congress, Washington, D.C.

WJN: Gov. William J. Northen Papers, Georgia Archives and History Division, Morrow

INTRODUCTION

1   Prather, "We Have Taken a City"; Gilmore, "Murder, Memory, and the Flight of the Incubus."

   For three excellent recent studies of the 1906 race riot that examine it primarily as a culminating local event rather than a new beginning in both Atlanta's and America's history, see Mixon, *Atlanta Riot*; Dorsey, *To Build Our Lives Together*; and Bauerlein, *Negrophobia*.

2   For an insightful discussion of this discourse and its evolution, see Bederman, *Manliness and Civilization*, 20–22.

3   A number of scholars have capably analyzed the effects of the 1906 riot on American racial debates. My book builds on these studies in significant ways by examining the connections between local and national debates, by underscoring the varied interactions among diverse groups, and by providing the first detailed gender analyses of Du Bois's and Washington's ideologies and postriot interactions. For the best of the studies of postriot social and cultural struggles, see Capeci and Knight, "Reckoning with Violence" and "W. E. B. Du Bois's Southern Front"; Harlan, *Wizard of Tuskegee*, 295–304; Lewis, *Biography of a Race*, 343–85; Litwack, *Trouble in Mind*, 319–22; and Shapiro, *White Violence and Black Response*, 96–103, 129–41.

4   Egerton, *Speak Now against the Day*, 48.

5   Janken, *White*, iii–20; Mitchell, *Gone with the Wind*, 54–56, 777–89; Pyron, *Southern Daughter*, 31–32; King with Riley, *Daddy King*, 85; Garrow, *Bearing the Cross*, 577.

6 Painter, *Southern History across the Color Line*, 2–3; Higginbotham, "African-American Women's History," 13–18; Brown, " 'What Has Happened Here,' " 41–48; Gilmore, *Gender and Jim Crow*; Ayers, *Promise of the New South*, vi–x; Bender, "Wholes and Parts."

7 Bauerlein, *Negrophobia*, 279–80; Capeci and Knight, "Reckoning with Violence"; Lewis, *Biography of a Race*, 365–66.

8 Holt, "Marking," 8.

9 Fields, "Ideology and Race"; Kolchin, "Whiteness Studies."

10 Woodward, *Thinking Back*, 32–36; Woodward, *Tom Watson*, 220–22, 370–80.

11 Fields, "Ideology and Race," 144 (quotation); Woodward, *Thinking Back*, 33.

12 Williamson, *Crucible of Race*, 220–21; Bauerlein, *Negrophobia*, 261.

13 A rich and rapidly growing scholarship has influenced my analyses of postriot discursive and social struggles. Drawing on this research, I emphasize the potential instability of social identities, the complex interactions among diverse social identity claims, the role of discursive and social relations in structuring these interactions, and the connections and ruptures between local and national identity struggles. The following have been especially useful in my analysis: Bederman, *Manliness and Civilization*, 23–31; Hunter, *To 'Joy My Freedom*; Kelley, *Race Rebels*; Feimster, " 'Ladies and Lynching,' " 8–13, 97–103; MacLean, "Leo Frank Case Reconsidered"; Gilmore, *Gender and Jim Crow*; Simon, *Fabric of Defeat*; Kantrowitz, *Ben Tillman*; Roediger, *Wages of Whiteness*; Hall, " 'Mind That Burns in Each Body' "; Hall, "Private Eyes, Public Women"; Hall, *Revolt against Chivalry*; Brown, "Negotiating and Transforming the Public Sphere"; Dailey, *Before Jim Crow*; Hewitt, *Southern Discomfort*; and Judson, "Building the 'New South' City."

14 Higginbotham, *Righteous Discontent*, 14–15, 185–229; Gaines, *Uplifting the Race*; Ferguson, *Black Politics*, 19–45.

15 White, *Man Called White*, 11–12; Janken, *White*, 15.

16 For a nice overview of whiteness studies, a scholarship that highlights whites' deployment of racial identity claims, see Kolchin, "Whiteness Studies." For a pioneering work in this area, see Roediger, *Wages of Whiteness*.

17 Hopkins quoted in Baker, *Following the Color Line*, 21.

18 Higginbotham's notion of a politics of respectability is one of the most brilliant and influential recent insights into African American history. Her analysis of this phenomenon, in *Righteous Discontent*, focuses primarily on its cultural and social origins rather than its dynamic evolution in relation to changing class relationships within institutions. Gaines's *Uplifting the Race* offers an illuminating discussion of the cultural and ideological manifestations of black elite notions of propriety. Ferguson's brilliant discussion of Atlanta's politics of respectability, in *Black Politics*, stresses the similarities among the city's black elites. White's *Too Heavy a Load* provides an insightful discussion of elitist notions of respectability among black clubwomen.

19 A growing number of political scientists and sociologists are turning their attention to the role of organizational structures in promoting or discouraging feelings of commitment, trust, and empathy. Elegant introductions to this scholarship include Ostrom, "Behavioral Approach," and Polletta, *Freedom Is an Endless Meeting*, 1–5, 209–10.

20 Higginbotham, "African-American Women's History," 18; Griffin, Clark, and Sandberg, "Narrative and Event," 24–25.

21 Chafe's *Civilities and Civil Rights* remains the most influential study of the potential social

control functions of white civility. In contrast to Chafe, historians of the Progressive Era have generally highlighted the potential role of biracialism in offering African Americans additional social resources and undermining white supremacy. Hahn's *Nation under Our Feet* has noted that this perspective inherently privileges the ideals of "inclusion and assimilation" over "separatism and community development . . . [and] protonationalism" (6). The historiography on biracial cooperation has also been influenced by more thoughtful approaches than those that Hahn criticizes, often revealing stunning insights. For an elegant exploration of the potential of late nineteenth-century interracial alliances among white yeoman farmers and freedmen, see Fields, "Ideology and Race," 166–68. On black women as "diplomats" who deployed interracial cooperation to enhance African Americans' access to social and governmental resources, see Gilmore, *Gender and Jim Crow*, 177–202. For a masterful study of how shared class concerns encouraged interracial alliances among black and white coal miners, see Kelly, *Race, Class, and Power*. In a brief postscript, Kelly argues that white elites disingenuously deployed the 1906 riot to posit themselves as the southern guardians of racial progressivism (203–7). I share Kelly's doubts regarding the validity of these claims among white elites, but I highlight the role that struggles over the riot's meaning played in convincing many Americans that interracial cooperation among elites offered the surest solution to the race problem.

22 Both Ferguson's dazzling *Black Politics* and my own book highlight the interconnections between black Atlantans' intraracial and interracial political and social struggles. My narrative begins much earlier than hers, it more intensively highlights black and white interactions, and it pays closer attention to the interrelationships among a wider range of social groups on a larger number of issues. Ferguson's focus on a relatively small number of black decision makers during the New Deal encourages her to underscore black elites' ideological unity during this period and to trace black Atlantans' entry into the public realm to the 1930s and 1940s. I argue that riot-associated developments played a key role in laying the foundations of biracialism in the city. For a discussion of Atlanta's interracial traditions emphasizing their positive accomplishments, see Pomerantz, *Where Peachtree Meets*. For an account of the rise of Atlanta's social inequalities focusing almost exclusively on race (rather than class and gender), see Bayor, *Race and the Shaping*.

CHAPTER 1

1 Doyle, *New Men*, 34; Rutheiser, *Imagineering Atlanta*, 15–19; Deaton, "Atlanta during the Progressive Era," 35; Atlanta Chamber of Commerce, *Annual Report* (1905), 7–8, 43; Dray, *At the Hands*, 162–64. In his very brief analysis of the Atlanta riot's origins, Dray draws on my dissertation and the scholarship of others to similarly highlight white fears of white women and black men adrift from traditional social controls.

2 U.S. Bureau of the Census, *Thirteenth Census*, 9:236–37 (tab. 3); Doyle, *New Men*, 44, 103.

3 Martin, *Atlanta and Its Builders*, 2:120, 115 (quotations); Rutheiser, *Imagineering Atlanta*, 19–30.

4 Martin, *Atlanta and Its Builders*, 2:519 (first quotation); Frith, "Manger of the Movement," 29 (second quotation); Brundage, *Lynching in the New South*, 270–74.

5 Jacobs, *Step Down, Dr. Jacobs*, 141; Doyle, *New Men*, 103, 143, 190–99; Pendergrast, *For*

God, Country, and Coca-Cola, 97–99; Atlanta Chamber of Commerce, *Annual Report* (1906), 5.

6   Wrigley, "Triumph of Provincialism," 30; Kuhn, *Contesting the New South Order*, 36; Ayers, *Promise of the New South*, 10–14, 86–88.

7   Du Bois, *Souls of Black Folk*, 87 (quotation); Baker, *Following the Color Line*, 94, 96; Dittmer, *Black Georgia*, 23.

8   Kuhn, " 'Full History of the Strike,' " 42; Hahn, *Roots of Southern Populism*, 139–86; Flamming, *Creating the Modern South*, 15–75; Bryant, *How Curious a Land*, 147–65; Wrigley, "Triumph of Provincialism," 34.

9   Du Bois, *Souls of Black Folk*, 97; Dittmer, *Black Georgia*, 23–26.

10 Du Bois, *Souls of Black Folk*, 85 (quotation); Brundage, *Lynching in the New South*, 108–13; Wrigley, "Triumph of Provincialism," 85–97; Dittmer, *Black Georgia*, 131–40.

11 Hunter, "Household Workers in the Making," 293–95 (tab. 1); Maclachlan, "Women's Work," 376 (tab. A.1); U.S. Bureau of the Census, *Occupations at the Twelfth Census*, 486–88 (tab. 43). Because the 1890 census did not distinguish between African Americans and other people of color, the number of African Americans in Atlanta in this year can be only roughly estimated.

12 U.S. Bureau of the Census, *Occupations at the Twelfth Census*, 486–88 (tab. 43).

13 Jones, *Labor of Love*, 113–14; Hunter, *To 'Joy My Freedom*, 71–73; Dorsey, *To Build Our Lives Together*, 49–51, 108–9, 116–17.

14 Ayers, *Promise of the New South*, 68–69; Jones, *Labor of Love*, 124–25; Brundage, *Lynching in the New South*, 113–14.

15 Henderson, *Atlanta Life Insurance Company*, 21–25; Ellis, "Southern Negro as Property Owner," 431.

16 Du Bois, *Souls of Black Folk*, 58 (quotation); Torrence, *Story of John Hope*, 139–40; *Chicago Defender*, 31 Oct. 1925; Porter, "Black Atlanta," 89–110.

17 Maclachlan, "Women's Work," 44–46, 60–65, 376 (tab. A.1); Kuhn, *Contesting the New South Order*, 34; Dinnerstein, *Leo Frank Case*, 7–8.

18 Maclachlan, "Women's Work," 377 (tab. A.1), 382 (tab. A.8), 383 (tab. A.9); MacLean, "Leo Frank Case Reconsidered," 186; Hall, "Private Eyes, Public Women," 261–62.

19 *AE*, 20 Aug. 1906 (quotation); Hall, " 'Mind That Burns in Each Body,' " 333–37; Hall, *Revolt against Chivalry*, 150–57; MacLean "Leo Frank Case Reconsidered," 194–99.

20 Hall, "Private Eyes, Public Women," 261–62; Friedman, *Crime and Punishment*, 193–97; Ayers, *Promise of the New South*, 157; Gilmore, *Gender and Jim Crow*, 95.

21 *AG*, 1 Sept. 1906 (quotation); Hall, "Private Eyes, Public Women," 260–61; Hickey, *Hope and Danger*, 5, 33, 69–70, 73–78; MacLean, "Leo Frank Case Reconsidered," 194–99.

22 *AE*, 17 Aug. 1906; Jacobs, *Law of the White Circle*, 168–71; Watson, "Ungrateful Negro," 165–67; Ohmann, *Selling Culture*, 257–58; Bederman, *Manliness and Civilization*, 25–30; Gilmore, *Gender and Jim Crow*, 61–68.

23 Bruce, *Plantation Negro*, 126–27 (first quotation), 84–85 (second quotation); Page, *Negro*, 80 (third quotation).

24 Tillman quoted in Williamson, *Crucible of Race*, 120, 116; Bruce, *Plantation Negro*, 84; Page, *Negro*, 112.

25 Baker, *Following the Color Line*, 6.

26 Ibid., 38–39 (first quotation); Watson, "Negro Secret Societies," 167 (second quotation).

27 Bayor, *Race and the Shaping*, 198–99.

28 Broyles quoted in Martin, *Atlanta and Its Builders*, 2:205; "Twenty-sixth Annual Report of the Chief of Police for the Year 1906, Atlanta, Georgia," Jenkins Papers, AHC, 20–25; Baker, *Following the Color Line*, 45–46, 52–54; Bayor, *Race and the Shaping*, 20–25, 198.

29 Terrell, "Peonage in the United States," 267; Berry, "Free Labor He Found Unsatisfactory," 37, 56; Taylor, "Abolition of the Convict Lease System in Georgia," 282.

30 *AC*, 13 Mar. 1905, 10 Aug. 1906.

31 Du Bois, *Souls of Black Folk*, 54, and Page, "Journey through the Southern States," 9025 (quotations); Baker, *Following the Color Line*, 27; Atlanta Chamber of Commerce, *Annual Report* (1906), 12.

32 *AJ*, 23 Sept. 1906; Hickey, *Hope and Danger*, 63–65; Garrett, *Atlanta and Environs*, 2:607–9.

33 *AJ*, 23 Sept. 1906 (first quotation); *Journal of Labor*, 15 Feb. 1907 (second quotation); Goodson, *Highbrows, Hillbillies, and Hellfire*, 70–73; Jacobs, *Law of the White Circle*, 188; Hickey, *Hope and Danger*, 63–65.

34 *AC*, 13 July 1902; Baker, *Following the Color Line*, 47; Hickey, *Hope and Danger*, 61–70; Hunter, *To 'Joy My Freedom*, 175.

35 Perry Bradford quoted in Hunter, *To 'Joy My Freedom*, 162; Baker, *Following the Color Line*, 45.

36 Kuhn, " 'Full History of the Strike,' " 80–81; Goodson, *Highbrows, Hillbillies, and Hellfire*, 140; Baker, *Following the Color Line*, 30–31. For an insightful discussion of white supremacy during this period as being increasingly "detached from the personalized relations of local power," see Hale, " 'For Colored' and 'For White,' " 162–66.

37 *Macon Daily Telegraph*, 4 Sept. 1906; Porter, "Black Atlanta," 141–50; Baker, *Following the Color Line*, 32–33, 48; Daniel, *Black Journals of the United States*, 377. Hickey's *Hope and Danger* insightfully describes Decatur Street as "a kind of a borderland where Atlanta's social divisions blurred" (63). Hunter's *To 'Joy My Freedom* similarly describes Five Points and downtown Atlanta, especially Decatur Street, as an area "where urban dwellers crossed the color line more freely than elsewhere in the city" (152–53).

38 Deaton, "Atlanta during the Progressive Era," 41; Jacobs, *Law of the White Circle*, 20, 25; *AC*, 4 Nov. 1906; Watson, "Suggestions for Black Atlanta," 653.

39 On fears of white women adrift in Atlanta, see Hall, "Private Eyes, Public Women," 261–62; Hickey, *Hope and Danger*, 66–70.

40 Jacobs, *Law of the White Circle*, 10, 31, 148, 210, 237; White, *Flight*, 54–55; Douglas, *Purity and Danger*, 137–39; Melnick, *Black-Jewish Relations on Trial*, 51–57; Williamson, *Crucible of Race*, 468–72; MacLean, "Leo Frank Case Reconsidered," 192–93.

41 Moore, *Moral Purity and Persecution*, ix–x; Patterson, *Rituals of Blood*, 185–93.

42 Du Bois, *Souls of Black Folk*, 72; Patterson, *Slavery and Social Death*, 1–14.

43 Patterson, *Rituals of Blood*, 181, 192–93; Capeci, *Lynching of Cleo Wright*.

CHAPTER 2

1 *AE*, 8 Sept. (quotation), 28 Sept. 1906; *AG*, 21 Aug. 1906; Baker, *Following the Color Line*, 6–7, 9; Bauerlein, *Negrophobia*, 68.

2 Nancy MacLean's "Leo Frank Case Reconsidered" has influenced this formulation.

3   Goodson, *Highbrows, Hillbillies, and Hellfire*, 42–43; Williamson, *Crucible of Race*, 173.

4   Baker, *Atlanta Riot*, 23 (quotation); Barber, "Atlanta Tragedy," 478; *AE*, 1 Aug. 1906.

5   *AG*, 21 Aug. 1906; Baker, *Following the Color Line*, 5–7; Baker, *Atlanta Riot*, 24; Barber, "Atlanta Tragedy," 478.

6   *AG*, 21 Aug. 1906 (quotation); *AJ*, 23, 25 Aug. 1906; *AC*, 16 Sept. 1906.

7   *AG*, 5 Sept. 1906; *AJ*, 21 Sept. 1906; *AC*, 21 Sept. 1906.

8   *AC*, 21, 22 Sept. 1906; *AJ*, 21 Sept. 1906; *AC*, 28 Nov. 1906.

9   *AC*, 22, 23 Sept. 1906; *AE*, 22, 23 Sept. 1906; *AJ*, 22, 23 Sept. 1906; Barber, "Atlanta Tragedy," 478.

10 Baker, *Following the Color Line*, 5; Ovington, *Walls Came Tumbling Down*, 58.

11 *AG*, 5 Sept. 1906.

12 *AE*, 26 Aug. 1906 (first quotation); *AG*, 5 Sept. 1906 (second quotation); *AE*, 21 Sept. 1906 (third quotation).

13 *AG*, 27 Aug. 1906 (quotation). For discussions of this code of honor and chivalry, see Wyatt-Brown, *Southern Honor*, 50–55; Hall, " 'Mind That Burns in Each Body,' " 328–47; Hall, *Revolt against Chivalry*, 145–57; and MacLean, "Leo Frank Case Reconsidered." For a discussion of the role that an adherence to Victorian values played in the rise of the gender ideologies underlying lynching, see Williamson, *Crucible of Race*, 181–86.

14 *AG*, 24 Aug. 1906.

15 "A Georgia Woman," letter to the editor, *AG*, 27 Aug. 1906 (first and second quotations); Baker, *Following the Color Line*, 7 (third quotation); Meyers interview, LAC.

16 *AE*, 17 Aug. 1906 (quotation); Wyatt-Brown, *Southern Honor*, 48–50. Hodes, *White Women, Black Men*, 165–75, dates this conflation of interracial sex with black political power to the Reconstruction Era.

17 *AE*, 17, 25 Aug. 1906.

18 *AE*, 24 Aug. 1906 (first quotation); *AG*, 10 Sept. 1906 (second quotation).

19 *AG*, 10 Sept. 1906.

20 *AG*, 25 Aug. 1906.

21 Graves in Southern Society for the Promotion, *Race Problems of the South*, 56 (first quotation); *AG*, 21 Aug. 1906 (second quotation).

22 *AE*, 25 Aug. 1906.

23 This analysis of the multivalent meanings that different groups ascribed to these social transformations is influenced by MacLean's discussions of the ways in which class, gender, and ethnicity similarly affected reactions to the Leo Frank case. See MacLean, "Leo Frank Case Reconsidered," 186–89.

24 Watson, "Negro Question in the South," 125, 128; Woodward, *Tom Watson*, 216–43; Ayers, *Promise of the New South*, 273–74.

25 For excellent discussions of the complexities of turn-of-the-century working-class views on race, see Kuhn's " 'Full History of the Strike,' " 145–49, and his *Contesting the New South Order*, 25–34.

26 Watson, "Mr. Graves's Appeal," 12 (first quotation); Watson, "Ungrateful Negro," 171 (second quotation); *Journal of Labor*, 29 June 1906, cited in Bauerlein, *Negrophobia*, 79; Kuhn, *Contesting the New South Order*, 25, 34; Perman, *Struggle for Mastery*, 283–87.

27 For an excellent discussion of these threats and the response of members of the working class and former yeoman farmers in the 1910s, see MacLean, "Leo Frank Case Reconsid-

ered." For a discussion of a broader "herrenvolk" racial ideology resulting from "an ideological marriage between egalitarian democracy and biological racism," see Fredrickson, *White Supremacy*, xi–xii, 154–55.

28   *AG*, 25 Aug. 1906 (first quotation); *AE*, 24 Aug. 1906 (second quotation).

29   *AG*, 27 Aug. (first quotation), 1 Sept. (second quotation), 10 Sept. 1906 (third quotation).

30   *AE*, 17 Aug. (first quotation), 26 Aug. 1906 (second quotation); *AJ*, 28 Aug. 1906; Bauerlein, *Negrophobia*, 94.

31   *AJ*, 31 Aug. 1906; *AC*, 1 Sept. 1906.

32   *AG*, 8 Sept. 1906.

33   *AJ*, 31 Aug. 1906; *AC*, 1 Sept. 1906; *AG*, 19 Sept. 1906.

34   *AE*, 21 Sept. 1906; *AJ*, 5 Aug. 1906; Letter Book, ser. 4, box 25, Smith Collection, Richard B. Russell Library, University of Georgia, Athens, 87.

35   Dittmer, *Black Georgia*, 100 (quotations); Grantham, *Hoke Smith*, 131–55; Perman, *Struggle for Mastery*, 286–90; Bauerlein, *Negrophobia*, 22.

36   *AJ*, 1 Aug. 1906.

37   *AJ*, 2 Aug. 1906 (quotation); Dittmer, *Black Georgia*, 94–104; Grantham, *Hoke Smith*, 131–55.

38   *AC*, 5 July 1906; Moore, "Negro and Prohibition"; Rabinowitz, *Race Relations in the Urban South*, 314–18; Ansley, *History of the Georgia Woman's Christian Temperance Union*, 76–78, 140–53; Bacote, "Negro in Atlanta Politics," 337–39. According to Bacote, the Democratic Party first instituted the white primary in Atlanta in 1892, suspended it in 1895, and then adopted it statewide in 1897.

39   *AJ*, 8 Sept. 1906 (quotation); *AG*, 10, 12 Sept. 1906; Williamson, *Crucible of Race*, 261; Nesbitt, "Social Gospel in Atlanta," 152–66.

40   *AE*, 23 Aug. 1906 (quotations). For a similar analysis in another setting, see Feimster, " 'Ladies and Lynching,' " 8–13, 97–103.

41   *New York Evening Post*, 22 Dec. 1906 (quotation). For similar findings in other locations, see Gilmore, *Gender and Jim Crow*, 101–4; Feimster, " 'Ladies and Lynching,' " 8–13, 49–51, 97–103. On white women's use of this discourse in Atlanta, see Kuhn, *Contesting the New South Order*, 26–28; Hickey, *Hope and Danger*, 18–24.

42   Hall, *Revolt against Chivalry*, 193–210.

43   Majette quoted in *AG*, 1 Sept. 1906; McLendon quoted in *AG*, 8 Sept. 1906.

44   McLendon quoted in *AG*, 8 Sept. 1906; Majette quoted in *AG*, 1 Sept. 1906.

45   For elegant overviews of the general scholarly consensus regarding black women's inability in the Jim Crow Era South to claim legal or chivalric protection from white rapists, see Higginbotham, *Righteous Discontent*, 189–90; Higginbotham, "African-American Women's History," 11–13; Brown, " 'What Has Happened Here,' " 47–48.

CHAPTER 3

1   *AG*, 24, 27 Aug. 1906.

2   For another discussion of this dilemma in a more general context, see Donaldson, "New Negroes in a New South," 85–90. Capeci and Knight's "W. E. B. Du Bois's Southern Front" also analyzes Du Bois's relationship with, and the Niagara Movement's influence on, black Georgians. My focus on Atlanta's New Black Men, especially Barber, and these black men's

preriot dilemmas differs from Capeci and Knight's work. I also build on these scholars' discussions of black masculinity and highlight Du Bois and his allies' dynamic interaction with both whites and other African American groups.

3   Washington, *Up from Slavery*, 94; Gaines, *Uplifting the Race*, 38–39.

4   Washington quoted in Litwack, *Trouble in Mind*, 148; "The Standard Printed Version of the Atlanta Exposition Address," in *BTW Papers*, 3:587; Harlan, *Making of a Black Leader*, 217–27. For an insightful discussion of Washington's attitudes and actions regarding lynching, see Shapiro, *White Violence and Black Response*, 132–37.

5   Washington, *Up from Slavery*, 75, 147; Harlan, *Booker T. Washington in Perspective*, 110–15; Gaines, *Uplifting the Race*, 37–39.

6   For overviews of these black civil rights losses, see Woodward, *Strange Career of Jim Crow*, 83–85, 97–102; Litwack, *Trouble in Mind*, 218–46; Fredrickson, *White Supremacy*, 257–74. On these educational strides, see Anderson, *Education of Blacks in the South*, 246 (tab. 7.1).

7   Harlan, *Booker T. Washington in Perspective*, 5–7, 103–4.

8   Thornbrough, "National Afro-American League," 502; Harlan, *Booker T. Washington in Perspective*, 110–38; Johnson and Johnson, *Propaganda and Aesthetics*, 18.

9   Dittmer, *Black Georgia*, 92–94.

10 Adams, "William Edward Burghardt DuBois," 178 (first quotation); Du Bois, *Autobiography*, 222 (second quotation); Donaldson, "New Negroes in a New South," 7–9, 79–80; Dittmer, *Black Georgia*, 151–54; Torrence, *Story of John Hope*, 135; Litwack, *Trouble in Mind*, 280–83; Lewis, *Biography of a Race*, 226–28; Ovington, *Portraits in Color*, 79; Du Bois, *Souls of Black Folk*, 10; Washington, *Up from Slavery*, 75, 147; Capeci and Knight, "Reckoning with Violence," 731.

11 Du Bois, *Souls of Black Folk*, 11 (quotation), 10 n. 7. For an insightful exegesis on the metaphor of the veil, see Rampersad, *Art and Imagination*, 68–69, 79–80.

12 Ovington, *Portraits in Color*, 86 (first quotation); Du Bois, *Souls of Black Folk*, 74 (second quotation).

13 Du Bois, *Souls of Black Folk*, 9–11, 15, 73.

14 Ibid., 15, 43.

15 Adams, "New Negro Man," 450–52 (first and second quotations); Mellinger, "John Henry Adams," 30; "Our Symposium" (third quotation). For Du Bois's faith in the possibilities of interracial cooperation, see Du Bois, *Souls of Black Folk*, 119.

16 J. W. E. Bowen to BTW, 2 Nov. 1906, reel 265, *Papers of BTW* (quotation); undated notes by Lugenia Burns Hope, folder 11, box 71, ELL; Brawley, *Two Centuries of Methodist Concern*, 315–32; Davis, *Clashing of the Soul*, 75, 80, 94, 154–63; "Word of Sympathy."

17 Pickens, "Jesse Max Barber," 485–86 (quotations); Harlan, *Booker T. Washington in Perspective*, 133–36.

18 Barber, "Morning Cometh," 38 (quotation); Daniel, *Black Journals of the United States*, 369–77; Gaines, *Uplifting the Race*, 61–66.

19 Barber, "Morning Cometh," 38.

20 "University the Birthplace of Reform," 433.

21 Williams, "Woman's Part in a Man's Business"; Hope, "Our Atlanta Schools"; Love, "Proclamation of Haitian Independence"; Miller, "Achievements of the Negro Race"; Gaines, *Uplifting the Race*, 60–65; Johnson and Johnson, *Propaganda and Aesthetics*, 16–23.

22 Bowen, "Doing Things at the Tuskegee Institute," 249 (first quotation); Washington

quoted in Harlan, *Booker T. Washington in Perspective*, 137–39; Pauline E. Hopkins to J. Max Barber, 18 Apr. 1905, reel 1, *Du Bois Papers*.

23 "Personal Issue" (quotation). For Barber's reaction to these developments, see "Stand by Your Guns" and "Georgia's Political Mess." For perceptive discussions of these changes in the policy of Theodore Roosevelt toward African Americans, see Bacote, "Georgia's Reaction to the Negro Policy of Theodore Roosevelt"; Williamson, *Crucible of Race*, 342–56; Harlan, *Wizard of Tuskegee*, 309.

24 Du Bois, *Autobiography*, 241.

25 Ibid., 242–48; Harlan, *Wizard of Tuskegee*, 52–62; Lewis, *Biography of a Race*, 274–75, 314–15.

26 Lewis, *Biography of a Race*, 317 (quotation), 318–22; Du Bois, *Autobiography*, 248.

27 W. E. B. Du Bois to Dear Colleague, 28 Feb. 1906, reel 2; Treasurer's Report, Niagara Movement, 18 Aug. 1906, reel 2; Niagara Movement Annual Meeting, reel 2; The Niagara Meeting, reel 2; and "Georgia Equal Rights Convention," 13, 14 Feb. 1906, reel 1, 6–7, all in *Du Bois Papers*. My analysis of the growing radicalization of Du Bois and other black Georgians preceding the riot has been influenced by Capeci and Knight's "Reckoning with Violence" and "W. E. B. Du Bois's Southern Front."

28 Simmons, *Men of Mark*, 813–14; Drago, *Black Politicians*, 24–27; Donaldson, "Standing on a Volcano," 135–43; Gaines, *Uplifting the Race*, 31–32.

29 Du Bois, *Autobiography*, 253 (first quotation); Barber, "Niagara Movement at Harpers Ferry," 405 (second quotation); Turner quoted in Angell, *Bishop Henry McNeal Turner*, 240 (third quotation); Du Bois, "Growth of the Niagara Movement," 44.

30 "Georgia Equal Rights Convention," reel 1, *Du Bois Papers*, 4.

31 Ibid., 15–16 (quotations); W. E. B. Du Bois to Dear Colleague, 28 Feb. 1906, reel 2, *Du Bois Papers*; Lewis, *Biography of a Race*, 326–27.

32 "Georgia Equal Rights Convention," reel 1, *Du Bois Papers*, 15–16.

33 Turner, *Respect Black*, 196–97 (first quotation); "Macon Convention," 164 (second quotation); Angell, *Bishop Henry McNeal Turner*, 244; *Macon Daily Telegraph*, 19 Feb. 1906.

34 W. J. White to W. E. B. Du Bois, 3 Mar. 1906, reel 2, *Du Bois Papers* (quotation); "Macon Convention," 164.

35 Bryant, "Negro Inferiority and Disfranchisement," 514 (quotation); Treasurer's Report, Niagara Movement, 18 Aug. 1906, reel 2, *Du Bois Papers*; Capeci and Knight, "Reckoning with Violence," 736–40.

36 *AI*, 28 July (first quotation), 21 July 1906 (second quotation).

37 "The Niagara Movement: Address to the Country," in Aptheker, *Pamphlets and Leaflets by W. E. B. Du Bois*, 63–64 (quotation); Barber, "Niagara Movement at Harpers Ferry," 405–8; "Niagara Movement"; W. E. B. Du Bois to Dear Colleague, 13 June 1906, reel 2, *Du Bois Papers*; Lewis, *Biography of a Race*, 228–30.

38 *AG*, 22 Aug. 1906.

39 *AG*, 25 Aug. 1906 (quotation); Gilmore, *Gender and Jim Crow*, 105–6.

40 *AE*, 9 Sept. 1906; *AG*, 10 Sept. 1906.

41 *AI*, 1 Sept. 1906 (first quotation); *AC*, 30 Aug. 1906 (second quotation).

42 *AJ*, 26 Feb. 1895, cited in Bacote, "Negro in Georgia Politics," 19 (first quotation); *Savannah Tribune*, 9 Dec. 1905 (second quotation); Aptheker, *Pamphlets and Leaflets by W. E. B. Du Bois*, 13–15, 19–21, 23–25; "Georgia Equal Rights Convention," reel 2, *Du Bois Papers*;

AC, 7 Jan. 1905; Proctor, "Day at Andersonville," 237; Proctor, *Between Black and White*, 4, 26, 39; Gatewood, *Aristocrats of Color*, 291.

43 AC, 12 Sept. 1904 (quotation); Stanley, *Children Is Crying*, 39–71; Luker, *Social Gospel in Black and White*, 12–18.

44 AJ, 22 Sept. 1906; AG, 1 Sept. 1906.

45 Proctor, *Between Black and White*, 97.

46 Du Bois quoted in Gaines, *Uplifting the Race*, 165. Although Gaines does not focus primarily on differing gender constructions of black masculinity, I am indebted to his keen insights. Especially helpful for understanding the GERC is Gaines's emphasis on the "tension between black elites' *perception* of themselves as middle class and the social and cultural forces that relentlessly denied that status" (14).

47 Bederman, *Manliness and Civilization*, 57–60; Higginbotham, "African-American Women's History," 13; Brown, " 'What Has Happened Here,' " 46–47; Hunton, "Negro Womanhood Defended," 281–82; Lutz, "Dizzy Steep to Heaven," 146–51.

48 Du Bois, *Souls of Black Folk*, 72 (first quotation); Adams, "Study of the Features of the New Negro Woman," 325 (second quotation); John Hope, undated speech, ["Woman's Club"], reel 21, *Hope Papers* (third quotation); "Georgia Equal Rights Convention," reel 1, *Du Bois Papers*, 16; Hall, *Revolt against Chivalry*, 145–57; Gaines, *Uplifting the Race*, 2–17; Bederman, *Manliness and Civilization*, 20–22. For similar discussions of Du Bois and the crowding out of women's voices, see Schechter, *Ida B. Wells-Barnett and American Reform*, 129–32; White, *Too Heavy a Load*, 56–68.

49 Hattie Rutherford Watson, "Work of the Neighborhood Union," *Spelman Messenger*, Nov. 1916, folder 8, box 5, NU, 5 (quotation); Higginbotham, *Righteous Discontent*, 31–40; White, *Too Heavy a Load*, 38–40; Hunton, "Negro Womanhood Defended," 282.

50 AG, 22, 24 Aug. 1906.

51 AG, 19, 21 Sept. 1906.

52 AJ, 22, 23 Sept. 1906; AC, 22, 23 Sept. 1906.

53 AC, 30 Aug. 1906; AE, 30 Aug. 1906; Bauerlein, *Negrophobia*, 113; Harlan, *Wizard of Tuskegee*, 297.

54 Torrence, *Story of John Hope*, 152; Dittmer, *Black Georgia*, 126.

CHAPTER 4

1 AE, 21, 22 Sept. 1906; headlines quoted in Baker, *Following the Color Line*, facing p. 7.

A number of scholars, particularly Bauerlein in *Negrophobia*, have written finely detailed and compelling analyses of the race riot and its immediate aftermath. My emphasis is on exploring both what the riot meant to different groups in Atlanta and how it influenced their senses of identity—issues largely missing from this earlier scholarship. Indeed, what is striking about earlier scholars' work is their relative disinterest both in exploring divisions within racial groups and in analyzing the complicated ways in which the riot changed how Atlantans viewed themselves and others. More recently, Ferguson has addressed these riot questions but only as a means of providing background information for her study of the 1930s and 1940s. This author's brief conclusions are insightful and elegantly argued, particularly her description of the rioters' aims of showing "black residents that they had no claim on public space and no legitimate place in the city's economy"; see her *Black Politics*, 20–25. For other important 1906 Atlanta race riot studies, see Crowe, "Racial Massacre in Atlanta" and "Racial Violence and Social Reform"; Williamson, *Crucible of Race*, 209–23; Dittmer, *Black Georgia*, 123–31; Mixon, *Atlanta Riot*; Rainey, "Race Riot of 1906"; Tagger, "Atlanta Race Riot of 1906"; and Dray, *At the Hands*, 162–67.

2 "Atlanta Massacre," 800.

3 White, *Man Called White*, 3, 11–12, 15 (quotations).

4 Baker, *Following the Color Line*, 17.

5 Griffin, Clark, and Sandberg, "Narrative and Event," 24–25 (first quotation); Baker, *Atlanta Riot*, 20 (second quotation); Brundage, *Lynching in the New South*, 123–24. More than any other scholar, Brundage has elucidated both the contingent nature of racial violence and the complexities of its aims.

6 Gibson, "Anti-Negro Riots," 1457 (quotations); *Washington Post*, 24 Sept. 1906.

7 *AC*, 23 Sept. 1906 (quotation); *AJ*, 23 Sept. 1906; *NYT*, 24 Sept. 1906; Gibson, "Anti-Negro Riots," 1457; Baker, *Atlanta Riot*, 19.

8 *AC*, 23 Sept. 1906, 23 Feb. 1907; *AJ*, 23 Sept. 1906.

9 *AE*, 23 Sept. 1906 (first quotation); *Boston Evening Transcript*, 24 Sept. 1906 (second quotation); Gibson, "Anti-Negro Riots," 1457; undated notebook by Lugenia Burns Hope, folder 11, box 71, ELL; Torrence, *Story of John Hope*, 152.

10 *Washington Post*, 24 Sept. 1906; *AC*, 23 Sept. 1906; *AE*, 23 Sept. 1906.

11 C. B. Wilmer, "Story of the Atlanta Race Riot of 1906," n.d., reel 19, *CIC*, 8.

12 *AC*, 23 Sept. 1906 (first quotation); *AI*, 29 Sept. 1906 (second quotation); *AC*, 26 Oct. 1906; Baker, *Atlanta Riot*, 19.

13 *AC*, 23 Sept. 1906; Baker, *Following the Color Line*, 32.

14 *AC*, 23 Sept. 1906; Baker, *Atlanta Riot*, 22 (quotation).

15 *AE*, 23 Sept. 1906 (quotation); *AC*, 23 Sept. 1906; *AJ*, 23 Sept. 1906; Baker, *Atlanta Riot*, 19.

16 *AC*, 23 Sept. 1906.

17 Ibid.

18 Ibid.

19 *AJ*, 23 Sept. 1906.

20 *NYA*, 8 Nov. 1906; Crowe, "Racial Massacre in Atlanta," 158–59; Bauerlein, *Negrophobia*, 244.

21 *AG*, 24 Sept. 1906; *AC*, 23 Sept. 1906; *AJ*, 23 Sept. 1906; Baker, *Atlanta Riot*, 19.

22 John Slaton to Monroe L. Bickhart, folder b, box 6, 24 Sept. 1906, Slaton Papers, GAHD (first quotation); *AE*, 25 Aug. 1906 (second quotation); Baker, *Atlanta Riot*, 20 (third quotation); *AE*, 23 Sept. 1906; *AC*, 23 Sept. 1906; *AJ*, 23 Sept. 1906.

23 *AG*, 24 Sept. 1906.

24 *AC*, 23 Sept. 1906; *AJ*, 23 Sept. 1906; *NYT*, 24 Sept. 1906; *San Francisco Chronicle*, 23 Sept. 1906.

25 *AE*, 23 Sept. 1906 (quotations); *AC*, 23 Sept. 1906; *AJ*, 23 Sept. 1906.

26 *AJ*, 23, 26, 27 Sept. 1906; Du Bois, "Tragedy at Atlanta," 1173; Crowe, "Racial Massacre in Atlanta," 157–58; *AC*, 26, 30 Oct., 1, 10 Nov. 1906; Barber, "Atlanta Tragedy," 479.

27 *AG*, 24 Sept. 1906, cited in Bauerlein, *Negrophobia*, 159 (first quotation); *Constitution* in "Southern Press on the Atlanta 'Pogrom,'" 453 (second quotation).

28 *Boston Evening Transcript*, 24 Sept. 1906 (first quotation); *AC*, 24 Sept. 1906 (second quotation); *AG*, 24 Sept. 1906.

29 *AC*, 24 Sept. 1906; *NYT*, 24 Sept. 1906.

30 *AJ*, 24 Sept. 1906.

31 Torrence, *Story of John Hope*, 153; Rawick, *American Slave*, ser. 1, vol. 4, Georgia Narratives, pt. 2, 407, cited in Litwack, *Trouble in Mind*, 540.

32 *AG*, 24 Sept. 1906.

33 Sinclair interview, LAC, untranscribed; White, *Man Called White*, 19.

34 *AG*, 24, 28 Sept. 1906; *AC*, 23, 29 Sept. 1906; *NYT*, 26 Sept. 1906; *AE*, 25 Sept. 1906; Dittmer, *Black Georgia*, 126. For a seminal discussion of violence and vocal resistance as forms of "infrapolitics," see Kelley, *Race Rebels*, 56–72.

35 Du Bois, "Tragedy at Atlanta," 1174 (quotation); White, *Man Called White*, 10–11; Merritt, *Herndons*, 94.

36 Baker, *Following the Color Line*, 11–12; *AG*, 25 Sept. 1906; *NYT*, 26 Sept. 1906.

37 *AG*, 25 Sept. 1906; Baker, *Following the Color Line*, 12; Dittmer, *Black Georgia*, 128–29.

38 *AC*, 25 Sept. 1906; *AG*, 25 Sept. 1906.

39 Baker, *Following the Color Line*, 13; *AC*, 26 Sept. 1906; *AG*, 25 Sept. 1906; *NYT*, 26 Sept. 1906; Baker, *Atlanta Riot*, 19.

40 Baker, *Following the Color Line*, 13; *AG*, 25 Sept. 1906; *AC*, 25 Sept. 1906; *AJ*, 25 Sept. 1906; Bauerlein, *Negrophobia*, 203.

41 *AC*, 29 Dec. (quotation), 23, 24 Sept. 1906; *AE*, 23 Sept. 1906; *AG*, 24 Sept. 1906.

42 John Slaton to Monroe L. Bickhart, folder b, box 6, 24 Sept. 1906, Slaton Papers, GAHD (quotation); Francis Garrison to Oswald Garrison Villard, 24 Oct. 1906, bMS Am 1323 (1443), OGV; Dittmer, *Black Georgia*, 129.

43 Gibson, "Anti-Negro Riots," 1459; Witherspoon interview, LAC; Crowe, "Racial Massacre in Atlanta," 168; Barber, "Atlanta Tragedy," 473; C. B. Wilmer, "Story of the Atlanta Race Riot of 1906," n.d., reel 19, *CIC*, 21; *AC*, 24 Sept. 1906; *NYT*, 24 Sept. 1906.

44 Baker, *Following the Color Line*, 15 (quotation); *AC*, 24 Sept. 1906; *AE*, 25 Sept. 1906; Barber, "Atlanta Tragedy," 473.

45 Hunton, *William Alphaeus Hunton*, 133, 163–64; Lutz, "Dizzy Steep to Heaven," 138–39, 155–57.

46 Baker, *Following the Color Line*, 16–17.

47 Horowitz, *Deadly Ethnic Riot*, 121–22 (quotation); Brundage, *Lynching in the New South*, 120–30.

48 Dittmer, *Black Georgia*, 29–34, 131; "Atlanta Massacre," 799; Porter, "Black Atlanta," 124–60.

49 Baker, *Following the Color Line*, 31; *AC*, 27 Apr. 1906; Kuhn, Joye, and West, *Living Atlanta*, 77–82; Kelley, *Race Rebels*, 62–75.

50 J. Max Barber, "The 'Atlanta Race Riots': 'A Tale of Man's Inhumanity to Man,'" filed with a letter from Jesse Max Barber to Brother, 20 Oct. 1906, reel 265, *Papers of BTW*, 8. For examples of these institutions, see Hunter, *To 'Joy My Freedom*, 68–73, and Dittmer, *Black Georgia*, 50–71.

51 Graves, "Tragedy at Atlanta," 1172 (first quotation); Barber, "Atlanta Tragedy," 475 (second quotation).

52 Sinclair interview, LAC.

53 Du Bois, *Autobiography*, 286 (quotation); Pomerantz, *Where Peachtree Meets*, 77.

54 *Los Angeles Times*, 24 Sept. 1906 (quotation); Janken, *White*, 16–19; *AC*, 23 Sept. 1906; Bauerlein, *Negrophobia*, 165.

55 Rouse, *Lugenia Burns Hope*, 44 (first quotation); Baker, *Following the Color Line*, 28 (second quotation).

56 Ovington, *Walls Came Tumbling Down*, 65 (first quotation); Kletzing and Crogman, *Progress of a Race*, 170, 190 (second quotation); Francis Garrison to Oswald Garrison Villard, 24 Oct. 1906, bMS Am 1323 (1443), OGV (third quotation; used with permission of the Houghton Library, Harvard University).

57 White, *Man Called White*, 366; Fields, "Ideology and Race."

58 White, *Man Called White*, 9–12; Janken, *White*, 18–19, xiii–xvi.

59 White, *Man Called White*, 12.

60 Ibid. (first quotation); Ovington, *Portraits in Color*, 107–8 (second quotation).

61 *Macon Daily Telegraph*, 26, 27 Sept. 1906; Dittmer, *Black Georgia*, 164–65.

CHAPTER 5

1 Waring, *Work of the Colored Law and Order League*, 3 (first quotation); *New York Daily Tribune*, 25 Sept. 1906 (second quotation); *NYW*, 24 Sept. 1906 (third quotation).

2 *San Francisco Chronicle*, 23 Sept. 1906.

3 *Washington Post*, 25 Sept. 1906 (first headline); *NYT*, 25 Sept. 1906 (second headline); *San Francisco Chronicle*, 25 Sept. 1906 (quotation).

4 Bederman, *Manliness and Civilization*, 20–22.

5 Shapiro offers a particularly insightful discussion of Washington's and Du Bois's differing reactions to the riot, incorporating many of the sources on which I rely; see his *White Violence and Black Response*, 127–39. My emphasis on those leaders' varying constructions of black masculinity and my placement of those men's responses within the context of broader local and national discursive struggles expands upon Shapiro's pioneering work.

6 Barber, "Atlanta Tragedy," 474 (quotation); *NYW*, 27 Sept. 1906.

7 *NYW*, 24 Sept. 1906; *N. W. Ayer and Son's American Newspaper Annual* (1906), 621.

8 *NYW*, 27 Sept. 1906.

9 *Boston Guardian*, 5 Oct. 1906, in Vertical File, "Atlanta Race Riot," AUC (quotation); *AC*, 29 Sept. 1906.

10 Jesse Max Barber to Brother, 20 Oct. 1906, reel 265, *Papers of BTW* (quotation); *Boston Guardian*, 5 Oct. 1906, in Vertical File, "Atlanta Race Riot," AUC.

11 *Boston Guardian*, 5 Oct. 1906, in Vertical File, "Atlanta Race Riot," AUC; J. Max Barber to Brother, 20 Oct. 1906, reel 265, *Papers of BTW*.

12 J. Max Barber, "The 'Atlanta Race Riots': 'A Tale of Man's Inhumanity to Man,'" filed with a letter from Jesse Max Barber to Brother, 20 Oct. 1906, reel 265, *Papers of BTW*, 3, 10–11.

13 McPherson, *Abolitionist Legacy*, 5; Lewis, *Biography of a Race*, 289, 311, 318–19, 427–28; Harlan, *Wizard of Tuskegee*, 95; Thornbrough, "National Afro-American League," 503.

14 BTW to Francis Jackson Garrison, 2 Oct. 1906, in *BTW Papers*, 9:84 (first quotation); BTW to Oswald Garrison Villard, 1 Oct. 1906, in ibid., 81 (second quotation).

15 *AC*, 30 Aug. 1906; *Chicago Broad Ax*, 13 Oct. 1906 (quotation); Harlan, *Wizard of Tuskegee*, 297–98.

16 To the editor of the *New York World*, in *BTW Papers*, 9:74–75.

17 To the editor of the *New York Age*, in ibid., 82–83 (quotation); Harlan, *Wizard of Tuskegee*, 300.

18 Du Bois, "Litany of Atlanta," 857. For a similar point, see Shapiro, *White Violence and Black Response*, 128–31.

19 Grimké, "Atlanta Riot," 407–8 (first quotation); "Atlanta Massacre," 799 (second quotation). On Grimké's views of Du Bois, see Lewis, *Biography of a Race*, 292, 313; Perry, *Lift Up Thy Voice*, 316–23, 328–30.

20 Shapiro, *White Violence and Black Response*, 128–31.

21 Du Bois, *Souls of Black Folk*, 128 (first quotation); "The Niagara Movement: Address to the Country," in Aptheker, *Pamphlets and Leaflets by W. E. B. Du Bois*, 64 (second quotation); Du Bois, "Litany of Atlanta," 858 (third quotation); "Violence," *Crisis*, 41 (May 1934): 148. Shapiro draws similar conclusions regarding Du Bois's evolving ideas on the use of retaliatory and defensive violence; see his *White Violence and Black Response*, 127–29, 130–31.

22 Capeci and Knight, "Reckoning with Violence," 745–52; Du Bois, "Tragedy at Atlanta," 1173–75.

23 Du Bois, "Tragedy at Atlanta," 1173–75 (quotation 1174); Du Bois, "Shadow of Years," 70.

24 Capeci and Knight, "Reckoning with Violence," 745–48; Du Bois, "Litany of Atlanta," 857; Du Bois, "Tragedy at Atlanta," 1175 (quotations).

25 Du Bois, *Autobiography*, 253; Du Bois, "Niagara Movement"; Du Bois, "Value of Agitation," 110 (quotation).

26 Miller, "Appeal to Reason," 74.

27 *Washington Bee*, 29 Sept. 1906; Grimké, "Atlanta Riot," 415, 417; *Wichita Searchlight*, 29 Sept. 1906; Perry, *Lift Up Thy Voice*, 240–41.

28 Telegram from BTW to Oswald Garrison Villard, 8 Oct. 1906, bMS Am 1323 (4098), OGV (quotation; used with permission of the Houghton Library, Harvard University); Thornbrough, "National Afro-American League," 503.

29 *NYA*, 11 Oct. 1906; Thornbrough, "National Afro-American League," 509–10.

30 Mary Church Terrell quoted in Miscellany Clippings, Bound Press Notes, 1906–1907, reel 31, *Papers of Mary Church Terrell*.

31 *New York Herald*, 11 Oct. 1906 (first quotation); *NYT*, 12 Oct. 1906 (second quotation).

32 Villard, "Aims of the Afro-American Council," 349–50.

33 Ibid., 352–53.

34 Ibid., 350.

35 BTW, Extracts from an Address Before the Afro-American Council, in *BTW Papers*, 9:95–96.

36 Walters and Miller, "Address to the Public," 332–33.

37 *NYA*, 27 Sept. (first and second quotations), 1 Nov. 1906 (third quotation); Fortune in Thornbrough, *T. Thomas Fortune*, 279 (fourth quotation).

38 BTW to Charles Waddell Chesnutt, 29 Oct. 1906, in *BTW Papers*, 9:112 (quotation); Charles Waddell Chesnutt to BTW, 9 Oct. 1906, in ibid., 92–94.

39 *San Francisco Chronicle*, 24 Sept. 1906 (first quotation); "American Kishinev" (second quotation); "Facts about the Atlanta Murders," 8147 (third quotation).

40 "Racial Self-Restraint," 309 (*Outlook* quotations); Gibson, "Anti-Negro Riots," 1459 (final quotation).

41 "Racial Self-Restraint," 310.

42 *Brooklyn Daily Eagle*, 25 Sept. 1906 (first quotation); "Facts about the Atlanta Murders," 8147 (second quotation); *AC*, 7 Nov. 1906; *AJ*, 26 Sept. 1906.

43 BTW to Christopher James Perry, 5 Oct. 1906, in *BTW Papers*, 9:86.

CHAPTER 6

1 *Boston Evening Transcript*, 24 Sept. 1906 (first quotation); *AJ*, 24 Sept. 1906 (second quotation).

2 *AJ*, 25 Sept. 1906; *AG*, 24, 25, 26 Sept. 1906; *AC*, 30 Sept. 1906.

3 On the city's governmental structure, see Deaton, "James G. Woodward," 11–12.

4 *AG*, 25 Sept. 1906.

5 Ibid. (quotations); *AJ*, 25 Sept. 1906.

6 *AG*, 26 Sept. 1906; *AJ*, 26 Sept. 1906.

7 Hopkins quoted in C. B. Wilmer, "Story of the Atlanta Race Riot of 1906," n.d., reel 19, *CIC*, 14, and in Baker, *Following the Color Line*, 18–19; *AG*, 26 Sept. 1906; *AJ*, 26 Sept. 1906; *AC*, 26 Sept. 1906.

8 Baker, *Following the Color Line*, 19–20.

9 Ibid., 20 (first quotation); *AC*, 26 Sept. 1906 (second quotation); Bauerlein, *Negrophobia*, 196.

10 Baker, *Following the Color Line*, 20; *AE*, 21, 27 Sept. 1906.

11 Baker, *Following the Color Line*, 18–19 (first quotation); *AG*, 26 Sept. 1906 (second quotation).

12 *Georgia Baptist*, 13 July, 16 Nov. 1899; *AC*, 15 July, 16 Sept., 11 Nov., 16 Dec. 1900; Torrence, *Story of John Hope*, 135.

13 Porter, "Black Atlanta," 125–47; Pomerantz, *Where Peachtree Meets*, 76. Capeci and Knight make a similar point in "Reckoning with Violence," 731.

14 *AG*, 26 Sept. 1906 (quotation); *Savannah Tribune*, 29 Sept. 1906; Ovington, *Walls Came Tumbling Down*, 65.

15 J. W. E. Bowen to Rev. M. C. B. Mason, undated, reel 5, GTS; J. W. E. Bowen to BTW, 2 Nov. 1906, reel 265, *Papers of BTW*.

16 BTW to the editor of the *Houston Texas Freeman*, 29 Sept. 1906, in *BTW*, 9:78; J. W. E. Bowen to M. C. B. Mason, undated, and to Brother, 29 Sept. 1906, reel 5, GTS; Davis, *Clashing of the Soul*, 169–73, 184–99.

17 *NYW* quoted in *NYA*, 6 Oct. 1906; Capeci and Knight, "Reckoning with Violence," 746.

18 Undated notes by Lugenia Burns Hope, folder 11, box 71, ELL; Torrence, *Story of John Hope*, 152–56, 376 (quotation).

19 Hopkins in Baker, *Following the Color Line*, 21 (first quotation); BTW to Francis Jackson Garrison, 2 Oct. 1906, in *BTW Papers*, 9:79 (second quotation).

20 *AC*, 26, 27, 30 Sept., 1, 2, 3 Oct. 1906; *AG*, 20 July 1906; City Council Minutes, 25 Sept. 1906, AHC.

21 City Council Minutes, 3, 4, 15 Oct. 1906, AHC; *AC*, 1, 2, 3, 16, 17, 18, 19 Oct., 4 Nov. 1906, 3 Jan. 1907; *AG*, 20 July 1906.

22 *AI*, 3 Nov. 1906 (quotation); *AJ*, 22, 23 Sept. 1906.

23 Upshaw quoted in *AC*, 27 Sept. 1906. See also *AC*, 29 Sept., 1, 6 Oct., 2 Dec. 1906.

24 *AC*, 17, 29 Dec. 1906, 4, 7 Jan. 1907; *AJ*, 7 Jan. 1907.

25 *AJ*, 24, 26 Sept. 1906.

26 *AC*, 23, 25, 29 Sept., 4, 9, Oct. 1906; *AG* 24, 26, 27, 28 Sept. 1906; *AJ*, 24 Sept. 1906; *AE*, 1 Oct. 1906.

27 *AC*, 30 Sept., 13 Oct., 1 Nov. 1906; *AJ*, 29 Sept. 1906; Bauerlein, *Negrophobia*, 241.

28 *AC*, 26 Oct., 7, 10, 13, 21 Nov. 1906; Case #4637, 4 Oct. 1906, *State v. John Jailette*, Superior Court Criminal Cases (Indictments), Fulton County Superior Court; Bauerlein, *Negrophobia*, 241.

29 *AC*, 16 Oct. 1906, 15 June 1907; Baker, *Following the Color Line*, 6–7; Cases #4572, #4573, 24 Sept. 1906, *State v. Robert Branham*, Superior Court Criminal Cases (Indictments), Fulton County Superior Court.

30 *AC*, 21, 22 Sept., 28 Nov. 1906.

31 Baker, *Atlanta Riot*, 25–26.

32 *New York Evening Post*, 22 Dec. 1906 (quotation); *AC*, 14, 17 Nov. 1906; *AE*, 18 Nov. 1906; *AI*, 15 Dec. 1906; Baker, *Following the Color Line*, 22–23.

33 Baker, *Following the Color Line*, 23–24; *AC*, 15 June 1907; Baker, *Atlanta Riot*, 24.

34 Baker, *Atlanta Riot*, 24.

35 *AC*, 17 Nov. 1906 (quotation); *AE*, 25 Oct. 1906. On the potentially open-ended nature of black-on-white assault trials in Virginia, see Dorr, *White Women, Rape, and the Power of Race*, 167–68.

36 Baker, *Atlanta Riot*, 23–24; *AC*, 15 June 1907; *Johnson v. State*, 128 Ga. 102, 57 S.E. 353 (1907).

37 *AC*, 30 Nov., 7 Dec., 1906; *New York Evening Post*, 22 Dec. 1906; Baker, *Following the Color Line*, 20–21.

38 *AC*, 30 Nov. 1906 (quotation); Baker, *Following the Color Line*, 21; *AI*, 13 Apr. 1907; C. B. Wilmer, "Story of the Atlanta Race Riot of 1906," n.d., reel 19, *CIC*, 17.

39 Muse quoted in Baker, *Following the Color Line*, 14; *New York Evening Post*, 22 Dec. 1906; *AG*, 12 Dec. 1906; *AC*, 31 Oct., 1 Nov., 12, 13 Dec. 1906; *AG*, 31 Oct. 1906.

40 BTW, Extracts from an Address in Atlanta, Georgia, in *BTW Papers*, 9:161 (quotation); *AC*, 23, 25 Dec. 1906; Baker, *Following the Color Line*, 21–22; Bauerlein, *Negrophobia*, 257.

41 Baker, *Following the Color Line*, 21–22; *AGN*, 9 Mar. 1907.

42 *AC*, 30 Nov. 1906; *New York Evening Post*, 22 Dec. 1906.

43 *AI*, 15 Dec. 1906.

44 *AC*, 31 Oct. 1906 (first quotation); "Discussion between Dr. C. B. Wilmer, D.D. and Dr. Duboise," reel 47, RSB, 31 (second quotation); *AC*, 7 Dec. 1906 (third quotation); *AG*, 15 Nov. 1906; *AI*, 15 Dec. 1906.

45 Tuttle, "W. E. B. Du Bois' Confrontation with White Liberalism," 252 (quotation); Baker, *Following the Color Line*, 24–25.

46 Baker, *Following the Color Line*, 32 (quotation); "Discussion between Dr. C. B. Wilmer, D.D. and Dr. Duboise," reel 47, RSB, 22–23.

47 *AI*, 19 Jan. 1907 (quotation); City Council Minutes, 19 Nov. 1906, AHC; *AC*, 18 Dec. 1906; Bauerlein, *Negrophobia*, 244. In *Dark Journey*, 222, McMillen underscores the importance of black voting rights as a tool for discouraging racially biased law enforcement procedures.

48 "Discussion between Dr. C. B. Wilmer, D.D. and Dr. Duboise," reel 47, RSB, 32.

49 Ibid., 3–4.

50 Baker, *Following the Color Line*, 21 (first quotation); John E. White to Ray Stannard Baker, 23 Apr. 1908, reel 26, RSB (second quotation).

51 Proctor, *Between Black and White*, 119; "Souvenir Program: Exercises Commemorative of the Breaking of Ground for the Institutional Building of the First Congregational Church," 2 July 1908, OCB; Hoke Smith to ——, 5 Oct. 1907, box 1, Proctor Papers.

52 Proctor, *Between Black and White*, 99.

53 *AC*, 17 Dec. 1906 (quotation), 28 Jan. 1907; *AI*, 27 Jan. 1912, 6 Apr. 1913.

54 "Discussion between Rev. Dr. C. B. Wilmer, D.D. and Dr. Duboise," reel 47, RSB, 32 (first quotation); Du Bois, "Value of Agitation," 109–10 (second quotation).

55 *AI*, 19 Jan. 1907 (first quotation); Proctor, *Between Black and White*, 97 (second quotation); *AC*, 31 Oct. 1906.

56 Proctor, *Between Black and White*, 97–99.

CHAPTER 7

1 Proctor, "Southerner of the New School," 406; *AC*, 3 Oct. 1906.

I was introduced to Northen's antilynching efforts by Williamson's *Crucible of Race*. Mixon also discusses Northen's early efforts in "Atlanta Riot of 1906," 693–706. This chapter supports Williamson's portrayal of Northen as a paternalistic "Conservative" on the race issue, heavily influenced by his memories of slavery and a distrust of the white masses. My analysis, however, expands on Williamson's research by detailing the evolution of Northen's movement and placing it within Georgia's larger social and cultural contexts. This chapter was also influenced by MacLean's *Behind the Mask of Chivalry* and Bederman's *Manliness and Civilization*, 46–53. Like MacLean's Klan, Northen's fears of disorder and social change were expressed in metaphors of pollution and sexual impurity. In contrast to the Klan's support of vigilantism and a "reactionary populism," however, Northen rejected mob violence and attempted to augment the power of a small white elite. As suggested by Bederman's research, Northen legitimized the authority of this elite on the basis of the restrained "white manliness" that Northen believed distinguished it from the "savagery" of black rapists and white mob participants. Northen's representation of lynching as "unmanly" and his desires to provide elite "law-abiding" black men with positions of partial authority in his antilynching leagues set the ex-governor apart from virtually all white southerners and even many white northerners of his era. My narrative has also benefited from Donaldson's exhaustive investigative work on William J. White in "Standing on a Volcano."

2 *AGN*, 13, 28 Mar. 1907.

3 W. J. Northen, "Christianity and the Negro Problem in Georgia: Address Delivered before the Evangelical Ministers' Association of Atlanta," 4 Sept. 1911, box 3, WJN, 15 (quotation); W. J. Northen, "The Negro at the South," 22 May 1899, box 3, WJN, 7, 15; *AC*, 26 Mar. 1913; Bonner, "Gubernatorial Career of W. J. Northen," 15–17, 47–71; Shaw, *Wool-Hat Boys*, 22–29; Williamson, *Crucible of Race*, 288; Woodward, *Tom Watson*, 239; Ayers, *Promise of the New South*, 274.

4 *AG*, 18 Jan. 1907 (quotation); *AGN*, 28 Mar. 1907. On Georgia's social transformations and these new fears, see MacLean, "Leo Frank Case Reconsidered"; Wrigley, "Triumph of

Provincialism," 30–41; Baker, *Following the Color Line*, 69–70; Friedman, *Crime and Punishment*, 193–97; Ayers, *Promise of the New South*, 157.

5   *AGN*, 28 Mar. 1907 (quotation).

6   *AE*, 22 Nov. 1906; *AC*, 1, 9, 23 Dec. 1906; *AG*, 3, 18 Jan. 1907; *AGN*, 20, 28 Mar. 1907; Bauerlein, *Negrophobia*, 257.

7   *AG*, 30 Jan. 1907.

8   *AG*, 18 Jan. 1907; *AGN*, 13, 28 Mar. 1907.

9   *AGN*, 28 Mar. 1906 (first quotation); Northen, "Christianity and the Negro Problem in Georgia," box 3, WJN, 13 (second quotation).

10 *AGN*, 28 Mar. 1907 (quotations); Hall, *Revolt against Chivalry*, 149–57; MacLean, *Behind the Mask of Chivalry*, 162–65; Tolnay and Beck, *Festival of Violence*, 76–77.

11 [W. J. Northen], "The Evolution of LAWLESSNESS and Unchallenged CRIME," n.d., box 3, WJN, 4–5.

12 *AGN*, 28 Mar. 1907.

13 Ibid.

14 Ibid.; Bederman, *Manliness and Civilization*, 57–67.

15 *AGN*, 13, 28 Mar. 1907; *AC*, 14 Mar. 1907.

16 *AGN*, 28 Mar. 1907.

17 Ibid.; W. J. Northen, "Printed Circular Concerning 'Active Co-operation of Our Best Citizens for the Enforcement of Law . . . ,' " 1907, box 3, WJN; Zangrando, *NAACP Crusade against Lynching*, 14; Brundage, *Lynching in the New South*, 195.

18 White, "Need of a Southern Program," 177.

19 Ibid., 188 (quotation); *AGN*, 9 Mar. 1906.

20 *AC*, 10 Oct. 1906 (first quotation); White, "Need of a Southern Program," 186 (second quotation).

21 John E. White to Ray Stannard Baker, 7 Oct. 1907, and "Southern Commission on the Race Problem," reel 26, RSB.

22 *AC*, 9 Oct. 1906.

23 *AC*, 15 Oct. (first quotation), 20 Oct. 1906 (second quotation).

24 Foner, *Reconstruction*, 88–95, 612; Genovese, *Roll, Jordan, Roll*, 161–284; Levine, *Black Culture and Black Consciousness*, 80; Litwack, *Been in the Storm So Long*, 466–71; Eskew, "Black Elitism and the Failure of Paternalism in Postbellum Georgia," 650–66.

25 W. J. Northen to BTW, 17 Jan. 1907, reel 282, *Papers of BTW*; W. E. B. Du Bois to Ray Stannard Baker, 6 May 1909, reel 27, RSB; Gaines, *Uplifting the Race*, 2–17; Higginbotham, *Righteous Discontent*, 42–58.

26 Donaldson, "Standing on a Volcano," 135–43; *Georgia Baptist*, 9, 30 Mar., 4, 18 May 1899.

27 *NYA*, 18 Oct. 1906 (quotation); Dittmer, *Black Georgia*, 164–65; Donaldson, "Standing on a Volcano," 160–61, 165–66.

28 Clipping from *Georgia Baptist*, n.d., Scrapbooks, WJN, 5:160 (quotation); *AC*, 9 Dec. 1906, 8 Feb. 1907.

29 *Macon Daily Telegraph*, 14 Feb. 1907 (quotations); Du Bois to William J. White, 24 Jan. 1907, reel 2, *Du Bois Papers*; Capeci and Knight, "Reckoning with Violence," 752.

30 *Macon Daily Telegraph*, 14 Feb. 1907.

31 *AC*, 14 Feb. 1907.

32 *AGN*, 13 Mar. 1907.

33 Clipping, n.d., Scrapbooks, WJN, 5:169.

34 *AGN*, 28 Mar. 1907 (quotation); Baker, *Following the Color Line*, 68–69.

35 *AGN*, 28 Mar. 1907; Brundage, *Lynching in the New South*, 108–13; Wrigley, "Triumph of Provincialism," 85–94; Dittmer, *Black Georgia*, 131–40.

36 Clipping, n.d., Scrapbooks, WJN, 5:198 (quotation); Gaston, *New South Creed*, 126.

37 *AJ*, 5 Apr. 1907; clipping, n.d., Scrapbooks, WJN, 5:192; Flamming, *Creating the Modern South*, 39–49.

38 Clipping, n.d., Scrapbooks, WJN, 5:192 (first quotation), and 5:150 (second quotation); "Ex-Governor Northen's Campaign."

39 *AJ*, 17 Mar. 1907 (quotation); Grantham, *Hoke Smith*, 144–53.

40 *AJ*, 17, 24 Mar. 1907.

41 W. J. Northen to Shailer Matthews, 22 June 1907, box 2, WJN (quotation); Evangelical Ministers' Association, Minutes, 1 Apr. 1907, CCA.

42 *Golden Age*, 11 Apr. 1907.

43 Bacote, "Negro in Georgia Politics," 428, 466; *AC*, 21, 30 June 1907; Link, *Paradox of Southern Progressivism*, 70–72; Dittmer, *Black Georgia*, 111–12.

44 *AC*, 13 July 1907.

45 *AGN*, 8 July (first quotation), 6 July 1907 (second quotation).

46 *Golden Age*, 8 Aug. 1906.

47 Hall quoted in Grantham, *Hoke Smith*, 160; Perman, *Struggle for Mastery*, 290–93.

48 Wrigley, "Triumph of Provincialism," 117–20; Dittmer, *Black Georgia*, 101–4; Perman, *Struggle for Mastery*, 291–93.

49 Colored Citizens, *Memorial to the Georgia Legislature*, 4.

50 Ibid., 6.

51 Ibid., 11; *AC*, 28 July 1907.

52 Bacote, "Negro in Georgia Politics," 488–90.

53 Ibid., 492–96; *AC*, 23 July 1907 (quotations).

54 Bacote, "Negro in Georgia Politics," 496–505; Grantham, *Hoke Smith*, 161–62; Dittmer, *Black Georgia*, 103–4; Kousser, *Shaping of Southern Politics*, 231–37; Sullivan, *Days of Hope*, 66, 105.

55 *AJ*, 17 Mar. 1907.

56 White, "Prohibition," 136–37.

57 Massey and Meyers, "Patterns of Repressive Social Control in Post-Reconstruction Georgia," 468; Brundage, *Lynching in the New South*, 263, 275.

58 W. J. Northen to My Dear Brother, 18 Dec. 1911, box 1, WJN; Williamson, *Crucible of Race*, 291.

59 *AGN*, 20 Mar. 1907.

60 *AC*, 14 Mar. 1907; *AGN*, 20, 28 Mar. 1907.

61 Clipping, n.d., Scrapbooks, WJN, 5:176.

CHAPTER 8

1 "Law Re-established," 297 (first quotation); Page, "Journey through the Southern States," 9025–26 (second quotation). On the powerful hold that these images of masculinity

exercised over early twentieth-century American minds, see Bederman, *Manliness and Civilization*, 46–53.

2 "The Week."

3 *AI*, 15 Dec. 1906 (quotation); Foner, *Reconstruction*, 610–12; Proctor, "Atlanta Riot," 424–26.

4 *NYA*, 24 Dec. 1907 (quotation); Proctor, *Between Black and White*, 100, 109, 112–13; Hoke Smith to ——, 5 Oct. 1907, box 1, Proctor Papers.

5 Proctor, *Between Black and White*, 117–25 (quotation, 117); Henry Hugh Proctor to Rev. C. H. Richards, 23 Feb. 1909, OCB; Proctor, *Between Black and White*, 101; BTW to Whom It May Concern, 19 Sept. 1907, box 1, and "Biggest City of Its Size," box 3, Proctor Papers; Capeci and Knight, "W. E. B. Du Bois's Southern Front," 498–99.

6 *NYW*, 26 Sept. 1906 (first quotation); BTW to Edgar Gardner Murphy, 2 Dec. 1906, and to Quincy Ewing, 22 Oct. 1906, in *BTW Papers*, 9:152 (second quotation), 98–99.

7 BTW to Theodore Roosevelt, 26 Nov. 1906, in *BTW Papers*, 9:147 (quotation); Gerstle, *American Crucible*, 62; Harlan, *Wizard of Tuskegee*, 309–13; Lewis, *Biography of a Race*, 330–33, 341–42.

8 BTW to Charles William Anderson, 7 Nov. 1906; Charles William Anderson to BTW, 10 Nov. 1906; and BTW to Theodore Roosevelt, 26 Nov. 1906, all in *BTW Papers*, 9:118 (quotation), 122, 147.

9 "President Roosevelt's Message," supplement, *NYT*, 5 Dec. 1906, 2; Wilson, "Negro in the President's Message," 579; Harlan, *Wizard of Tuskegee*, 319–20.

10 "President Roosevelt's Message," Supplement *NYT*, 5 Dec. 1906, 2 (quotation); "Negro in the Message," 537; Wilson, "Negro in the President's Message," 576.

11 "President Roosevelt's Message," Supplement *NYT*, 5 Dec. 1906, 2.

12 *NYA*, 13 Dec. 1906 (first quotation); "President's Message to Congress," 536 (second quotation); Kelly Miller to BTW, 16 Nov. 1906, in *BTW Papers*, 9:130–31.

13 *AC*, 5 Dec. 1906 (quotation); Theodore Roosevelt to Clark Howell, 26 Oct., 5 Nov. 1906, in Morison, *Big Stick*, 472, 487–88; Theodore Roosevelt to Governor Montague, 5 Nov. 1906, reel 343, Theodore Roosevelt Papers, LC.

14 Kelly Miller to BTW, 16 Nov. 1906, and Timothy Thomas Fortune to BTW, 8 Dec. 1906, in *BTW Papers*, 9:130–31 (first quotation), 157 (second quotation).

15 BTW to Whitefield McKinlay, 8 Nov. 1906; to Theodore Roosevelt, 2 Nov. 1906; and to Charles William Anderson, 7 Nov. 1906, all in ibid., 9:119 (first quotation), 113 (second quotation), 119 (third quotation).

16 BTW, Extracts from an Address in Atlanta, Georgia, and BTW, An Article in the *Outlook*, in ibid., 9:158–61 (first quotation), 168–74 (second quotation).

17 BTW, Extracts from an Address in Atlanta, Georgia, in ibid., 9:159, 161.

18 BTW, "The Standard Printed Version of the Atlanta Exposition Address," in ibid., 3:587.

19 Thornbrough, *T. Thomas Fortune*, 312–13, 325–31, 351–56.

20 BTW to John Thompson, 13 June 1908, in *BTW Papers*, 9:572 (first quotation); Du Bois, "Plucky Man"; Harlan, *Wizard of Tuskegee*, 320–21; Harlan, *Booker T. Washington in Perspective*, 145–48.

21 Grantham, introduction to *Following the Color Line*, vi–vii; Roper, *C. Vann Woodward*, 90–91; Theodore Roosevelt to Ray Stannard Baker, Mar. 30, 1907, reel 25, RSB.

22 Morris, *Theodore Rex*, 437; Ohmann, *Selling Culture*, 28–29, 48–49, 118–19, 246–58, 273–

79; *N. W. Ayer and Son's American Newspaper Annual* (1906), 603, 611; Bannister, *Ray Stannard Baker*, 147.

23 John S. Phillips to Ray Stannard Baker, 26 July 1906 (first quotation), and Ray Stannard Baker to Father, 31 Oct. 1906 (second quotation), reel 25, RSB; Bannister, *Ray Stannard Baker*, 102–13, 127; Semonche, *Ray Stannard Baker*, 156–59; Ohmann, *Selling Culture*, 255–59.

24 Ray Stannard Baker to Father, 31 Oct. 1906 (first quotation), and John S. Phillips to Ray Stannard Baker, 18 Apr. 1907 (second quotation), reel 25, RSB.

25 Baker, *Following the Color Line*, vii, 7; Mary White Ovington to Ray Stannard Baker, 12 Nov. 1906, reel 25, RSB (quotation).

26 Mary White Ovington quoted in Wedin, *Inheritors of the Spirit*, 87.

27 W. E. B. Du Bois to Ray Stannard Baker, 3 Apr. 1907, reel 25, RSB.

28 Baker, *Following the Color Line*, 219 (quotation).

29 Ibid., 199.

30 Undated, anonymous letter to Ray Stannard Baker, Nov.–Dec. 1907, reel 26, and W. E. B. Du Bois to Ray Stannard Baker, 3 Apr. 1907, and 1907 Memorandum, reel 25, RSB.

31 Baker, "A Race Riot, and After," 569 (first quotation), 564 (second quotation), 575 (third quotation), 579 (fourth quotation); Semonche, *Ray Stannard Baker*, 120, 125, 154.

32 BTW to Emmett Jay Scott, 21 Oct. 1907, in *BTW Papers*, 9:384 (first quotation); Baker, *Following the Color Line*, 235 (second quotation), 302–3 (third quotation), 305 (fourth quotation).

33 Baker, *Following the Color Line*, 304 (first quotation), 307 (second quotation), 273 (third quotation); Semonche, *Ray Stannard Baker*, 207.

34 Ray Stannard Baker to W. E. B. Du Bois, 6 May 1907, reel 1, *Du Bois Papers*; Ray Stannard Baker to Father, 3 Apr. 1907, reel 25, RSB.

35 *AGN*, 28 Mar. 1907.

36 J. Max Barber to Ray Stannard Baker, 24 June 1908, reel 26, RSB.

37 W. E. B. Du Bois to Ray Stannard Baker, 6 May 1909, reel 27, RSB.

38 Tuttle, "W. E. B. Du Bois' Confrontation with White Liberalism," 241–58; Ray Stannard Baker to W. E. B. Du Bois, 11 Oct., 10 May 1907, reel 25, and 26 May, 2 Oct. 1908, reel 26, RSB; John Phillips to W. E. B. Du Bois, 24, 29 Dec. 1908, reel 1, *Du Bois Papers*.

39 *N. W. Ayer and Son's American Newspaper Annual* (1907), 605–6, 621, 629; Daniel, *Black Journals of the United States*, 210, 377.

40 Du Bois, "Postscript," 244.

41 Du Bois, "Shadow of Years," 170–71 (quotations); W. E. B. Du Bois to My Dear Colleagues, 1907, and to Mr. Waldron, 6 Dec. 1907, microfilm, reel 2, *Du Bois Papers*. See Capeci and Knight, "Reckoning with Violence," 745–52, for an alternative interpretation of the riot's effects on Du Bois, arguing that its violence triggered a far more profound mental breakdown.

42 *Baltimore Sun* quoted in Thornbrough, "National Afro-American League," 510; Harlan, *Wizard of Tuskegee*, 338–47; Thornbrough, *T. Thomas Fortune*, 302; A. Walters to Dr. W. E. B. DuBois, 11 Apr. 1908, reel 2, *Du Bois Papers*; Aptheker, *Selections from the Horizon*, 60.

43 William Walling quoted in Kellogg, *NAACP*, 1:9–10; McPherson, *Abolitionist Legacy*, 377–93.

44   Kellogg, *NAACP*, 1:10–14, 11 (quotation); Lewis, *Biography of a Race*, 386–90; Harlan, *Wizard of Tuskegee*, 360–62.

45   Kellogg, *NAACP*, 1:297–99 (quotations); Harlan, *Wizard of Tuskegee*, 360–62.

46   Aptheker, *Selections from the Horizon*, 70 (quotation); Lewis, *Biography of Race*, 471.

47   BTW quoted in Harlan, *Wizard of Tuskegee*, 361 (quotation), 369–75; Kellogg, *NAACP*, 1:39–45, 300–303; Lewis, *Biography of a Race*, 391–407, 513.

48   BTW, A Manuscript of an Article [1911], in *BTW Papers*, 11:444–49; Baker, "Negro Suffrage in a Democracy," 617, 619.

49   Harlan, *Wizard of Tuskegee*, 367 (quotation); Bannister, *Ray Stannard Baker*, 154–55.

50   J. Max Barber to Ray Stannard Baker, 24 June 1908, reel 26, RSB (quotation); Harlan, *Booker T. Washington in Perspective*, 147–48.

CHAPTER 9

1   Gilmore, *Gender and Jim Crow*, 147–50.

2   Higginbotham, *Righteous Discontent*, 14–15.

3   Proctor, *Between Black and White*, 106–11; McEwen, "First Congregational Church, Atlanta"; Luker, *Social Gospel in Black and White*, 184–90; Goodson, *Highbrows, Hillbillies, and Hellfire*; "The Fifteenth Century Drama, 'Everyman,'" OCB; "A Model Church for the Colored People," Proctor Papers.

4   Proctor, *Between Black and White*, 106–9; "Report of the Institutional Department, 1916" and "Report of the Institutional Department," 6 Jan. 1919, First Congregational Church Minutes, GAHD; "A Model Church for the Colored People," Proctor Papers; *AI*, 6 Nov. 1915.

5   Proctor, *Between Black and White*, 108 (quotation); Proctor, *Living Fountain*, 6.

6   Women's Missionary Society Minutes, First Congregational Church, Atlanta, 18 May 1909, 4 Mar. 1913, 23 Feb., 1 June 1915, 21 Feb., 14 Mar. 1916; Gilmore, *Gender and Jim Crow*, 147–53.

7   Proctor, *Negro Womanhood*, 4 (first quotation); Proctor, *Living Fountain*, 5 (second quotation).

8   Proctor, *Living Fountain*, 6–7; *AI*, 13 May 1916.

9   Proctor, *Negro Womanhood*, 4 (first quotation); Proctor (second quotation) and *AC* (third quotation) in Goodson, *Highbrows, Hillbillies, and Hellfire*, 156, 157.

10   Proctor, "Southerner of the New School," 402; Galloway, *Inman Family*, 115.

11   Proctor, "Southerner of the New School," 402 (quotation); Oney, *And the Dead Shall Rise*, 150; Campbell, *Music and the Making of a New South*, 83–91; Evangelical Ministers' Association, Minutes, 3 Oct., 7 Nov. 1910, 4 Sept. 1911, CCA; Proctor, "Southerner of the New School," 404; Frith, "Manger of the Movement," 36, 119–22; Lefever, "Involvement of the Men and Religion Forward Movement," 523, 534; *AC*, 10 Oct. 1915.

12   Dittmer, *Black Georgia*, 203–11; Brundage, *Lynching in the New South*, 227–30; Dray, *At the Hands*, 247–48, 254–56; Frith, "Manger of the Movement," 99–100; Proctor, "Atlanta Plan," 11.

13   Jones, "Counting the Cost," 12 (first quotation); Speer, *John J. Eagan*, 92 (second quotation); Proctor, "Atlanta Plan," 10–11.

14　C. B. Wilmer, "Story of the Atlanta Race Riot of 1906," n.d., reel 19, *CIC*, 21; Proctor, "Atlanta Plan," 9.

15　Jones, "Counting the Cost," 13–14.

16　Proctor, "Atlanta Plan," 9 (quotation); Jones, "Counting the Cost," 13.

17　Proctor, *Between Black and White*, 178; Adams interview, LAC.

18　White, *Man Called White*, 21 (first quotation); Rucker Sisters (Lucy Rucker Aiken, Neddie Rucker Harper, and Hazel Rucker) interview, in Hill, *Black Women Oral History Project*, 8:287 (second quotation); Pomerantz, *Where Peachtree Meets*, 108.

19　Pomerantz, *Where Peachtree Meets*, 79 (first quotation); White, *Man Called White*, 24 (second quotation); Jenness, *Twelve Negro Americans*, 56 (third quotation).

20　*Journal* quoted in Goodson, *Highbrows, Hillbillies, and Hellfire*, 157; Proctor, "Puritans in Bronze."

21　Proctor, "Need of Friendly Visitation."

22　*AC*, 15 Sept. 1912, cited in Hunter, *To 'Joy My Freedom*, 210.

23　Hunter, *To 'Joy My Freedom*, 27–28, 33–34, 51–52, 132–33.

24　*AI*, 5 Oct. 1912.

25　Proctor, *Between Black and White*, 121 (first quotation); White, *Man Called White*, 21 (second quotation).

26　*AI*, 27 Dec. 1913, 10, 17, 31 Jan. 1914, 21 Feb., 25 Apr., 7 Nov. 1914.

27　*AI*, 7 Sept. 1912 (quotation); Davis, *Communist Councilman*, 27. For Davis's background, see Matthews, "Black Newspapermen," 365–72; Bacote, "Negro Officeholders in Georgia"; Dittmer, *Black Georgia*, 90–109, 55–64. For previous and much briefer examinations of Davis's and Proctor's conflicts, see Dittmer, *Black Georgia*, 61–62; Gatewood, *Aristocrats of Color*, 290–92.

28　*AI*, 2, 9 Apr. 1904; Matthews, "Black Newspapermen," 365–72; Bacote, "Negro Officeholders in Georgia"; Dittmer, *Black Georgia*, 90–109, 55–64.

29　*AI*, 2 July 1910 (quotation); Dittmer, *Black Georgia*, 107–9.

30　Davis, *Communist Councilman*, 33 (quotation); *AI*, 27 Mar., 23 Oct. 1915; Summers, *Manliness and Its Discontents*, 33–44.

31　*AI*, 15 Dec. 1906, 19 Jan. 1907, 23 May 1908; Gatewood, *Aristocrats of Color*, 158.

32　*AI*, 31 Aug. (quotation), 7 Sept. 1912.

33　*AI*, 19 June 1915 (quotation), 1 Nov. 1913, 20 Nov. 1915.

34　*AC*, 4 Oct. (quotation), 2 Aug. 1915.

35　*AI*, 2 (quotation), 9 Oct. 1915.

36　*AI*, 9 Oct. 1915, 20 Jan. 1917.

37　*AI*, 16 (quotation), 23 Oct. 1915.

38　*AC*, 10 Oct. 1915; *AI*, 16 Oct. 1915; Bayor, *Race and the Shaping*, 59–60.

39　Walter White to James W. Johnson, 5 Dec. 1906, pt. 12, ser. A, reel 9, Atlanta Branch Files, *NAACP*.

40　Watson, "Suggestions for Black Atlanta," 654; Frith, "Manger of the Movement," 84; Du Bois, *Autobiography*, 253. Dorsey's *To Build Our Lives Together* traces a gradual hardening of black intraracial divisions in Atlanta between the Civil War and the early 1900s as African American economic development and white racism intensified class and status tensions among black residents. As Dorsey demonstrates, virtually all African Americans, despite their differences, remained committed to the ideals of racial solidarity and mutual uplift. In *Stone of Hope*, Chappell argues that both white and black solidarity was limited in the South even during the 1960s civil rights struggles. This insight suggests that the central problem of black political history is not African American disunity. A better question to ask, perhaps, is What has allowed African Americans, in the face of brutal racism and discrimination, to repeatedly overcome class and status divisions in pursuit of shared interests and goals? This question is addressed in relationship to Atlanta in the next chapter.

CHAPTER 10

1 Research Notes, folder 22, box 1, NU; Frazier, "Neighborhood Union," 438.

    The Neighborhood Union, Lugenia Burns Hope, and the "politics of respectability" have attracted the attention of many leading scholars of U.S. history. While each of their works has a different insight and emphasis, these scholars have rightly emphasized the union's (or in some cases, other women's groups') "maternalist" ideology, the class implications of both its politics of respectability and law-and-order concerns, and its political role in the school campaigns between 1919 and 1921. This chapter builds on the insights of these scholars. My focus differs from that of other authors in placing the organization in the context of black men's political struggles, in detailing its role in politically mobilizing the black community, in emphasizing members' dissimulation in the public realm of black-white contact, and in locating the Neighborhood Union within an urban setting where vice posed real dangers to women and children. What is striking from these perspectives is the union's democratic and egalitarian emphasis, its success in grassroots organizing, and its singular achievement in uniting black Atlantans across the traditional barriers of religious and class differences. The most helpful studies of the Neighborhood Union and the politics of respectability include Rouse, *Lugenia Burns Hope*, 57–90; Neverdon-Morton, *Afro-American Women of the South*, 145–63; Gordon, "Black and White Visions of Welfare"; Shaw, "Black Club Women," 10–25; Beardsley, *History of Neglect*, 105–8; Higginbotham, *Righteous Discontent*, 185–229; Lasch-Quinn, *Black Neighbors*, 115–26; Hunter, *To 'Joy My Freedom*, 136–44; Ferguson, *Black Politics*, 4–5, 9–11, 49–57; Judson, "Building the 'New South' City," 116–34; Shivery, "History of Organized Social Work"; Hickey, *Hope and Danger*, 97–102, 118–19.

2 Speeches and Lectures, folder 24, box 1, NU.

3 Ibid.

4 Watson, "Work of the Neighborhood Union," NU, 5 (quotation); *Chicago Defender*, 31 Oct. 1925; Torrence, *Story of John Hope*, 138–39; Shivery, "History of Organized Social Work," 74–78; Rouse, *Lugenia Burns Hope*, 60–63.

5 Torrence, *Story of John Hope*, 139; Watson, "Work of the Neighborhood Union," NU, 5; *Chicago Defender*, 31 Oct. 1925; Shivery, "History of Organized Social Work," 74–78; Rouse, *Lugenia Burns Hope*, 60–63; Judson, "Building the 'New South' City," 93; Oney, *And the Dead Shall Rise*, 54.

6 Du Bois, *Negro American Family*, 58; Watson, "Work of the Neighborhood Union," NU, 5; *Chicago Defender*, 31 Oct. 1925; Torrence, *Story of John Hope*, 138–39; Shivery, "History of Organized Social Work," 49, 74–78; Rouse, *Lugenia Burns Hope*, 60–63.

7 Shivery, "History of Organized Social Work," 43; Neighborhood Union Minute Book,

1908–1918, "Bylaws," and entry dated 8 July 1908, folder 1, box 4, NU; Rouse, *Lugenia Burns Hope*, 65.

8   *AI*, 7 Dec. 1912; White, *Too Heavy a Load*, 21–36; Hunter, *To 'Joy My Freedom*, 44–73.

9   "Community Organization and Leadership," 1922, folder 25, box 1, NU; Adrienne McNeil Herndon to BTW, 12 Feb. 1907, in *BTW Papers*, 9:216–17.

10 John Hope, undated speech, ["Woman's Club"], reel 21, *Hope Papers*. Deborah White also discusses Hope's speech in *Too Heavy a Load*, 57–58. White rightly emphasizes the sexist undertones of the speech. At the same time, John's speech opened up a potential realm of civic participation that could be claimed by Lugenia and other Neighborhood Union members. For a perceptive discussion of the rising importance of the home and neighborhood spheres as sites of "congregation" among African Americans during the early twentieth century, see Lewis, *In Their Own Interests*, 5–6, 89–90. On the marital conflicts arising from Lugenia's refusal to confine her activities to the home, see Davis, *Clashing of the Soul*, 217; Rouse, *Lugenia Burns Hope*, 22–24, 35–38.

11 *AI*, 7 Dec. 1912; Shivery, "History of Organized Social Work," 48, 86–87; Rouse, *Lugenia Burns Hope*, 66–67; Neverdon-Morton, *Afro-American Women of the South*, 152.

12 *Chicago Defender*, 31 Oct. 1925 (quotation); Meeting Notes—Neighborhood Union, 1919–1924, folder 18, box 1, NU; Frazier, "Neighborhood Union in Atlanta," 438; Hope's-Notes, folder 44, box 13, NU; Shivery, "History of Organized Social Work," 447; Rouse, *Lugenia Burns Hope*, 69–72; Neverdon-Morton, *Afro-American Women of the South*, 152.

13 Meeting Notes—Neighborhood Union, folder 18, box 1, NU (quotation).

14 Watson, "Work of the Neighborhood Union," NU, 5 (quotation); Meeting Notes—Neighborhood Union, folder 18, box 1, NU; Frazier, "Neighborhood Union," 437; Shivery, "History of Organized Social Work History," 69–73; *Chicago Defender*, 31 Oct. 1925; Neighborhood Union Minute Book, 1908–1918, "Bylaws," and entries dated 12 Aug. 1908, 28 May 1909, folder 1, box 4, NU; Lasch-Quinn, *Black Neighbors*, 122; Hickey, *Hope and Danger*, 98–99.

15 Watson, "Work of the Neighborhood Union," NU, 6; Meeting Notes—Neighborhood Union, folder 18, box 1, NU; Lasch-Quinn, *Black Neighbors*, 124; Shivery, "History of Organized Social Work," 111.

16 Hope's-Notes, folder 44, box 13, NU (first quotation); *Chicago Defender*, 31 Oct. 1925 (second quotation); Lasch-Quinn, *Black Neighbors*, 124; Hunter, *To 'Joy My Freedom*, 141–42.

17 *AI*, 7 Dec. 1912; Public School 1913 Campaign, Neighborhood Union, folder 4, box 4, NU; Research Notes, folder 22, box 1, NU; Neighborhood Union Minute Book, 1908–1918, 11 June 1914, folder 1, box 4, NU; Frazier, "Neighborhood Union," 437; Shivery, "History of Organized Social Work," 12–16; Neverdon-Morton, *Afro-American Women of the South*, 141–43.

18 Speeches and Lectures, folder 24, box 1, NU.

19 Watson, "Work of the Neighborhood Union," NU, 6; Shivery, "History of Organized Social Work," 116–17.

20 Neighborhood Union Minute Book, 1908–1918, 9 Sept., 14 Oct., 11 Nov. 1909, Aug. 1910, June, 9 Nov. 1911; 8 Aug., 7 Mar. 1912, folder 1, box 4, NU; Watson, "Work of the Neighborhood Union," NU, 6. For additional discussions of these campaigns, see White, *Too Heavy a Load*, 72; Hunter, *To 'Joy My Freedom*, 138–40; Rouse, *Lugenia Burns Hope*, 70.

21 Speeches and Lectures, folder 24, box 1, NU (quotation); White, *Too Heavy a Load*, 56–86; Higginbotham, *Righteous Discontent*, 188–205.

22 John B. Watson to John Hope, 2 Aug. 1912, reel 13, *Hope Papers* (first quotation); *AJ*, 12 Dec. 1909 (second quotation).

23 Undated letter to Honorable ——, folder 31, box 3, NU (quotation); Watson, "Work of the Neighborhood Union," NU, 5; Neighborhood Union Minute Book, 1908–1918, 9 Sept., 14 Oct., 11 Nov. 1909, Aug. 1910, Feb., June, 9 Nov. 1911, 8 Aug., 7 Mar. 1912.

24 Annual Report of the Atlanta Anti-Tuberculosis Association, 1919, folder 6, box 10, NU, 21–22 (quotation); Report of Negro National Health Week, 3–9 Apr. 1921, folder 7, box 10, NU; Judson, "Building the 'New South' City," 113–14; Neverdon-Morton, *Afro-American Women of the South*, 53–54; Hickey, *Hope and Danger*, 107–19.

25 Litwack, *Trouble in Mind*, 439 (quotation); Rouse, *Lugenia Burns Hope*, 43–44; Hunter, *To 'Joy My Freedom*, 120–25. More than any other scholar, Robin D. G. Kelley has illuminated the complex forms of resistance in which African Americans have engaged; see Kelley, *Race Rebels*, chaps. 1–4.

26 Hunter, *To 'Joy My Freedom*, 177–78, 180–83.

27 Gutman, *Black Family*, 448–49; Judson, "Building the 'New South' City," 33; Hunter, "Household Workers in the Making," 293 (tab. 1).

28 Watson, "Work of the Neighborhood Union," NU, 6; Neighborhood Union Minute Book, 1908–1918, 7 Mar. 1912, folder 1, box 4, NU; Wardlaw, "Leisure Time Activities of Negro Boys," 29.

29 Watson, "Work of the Neighborhood Union," NU, 6.

30 *Chicago Defender*, 31 Oct. 1925 (quotation); Hattie Watson, "Annual Report of the Neighborhood Union, 1913–1914," folder 7, box 5, NU. Lasch-Quinn, in *Black Neighbors*, 124, also emphasizes the Neighborhood Union's responsiveness to community members.

31 For an elegant introduction to these increasingly influential ideas, see Kelling and Coles, *Fixing Broken Windows*, 14–27.

32 Torrence, *Story of John Hope*, 140.

33 Hattie Watson, "Annual Report of the Neighborhood Union, 1913–1914," folder 7, box 5, NU; Research Notes, folder 22, box 1, NU; Davis, *Clashing of the Soul*, 200; Gilmore, *Gender and Jim Crow*, 14; Litwack, *Trouble in Mind*, 52–102.

34 Minutes of Women's Social Improvement Committee, 19 Aug., 2 Sept., 28 Oct. 1913, folder 1, box 4, NU; Public School 1913 Campaign Notebook, folder 4, box 4, NU; *AI*, 13 Dec. 1913; Rouse, *Lugenia Burns Hope*, 79; Neverdon-Morton, *Afro-American Women of the South*, 152–58.

35 Minutes of the Woman's Social Improvement Committee, 19 Aug., 2 Sept., 28 Oct., 2 Dec. 1913, folder 3, box 4, NU; Rouse, *Lugenia Burns Hope*, 74–79; Neverdon-Morton, *Afro-American Women of the South*, 152–58.

36 White, *Man Called White*, 30 (quotation); Bayor, *Race and the Shaping*, 201–2.

37 *AI*, 24 Feb. 1917; Atlanta Branch, National Association for the Advancement of Colored People, to Dear Friend, 1917, pt. 12, ser. A, reel 9, Atlanta Branch Files, *NAACP*; Bayor, *Race and the Shaping*, 201–3.

38 Walter White to James W. Johnson, 1 Oct. 1917, pt. 12, ser. A, reel 9, Atlanta Branch Files, *NAACP* (first quotation); *AI*, 3 Feb. 1917 (second quotation); White, *Man Called White*, 34;

Walter White to James Weldon Johnson, 27 Sept. 1917, pt. 12, ser. A, reel 9, Atlanta Branch Files, *NAACP*; Toppin, "Walter White," 8–9.

39 Walter White to James Weldon Johnson, 23 Feb. (first quotation) and 5 Dec. 1917 (second quotation), pt. 12, ser. A, reel 9, Atlanta Branch Files, *NAACP*.

40 Toppin, "Walter White," 10, 15; Carson, *Called to Serve*, 15.

41 Harry Pace to Mr. James Weldon Johnson, 15 July 1918, and to Friend, 7 July 1918, pt. 12, ser. A, reel 9, Atlanta Branch Files, *NAACP* (quotations); Carson, *Called to Serve*, 15.

42 Carson, *Called to Serve*, 15–16; Bayor, *Race and the Shaping*, 202–3.

43 T. K. Gibson to James W. Johnson, 7 Mar. 1919, pt. 12, ser. A, reel 9, Atlanta Branch Files, *NAACP* (quotations); Bayor, *Race and the Shaping*, 203.

44 L. C. Crogman to J. R. Shillady, 18 Apr. 1919, pt. 12, ser. A, reel 9, Atlanta Branch Files, *NAACP* (first quotation); *AI*, 22 Mar. 1919 (second quotation); Carson, *Called to Serve*, 16 (third quotation).

45 A. D. Williams to Whom It Concerns, 1 Oct. 1919, folder 33, box 2, NU.

46 Torrence, *Story of John Hope*, 230; Davis, *Clashing of the Soul*, 263.

47 Toppin, "Walter White," 20–21; Bayor, *Race and the Shaping*, 204–5.

48 Bayor, *Race and the Shaping*, 205–11.

49 "Community Organization and Leadership," 1922, folder 25, box 1, NU (quotation). On these frustrations, see Rouse, *Lugenia Burns Hope*, chap. 5 (91–121).

50 Hickey, *Hope and Danger*, 180–82; Judson, "Building the 'New South' City," 329–36, 381–89.

51 Eugene Kinckle Jones to Mrs. John Hope, 27 Apr. 1917, folder 28, box 2, NU (first quotation); Thomas, *My Story in Black and White*, 96–97 (second quotation), 112.

52 M. W. Bullock to Mrs. John Hope, 10 July 1926, folder 7, box 1, NU; Judson, "Building the 'New South' City," 245–50; Thomas, *My Story in Black and White*, 96–100, 111–12; Spritzer and Bergmark, *Grace Towns Hamilton*, 87.

53 Judson, "Building the 'New South' City," 250–54; Shivery, "History of Organized Social Work," 518 (quotation), 519–21.

54 Mrs. John Hope to Co-Worker, 11 Nov. 1925 (quotation), and L. B. Hope to Wallace Buttrick, 21 Sept. 1925, folder 46, box 2, NU; M. W. Bullock to Mrs. John Hope, 10 July 1926, folder 7, box 1, NU.

55 Shivery, "History of Organized Social Work," 518 (quotation), 522; Ferguson, *Black Politics*, 49–52.

56 Research Notes, folder 22, box 1, NU.

57 Hope to Co-Workers, 8 July 1935, folder 28, box 3, NU (quotation); Meeting Notes—Neighborhood Union, 1919–1924, folder 18, box 1, NU; Shivery, "History of Organized Social Work," 393; Minutes of NAACP 1934, folder 37, box 12, NU, 6–7; Ferguson, *Black Politics*, 148–55; Janken, *Rayford W. Logan*, 103–4, 107–8; Rouse, *Lugenia Burns Hope*, 123–27.

58 E. Franklin Frazier to Robert W. Bagnall, 8 Jan., 2 Feb. 1925, pt. 12, ser. A, reel 9, Atlanta Branch Files, *NAACP*. Frazier's 1925 letters anticipated his 1955 portrayal of a "black bourgeoisie" whose gaudy worlds of "make-believe" and "conspicuous consumption" temporarily distracted them from the realities of white racism and black exclusion. For an elegant summary of Frazier's famous work and its reception, see Teele, introduction to *E. Franklin Frazier and Black Bourgeoisie*, 1–13.

59　On the high costs imposed by brutal and sustained white violence on black political and social movements, see Payne, *I've Got the Light of Freedom*, 7–21, and McMillen, *Dark Journey*, 311–18.

60　For a masterful study of these continuing divisions, see Ferguson, *Black Politics*, 253–68.

CHAPTER 11

1　Witherspoon interview, LAC, 3 (first quotation); Brown, *Charlie Brown Remembers*, 43 (second quotation); Kuhn, Joye, and West, *Living Atlanta*, xiii–xix.

2　Ellsworth, *Death in a Promised Land*, 98, 104–7; Lewis interview, LAC.

3　Georgia Writers' Program, *Atlanta*, 33–34 (quotation); Crowe, "Racial Massacre in Atlanta," 169.

4　Garrett, *Atlanta and Environs*, 2:503 (quotation); *AJ*, 22 Sept. 1980.

5　Pyron, *Southern Daughter*, 31–32.

6　Mitchell, *Gone with the Wind*, 745, 751, 77–78.

7　Lewis interview, LAC (first quotation); Rouse, *Lugenia Burns Hope*, 45 (second quotation); Usher interview, LAC, untranscribed.

8　Crowe, "Racial Massacre in Atlanta," 168–69.

9　Dinnerstein, *Leo Frank Case*, 36–61; Oney, *And the Dead Shall Rise*, 99–100, 184–85, 383–84; Dray, *At the Hands*, 207–14. For convincing gender analyses of the Frank case, see MacLean, "Leo Frank Case Reconsidered"; Williamson, *Crucible of Race*, 468–72; Melnick, *Black-Jewish Relations on Trial*, 85–87.

10　*Augusta Chronicle* quoted in Dinnerstein, *Leo Frank Case*, 60.

11　Roan quoted in ibid., 80; Dray, *At the Hands*, 211.

12　Dinnerstein, *Leo Frank Case*, 114–21; Oney, *And the Dead Shall Rise*, 500–503.

13　Watson quoted in Dinnerstein, *Leo Frank Case*, 119.

14　Dinnerstein, *Leo Frank Case*, 54–56, 132–33, 139–44; Dray, *At the Hands*, 211–14.

15　Dinnerstein, *Leo Frank Case*, 149–50, 158–60; Moseley, "Political Influence of the Ku Klux Klan"; MacLean, *Behind the Mask of Chivalry*, 17–18; Pomerantz, *Where Peachtree Meets*, 93–94; Jenkins, *Keeping the Peace*, 4 (quotation).

16　*Milwaukee Leader* quoted in Dray, *At the Hands*, 214; MacLean, "Leo Frank Case Reconsidered," 201; Pomerantz, *Where Peachtree Meets*, 97–98; Newman, *Southern Hospitality*, 82–83, 101–2.

17　Newman, *Southern Hospitality*, 83, 103–4; Pomerantz, *Where Peachtree Meets*, 93–94.

18　John Hope to Dr. D. W. Abercrombie, 30 Aug. 1915, reel 13, *Hope Papers* (quotation); Rowley, "George Alexander Towns," 37–38.

19　Davis, *Clashing of the Soul*, 313–14.

20　John Hope to Dr. D. W. Abercrombie, 30 Aug. 1915, reel 13, *Hope Papers* (first quotation); Pomerantz, *Where Peachtree Meets*, 266 (second quotation).

21　Alexander quoted in Speer, *John J. Eagan*, 106; C. B. Wilmer, "Story of the Atlanta Race Riot of 1906," n.d., reel 19, *CIC*, 21; Brundage, *Lynching in the New South*, 216–18, 234–35; Sosna, *In Search of the Silent South*, 21–22; Davis, *Clashing of the Soul*, 260–63; Hall, *Revolt against Chivalry*, 60–63; Chappell, *Inside Agitators*, 35–36.

22　Speer, *John J. Eagan*, 87 (quotations); Sosna, *In Search of the Silent South*, 23–24; Chappell, *Inside Agitators*, 35–37.

23 Dray, *At the Hands*, 280; Dykeman and Stokely, *Seeds of Southern Change*, 41.

24 Sosna, *In Search of the Silent South*, 25–26; Chappell, *Inside Agitators*, 36–37; Hall, *Revolt against Chivalry*, 237–41.

25 Janken, *White*, 366–72.

26 Hall, " 'You Must Remember This,' " 460–64; Hall, *Revolt against Chivalry*, 194–97; Chappell, *Inside Agitators*, 37–39; Sosna, *In Search of the Silent South*, 33–34; Egerton, *Speak Now against the Day*, 158–62, 289, 567–69.

27 Egerton, *Speak Now against the Day*, 333, 432–39, 564–65; Chappell, *Inside Agitators*, 46–49.

28 Chappell, *Inside Agitators*, 49 (quotation); Sosna, *In Search of the Silent South*, 39–41; Hall, *Revolt against Chivalry*, 258–60.

29 Ferguson, *Black Politics*, 84–86, 96–97, 145–47, 226–32; Tuck, *Beyond Atlanta*, 26–27.

30 Tuck, *Beyond Atlanta*, 41–43; Egerton, *Speak Now against the Day*, 225–27.

31 Pomerantz, *Where Peachtree Meets*, 148; Tuck, *Beyond Atlanta*, 40–42; Bayor, *Race and the Shaping*, 21.

32 Tuck, *Beyond Atlanta*, 62–64; Bayor, *Race and the Shaping*, 23–25; Stone, *Regime Politics*, 26–38.

33 Martin, *William Berry Hartsfield*, 156; Roche, *Restructured Resistance*, 24–39; Pomerantz, *Where Peachtree Meets*, 350–51; Stone, *Regime Politics*, 26–38.

34 Hartsfield, quoted in Martin, *William Berry Hartsfield*, 142; Bayor, *Race and the Shaping*, 29–32.

35 Allen with Hemphill, *Mayor*, 82 (quotation); Jenkins, *Keeping the Peace*, 53; Stone, *Regime Politics*, 48, 161.

36 Pomerantz, *Where Peachtree Meets*, 293; Stone, *Regime Politics*, 52–55; Jenkins, *Keeping the Peace*, 34–39.

37 Patrick, "Nail in the Coffin of Racism," 246 (quotation); Mays, *Born to Rebel*, 18; King with Riley, *Daddy King*, 85; Pomerantz, *Where Peachtree Meets*, 76–77.

38 Allen with Hemphill, *Mayor*, 90 (quotation); Spritzer and Bergmark, *Grace Towns Hamilton*, 19–24; Clowse, *Ralph McGill*, 139; Ferguson, *Black Politics*, 153–57; Stone, *Regime Politics*, 25–26.

39 Allen with Hemphill, *Mayor*, 92 (quotation); Spritzer and Bergmark, *Grace Towns Hamilton*, 92–99, 137–44; Stone, *Regime Politics*, 32–42; Bayor, *Race and the Shaping*, 59–60, 82; Ferguson, *Black Politics*, 266–67; Newman, *Southern Hospitality*, 138–40. Birmingham faced a similar crisis in housing for black residents during this period. There, as Eskew points out, the refusal of whites to negotiate a settlement with African Americans helped transform a black struggle for access to housing into a movement opposing segregation. See Eskew, *But for Birmingham*, 82, 347 n. 1, 349 n. 29.

40 Pomerantz, *Where Peachtree Meets*, 282–83; Roche, *Restructured Resistance*, 185–87; Stone, *Regime Politics*, 46–50; Bayor, *Race and the Shaping*, 224–27.

41 Dobbs in Pomerantz, *Where Peachtree Meets*, 244 (first quotation); King with Riley, *Daddy King*, 155 (second quotation); Jenkins, *Keeping the Peace*, 40 (third quotation); Pomerantz, *Where Peachtree Meets*, 216–17; Tuck, *Beyond Atlanta*, 105.

42 King in Raines, *My Soul Is Rested*, 461 (first quotation); King with Riley, *Daddy King*, 155 (second quotation).

43 Bond in Greene, *Temple Bombing*, 385 (first quotation); Bond in Raines, *My Soul Is Rested*, 85 (second quotation); Stone, *Regime Politics*, 54.

44 King with Riley, *Daddy King*, 164; Stone, *Regime Politics*, 54–55.

45 Pomerantz, *Where Peachtree Meets*, 259–63.

46 Ibid., 264–68.

47 Ibid., 270 (quotation), 264–72.

48 Allen with Hemphill, *Mayor*, 40 (quotation); Tuck, *Beyond Atlanta*, 114–15.

49 Pomerantz, *Where Peachtree Meets*, 313 (first quotation), 324 (second quotation).

50 King in Tuck, *Beyond Atlanta*, 112 (first quotation); King, *Autobiography*, 195 (second quotation); Stone, *Regime Politics*, 58; Pomerantz, *Where Peachtree Meets*, 254.

51 King with Riley, *Daddy King*, 99, 112.

52 Ibid., 99 (quotation); Ferguson, *Black Politics*, 265–67; Stone, *Regime Politics*, 52–54.

53 Chappell, *Inside Agitators*, 221–23.

54 King with Riley, *Daddy King*, 137 (first quotation); Garrow, *Bearing the Cross*, 577 (second quotation). Chafe, in his pioneering studies of Greensboro, North Carolina, has explored how the "progressive mystique" of "civility" has often proved "an exquisite instrument of social control" and "virtually impossible to break through"; see Chafe, *Civilities and Civil Rights* and "Epilogue from Greensboro," 277–86.

55 Stone, *Regime Politics*, 96–98, 107–8; Pomerantz, *Where Peachtree Meets*, 511–15.

56 Bayor, *Race and the Shaping*, 48–52, 123–24; Stone, *Regime Politics*, 96–98; Pomerantz, *Where Peachtree Meets*, 459–60; Rutheiser, *Imagineering Atlanta*, 173, 180–82.

57 Bayor, *Race and the Shaping*, 48–52, 123–24; Stone, *Regime Politics*, 96–98; Rutheiser, *Imagineering Atlanta*, 173, 180–82.

58 Stone, *Regime Politics*, 103–7; Bayor, *Race and the Shaping*, 247–50.

59 Sjoquist, introduction to *Atlanta Paradox*, 1–2; Bayor, *Race and the Shaping*, 84, 251.

60 Stone, *Regime Politics*, 189, 213.

61 King, *Autobiography*, 346 (quotation); Garrow, *Bearing the Cross*, 583–84; Bayor, *Race and the Shaping*, 27.

62 Young, *Way Out of No Way*, 148 (quotation); Newman, *Southern Hospitality*, 261–65.

63 Von Hoffman, *House by House*, 164–68.

64 Ibid., 169–71.

65 Ibid., 201–2; Youngblood interview, in "Beyond Gentrification"; Historic District Development Corporation, <http://www.hddc.net>.

66 Von Hoffman, *House by House*, 202–4; "About Reynoldstown," <http://www.reynoldstown.org/rcil/about.htm>.

67 Young, *Easy Burden*, 524–25.

68 Young, *Way Out of No Way*, 142, 148.

69 Proctor, *Between Black and White*, 189.

70 Young, *Easy Burden*, 529, 531.

CONCLUSION

1 Du Bois, *Ordeal of Mansart*, 316 (first quotation), 275 (second quotation). For an outstanding analysis of the *Black Flame* trilogy and its place in Du Bois's life, see Rampersad,

Art and Imagination, 266–87. Rampersad rightfully emphasizes the destructiveness of broad social forces in the novel, over which, he argues, its fictional characters, including Mansart, can exert relatively little power or influence. Yet while Rampersad describes Mansart as a figure of "pathos," he also notes the ultimately triumphant portrayal of Mansart at the end of the novel. In contrast to Rampersad's interpretation, my reading of the novel suggests Du Bois's emphasis on historical contingency and human agency.

2   Du Bois, *Ordeal of Mansart*, 238, 240, 253.

3   Ibid., 246–52.

4   Ibid., 249, 273, 276.

5   Ibid., 310–11.

6   Ibid., 313–14.

7   Du Bois, *Worlds of Color*, 348–49.

SELECTED BIBLIOGRAPHY

MANUSCRIPT COLLECTIONS

Amherst, Massachusetts
 University of Massachusetts Amherst, W. E. B. Du Bois Library,
 Special Collections and Archives
  W. E. B. Du Bois Papers

Athens, Georgia
 University of Georgia
  Hargrett Rare Book and Manuscript Library
   Margaret Mitchell Marsh Papers
  Richard B. Russell Library
   Hoke Smith Collection

Atlanta, Georgia
 Atlanta History Center, James G. Kenan Research Center
  Atlanta City Council Minutes
  Atlanta Lung Association Collection
  Aldine Chambers Papers
  Christian Council of Atlanta Collection
  John J. Eagan Collection, 1870–1924
  Herbert T. Jenkins Papers
  Long-Rucker-Aiken Family Papers
  Robert F. Maddox Papers
 Atlanta University Center, Robert W. Woodruff Library,
 Archives and Special Collections
  Atlanta University Archives Collection
  Records of Gammon Theological Seminary. Microfilm.

Neighborhood Union Collection
Watson, Hattie Rutherford. "Work of the Neighborhood Union."
Spelman Messenger, November 1916. Folder 8, box 5.
Vertical Files
Emory University, Robert W. Woodruff Library, Special Collections and Archives
Asa Griggs Candler Papers
Warren Akin Candler Papers
Georgia Woman's Christian Temperance Union Records
Joel Chandler Harris Papers
Julian LaRose Harris Papers
Charles Forrest Palmer Papers
First Congregational Church
Women's Missionary Society Minutes

Cambridge, Massachusetts
Harvard University, Houghton Library
Oswald Garrison Villard Papers

Chapel Hill, North Carolina
University of North Carolina, Southern Historical Collection
Thomas E. Watson Papers

Chicago, Illinois
University of Illinois, Richard J. Daley Library, Special Collections
Emma and Lloyd Lewis Family Papers

Durham, North Carolina
Duke University, Rare Book, Manuscript, and Special Collections Library
Ernest Sevier Cox Papers
W. A. Pledger Letter Book

Morrow, Georgia
Georgia Archives and History Division
First Congregational Church Minutes. Microfilm.
Gov. William J. Northen Papers
John M. Slaton Papers

New Orleans, Louisiana
Tulane University, Tilton Hall, Amistad Research Center
Office of Church Building of the United Church Board for
Homeland Ministries Archives
Henry Hugh and Adeline L. Proctor (Davis) Papers

Washington, D.C.
Library of Congress, Manuscript Division
Ray Stannard Baker Papers. Microfilm.

MANUSCRIPTS PUBLISHED ON MICROFILM

Commission on Interracial Cooperation Papers. Glen Rock, N.J.: Microfilming Corporation of America, 1984.

Papers of Booker T. Washington. Washington, D.C.: Library of Congress, Photoduplication Service, 1981.

Papers of John and Lugenia Burns Hope. Frederick, Md.: University Publications of America, 1984.

Papers of Mary Church Terrell. Washington, D.C.: Library of Congress, Photoduplication Service, 1977.

Papers of the NAACP. Frederick, Md.: University Publications of America, 1981.

W. E. B. Du Bois Papers. Sanford, N.C.: Microfilming Corporation of America, 1980.

INTERVIEWS

Atlanta History Center, James G. Kenan Research Center,
Library and Archives, Living Atlanta Collection
Adams, Kathleen R. Interview by E. Bernard West, 11 March 1980.
Fiebelman, Clarence. Interview by Cliff Kuhn, 18 March 1980.
Griffin, John. Interview by Cliff Kuhn, 27 March 1980.
Lewis, E. T. Interview by E. Bernard West, 18 March 1980.
Meyers, Ethel. Interview by Cliff Kuhn, 6 March 1980.
Morton, Mary. Interview by E. Bernard West, 11 February 1980.
Owens, Ruby. Interview by E. Bernard West, 23 January 1979.
Sinclair, Horace. Interview by E. Bernard West, 18 July 1979.
Usher, Bazoline. Interview by E. Bernard West, 5 September 1979.
Washburn, Nannie L. Interview by Cliff Kuhn, 8 December 1978.
Witherspoon, Evelyn. Interview by Cliff Kuhn, 13 March 1979.

"Beyond Gentrification: Strategies for Managing Community Change." *P.O.V.*
<http://www.pbs.org/pov/pov2003/flagwars/special—roundtablemy.html>.
29 January 2005.

Youngblood, Mtamanika. Interview by Harold Simon, [ca. 2003].

GOVERNMENT DOCUMENTS

Fulton County Superior Court, Fulton County, Georgia. Superior Court Criminal Cases (indictments).

Georgia Reports. Johnson v. State, 128 Ga. 102, 57 S.E. 353 (1907).

U.S. Bureau of the Census. *Occupations at the Twelfth Census, 1900.* Washington, D.C.: Government Printing Office, 1904.

———. *Thirteenth Census of the United States, 1910.* Vol. 9. *Manufactures.* Washington, D.C.: Government Printing Office, 1912.

NEWSPAPERS

Atlanta Constitution
Atlanta Evening News
Atlanta Georgian
Atlanta Independent
Atlanta Journal
Boston Evening Transcript
Brooklyn Eagle
Brooklyn Standard Union
Chicago Broad Ax
Chicago Defender
Congregationalist
Georgia Baptist
Golden Age
Journal of Labor
Los Angeles Times
Macon Daily Telegraph
New York Age
New York Daily Tribune
New York Evening Post
New York Herald
New York Times
New York World
San Francisco Chronicle
Washington Bee
Washington Post

PERIODICALS AND ANNUALS

American Magazine
Atlanta City Directory
Atlantic Monthly
N. W. Ayer and Son's American Newspaper Annual
Bulletin of Atlanta University
Collier's
Colored American Magazine
Crisis
Harper's Weekly
Independent
Literary Digest
Nation
Outlook
Phylon
South Atlantic Quarterly

Southern Workman
Spelman Messenger
Tom Watson's Magazine
Voice
Voice of the Negro
Watson's Jeffersonian Magazine
Watson's Magazine
World To-Day
World's Work

BOOKS, ARTICLES, DISSERTATIONS, AND THESES

Adams, John Henry. "Rough Sketches: A Study of the Features of the New Negro Woman."
    Voice of the Negro 1 (August 1904): 323–26.
——. "Rough Sketches: The New Negro Man." *Voice of the Negro* 1 (October 1904): 447–52.
——. "Rough Sketches: William Edward Burghardt DuBois, Ph.D." *Voice of the Negro* 2 (March
    1905): 176–81.
Allen, Ivan, Jr., with Paul Hemphill. *Mayor: Notes on the Sixties*. New York: Simon and
    Schuster, 1971.
"An American Kishinev." *Outlook* 84 (29 September 1906): 241–42.
Anderson, James D. *The Education of Blacks in the South, 1860–1935*. Chapel Hill: University of
    North Carolina Press, 1988.
Angell, Stephen Ward. *Bishop Henry McNeal Turner and African-American Religion in the
    South*. Knoxville: University of Tennessee Press, 1992.
Ansley, Lula Barnes. *History of the Georgia Woman's Christian Temperance Union: From Its
    Organization, 1883–1907*. Columbus, Ga.: Gilbert Printing Co., 1914.
Aptheker, Herbert, ed. *1891–1909*. Vol. 1 of *Writings by W. E. B. Du Bois in Periodicals Edited by
    Others*. Millwood, N.Y.: Kraus-Thomson, 1982.
——, ed. *Contributions by W. E. B. Du Bois in Government Publications and Proceedings*.
    Millwood, N.Y.: Kraus-Thomson, 1980.
——, ed. *The Correspondence of W. E. B. Du Bois*. 3 vols. Amherst: University of Massachusetts
    Press, 1973–78.
——, ed. *Pamphlets and Leaflets by W. E. B. Du Bois*. White Plains, N.Y.: Kraus-Thomson,
    1986.
——, ed. *Selections from the Horizon*. Vol. 1 of *Writings in Periodicals Edited by W. E. B.
    Du Bois*. Millwood, N.Y.: Kraus-Thomson, 1985.
Atlanta Centennial Year Book, 1837–1937. Atlanta: G. Murphy, 1937.
Atlanta Chamber of Commerce. *Annual Report*, 1905, 1906.
——. *Atlanta: A Twentieth Century City*. Atlanta: Foote and Davies, 1903.
"The Atlanta Massacre." *Independent* 61 (4 October 1906): 799–800.
"Atlanta's Race War." *Collier's* 38 (6 October 1906): 13–14.
Ayers, Edward. *The Promise of the New South: Life after Reconstruction*. New York: Oxford
    University Press, 1992.
——. *Vengeance and Justice: Crime and Punishment in the Nineteenth-Century American South*.
    New York: Oxford University Press, 1984.

Bacote, Clarence A. "Georgia's Reaction to the Negro Policy of Theodore Roosevelt." *Atlanta Historical Bulletin* 21 (Spring 1977): 72–94.

——. "The Negro in Atlanta Politics." *Phylon* 16 (4th quarter 1955): 333–50.

——. "The Negro in Georgia Politics, 1880–1908." Ph.D. diss., University of Chicago, 1955.

——. "Negro Officeholders in Georgia under President McKinley." *Journal of Negro History* 44 (July 1959): 217–39.

——. *The Story of Atlanta University: A Century of Service, 1896–1965.* Atlanta: Atlanta University, 1969.

Baker, Ray Stannard. *The Atlanta Riot.* New York: Philips, 1907.

——. *Following the Color Line: An Account of Negro Citizenship in the American Democracy.* New York: Doubleday, Page, 1908.

——. "Following the Color Line—A Race Riot, and After." *American Magazine* 63 (April 1907): 563–79.

——. "Negro Suffrage in a Democracy." *Atlantic Monthly* 106 (November 1910): 612–19.

Bannister, Robert C. *Ray Stannard Baker: The Mind and Thought of a Progressive.* New Haven: Yale University Press, 1966.

Barber, J. Max. "The Atlanta Tragedy." *Voice* 3 (November 1906): 473–79.

——. "The Morning Cometh." *Voice of the Negro* 1 (January 1904): 37–38.

——. "The Niagara Movement at Harpers Ferry." *Voice of the Negro* 3 (October 1906): 402–11.

——. "Why Mr. Barber Left Atlanta." *Voice* 3 (November 1906): 470–72.

Bartley, Numan V. *The Creation of Modern Georgia.* 2nd ed. Athens: University of Georgia Press, 1990.

Bauerlein, Mark. *Negrophobia: A Race Riot in Atlanta, 1906.* San Francisco: Encounter Books, 2001.

Bauman, Mark K. *Warren Akin Candler: The Conservative as Idealist.* Metuchen, N.J.: Scarecrow Press, 1981.

Bay, Mia. *The White Image in the Black Mind: African-American Ideas about White People, 1830–1925.* New York: Oxford University Press, 2000.

Bayor, Ronald H. *Race and the Shaping of Twentieth-Century Atlanta.* Chapel Hill: University of North Carolina Press, 1996.

Beard, Annie R. "Mrs. John Hope, Black Community Builder in Atlanta, Georgia, 1900–1936." Master's thesis, Atlanta University, 1975.

Beardsley, Edward H. *A History of Neglect: Health Care for Blacks and Mill Workers in the Twentieth-Century South.* Knoxville: University of Tennessee Press, 1987.

Bederman, Gail. *Manliness and Civilization: A Cultural History of Gender and Race in the United States, 1880–1917.* Chicago: University of Chicago Press, 1995.

Bender, Thomas. "Wholes and Parts: The Need for Synthesis in American History." *Journal of American History* 73 (June 1986): 120–36.

Bernstein, Iver. *The New York City Draft Riots: Their Significance for American Society and Politics in the Age of the Civil War.* New York: Oxford University Press, 1990.

Berry, David Charles. "Free Labor He Found Unsatisfactory: James W. English and Convict Lease Labor at the Chattahoochee Brick Company." Master's thesis, Georgia State University, 1991.

Bolden, Willie Miller. "The Political Structure of Charter Revision Movements in Atlanta during the Progressive Era." Ph.D. diss., Emory University, 1978.

Bonner, James Calvin. "The Gubernatorial Career of W. J. Northen." Master's thesis, University of Georgia, 1936.

Borchert, James. *Alley Life in Washington: Family, Community, Religion, and Folklife in the City, 1850–1970*. Urbana: University of Illinois Press, 1980.

Bowen, J. W. E. "Doing Things at the Tuskegee Institute." *Voice of the Negro* 2 (April 1905): 249–53.

Boyer, Paul. *Urban Masses and Moral Order in America, 1820–1920*. Cambridge: Harvard University Press, 1978.

Brawley, James P. *Two Centuries of Methodist Concern: Bondage, Freedom, and Education of Black People*. New York: Vantage, 1974.

Brown, Charlie. *Charlie Brown Remembers Atlanta: Memoirs of a Public Man as Told to James C. Bryant*. Columbia, S.C.: R. L. Bryan Co., 1982.

Brown, Elsa Barkley. "Negotiating and Transforming the Public Sphere: African American Political Life in the Transition from Slavery to Freedom." In *Jumpin' Jim Crow: Southern Politics from Civil War to Civil Rights*, edited by Jane Dailey, Glenda Elizabeth Gilmore, and Bryant Simon, 28–64. Princeton: Princeton University Press, 2000.

———. " 'What Has Happened Here': The Politics of Difference in Women's History and Feminist Politics." In *"We Specialize in the Wholly Impossible": A Reader in Black Women's History*, edited by Darlene Clark Hine, Wilma King, and Linda Reed, 39–54. Brooklyn: Carlson Publishing, 1995.

Brown, Richard Maxwell. *Strain of Violence: Historical Studies of American Violence and Vigilantism*. New York: Oxford University Press, 1975.

Bruce, Philip A. *The Plantation Negro as a Freeman: Observations on His Character, Condition, and Prospects in Virginia*. 1889. Reprint. Williamstown, Mass.: Corner House Publishers, 1970.

Brundage, W. Fitzhugh. *Lynching in the New South: Georgia and Virginia, 1880–1930*. Urbana: University of Illinois Press, 1993.

Bryant, Jonathan M. *How Curious a Land: Conflict and Change in Greene County, Georgia, 1850–1885*. Chapel Hill: University of North Carolina Press, 1996.

Bryant, Peter James. "Negro Inferiority and Disfranchisement." *Voice of the Negro* 3 (July 1906): 510–14.

Bullock, Penelope L. *The Afro-American Periodical Press, 1838–1909*. Baton Rouge: Louisiana State University Press, 1981.

———. "Profile of a Periodical: The 'Voice of the Negro.' " *Journal of Negro History* 54 (April 1969): 150–73.

"The Burdened South." *World's Work* 13 (November 1906): 8148.

Campbell, Gavin James. *Music and the Making of a New South*. Chapel Hill: University of North Carolina Press, 2004.

Candler, Charles Howard. *Asa Griggs Candler*. Atlanta: Emory University Press, 1950.

Capeci, Dominic J., Jr. *The Lynching of Cleo Wright*. Lexington: University Press of Kentucky, 1998.

Capeci, Dominic J., Jr., and Jack C. Knight. "Reckoning with Violence: W. E. B. Du Bois and the 1906 Atlanta Race Riot." *Journal of Southern History* 62 (November 1996): 727–66.

———. "W. E. B. Du Bois's Southern Front: Georgia's 'Race Men' and the Niagara Movement, 1905–1907." *Georgia Historical Quarterly* 83 (Fall 1999): 479–507.

Carson, Clayborne, ed. *Called to Serve, January 1929–June 1951*. Vol. 1 of *The Papers of Martin Luther King, Jr*. Berkeley: University of California Press, 1992.

Carter, Edward R. *The Black Side: A Partial History of the Business, Religious, and Education Side of the Negro in Atlanta, Ga*. 1894. Reprint. Freeport, N.Y.: Books for Libraries Press, 1971.

Cell, John. *The Highest Stage of White Supremacy: The Origins of Segregation in South Africa and the American South*. Cambridge: Cambridge University Press, 1982.

Chafe, William H. *Civilities and Civil Rights: Greensboro, North Carolina, and the Black Struggle for Freedom*. New York: Oxford University Press, 1980.

——. "Epilogue from Greensboro, North Carolina." In *Democracy Betrayed: The Wilmington Race Riot of 1898 and Its Legacy*, edited by David S. Celeski and Timothy B. Tyson, 277–86. Chapel Hill: University of North Carolina Press, 1998.

Chappell, David L. *Inside Agitators: White Southerners in the Civil Rights Movement*. Baltimore: Johns Hopkins University Press, 1994.

——. *A Stone of Hope: Prophetic Religion and the Death of Jim Crow*. Chapel Hill: University of North Carolina Press, 2004.

Cleaton, J. D. *Atlanta: The Metropolis of the South*. Atlanta: Franklin-Turner, 1907.

Clifford, Carrie. "Atlanta's Shame." *Voice* 3 (November 1906): 497.

——. "The Atlanta Riots II—A Northern Black Point of View." *Outlook* 84 (3 November 1906): 562–64.

Clowse, Barbara Barksdale. *Ralph McGill: A Biography*. Macon, Ga.: Mercer University Press, 1998.

The Code of the State of Georgia, Adopted December 15th, 1895. Vol. 3. Atlanta: Foote and Davies, 1896.

Coleman, Kenneth, and Charles Stephen Gurr. *Dictionary of Georgia Biography*. 2 vols. Athens: University of Georgia Press, 1983.

Colored Citizens. *A Memorial to the Georgia Legislature on the Disfranchisement Bill*. Atlanta: Franklin Publishing, 1907.

Cooper, Walter G. *Official History of Fulton County*. Atlanta: Walter W. Brown Publishing, 1934.

Courtwright, David T. *Violent Land: Single Men and Social Disorder from the Frontier to the Inner City*. Cambridge: Harvard University Press, 1996.

"Crime." *Crisis* 3 (March 1912): 189.

Crowe, Charles. "Racial Massacre in Atlanta, September 22, 1906." *Journal of Negro History* 54 (April 1969): 150–73.

——. "Racial Violence and Social Reform—Origins of the Atlanta Riot of 1906." *Journal of Negro History* 53 (July 1968): 234–56.

Cutler, James Elbert. *Lynch-Law: An Investigation into the History of Lynching in the United States*. 1905. Reprint. Montclair, N.J.: Patterson Smith, 1969.

Dailey, Jane Elizabeth. *Before Jim Crow: The Politics of Race in Postemancipation Virginia*. Chapel Hill: University of North Carolina Press, 2000.

Dailey, Jane, Glenda Elizabeth Gilmore, and Bryant Simon, eds. *Jumpin' Jim Crow: Southern Politics from Civil War to Civil Rights*. Princeton: Princeton University Press, 2000.

Daniel, Walter C. *Black Journals of the United States*. Westport, Conn.: Greenwood Press, 1982.

Davis, Benjamin J. *Communist Councilman from Harlem: Autobiographical Notes Written in a Federal Penitentiary*. New York: International Publishers, 1969.

Davis, Harold E. *Henry Grady's New South: Atlanta, a Brave and Beautiful City*. Tuscaloosa: University of Alabama Press, 1990.

Davis, Leroy. *A Clashing of the Soul: John Hope and the Dilemma of African American Leadership and Black Higher Education in the Early Twentieth Century*. Athens: University of Georgia Press, 1998.

Deaton, Thomas Mashburn. "Atlanta during the Progressive Era." Ph.D. diss., University of Georgia, 1969.

——. "James G. Woodward: The Working Man's Mayor." *Atlanta History: A Journal of Georgia and the South* 31 (Fall 1987): 11–23.

D'Emilio, John, and Estelle B. Freedman. *Intimate Matters: A History of Sexuality in America*. New York: Harper and Row, 1988.

Dinnerstein, Leonard. *The Leo Frank Case*. New York: Columbia University Press, 1968.

Dittmer, John. *Black Georgia in the Progressive Era, 1900–1920*. Urbana: University of Illinois Press, 1977.

Donaldson, Bobby J. "New Negroes in a New South: Race, Power, and Ideology in Georgia, 1890–1925." Ph.D. diss., Emory University, 2002.

——. "Standing on a Volcano: The Leadership of William Jefferson White." In *Paternalism in a Southern City: Race, Religion, and Gender in Augusta*, edited by Edward J. Cashin and Glenn T. Eskew, 135–75. Athens: University of Georgia Press, 2001.

Dorr, Lisa Lindquist. *White Women, Rape, and the Power of Race in Virginia, 1900–1960*. Chapel Hill: University of North Carolina Press, 2004.

Dorsey, Allison. *To Build Our Lives Together: Community Formation in Black Atlanta, 1875–1906*. Athens: University of Georgia Press, 2004.

Douglas, Mary. *Purity and Danger: An Analysis of Concepts of Pollution and Taboo*. 1966. Reprint. London: Routledge, 1992.

Doyle, Don H. *New Men, New Cities, New South: Atlanta, Nashville, Charleston, Mobile, 1860–1910*. Chapel Hill: University of North Carolina Press, 1990.

Drago, Edmund. *Black Politicians and Reconstruction in Georgia: A Splendid Failure*. Baton Rouge: Louisiana State University Press, 1982.

Dray, Philip. *At the Hands of Persons Unknown: The Lynching of Black America*. New York: Random House, 2002.

Du Bois, W. E. B. *The Autobiography of W. E. B. Du Bois: A Soliloquy on Viewing My Life from the Last Decade of Its First Century*. New York: International Publishers, 1968.

——. "Growth of the Niagara Movement." *Voice of the Negro* 3 (January 1906): 43–45.

——. "A Litany of Atlanta." *Independent* 61 (11 October 1906): 856–58.

——. *Mansart Builds a School*. Vol. 2 of *The Black Flame: A Trilogy*. New York: Mainstream Publishers, 1959.

——, ed. *Morality among Negroes in Cities*. Atlanta University Publication 1. Atlanta: Atlanta University Press, 1896.

——, ed. *The Negro American Family*. Atlanta University Publication 13. Atlanta: Atlanta University Press, 1908.

——. "The Negro in the Black Belt: Some Social Sketches [1899]." In *Contributions by W. E. B.*

Du Bois in Government Publications and Proceedings, edited by Herbert Aptheker, 45–63. Millwood, N.Y.: Kraus-Thomson, 1980.

——. "The Niagara Movement." In *The Oxford W. E. B. Du Bois Reader*, edited by Eric J. Sundquist, 373–76. New York: Oxford University Press, 1996.

——, ed. *Notes on Negro Crime Particularly in Georgia*. Atlanta University Publication 9. Atlanta: Atlanta University Press, 1904.

——. *The Ordeal of Mansart*. Vol. 1 of *The Black Flame: A Trilogy*. New York: Mainstream Publishers, 1957.

——. "A Plucky Man." *Crisis* 5 (November 1912): 16.

——. "Postscript: Looking Seventy-five Years Backward." *Phylon* 3 (2nd quarter 1942): 238–48.

——. "The Shadow of Years." *Crisis* 15 (February 1918): 167–71.

——, ed. *Social and Physical Conditions of Negroes in Cities*. Atlanta University Publication 2. Atlanta: Atlanta University Press, 1897.

——. *The Souls of Black Folk: Authoritative Text, Contexts, Criticism*. Edited by Henry Louis Gates Jr. and Terry Hume Oliver. New York: Norton, 1999.

——. "The Tragedy at Atlanta II—From the Point of View of the Negroes." *World To-Day* 11 (November 1906): 1173–75.

——. "The Value of Agitation." *Voice* 4 (March 1907): 109–10.

——. *Worlds of Color*. Vol. 3 of *The Black Flame: A Trilogy*. New York: Mainstream Publishers, 1961.

Durrett, Dan, and Dana White. *An-Other Atlanta: The Black Heritage*. Atlanta: History Group, 1975.

Dyer, Thomas G. *Theodore Roosevelt and the Idea of Race*. Baton Rouge: Louisiana State University Press, 1980.

Dykeman, Wilma. *Prophet of Plenty: The First Ninety Years of W. D. Weatherford*. Knoxville: University of Tennessee Press, 1966.

Dykeman, Wilma, and James Stokely. *Seeds of Southern Change: The Life of Will Alexander*. New York: Norton, 1976.

Egerton, John. *Speak Now against the Day: The Generation before the Civil Rights Movement in the South*. New York: Knopf, 1994.

Ellis, Ann W. "The Commission on Interracial Cooperation, 1919–1944: Its Activities and Results." Ph.D. diss., Georgia State University, 1975.

Ellis, Lenora Beck. "The Southern Negro as Property Owner." *Tom Watson's Magazine* 1 (June 1905): 429–34.

Ellsworth, Scott. *Death in a Promised Land: The Tulsa Race Riot of 1921*. Baton Rouge: Louisiana State University Press, 1982.

Eskew, Glenn T. "Black Elitism and the Failure of Paternalism in Postbellum Georgia: The Case of Bishop Lucius Holsey." *Journal of Southern History* 58 (November 1992): 637–66.

——. *But for Birmingham: The Local and National Movements in the Civil Rights Struggle*. Chapel Hill: University of North Carolina Press, 1997.

"Ex-Governor Northen's Campaign for Law and Order." *Bulletin of Atlanta University* 171 (March 1907): 1.

"Facts about the Atlanta Murders." *World's Work* 13 (November 1906): 8147–48.

Feimster, Crystal Nicole. " 'Ladies and Lynching': The Gendered Discourse of Mob Violence in the New South." Ph.D. diss., Princeton University, 2000.

Fennel, Dwight. "A Demographic Study of Black Business, 1905–1908, with Respect to the Race Riot of 1906." Master's thesis, Atlanta University, 1977.

Ferguson, Karen. *Black Politics in New Deal Atlanta*. Chapel Hill: University of North Carolina Press, 2002.

"A Few of the Thousand Letters from Our Friends." *Voice* 3 (November 1906): 500–503.

Fields, Barbara J. "Ideology and Race in American History." In *Region, Race, and Reconstruction: Essays in Honor of C. Vann Woodward*, edited by J. Morgan Kousser and James M. McPherson, 143–77. New York: Oxford University Press, 1982.

Flamming, Douglas. *Creating the Modern South: Millhands and Managers in Dalton, Georgia, 1884–1984*. Chapel Hill: University of North Carolina Press, 1992.

——. " 'Give Her Some out of That': Cotton Mill Girls, Family Wages, and the Question of Female Independence in the New South." In *Labor in the Modern South*, edited by Glen T. Eskew, 47–61. Athens: University of Georgia Press, 2001.

Foner, Eric. *Reconstruction: America's Unfinished Revolution, 1863–1877*. New York: Harper and Row, 1988.

"For Law and Order." *Independent* 63 (11 July 1907): 106–7.

Foucault, Michel. *Discipline and Punish: The Birth of the Prison*. Translated by Alan Sheridan. New York: Vintage, 1979.

——. *An Introduction*. Vol. 1 of *The History of Sexuality*. Translated by Robert Hurley. New York: Vintage, 1978.

Franklin, John Hope, and August Meier, eds. *Black Leaders of the Twentieth Century*. Urbana: University of Illinois Press, 1982.

Fraser, Nancy. *Unruly Practices: Power, Discourse, and Gender in Contemporary Social Theory*. Minneapolis: University of Minnesota Press, 1989.

Frazier, Edward Franklin. "Neighborhood Union in Atlanta." *Southern Workman* 52 (September 1923): 437–42.

Fredrickson, George M. *The Arrogance of Race: Historical Perspectives on Slavery, Racism, and Social Inequality*. Middletown, Conn.: Wesleyan University Press, 1988.

——. *The Black Image in the White Mind: The Debate on Afro-American Character and Destiny, 1817–1914*. New York: Harper and Row, 1972.

——. *White Supremacy: A Comparative Study in American and South African History*. New York: Oxford University Press, 1981.

Friedman, Lawrence M. *Crime and Punishment in American History*. New York: Basic Books, 1993.

Friedman, Lawrence M., and Robert V. Percival. *The Roots of Justice: Crime and Punishment in Alameda County, California, 1870–1910*. Chapel Hill: University of North Carolina Press, 1981.

Frith, Aaron. "The Manger of the Movement: Atlanta and the Black Freedom Struggle, 1890–1950." Ph.D. diss., Yale University Press, 1997.

Gaines, Kevin K. *Uplifting the Race: Black Leadership, Politics, and Culture in the Twentieth Century*. Chapel Hill: University of North Carolina Press, 1996.

Galloway, Tammy Harden. *The Inman Family: An Atlanta Family from Reconstruction to World War*. Macon, Ga.: Mercer University Press, 2002.

Garrett, Franklin M. *Atlanta and Environs: A Chronicle of Its People and Events*. Vol. 2. 1954. Reprint. Athens: University of Georgia Press, 1969.

Garrow, David J., ed. *Atlanta, Georgia, 1960–61: Sit-Ins and Student Activism*. Brooklyn: Carlson Publishing, 1989.

——. *Bearing the Cross: Martin Luther King, Jr., and the Southern Christian Leadership Conference*. New York: William Morrow, 1986.

Gaston, Paul M. *The New South Creed: A Study in Southern Mythmaking*. New York: Knopf, 1970.

Gatewood, Willard B. *Aristocrats of Color: The Black Elite, 1880–1920*. Bloomington: University of Indiana Press, 1990.

Gaventa, John. *Power and Powerlessness: Quiescence and Rebellion in an Appalachian Valley*. Urbana: University of Illinois Press, 1980.

Genovese, Eugene D. *Roll, Jordan, Roll: The World the Slaves Made*. New York: Pantheon, 1974.

"Georgia's Political Mess." *Voice of the Negro* 3 (January 1906): 62–63.

Georgia Writers' Program. *Atlanta: A City of the Modern South*. 1942. Reprint. St. Clair Shores, Mich.: Somerset Publishers, 1973.

Gerstle, Gary. *American Crucible: Race and Nation in the Twentieth Century*. Princeton: Princeton University Press, 2001.

Gibson, Thomas. "The Anti-Negro Riots in Atlanta." *Harper's Weekly* 50 (13 October 1906): 1457–59.

Giddings, Paula. *When and Where I Enter: The Impact of Black Women on Race and Sex in America*. New York: William Morrow, 1984.

Gilmore, Glenda Elizabeth. *Gender and Jim Crow: Women and the Politics of White Supremacy in North Carolina, 1896–1920*. Chapel Hill: University of North Carolina Press, 1996.

——. "Murder, Memory, and the Flight of the Incubus." In *Democracy Betrayed: The Wilmington Race Riot of 1898 and Its Legacy*, edited by David S. Celeski and Timothy B. Tyson, 73–93. Chapel Hill: University of North Carolina Press, 1998.

Gladwell, Malcolm. *The Tipping Point: How Little Things Can Make a Big Difference*. Boston: Little, Brown, 2000.

Godshalk, David Fort. "In the Wake of Riot: Atlanta's Struggle for Order, 1899–1919." Ph.D. diss., Yale University, 1992.

——. "William J. Northen's Public and Personal Struggles against Lynching." In *Jumpin' Jim Crow: Southern Politics from Civil War to Civil Rights*, edited by Jane Dailey, Glenda Elizabeth Gilmore, and Bryant Simon, 140–61. Princeton: Princeton University Press, 2000.

Goldfield, David R. "The Urban South: A Regional Framework." *American Historical Review* 86 (December 1981): 1009–34.

"A Good Sequel to the Atlanta Riot." *World's Work* 13 (March 1907): 8592.

Goodson, Steve. *Highbrows, Hillbillies, and Hellfire: Public Entertainment in Atlanta, 1880–1930*. Athens: University of Georgia Press, 2002.

Gordon, Linda. "Black and White Visions of Welfare: Women's Welfare Activism, 1890–1945." *Journal of American History* 78 (September 1991): 559–90.

Grantham, Dewey W. Jr. *Hoke Smith and the Politics of the New South*. Baton Rouge: Louisiana State University Press, 1958.

——. Introduction to *Following the Color Line: American Negro Citizenship in the Progressive Era*, by Ray Stannard Baker. 1908. Reprint. New York: Harper and Row, 1964.

——. "Review Essay: The Contours of Southern Progressivism." *American Historical Review* 86 (December 1981): 1035–59.

———. *Southern Progressivism: The Reconciliation of Progress and Tradition.* Knoxville: University of Tennessee Press, 1983.

Graves, John Temple. "The Tragedy at Atlanta I—From the Point of View of Whites." *World To-Day* 11 (November 1906): 1169–73.

Greene, Melissa Fay. *The Temple Bombing.* Reading, Mass.: Addison-Wesley, 1996.

Griffin, Larry J., Paula Clark, and Joanne C. Sandberg. "Narrative and Event: Lynching and Historical Sociology." In *Under Sentence of Death: Lynching in the South,* edited by W. Fitzhugh Brundage, 24–47. Chapel Hill: University of North Carolina Press, 1997.

Grimké, Francis J. "The Atlanta Riot." In *Addresses Mainly Personal and Racial,* vol. 1 of *The Works of Francis J. Grimké,* edited by Carter G. Woodson, 406–18. Washington, D.C.: Associated Publishers, 1942.

Gutman, Herbert G. *The Black Family in Slavery and Freedom, 1750–1925.* New York: Pantheon, 1976.

Guy-Sheftall, Beverly. *Daughters of Sorrow: Attitudes toward Black Women, 1880–1920.* Brooklyn: Carlson Publishing, 1990.

Hahn, Steven. *A Nation under Our Feet: Black Political Struggles in the Rural South from Slavery to the Great Migration.* Cambridge: Harvard University Press, 2003.

———. *The Roots of Southern Populism: Yeoman Farmers and the Transformation of the Georgia Upcountry, 1850–1890.* New York: Oxford University Press, 1983.

Hale, Grace Elizabeth. " 'For Colored' and 'For White': Segregating Consumption in the South." In *Jumpin' Jim Crow: Southern Politics from Civil War to Civil Rights,* edited by Jane Dailey, Glenda Elizabeth Gilmore, and Bryant Simon, 162–82. Princeton: Princeton University Press, 2000.

Hall, Jacquelyn Dowd. "Disorderly Women: Gender and Labor Militancy in the Appalachian South." In *Unequal Sisters,* edited by Ellen Carol Dubois and Vicki L. Ruiz, 298–321. New York: Routledge, 1990.

———. " 'The Mind That Burns in Each Body': Women, Rape, and Racial Violence." In *Powers of Desire: The Politics of Sexuality,* edited by Ann Snitow, Christine Stansell, and Sharon Thompson, 328–49. New York: Monthly Review Press, 1983.

———. "O. Delight Smith's Progressive Era: Labor, Feminism, and Reform in the Urban South." In *Visible Women: New Essays on American Activism,* edited by Nancy A. Hewitt and Suzanne Lebsock, 166–98. Urbana: University of Illinois Press, 1993.

———. "Partial Truths: Writing Southern Women's History." In *Southern Women: Histories and Identities,* edited by Virginia Bernhard, Betty Brandon, Elizabeth Fox-Genovese, and Theda Perdue, 11–29. Columbia: University of Missouri Press, 1992.

———. "Private Eyes, Public Women: Images of Class and Sex in the Urban South, Atlanta, Georgia, 1913–1915." In *Work Engendered: Toward a New History of American Labor,* edited by Ava Baron, 243–72. Ithaca: Cornell University Press, 1991.

———. *Revolt against Chivalry: Jessie Daniel Ames and the Women's Campaign against Lynching.* New York: Columbia University Press, 1979.

———. " 'You Must Remember This': Autobiography as Social Critique." *Journal of American History* 85 (September 1998): 436–65.

Hall, Jacquelyn Dowd, James Leloudis, Robert Korstad, Mary Murphy, Lu Ann Jones, and Christopher B. Daly. *Like a Family: The Making of a Southern Cotton Mill World.* Chapel Hill: University of North Carolina Press, 1987.

Harlan, Louis R. *Booker T. Washington in Perspective: Essays of Louis R. Harlan*. Edited by
Raymond W. Smock. Jackson: University Press of Mississippi, 1988.

———. *Booker T. Washington: The Making of a Black Leader, 1856–1901*. New York: Oxford
University Press, 1972.

———. *Booker T. Washington: The Wizard of Tuskegee, 1901–1915*. New York: Oxford University
Press, 1983.

Harlan, Louis R., and Raymond W. Smock, eds. *The Booker T. Washington Papers*. 14 vols.
Urbana: University of Illinois Press, 1972–89.

Harley, Sharon. "When Your Work Is Not Who You Are: The Development of a Working-
Class Consciousness among Afro-American Women." In *"We Specialize in the Wholly
Impossible": A Reader in Black Women's History*, edited by Darlene Clark Hine, Wilma
King, and Linda Reed, 25–37. Brooklyn: Carlson Publishing, 1995.

Harris, Carl V. *Political Power in Birmingham, 1871–1921*. Knoxville: University of Tennessee
Press, 1977.

Harvey, Paul. *Redeeming the South: Religious Cultures and Racial Identities among Southern
Baptists, 1865–1925*. Chapel Hill: University of North Carolina Press, 1997.

Henderson, Alexa Benson. "Alonzo F. Herndon and Black Insurance in Atlanta, 1904–1915."
Atlanta Historical Society Bulletin 21 (Spring 1977): 34–47.

———. *Atlanta Life Insurance Company: Guardian of Black Economic Dignity*. Tuscaloosa:
University of Alabama Press, 1990.

Hewitt, Nancy A. *Southern Discomfort: Women's Activism in Tampa, Florida, 1880s–1920s*.
Urbana: University of Illinois Press, 2003.

Hickey, Georgina Susan. *Hope and Danger in the New South City: Working-Class Women and
Urban Development in Atlanta, 1890–1940*. Athens: University of Georgia Press, 2003.

———. "Visibility, Politics, and Urban Development: Working-Class Women in Early Twentieth
Century Atlanta." Ph.D. diss., University of Michigan, 1995.

Higginbotham, Evelyn Brooks. "African-American Women's History and the Metalanguage of
Race." In *"We Specialize in the Wholly Impossible": A Reader in Black Women's History*,
edited by Darlene Clark Hine, Wilma King, and Linda Reed, 3–24. Brooklyn: Carlson
Publishing, 1995.

———. *Righteous Discontent: The Women's Movement in the Black Baptist Church, 1880–1920*.
Cambridge: Harvard University Press, 1993.

Hill, Ruth Edmonds, ed. *The Black Women Oral History Project: From the Arthur and Elizabeth
Schlesinger Library on the History of Women in America, Radcliffe College*. 10 vols. Westport,
Conn.: Meckler, 1991.

Hodes, Martha. *White Women, Black Men: Illicit Sex in the Nineteenth Century South*. New
Haven: Yale University Press, 1997.

Holt, Thomas C. "Marking: Race, Race-making, and the Writing of History." *American
Historical Review* 100 (February 1995): 1–20.

Hope, John. "Our Atlanta Schools." *Voice of the Negro* 1 (January 1904): 10–16.

Horowitz, Donald L. *The Deadly Ethnic Riot*. Berkeley: University of California Press, 2001.

Hunter, Tera. "Domination and Resistance: The Politics of Wage Household Labor in New
South Atlanta." *Labor History* 34 (Spring/Summer 1993): 205–20.

———. "Household Workers in the Making: Afro-American Women in Atlanta and the New
South, 1861–1920." Ph.D. diss., Yale University, 1990.

——. *To 'Joy My Freedom: Southern Black Women's Lives and Labors after the Civil War*. Cambridge: Harvard University Press, 1997.

Hunton, Addie. "Negro Womanhood Defended." *Voice of the Negro* 1 (July 1904): 280–82.

——. *William Alphaeus Hunton: A Pioneer Prophet of Young Men*. New York: Association Press, 1938.

Jacobs, Thornwell. *The Law of the White Circle*. Nashville: Taylor-Trotwood Publishing Co., 1908.

——. *Step Down, Dr. Jacobs: The Autobiography of an Autocrat*. Atlanta: Westminster Publishers, 1945.

Jacoway, Elizabeth, and David R. Colburn. *Southern Businessmen and Desegregation*. Baton Rouge: Louisiana State University Press, 1982.

James, Joy. *Transcending the Talented Tenth: Black Leaders and American Intellectuals*. New York: Routledge, 1997.

Janken, Kenneth Robert. *Rayford W. Logan and the Dilemma of the African-American Intellectual*. Amherst: University of Massachusetts Press, 1993.

——. *White: The Biography of Walter White, Mr. NAACP*. New York: New Press, 2003.

Jenkins, Herbert T. *Keeping the Peace: A Police Chief Looks at His Job*. New York: Harper and Row, 1970.

Jenness, Mary. *Twelve Negro Americans*. New York: Friendship Press, 1936.

Johnson, Arthur Abby, and Ronald Maberry Johnson. *Propaganda and Aesthetics: The Literary Politics of Afro-American Magazines in the Twentieth Century*. Amherst: University of Massachusetts Press, 1979.

Johnson, Bethany. "Freedom and Slavery in the *Voice of the Negro*: Historical Memory and African-American Identity, 1904–1907." *Georgia Historical Quarterly* 84 (Spring 2000), 29–71.

Johnson, James Weldon. *Along This Way: The Autobiography of James Weldon Johnson*. New York: Viking, 1933.

Jones, Beverly Washington. *Quest for Equality: The Life and Writings of Mary Elizabeth Church Terrell, 1863–1954*. Brooklyn: Carlson Publishing, 1990.

Jones, Jacqueline. *Labor of Love, Labor of Sorrow: Black Women, Work, and the Family from Slavery to the Present*. New York: Basic Books, 1985.

Jones, M. Ashby. "Counting the Cost." *Southern Workman* 43 (January 1920): 12–14.

Judson, Sarah Mercer. "Building the 'New South' City: African-American and White Clubwomen in Atlanta, 1895–1930." Ph.D. diss., New York University, 1997.

"The Julius King Case." *Voice of the Negro* 3 (July 1906): 472–73.

Kantrowitz, Stephen. *Ben Tillman and the Reconstruction of White Supremacy*. Chapel Hill: University of North Carolina Press, 2000.

Katz, Michael B. *In the Shadow of the Poorhouse: A Social History of Welfare in America*. 10th anniversary ed. New York: Basic Books, 1996.

Kelley, Robin D. G. *Hammer and Hoe: Alabama Communists during the Great Depression*. Chapel Hill: University of North Carolina Press, 1990.

——. *Race Rebels: Culture, Politics, and the Black Working Class*. New York: Free Press, 1994.

——. " 'We Are Not What We Seem': Rethinking Black Working-Class Opposition in the Jim Crow South." *Journal of American History* 80 (June 1993): 75–112.

Kelling, George L., and Catherine M. Coles. *Fixing Broken Windows: Restoring Order and Reducing Crime in Our Communities*. New York: Martin Kessler Books, 1996.

Kellogg, Charles Flint. *NAACP: A History of the National Association for the Advancement of Colored People*. Vol. 1, *1909–1920*. Baltimore: Johns Hopkins University Press, 1967.

Kelly, Brian. *Race, Class, and Power in the Alabama Coalfields, 1908–1921*. Urbana: University of Illinois Press, 2001.

Kennedy, Randall. *Race, Crime, and the Law*. New York: Pantheon, 1997.

King, Martin Luther, Jr. *The Autobiography of Martin Luther King, Jr.* Edited by Clayborne Carson. New York: Warner Books, 1998.

King, Martin Luther, Sr., with Clayton Riley. *Daddy King: An Autobiography*. New York: William Morrow, 1980.

Kletzing, H. F., and W. H. Crogman. *The Progress of a Race: The Remarkable Advancement of the American Negro*. Atlanta: J. L. Nichols, 1897.

Knight, Lucian Lamar. *History of Fulton County, Georgia: Narrative and Biographical*. Atlanta: A. H. Cawston, 1930.

Kolchin, Peter. "Whiteness Studies: The New History of Race in America." *Journal of American History* 89 (June 2002): 154–73.

Kousser, J. Morgan. *The Shaping of Southern Politics: Suffrage Restriction and the Establishment of the One-Party South, 1880–1910*. New Haven: Yale University Press, 1974.

Kuhn, Clifford M. *Contesting the New South Order: The 1914–1915 Strike at Atlanta's Fulton Mills*. Chapel Hill: University of North Carolina Press, 2001.

——. " 'A Full History of the Strike as I Saw It': Atlanta's Fulton Bag and Cotton Mills Workers and Their Representations through the 1914–15 Strike." Ph.D. diss., University of North Carolina, 1993.

Kuhn, Clifford, Harlon E. Joye, and E. Bernard West. *Living Atlanta: An Oral History of the City, 1914–1948*. Atlanta and Athens: Atlanta Historical Society and University of Georgia Press, 1990.

Lane, Mills, ed. *Standing upon the Mouth of a Volcano: New South Georgia*. Savannah: Beehive Press, 1993.

Lane, Roger. *The Roots of Violence in Black Philadelphia, 1860–1900*. Cambridge: Harvard University Press, 1986.

Lasch-Quinn, Elizabeth. *Black Neighbors: Race and the Limits of Reform in the American Settlement House Movement, 1890–1945*. Chapel Hill: University of North Carolina Press, 1993.

"Law Re-established." *Outlook* 84 (6 October 1906): 296–97.

Lefever, Harry G. "The Involvement of the Men and Religion Forward Movement in the Cause of Labor Justice, Atlanta, Georgia, 1912–1916." *Labor History* 14 (Fall 1973): 521–35.

——. "Prostitution, Politics, and Religion: The Crusade against Vice in Atlanta in 1912." *Atlanta Historical Journal* 24 (Spring 1980): 7–19.

Levine, Lawrence. *Black Culture and Black Consciousness: Afro-American Folk Thought from Slavery to Freedom*. New York: Oxford University Press, 1977.

Lewis, David Levering. *W. E. B. Du Bois: Biography of a Race, 1868–1919*. New York: Henry Holt, 1993.

——. *W. E. B. Du Bois: The Fight for Equality and the American Century, 1919–1963*. New York: Henry Holt, 2000.

Lewis, Earl. *In Their Own Interests: Race, Class, and Power in Twentieth-Century Norfolk, Virginia*. Berkeley: University of California Press, 1990.

Lewis, John, with Michael D'Orso. *Walking with the Wind: A Memoir of the Movement*. New York: Simon and Schuster, 1998.

Link, William A. *The Paradox of Southern Progressivism, 1880–1930*. Chapel Hill: University of North Carolina Press, 1993.

Litwack, Leon. *Been in the Storm So Long: The Aftermath of Slavery*. New York: Vintage, 1980.

——. *Trouble in Mind: Black Southerners in the Age of Jim Crow*. New York: Knopf, 1998.

Love, J. Robert. "The Proclamation of Haitian Independence." *Voice of the Negro* 2 (September 1905): 634–38.

Luker, Ralph E. *The Social Gospel in Black and White: American Racial Reform, 1885–1912*. Chapel Hill: University of North Carolina Press, 1991.

Lutz, Christine Ann. "The Dizzy Steep to Heaven: The Hunton Family, 1850–1970." Ph.D. diss., Georgia State University, 2001.

"Lynching." *Crisis* 3 (January 1912): 101.

"Lynch Law in the South." *Independent* 61 (11 October 1906): 842–43.

Maclachlan, Gretchen Ehrmann. "Women's Work: Atlanta's Industrialization and Urbanization, 1879–1929." Ph.D. diss., Emory University, 1992.

MacLean, Nancy. *Behind the Mask of Chivalry: The Making of the Second Ku Klux Klan*. New York: Oxford University Press, 1994.

——. "The Leo Frank Case Reconsidered: Gender and Sexual Politics in the Making of Reactionary Populism." In *Jumpin' Jim Crow: Southern Politics from Civil War to Civil Rights*, edited by Jane Dailey, Glenda Elizabeth Gilmore, and Bryant Simon, 917–48. Princeton: Princeton University Press, 2000.

"The Macon Convention." *Voice of the Negro* 3 (March 1906): 163–64.

Martin, Harold H. *William Berry Hartsfield: Mayor of Atlanta*. Athens: University of Georgia Press, 1978.

Martin, Thomas H. *Atlanta and Its Builders: A Comprehensive History of the Gate City of the South*. 2 vols. Atlanta: Century Memorial Publishing Co., 1902.

Massey, James L., and Martha Meyers. "Patterns of Repressive Social Control in Post-Reconstruction Georgia, 1882–1935." *Social Forces* 68 (December 1989): 458–88.

Mathias, William J., and Stuart Anderson. *Horse to Helicopter: First Century of the Atlanta Police Department*. Atlanta: School of Urban Life, Georgia State University, 1973.

Matthews, John Michael. "Black Newspapermen and the Black Community in Georgia, 1890–1930." *Georgia Historical Quarterly* 68 (Fall 1984): 365–81.

——. "The Dilemma of Negro Leadership in the New South: The Case of the Negro Young People's Congress of 1902." *South Atlantic Quarterly* 73 (Winter 1974): 130–44.

——. "The Georgia 'Race Strike' of 1909." *Journal of Southern History* 40 (November 1974): 613–30.

Mays, Benjamin. *Born to Rebel*. 1971. Reprint. Athens: University of Georgia Press, 1987.

McCombs, McClure Person. " 'Pittsburgh': A Sociological Study of a 'Natural' Area." Master's thesis, Atlanta University, 1951.

McEwen, Homer C. "First Congregational Church, Atlanta." *Atlanta Historical Bulletin* 21 (Spring 1977): 129–41.

McKelway, A. J. "The Atlanta Riots I—A Southern White Point of View." *Outlook* 84 (3 November 1906): 557–62.

McMillen, Neil R. *Dark Journey: Black Mississippians in the Age of Jim Crow*. Urbana: University of Illinois Press, 1989.

McMurry, Linda O. *To Keep the Waters Troubled: The Life of Ida B. Wells*. New York: Oxford University Press, 1998.

McPherson, James M. *The Abolitionist Legacy: From Reconstruction to the NAACP*. Princeton: Princeton University Press, 1975.

Meier, August. *Negro Thought in America, 1880–1915: Racial Ideologies in the Age of Booker T. Washington*. Ann Arbor Paperback Edition. Ann Arbor: University of Michigan Press, 1966.

Meier, August, and David Lewis. "History of the Negro Upper Class in Atlanta, Georgia, 1890–1958." *Journal of Negro Education* 28 (Winter 1959): 128–39.

Meier, August, and Elliot Rudwick. *Along the Color Line: Explorations in the Black Experience*. Urbana: University of Illinois Press, 1976.

Mellinger, Wayne Martin. "John Henry Adams and the Image of the 'New Negro.'" *International Review of African American Art* 14 (1997): 29–33.

Melnick, Jeffrey. *Black-Jewish Relations on Trial: Leo Frank and Jim Conley in the New South*. Jackson: University of Mississippi Press, 2000.

Merritt, Carole. *The Herndons: An Atlanta Family*. Athens: University of Georgia Press, 2002.

Meyerowitz, Joanne. *Women Adrift: Independent Wage Earners in Chicago, 1880–1930*. Chicago: University of Chicago Press, 1988.

Miller, Kelly. "Achievements of the Negro Race." *Voice of the Negro* 2 (September 1905): 612–18.

———. "An Appeal to Reason on the Race Problem: An Open Letter to John Temples Graves Suggested by the Atlanta Riot, October, 1906." In *Radicals and Conservatives: And Other Essays on the Negro in America*, 71–101. 1908. Reprint. New York: Schocken Books, 1968.

Minnix, Kathleen. *Laughter in the Amen Corner: The Life of Evangelist Sam Jones*. Athens: University of Georgia Press, 1993.

Mitchell, Margaret. *Gone with the Wind*. New York: MacMillan, 1936.

Mixon, Gregory Lamont. "The Atlanta Riot of 1906." Ph.D. diss., University of Cincinnati, 1989.

———. *The Atlanta Riot: Race, Class, and Violence in a New South City*. Gainesville: University Press of Florida, 2005.

———. "'Good Negro–Bad Negro': The Dynamics of Race and Class in Atlanta during the Era of the 1906 Riot." *Georgia Historical Quarterly* 81 (Fall 1997): 593–621.

———. "The Political Career of Henry A. Rucker: A Survivor in a New South City." *Atlanta History: A Journal of Georgia and the South* 45 (Summer 2001): 4–26.

Montgomery, William E. *Under Their Own Vine and Fig Tree: The African American Church in the South, 1865–1900*. Baton Rouge: Louisiana State University Press, 1993.

Moore, Barrington, Jr. *Moral Purity and Persecution in History*. Princeton: Princeton University Press, 2000.

Moore, John Hammond. "The Negro and Prohibition in Atlanta, 1885–1887." *South Atlantic Quarterly* 69 (Winter 1970): 38–57.

Morison, Elting E., ed. *The Big Stick, 1906–1907*. Vol. 5 of *The Letters of Theodore Roosevelt*. Cambridge: Harvard University Press, 1952.

Morris, Edmund. *Theodore Rex*. New York: Random House, 2001.

Moseley, Clement Charlton. "The Political Influence of the Ku Klux Klan in Georgia, 1915–1925." *Georgia Historical Quarterly* 57 (Summer 1973): 235–55.

Myrick, Clarissa, Carolyn Seals, and Dan Moore. *Sweet Auburn: Street of Pride: A Pictorial History*. Atlanta: Apex, 1988.

Nasstrom, Kathryn L. "Down to Now: Memory, Narrative, and Women's Leadership in the Civil Rights Movement in Atlanta, Georgia." *Gender and History* 11 (April 1999): 113–44.

National Association for the Advancement of Colored People. *Thirty Years of Lynching in the United States, 1889–1918*. 1919. Reprint. New York: Arno Press, 1969.

"The Negro in the Message." *Voice* 3 (December 1906): 536–37.

Nesbitt, Martha Tovell. "The Social Gospel in Atlanta: 1900–1920." Ph.D. diss., Georgia State University, 1975.

Neverdon-Morton, Cynthia. *Afro-American Women of the South and the Advancement of the Race, 1895–1925*. Knoxville: University of Tennessee Press, 1989.

Newby, Idus A. *Plain Folk in the New South: Social Change and Cultural Persistence*. Baton Rouge: Louisiana State University Press, 1989.

Newman, Harvey K. *Southern Hospitality: Tourism and the Growth of Atlanta*. Tuscaloosa: University of Alabama Press, 1999.

"The Niagara Movement." *Voice of the Negro* 3 (July 1906): 476.

Ohmann, Richard M. *Selling Culture: Magazines, Markets, and Class at the Turn of the Century*. New York: Verso, 1996.

Oney, Steve. *And the Dead Shall Rise: The Murder of Mary Phagan and the Lynching of Leo Frank*. New York: Pantheon, 2003.

Ostrom, Elinor. "A Behavioral Approach to the Rational Choice Theory of Collective Action: Presidential Address, American Political Science Association, 1997." *American Political Science Review* 92 (March 1998): 1–22.

"Our Anniversary." *Voice of the Negro* 2 (January 1905): 694–95.

"Our Symposium." *Voice of the Negro* 2 (January 1905): 670.

Ovington, Mary White. *Portraits in Color*. New York: Viking, 1927.

——. *The Walls Came Tumbling Down*. New York: Harcourt, Brace, 1947.

Ownby, Ted. *Subduing Satan: Religion, Recreation, and Manhood in the Rural South, 1865–1920*. Chapel Hill: University of North Carolina Press, 1990.

Page, Thomas Nelson. *The Negro: The Southerner's Problem*. New York: Charles Scribner's Sons, 1904.

Page, Walter H. "A Journey through the Southern States." *World's Work* 14 (June 1907): 9003–36.

Painter, Nell Irvin. *Southern History across the Color Line*. Chapel Hill: University of North Carolina Press, 2002.

Patrick, Robert Pierce, Jr. "A Nail in the Coffin of Racism: The Story of the Columbians." *Georgia Historical Quarterly* 85 (Summer 2001): 245–63.

Patterson, Orlando. *Rituals of Blood: Consequences of Slavery in Two American Centuries*. Washington, D.C.: Civitas/Counterpoint, 1998.

——. *Slavery and Social Death: A Comparative Study*. Cambridge: Harvard University Press, 1982.

Payne, Charles M. *I've Got the Light of Freedom: The Organizing Tradition and Mississippi Freedom Struggle*. Berkeley: University of California Press, 1995.

Peiss, Kathy. *Cheap Amusements: Working Women and Leisure in Turn-of-the-Century New York*. Philadelphia: University of Pennsylvania Press, 1986.

Pendergrast, Mark. *For God, Country, and Coca-Cola: The Unauthorized History of the Great American Soft Drink and the Company That Makes It*. New York: Charles Scribner's Sons, 1993.

Penn, I. Garland, and J. W. E. Bowen. *The United Negro: His Problems and His Progress: Containing the Address and Proceedings of the Negro Young People's Christian and Educational Congress Held August 6–11, 1902*. Atlanta: D. E. Luther, 1902.

Perman, Michael. *Struggle for Mastery: Disfranchisement in the South, 1888–1908*. Chapel Hill: University of North Carolina Press, 2001.

Perry, Mark. *Lift Up Thy Voice: The Grimké Family's Journey from Slaveholders to Civil Rights Leaders*. New York: Viking, 2001.

"The Personal Issue." *Voice of the Negro* 1 (July 1904): 268.

Pickens, William. "Jesse Max Barber." *Voice* 3 (November 1906): 483–88.

Platt, Anthony. *E. Franklin Frazier Reconsidered*. New Brunswick: Rutgers University Press, 1991.

Polletta, Francesca. *Freedom Is an Endless Meeting: Democracy in American Social Movements*. Chicago: University of Chicago Press, 2002.

Pomerantz, Gary. *Where Peachtree Meets Sweet Auburn: The Saga of Two Families and the Making of Atlanta*. New York: Charles Scribner's Sons, 1996.

Porter, Michael Leroy. "Black Atlanta: An Interdisciplinary Study of Blacks on the East Side of Atlanta, 1890–1930." Ph.D. diss., Emory University, 1974.

The Possibilities of the Negro in Symposium. Atlanta: Franklin Printing and Publishing, 1904.

Prather, H. Leon, Sr. "We Have Taken a City: A Centennial Essay." In *Democracy Betrayed: The Wilmington Race Riot of 1898 and Its Legacy*, edited by David S. Celeski and Timothy B. Tyson, 15–41. Chapel Hill: University of North Carolina Press, 1998.

Proctor, H. H., and M. N. Work. "Atlanta and Savannah." In *Some Notes on Negro Crime, Particularly in Georgia*, edited by W. E. B. Du Bois. Atlanta University Publication 9. Atlanta: Atlanta University Press, 1904.

Proctor, Henry Hugh. "The Atlanta Plan of Inter-Racial Cooperation." *Southern Workman* 42 (January 1920): 9–12.

———. "The Atlanta Riot: Fundamental Causes and Reactionary Results." *Southern Workman* 36 (August 1907): 424–26.

———. *Between Black and White: Autobiographical Sketches*. Boston: Pilgrim Press, 1925.

———. "The Church as an Institution for Social Betterment." In *Some Efforts of American Negroes for Their Own Social Betterment*, edited by W. E. B. Du Bois, 50–51. Atlanta University Publication 3. Atlanta: Atlanta University Press, 1898.

———. "A Day at Andersonville." *Voice of the Negro* 1 (June 1904): 234–37.

———. *A Living Fountain*. New York: American Missionary Association, n.d.

———. "The Need of Friendly Visitation." In *Social and Physical Condition of Negroes in Cities*, edited by W. E. B. Du Bois, 44–45. Atlanta University Publication 2. Atlanta: Atlanta University Press, 1897.

———. "New Era of Reconstruction." *Bulletin of Atlanta University* 170 (February 1907): 1.

——. "Puritans in Bronze." *Congregationalist* 108 (2 August 1923): 148–49.

——. "A Southerner of the New School: William J. Northen." *Southern Workman* 42 (July 1913): 406–7.

Proctor, Mrs. H. H. *Negro Womanhood*. New York: American Missionary Society, n.d.

Pyron, Darden Asbury. *Southern Daughter: The Life of Margaret Mitchell*. New York: Oxford University Press, 1991.

Rabinowitz, Howard. "More than the Woodward Thesis: Assessing the Strange Career of Jim Crow." *Journal of American History* 75 (December 1988): 842–86.

——. *Race Relations in the Urban South, 1865–1890*. New York: Oxford University Press, 1978.

Rable, George C. *But There Was No Peace: The Role of Violence in the Politics of Reconstruction*. Athens: University of Georgia Press, 1984.

"Race Riots and Murders in Atlanta." *Independent* 61 (27 September 1906): 713–14.

"The Race-War in Atlanta." *World To-Day* 11 (November 1906): 1127–28.

"Racial Self-Restraint." *Outlook* 84 (6 October 1906): 308–10.

Raines, Howell. *My Soul Is Rested: Movement Days in the Deep South Remembered*. New York: Putnam, 1977.

Rainey, Glenn Weddington. "The Race Riot of 1906 in Atlanta." Master's thesis, Emory University, 1929.

Rampersad, Arnold. *The Art and Imagination of W. E. B. Du Bois*. 1976. Reprint. New York: Schocken Books, 1990.

Rawick, George P., ed. *The American Slave: A Composite Autobiography*. Supplement, ser. 1, 12 vols. Westport, Conn.: Greenwood Press, 1977.

"Reconstructive Movements in Atlanta." *Independent* 61 (20 December 1906): 1504–5.

Roche, Jeff. *Restructured Resistance: The Sibley Commission and the Politics of Desegregation in Georgia*. Athens: University of Georgia Press, 1998.

Roediger, David R. *The Wages of Whiteness: Race and the Making of the American Working Class*. London: Verso, 1991.

Roosevelt, Theodore. *State Papers as Governor and President, 1899–1909*. Vol. 17 of *The Works of Theodore Roosevelt*. Memorial ed. New York: Charles Scribner's Sons, 1925.

Roper, John Herbert. *C. Vann Woodward, Southerner*. Athens: University of Georgia Press, 1987.

Rosen, Ruth. *The Lost Sisterhood: Prostitution in America, 1900–1918*. Baltimore: Johns Hopkins University Press, 1982.

Rouse, Jacqueline Anne. *Lugenia Burns Hope: Black Southern Reformer*. Athens: University of Georgia Press, 1989.

Rowley, Dean. "George Alexander Towns: A Profile of His Atlanta University Experience, 1885–1929." Master's thesis, Atlanta University, 1975.

Rudwick, Elliott M. *W. E. B. Du Bois: Propagandist of the Negro Protest*. 1960. Reprint. New York: Atheneum, 1969.

Russell, James Michael. *Atlanta, 1847–1890: City Building in the Old South and the New*. Baton Rouge: Louisiana State University Press, 1988.

Rutheiser, Charles. *Imagineering Atlanta: The Politics of Place in the City of Dreams*. London: Verso, 1996.

Schechter, Patricia A. *Ida B. Wells-Barnett and American Reform, 1880–1930*. Chapel Hill: University of North Carolina Press, 2001.

Schudson, Michael. *Discovering the News: A Social History of American Newspapers*. New York: Basic Books, 1978.

Scott, James C. *Domination and the Arts of Resistance: Hidden Transcripts*. New Haven: Yale University Press, 1990.

Semonche, John E. *Ray Stannard Baker: A Quest for Democracy in Modern America, 1870–1918*. Chapel Hill: University of North Carolina Press, 1969.

Senechal, Roberta. *The Sociogenesis of a Race Riot: Springfield, Illinois, in 1908*. Urbana: University of Illinois Press, 1990.

Shapiro, Herbert. *White Violence and Black Response: From Reconstruction to Montgomery*. Amherst: University of Massachusetts Press, 1988.

Shaw, Barton C. *The Wool-Hat Boys: Georgia's Populist Party*. Baton Rouge: Louisiana State University Press, 1984.

Shaw, Stephanie J. "Black Club Women and the Creation of the National Association of Colored Women." *Journal of Women's History* 3 (Fall 1991): 10–25.

Shivery, Louie Delphia. "The History of Organized Social Work among Atlanta Negroes, 1890–1935." Master's thesis, Atlanta University, 1936.

Simmons, William. *Men of Mark: Eminent, Progressive, and Rising*. Cleveland: O. G. M. Rewell and Company, 1887.

Simon, Bryant. *A Fabric of Defeat: The Politics of South Carolina Millhands, 1910–1948*. Chapel Hill: University of North Carolina Press, 1998.

Sjoquist, David L. Introduction to *The Atlanta Paradox*, edited by David L. Sjoquist. New York: Russell Sage Foundation, 2000.

Sosna, Morton. *In Search of the Silent South*. New York: Columbia University Press, 1977.

"The Southern Press on the Atlanta 'Pogrom.'" *Literary Digest* 33 (6 October 1906): 452–54.

Southern Society for the Promotion of the Study of Race Conditions and Problems in the South. *Race Problems of the South: Report of the Proceedings of the First Annual Conference Held under the Auspices of the Southern Society for the Promotion of the Study of Race Conditions and Problems in the South at Montgomery, Alabama, May 8, 9, 10, A.D. 1900*. [1900?] Reprint. New York: Negro Universities Press, 1969.

Speer, Robert E. *John J. Eagan: A Memoir of an Adventurer for the Kingdom of God on Earth*. Birmingham, Ala.: American Cast Iron Pipe Company, 1939.

Spritzer, Lorraine Nelson, and Jen B. Bergmark. *Grace Towns Hamilton and the Politics of Southern Change*. Athens: University of Georgia Press, 1997.

"Stand by Your Guns." *Voice of the Negro* 3 (March 1906): 216.

Stanley, Alfred Knighton. *The Children Is Crying: Congregationalism among Black People*. New York: Pilgrim Press, 1979.

Stone, Clarence N. *Regime Politics: Governing Atlanta, 1946–1988*. Lawrence: University Press of Kansas, 1989.

Suggs, Henry Lewis, ed. *The Black Press in the South, 1864–1979*. Westport, Conn.: Greenwood Press, 1983.

Sullivan, Patricia. *Days of Hope: Race and Democracy in the New Deal Era*. Chapel Hill: University of North Carolina Press, 1996.

Summers, Martin. *Manliness and Its Discontents: The Black Middle Class and the Transformation of Masculinity, 1900–1930*. Chapel Hill: University of North Carolina Press, 2004.

Tagger, Barbara. "The Atlanta Race Riot of 1906 and the Black Community." Master's thesis, Atlanta University, 1984.

Talmadge, John E. *Rebecca Latimer Felton: Nine Stormy Decades*. Athens: University of Georgia Press, 1960.

Taylor, A. Elizabeth. "The Abolition of the Convict Lease System in Georgia." *Georgia Historical Quarterly* 26 (September–December 1942): 273–87.

Teele, James E. Introduction to *E. Franklin Frazier and Black Bourgeoisie*, edited by James E. Teele. Columbia: University of Missouri Press, 2002.

Terrell, Mary Church. "Peonage in the United States: The Convict Lease System and the Chain Gangs." In *Quest for Equality: The Life and Writings of Mary Eliza Church Terrell, 1863–1954*, edited by Beverly Washington Jones, 255–73. Brooklyn: Carlson Publishing, 1990.

Thelen, David. "Memory and American History." *Journal of American History* 75 (March 1989): 1117–29.

Thomas, Jesse O. *My Story in Black and White: The Autobiography of Jesse O. Thomas*. New York: Exposition Press, 1967.

Thornbery, Jerry John. "The Development of Black Atlanta, 1865–1885." Ph.D. diss., University of Maryland, 1977.

Thornbrough, Emma Lou. "The National Afro-American League." *Journal of Southern History* 27 (November 1961): 494–512.

——. "T. Thomas Fortune: Militant Editor in the Age of Accommodation." In *Black Leaders of the Twentieth Century*, edited by John Hope Franklin and August Meier, 19–37. Urbana: University of Illinois Press, 1982.

——. *T. Thomas Fortune: Militant Journalist*. Chicago: University of Chicago Press, 1972.

Thurman, Howard. *With Head and Heart: The Autobiography of Howard Thurman*. New York: Harcourt Brace Jovanovich, 1979.

Tindall, George Brown. *The Emergence of the New South, 1913–1945*. Vol. 10 of *A History of the South*. Baton Rouge: Louisiana State University Press, 1967.

Tolnay, Stewart E., and E. M. Beck. *A Festival of Violence: An Analysis of Southern Lynchings, 1882–1930*. Urbana: University of Illinois Press, 1995.

Toppin, Edgar A. "Walter White and the Atlanta NAACP's Fight for Equal Schools, 1916–1917." *History of Education Quarterly* 7 (Spring 1967): 3–21.

Torrence, Ridgely. *The Story of John Hope*. New York: Macmillan, 1948.

Trotter, Joe William. *Black Milwaukee: The Making of an Industrial Proletariat, 1915–1945*. Urbana: University of Illinois Press, 1985.

Tuck, Stephen G. N. *Beyond Atlanta: The Struggle for Racial Equality in Georgia, 1940–1980*. Athens: University of Georgia Press, 2001.

Tullos, Allen. *Habits of Industry: White Culture and the Transformation of the Carolina Piedmont*. Chapel Hill: University of North Carolina Press, 1989.

Turner, Henry McNeal. *Respect Black: The Writings and Speeches of Henry McNeal Turner*. Edited by Edwin S. Redkey. New York: Arno Press, 1971.

Tuttle, William F. "W. E. B. Du Bois' Confrontation with White Liberalism during the Progressive Era: A *Phylon* Document." *Phylon* 35 (September 1974): 241–58.

Tyson, Timothy B. "Robert F. Williams, 'Black Power,' and the Roots of the African American Freedom Struggle." *Journal of American History* 85 (September 1998): 540–70.

"The University the Birthplace of Reform." *Voice of the Negro* 1 (October 1904): 432–33.

Villard, Oswald Garrison. "The Aims of the Afro-American Council." *Colored American Magazine* 10 (November 1906): 349–53.

von Hoffman, Alexander. *House by House, Block by Block: The Rebirth of America's Urban Neighborhoods*. New York: Oxford University Press, 2003.

Walker, Eugene Pierce. "Attitudes towards Negroes as Reflected in the Atlanta Constitution, 1908–1918." Master's thesis, Atlanta University, 1969.

Walters, Bishop A. J., and Kelly Miller. "An Address to the Public." *Colored American Magazine* 10 (November 1906): 332–34.

Wardlaw, James Tapley. "Leisure Time Activities of Negro Boys in the First Ward of Atlanta, Georgia." Master's thesis, Atlanta University, 1934.

Ware, Edward T. "The Atlanta Riots III—From the Point of View of a Missionary College." *Outlook* 84 (3 November 1906): 564–66.

Waring, James H. N. *Work of the Colored Law and Order League: Baltimore, Md.* Cheney, Pa.: Committee of Twelve for the Advancement of the Interests of the Negro Race, [1908].

Washington, Booker T. "The Golden Rule in Atlanta." *Outlook* 84 (15 December 1906): 913–16.

———. *Up from Slavery*. In *Three Negro Classics*. New York: Avon Books, 1965.

Watson, H. B. "Suggestions for Black Atlanta." *Voice of the Negro* 3 (September 1906): 653–54.

Watson, Thomas E. "The Color Line." *Watson's Jeffersonian Magazine* 1 (May 1907): 438–40.

———. "Foreword." *Watson's Jeffersonian Magazine* 1 (January 1907): 3–28.

———. "Mr. Graves's Appeal to the Populists." *Tom Watson's Magazine* 3 (November 1905): 12–18.

———. "The Negro Question in the South." In *A Populist Reader: Selections from the Works of American Populist Leaders*, edited by George Brown Tindall, 118–28. New York: Harper and Row, 1966.

———. "Negro Secret Societies." *Watson's Jeffersonian Magazine* 1 (February 1907): 166–69.

———. "Populism." *Tom Watson's Magazine* 2 (September 1905): 257–59.

———. "Sam Spencer." *Watson's Magazine* 4 (April 1906): 161–65.

———. "Socialism and One of Its Great Books." *Watson's Magazine* 4 (May 1906): 321–30.

———. "The Ungrateful Negro." *Watson's Magazine* 4 (April 1906): 165–74.

Watters, Pat. *Coca-Cola: An Illustrated History*. Garden City, N.J.: Doubleday, 1978.

Watts, Eugene. "The Police in Atlanta, 1890–1905." *Journal of Southern History* 39 (May 1973): 165–82.

———. *The Social Bases of City Politics: Atlanta, 1865–1904*. Westport, Conn.: Greenwood Press, 1978.

Wedin, Carolyn. *Inheritors of the Spirit: Mary White Ovington and the Founding of the NAACP*. New York: John Wiley and Sons, 1998.

"The Week." *Nation* 84 (3 January 1907): 1.

White, Deborah Gray. *Too Heavy a Load: Black Women in Defense of Themselves, 1894–1994*. New York: Norton, 1999.

White, John E. "The Need of a Southern Program on the Negro Problem." *South Atlantic Quarterly* 6 (April 1907): 177–88.

———. "Prohibition: The New Task and Opportunity of the South." *South Atlantic Quarterly* 7 (April 1908): 130–42.

———. "The True and False in Southern Life." *South Atlantic Quarterly* 5 (April 1906): 97–113.

White, Walter. *Flight*. New York: Knopf, 1926.

——. *A Man Called White: The Autobiography of Walter White*. New York: Viking, 1948.

Wiebe, Robert H. *The Search for Order, 1877–1920*. New York: Hill and Wang, 1967.

Williams, Fannie Barrier. "The Woman's Part in a Man's Business." *Voice of the Negro* 1 (November 1904): 543–47.

Williamson, Joel. *The Crucible of Race: Black-White Relations in the American South since Emancipation*. New York: Oxford University Press, 1984.

Wilson, Edward E. "The Negro in the President's Message." *Voice* 3 (December 1906): 575–80.

"The Wind and the Whirlwind." *Independent* 61 (27 September 1906): 799–800.

Wingo, Horace C. "Race Relations in Georgia, 1872–1908." Ph.D. diss., University of Georgia, 1969.

Woodward, C. Vann. *Origins of the New South, 1877–1913*. Vol. 9 of *A History of the South*. Baton Rouge: Louisiana State University Press, 1951.

——. *The Strange Career of Jim Crow*. 3rd ed. New York: Oxford University Press, 1974.

——. *Thinking Back: The Perils of Writing History*. Baton Rouge: Louisiana State University Press, 1986.

——. *Tom Watson: Agrarian Rebel*. New York: Macmillan, 1938.

"A Word of Sympathy." *Voice of the Negro* 2 (August 1904): 341–42.

Wrigley, Steven Wayne. "The Triumph of Provincialism: Public Life in Georgia, 1898–1917." Ph.D. diss., Northwestern University, 1986.

Wyatt-Brown, Bertram. *Southern Honor: Ethics and Behavior in the Old South*. New York: Oxford University Press, 1982.

Young, Andrew. *An Easy Burden: The Civil Rights Movement and the Transformation of America*. New York: HarperCollins, 1996.

——. *A Way Out of No Way: The Spiritual Memoirs of Andrew Young*. Nashville: T. Nelson, 1994.

Zangrando, Robert L. *The NAACP Crusade against Lynching, 1909–1950*. Philadelphia: Temple University Press, 1980.

WEBSITES

"About Reynoldstown." Reynoldstown Civic Improvement League. <http://www.reynolds town.org/rcil/about.htm>. 29 January 2005.

Historic District Development Corporation. <http://www.hddc.net>. 29 January 2005.

INDEX

Atlanta Colored Music Festival, 211, 214, 219

Atlanta Constitution, 17, 120, 159, 163, 166, 167, 239, 260, 263; on the alleged black rapist and his punishment, 38; on disfranchisement, 49–50; and Henry Hugh Proctor, 77, 214, 222; and Theodore Roosevelt, 194

Atlanta Daily World, 268, 270

Atlanta Evening News, 54, 85, 139, 141, 189, 192; on the alleged black rapist and his punishment, 35–41, 43, 52, 74, 151; and News Protective League, 46–48; on white women and self-defense, 53; on white-on-black rape, 55; on Atlanta race riot, 105; criticized by blacks, 117, 120; and merger with *Atlanta Georgian*, 167

Atlanta Georgian, 42, 110, 137, 141, 159, 167, 202, 260; on the alleged black rapist and his punishment, 35, 37–40; on white women and self-defense, 53; on black elite, 57, 74–76, 78, 81–82; and merger with *Atlanta Evening News*, 167

Atlanta Georgian and News, 167

Atlanta Independent, 30, 140, 222, 226, 245. *See also* Davis, Benjamin J.

Atlanta Journal, 85, 133, 146, 183, 219, 239, 260, 263; on the black rapist and his punishment, 37–38; on disfranchisement, 48, 50–51, 177–78; and William J. Northen, 177–78, 185

Atlanta Negro Voters League, 270

Atlanta Neighborhood Development Partnership (ANDP), 282

Atlanta Paradox, 280

"Atlanta Plan," 273, 277, 278, 281, 283

Atlanta Plan of Inter-racial Cooperation, 216

Atlanta Project, 281–83

Atlanta race riot: causes of, 33–36, 55–56, 88, 107–10; and contingency of violence, 34, 86; and social identities, 86, 88, 109–14; black defensive violence during, 100–105, 109–14; invasion of Dark Town and black defensive response, 102, 109–10, 113; white raids on Brownsville, 102–4, 106, 109–10, 114; casualties during, 105–6; statewide

responses to, 114; historiography on, 292 (n. 1), 301–2 (n. 1)

—downtown antiblack massacre, 22 September 1906: outbreak of, 85–86, 88–90; white public officials' and elites' responses during, 86, 88–91, 93; attacks on black streetcar passengers, 90–93; attacks on white property, 93, 94, 95; attacks on black workers and businesses, 93–96, 96–97, 98–99; violence against black residences, 94–96, 97; composition of white mob, 98–99

Atlanta race riot, national commentators on: and mainstream white press, 2–3, 115–17, 131–33, 187–88; and blacks, 117–25, 130–31; and National Afro-American Council, 125–30; and Ray Stannard Baker, 200–203. *See also* Barber, Jesse Max; Black defensive violence; Du Bois, W. E. B.; Proctor, Henry Hugh; Washington, Booker T.

Atlanta race riot, public memories of, 3–4, 257–60; and interracial cooperation, 215–17, 270–71

—black memories: and intraracial unity, 109, 110–14, 259–60; and black defensive violence, 110–14, 259–60, 289; and Henry Hugh Proctor, 162, 187–90, 225; and Benjamin J. Davis, 225. *See also* Du Bois, W. E. B.; First Congregational Church; Hope, Lugenia Burns; White, Walter F.

—white memories, 288–89, 290; and white intraracial divisions, 86–87, 98–99, 109–10; and Margaret Mitchell, 259–60; and Leo Frank, 260–61; and white newspapers, 260–61, 263–64, 270, 275

Atlanta School of Social Work, 240

"Atlanta Spirit," 14–15, 262

Atlanta University, 229

Atlanta Urban League (AUL), 267, 268; and interracial cooperation, 252, 270–72, 277; and Neighborhood Union, 252, 280, 288; and residential segregation, 271–72

Atlanta Woman's Club (black), 81

Auburn Avenue, 20, 108, 224

Avery Congregational Working Girls' Home, 211

Bacote, Clarence, 260, 268

Baker, Ray Stannard, 3, 17, 157; on Atlanta, 24–40 passim, 200–203, 207; on black and white elites, 188, 200–202; on interracial cooperation, 188, 201, 207; background of and influences on, 198–200; and black civil rights, 201, 207. *See also* Barber, Jesse Max; Du Bois, W. E. B.; Proctor, Henry Hugh

Baptist Ministers Union (black), 75–76, 220

Barber, Jesse Max, 7, 31, 140, 288; and *Voice of the Negro*, 65–67, 196–97; manhood ideals of, 66, 117–19; and Booker T. Washington, 67–68, 120–21, 130, 195–97, 207–8; and black activism, 70, 72–74; on Atlanta race riot, 106, 109–10, 116–19, 124; exile from Atlanta, 118, 123, 143, 160, 192, 195, 197, 203, 208; and Theodore Roosevelt, 191–92; and NAACP, 196; and Ray Stannard Baker, 203–4, 207; and W. E. B. Du Bois, 204, 207–208. *See also* New Black Men; *Voice of the Negro*

Barton, Bruce, 189

Bauerlein, Mark, 6, 301 (n. 1)

Bayor, Ronald, 279

Beaver Slide, 229, 242

Bederman, Gail, 308 (n. 1), 310–11 (n. 1)

Belser, J. B., 93

Big Bethel AME Church, 223, 249

Birmingham, Ala., 262, 276, 320 (n. 39)

Black barbers and barbershops, 19, 20, 31; and Atlanta race riot, 93–94, 106, 108, 122; postriot closing of, 109, 137

Black children: and city stockade, 26; and neighborhood dangers to, 229–30, 243–44; and Lugenia Burns Hope, 236–38

Black colleges, 21, 61; and whites, 49, 172; and New Black Men, 64–66, 72; and Atlanta race riot, 100, 102–4, 123, 141; and student sit-ins, 273–75. *See also* Interracial cooperation; *and individual colleges and educational institutions*

Black defensive violence, 289; and Atlanta race riot, 100–105, 109–14; and black women and manhood, 111; and Booker T. Washington, 120; and national black com-

mentators, 125–26, 130–31; and W. E. B. Du Bois, 110–11, 123–24, 206; Oswald Garrison Villard on, 128–29, 206; and interracial cooperation, 135–36, 166, 259–60; and postriot criminal trials, 147–48. *See also* Black intraracial unity; Fortune, T. Thomas; Hope, Lugenia Burns; Niagara Movement

Black domestic workers, 19–20; and black respectability, 219–21; and Neighborhood Union, 236. *See also* Black women; Black working class

Black education: and public schools, 19, 25, 230, 245, 250–51; and alleged rapists, 41; and whites, 49–51, 172–73, 176, 194, 217, 246; Booker T. Washington on, 59–60, 67; and W. E. B. Du Bois, 63, 124; and New Black Men, 64–66, 67, 72; and Niagara Movement, 69–70, 72, 124; and William J. White, 70, 172–74; and Henry McNeal Turner, 72; schools as targets of white racial violence, 176; and Theodore Roosevelt, 192; and black intraracial unity, 244–45; and black women, 244–45; desegregation of public schools, 272, 276, 278, 279. *See also* City council; Disfranchisement; Hope, Lugenia Burns; Interracial cooperation; NAACP, Atlanta branch; Neighborhood Union; School bond elections

Black Flame trilogy, 285–88

Black home, 232

Black intraracial social divisions, 8–9, 228, 314–15 (n. 40); and First Congregational Church, 9, 210–11; and institutional organization structures, 9, 210–11; and interracial cooperation, 10–11, 156–57, 160–62, 210–11, 219–21, 264–67, 272–79; and Atlanta race riot, 112–14; and Benjamin J. Davis, 221–22, 226; and Henry Hugh Proctor, 223–24; and Niagara Movement, 227; and Neighborhood Union, 227; and denominationalism, 235. *See also* Black respectability; "Criminal element"

Black intraracial unity, 229, 293 (n. 19); and Atlanta race riot, 86, 109, 110–14, 210–11;

and black defensive violence, 110–14; and Neighborhood Union, 210, 228, 233–36; and black education, 244–45; and NAACP, 247–49

Black men "adrift," 14, 23, 26–27, 32–33, 34; and white women "adrift," 14, 26–30; white stereotypes and, 23–24; and rape, 40–41; black ministers on, 75–76; and Henry Hugh Proctor, 78

Black respectability, 8–9; and black social divisions, 79–80, 219–21, 240–44, 255–56; and Neighborhood Union, 237–39. *See also* Proctor, Henry Hugh

—politics of, 8–9, 210–11, 240–44, 293 (n. 18); and white backlash, 57–58; Jesse Max Barber on, 119; and civic leagues, 157; and black militancy, 218–19; and social divisions, 219–21; and Benjamin J. Davis, 222–23

Blackstock, George W., 95, 98, 148

Black voting, 10–11; voter mobilization, 10–11, 253–54, 268; and alleged black-on-white rapes, 50–51, 258; and W. E. B. Du Bois, 64; and NAACP school campaign, 248–50; and white mob violence, 255. *See also* Disfranchisement; White primary

Black women: and white stereotypes, 24, 238; New Black Women, 80–81; and black defensive violence, 111; and black churches, 212; and clubs and community organizations, 231–32, 236; and black gender roles, 232–33; black sexual mores and single mothers in Atlanta, 241–42; and social disorder, 243–44; and education, 244–45; and NAACP bond campaigns, 249–50. *See also* Black domestic workers; Black working class; Hope, Lugenia Burns; Neighborhood Union; Women's Social Improvement Committee

Black working class, 19–20: and leisure activities, 28–30; and black defensive violence, 100–105, 109–14; as target for temperance reform, 144; and black resistance, 240–41; and New Deal, 267; and neighborhood revitalization, 282–83

"Blind tigers," 229. *See also* Saloons

Blodgett, Thomas, 183

Bond, Julian, 274

Bond elections, 248–50

Booker T. Washington High School, 250–51

Boosterism, 14–16, 262

Borders, William Holmes, 270–73, 275

Boston Guardian, 61, 69

Boston Pilot, 127

Bowen, John Wesley Edward, 68; manhood ideals of, 65; and Gammon Theological Seminary, 65, 102, 104; riot experiences of, 102, 104; postriot concerns and strategies of, 141–42

Branham, Robert, 149, 152

Brooks, Wiley, 103

Brown, Charlie, 257

Brown, George, 219–20

Brown, J. Pope, 176

Brown, John, 74, 123

Brown, Milton, 96

Brownsville, Atlanta, 1, 8, 122, 124, 128, 200, 289; and Atlanta race riot, 102–4, 106, 109–10, 114; and postriot interracial cooperation, 141, 155; and postriot criminal trials, 154

Brownsville, Tex., affair, 190–96, 208

Brown v. the Board of Education of Topeka, Kansas, 285

Broyles, Nash, 25, 30, 155, 246; and postriot criminal trials, 147–48

Bruce, Philip, 23–24

Bryan, Orrie, 37–38, 39, 149

Bryant, Peter James, 70, 74, 100, 145, 153, 220

Bugg, Laura, 236

Bumstead, Horace, 112

Business Men's Gospel Union, 217

Camp, Annie, 150–52

Candler, Asa, 16, 159

Candler Building, 16

Cann, George, 149, 150

Cannon, W. S., 247

Capeci, Dominic J., Jr., 123, 298–99 (n. 2)

Carmichael, Frank, 36

race riot memories, 258–60; and Commission on Interracial Cooperation, 264–65; and post–World War II interracial cooperation, 269–70

—white, 54; and white temperance reformers, 146, 180; and Leo Frank lynching, 262

Criminal justice system, 79; and segregation, 25, 30; and black defendants, 25–26; and arrest rates in Atlanta, 25–26, 30; black resistance to, 26; whites' distrust of for punishing alleged black rapists, 41–43; and Georgia Equal Rights Convention, 72; and Atlanta's black elite, 75–76, 78–80; and postriot trials, 147–52, 161; and Neighborhood Union, 238–39, 243. *See also* Police

Crisis, 207–8

Crogman, William H., 112, 141

Crowe, Charles, 98, 106, 258

Dance halls and dancing, 28–30, 219; and alleged black rapes, 40–41, 48, 224–25; and Benjamin J. Davis, 224, 226; and Neighborhood Union, 237–38, 240, 241, 244, 255. *See also* Proctor, Henry Hugh

Daniel, Charles, 46–48

Dark Town, 1, 20–21, 26; and Atlanta race riot, 102, 109–10, 113; and debates on black defensive violence, 122, 124, 128, 289

Davis, Benjamin J., 30, 40, 245; and disfranchisement, 74, 158; and 1906 antiblack newspaper campaign, 75, 82; on interracial cooperation, 76; and temperance reform, 145–46; and civic leagues, 150, 158, 161, 223; professional and political career of, 222; manhood ideals of, 222–23, 225–26; and United Order of the Odd Fellows, 222–24, 226, 247; and black respectability, 224–26; and Odd Fellows Headquarters and Auditorium, 224–26; and black ministers, 226; and NAACP, 247–48. *See also* Proctor, Henry Hugh; Odd Fellows Roof Garden

Davis, Leroy, 233

Decatur Street, 41, 52, 82, 144; as center for

racial conflict and social fears, 27–31, 296 (n. 37); during Atlanta race riot, 88–90, 108, 109–10

Democratic Party, 44–45, 48–51, 165

Detroit Barbershop, 89

Deveaux, John H., 222

Disfranchisement: and 1906 Democratic gubernatorial primary, 48–51; and Booker T. Washington, 58, 59, 60, 131; black opposition to, 74, 126, 180–84; and W. E. B. Du Bois, 124, 158; and civic leagues, 157–58; and Georgia Equal Rights Convention, 175; and legislative battle over, 181–83; and voter participation rates, 183; and black institution building, 209–10; and black public schools, 246, 250–51. *See also* Black voting; Interracial cooperation; Northen, William J.

Dittmer, John, 108

Dives. *See* Saloons

Dixon, Thomas, 36, 143

Dobbs, John Wesley: and black armed resistance, 110; and civil rights, 218, 254, 268, 270–73, 278; and Atlanta race riot memories, 270

Donaldson, Bobby, 308 (n. 1)

Dorsey, Allison, 292 (n. 1), 314–15 (n. 40)

Dorsey, Hattie, 282

Dorsey, Hugh M., 260

Du Bois, W. E. B., 17–19, 77, 142–43, 190, 211; and New Black Men, 2, 61–62; and Booker T. Washington, 3, 67–69, 116, 121–22, 134; and racial protest, 4, 77; on rape and miscegenation, 33, 80–81; manhood ideals of, 62–64; and *The Souls of Black Folk*, 62–64, 123, 128; and the "veil," 62–64, 161, 286; and interracial cooperation, 64; and Niagara Movement, 69–74, 124, 204, 227; elitism of, 79; and Atlanta race riot, 110–11, 121–24, 204, 257, 286–88; on black defensive violence, 110–11; 123–24, 206; and Oswald Garrison Villard, 128, 206; and civic leagues, 153, 156–59, 160–61, 173, 203; and William J. Northen, 173; and Ray Stannard Baker, 199–203; and 1908 national election, 205; and NAACP, 206–8. *See also* Washington, Booker T.

Eagan, John J., 152, 216, 246, 264
East Point, Ga., 95, 99–100
Edmonds, Richard, 177
Edmunds, Walter, 92
Elites
—black, 1–2, 8–9, 20–21; and social composition of postriot interracial organizations, 140–41, 153. *See also* Atlanta Urban League; Black respectability; First Congregational Church; New Black Men; New Black Women; Proctor, Henry Hugh
—black and white, 10–11, 290; and national press on, 188, 198, 200–201; and composition of post–World War II interracial regime, 268–70; and post–World War II negotiated settlements, 271–84 passim. *See also* Atlanta, national image of; Civic leagues; Commission on Interracial Cooperation; Committee of Safety; Interracial cooperation; Religion; Southern Regional Council
—white, 1–2, 7; and response to the Atlanta race riot, 86, 88, 98–99, 111–12, 132–39; and participation in the riot, 98–99; and social composition of postriot interracial organizations, 139, 152. *See also* Chamber of Commerce, Atlanta; Evangelical Ministers' Association; Hopkins, Charles T.; Northen, William J.; White business leaders
Ellis, W. D., 47–48
English, James W., 26, 90, 152, 160; and Jesse Max Barber, 118–19, 204, 208; and Committee of Safety, 139, 142, 147
Eskew, Glenn T., 320 (n. 39)
Evangelical Ministers' Association (EMA), 178, 216

Fambro, Frank, 103
Fambro, Priscilla, 155
Federal Emergency Relief Administration, 267

Ferguson, Karen, 294 (n. 22), 301–2 (n. 1)
Fields, Barbara J., 6
First Congregational Church (First Church), 2, 223; and black respectability, 9, 77–78, 210–11, 254–56; building and financing of, 159, 189–90; social service activities of, 211–14; and black women, 212. *See also* Atlanta Colored Music Festival
—membership of, 78, 162, 218; Atlanta race riot memories of, 162, 218; and interracial cooperation, 214–15, 218; white Atlanta press on, 219; and "criminal element," 219–20; social isolation of, 220–21, 227; and Benjamin J. Davis, 223; and Neighborhood Union, 229, 236; and NAACP, 246–47; and Atlanta Urban League, 252. *See also* Dobbs, John Wesley; Hamilton, Grace Towns; Herndon, Adrienne McNeil; Herndon, Alonzo F.; Pace, Harry; Proctor, Adeline; Proctor, Henry Hugh; Proctor, Lillian; Rucker, Henry; Thomas, Jesse O.; White, Walter F.; Young, Andrew
Five Points, 20; as center of racial conflict and social fears, 27–31, 41; during Atlanta race riot, 85–86, 88–93, 96–97, 107–8
Flipper, Joseph S., 70
Following the Color Line: An Account of Negro Citizenship in the American Democracy, 3, 188, 197; public reactions to, 202–4
Forsyth Street, 92, 93, 95
Fortune, T. Thomas, 61; and black defensive violence, 130–31; postriot career of, 196–97. *See also* Roosevelt, Theodore; Washington, Booker T.
Fountain, William, 182
Fourth Ward, 20, 226
Frank, Leo, 2, 260–64, 270
Frazier, E. Franklin, 228, 254–55, 318 (n. 58)
Frazier, Lucius (Luther), 37–38, 39, 149
Fredrickson, George, 45
Friendship Baptist Church, 155, 166, 195

Gaines, Kevin K., 8, 293 (n. 18)
Gammon Theological Seminary, 102–5, 141
Garrett, Franklin, 258

Garrison, Francis Jackson, 105
Garrison, William Lloyd, 206
"Gate City," 13
Gates, Henry Louis, Jr., 62
Gauth, Larry, 175–76, 181
Georgia Baptist Convention, 165, 184
Georgia Department of Public Welfare, 251
Georgia Equal Rights Convention (GERC),
  77, 183, 204, 301 (n. 46); composition of,
  70, 72; 1906 meeting of, 70, 72–74, 186; and
  criminal justice system, 79, 175; and black
  women, 80–81; and Atlanta's white minis-
  try, 172; 1907 meeting of, 174–75; and dis-
  franchisement and segregation, 175. See
  also Interracial cooperation; White,
  William J.
Georgia Federation of Labor, 45
Georgia School of Technology, 100
Georgia Suffrage League, 182–83
Gilmore, Glenda, 210
Glenn, Joe, 150–52, 156
Golden Age, 51
Gone with the Wind, 3, 258
Goree, C. P., 182–83
Grady, Henry, 93
Grady Hospital, 97
Grantham, Dewey, 197
Graves, John Temple: on segregation, 42, 117;
  on black rapist, 42–43, 117; and black civic
  leaders, 75; on Atlanta race riot, 110, 117;
  and Henry Hugh Proctor, 159. See also
  Atlanta Georgian
Gray, James, 50–51, 177–78, 183
Gregory, J. H. (Mrs.), 37
Grimké, Archibald, 206
Grimké, Francis J., 119, 122, 125, 127

Hahn, Steven, 294 (n. 21)
Hall, Joseph Hill, 181
Hamilton, Grace Towns, 268, 270, 271–72
Hampton Institute, 189, 192
Harlan, Louis R., 208
Harpers Ferry, 74, 123
Hartsfield, William, 268–71, 274
Hartsfield International Airport, 278

Heard, Jim, 103, 104, 105, 141, 154
Hembree, Georgia, 37, 38, 151
Henry Grady Monument, 93
Herndon, Adrienne McNeil, 232
Herndon, Alonzo F., 70, 140, 181; business
  career of, 20, 30–31; and First Congrega-
  tional Church, 78, 218
Higginbotham, Evelyn Brooks, 8, 10, 210, 293
  (n. 18)
Hillyer, George, 48
Historic District Development Corporation
  (HDDC), 282–83
Holt, Thomas C., 5
"Holy Rollers" (Holiness Church), 229, 236,
  239, 241
Hope, John, 229, 244; manhood ideals of,
  62, 76, 142–43, 218, 263–64; and Niagara
  Movement, 70, 74; on gender roles, 81, 233;
  riot experiences of, 90, 100; and Lugenia
  Burns Hope, 142, 233, 254; effects of riot
  on, 142–43, 263–64; NAACP activism of,
  247
Hope, Lugenia Burns: and Atlanta race riot,
  90, 232; on black defensive violence, 111–
  12, 232, 243, 259–60; and black respectability, 210–11, 255–56; and founding of
  Neighborhood Union, 227, 230–31; on
  men's and women's activism, 228–29; and
  West Side's social environment, 229–30;
  on the black home, 232–33; as a community organizer, 233, 249–50; inclusiveness
  of, 235–36, 243; on vice and "social disorder," 236–38, 243–44; and white stereotypes of black women, 238; and interracial
  cooperation, 239–40, 246, 251, 260–61; and
  campaigns for better schools, 244–47,
  249–50; and vision of intraracial unity,
  251; and black voting, 253–54. See also
  Hope, John; Neighborhood Union;
  Women's Social Improvement Committee
Hopkins, Charles T., 8, 161, 167, 289; and
  Committee of Safety, 137–40, 143; and
  white chivalry, 138, 139–40; paternalism of,
  138, 156–58; and civic leagues, 150, 152–59
Hopkins, Linton, 48

Howard, David T., 106

Howell, Clark, 159; and 1906 gubernatorial primary, 49–51; black criticisms of 68, 123–24

Hunt, Cornelia, 149

Hunter, Tera, 236, 241

Hunton, Addie, 81, 106–7

Hunton, William, 106–7

International Council of Women of the Darker Races, 236

Interracial cooperation, 10–11, 293–94 (nn. 21–22); and labor, 44–45; and Populism, 44–45; and temperance reform, 51–52; and Booker T. Washington, 58–59, 120–21, 130, 133, 207; and Georgia Equal Rights Convention, 72–73, 174–75; and preriot antiblack discourse, 76, 83–84; and Henry Hugh Proctor, 78, 188–90, 214–18, 246, 258, 269, 277, 284, 289; and *Atlanta Georgian*, 81–82; white northern press on, 132–33; and Atlanta's national image, 135, 187–88, 269–70, 276; and black defensive violence, 135–36, 166, 259–60; and social identities of blacks, 136, 141, 161–62; and white fears of black crime, 136–37, 238–39, 255–56; and black colleges, 140–43, 153, 160, 270; and white threats of violence, 141–43, 152–53, 270–71; and selective pay-offs to blacks, 159–60, 277–78; and marginalization of black militant voices, 160–61, 264–67, 272–73, 275–79; and disfranchisement, 181–83; and First Congregational Church, 210–11; and Neighborhood Union, 210–11, 238–40, 246, 251–54; and white Atlanta race riot memories, 215–16; and white religious leaders, 216; and Church Cooperative Committees, 216–17; and residential segregation, 226–27; and white public health concerns, 239–40; and Lugenia Burns Hope, 239–40, 246, 251, 259–60; and black community organizing, 239–40, 255–56; and black education, 245–46; and NAACP school campaign, 250; and Atlanta Urban League, 252, 270–72,

277; during T. L. Martin murder trial, 263; and black public riot memories, 270; and public school segregation, 272, 279; black dissatisfaction with, 273; and sit-ins, 273–76; and black mayors, 278–79; and "Atlanta Paradox," 280; and Andrew Young, 281, 283–84; and neighborhood revitalization organizations, 282–83. *See also* Baker, Ray Stannard; Black intraracial social divisions; Civic leagues; Civil rights movement; Du Bois, W. E. B.; Northen, William J.; Religion; White, William J.; White business leaders

Interracial sex. *See* Miscegenation; Rape

Jackson, Maynard, 278–79, 281, 283

Jacobs, Thornwell, 15

Jaillette, William, 95, 108

Janken, Kenneth Robert, 113, 266

Jeffries, Jim, 216

Jenkins, Frank E., 172

Jenkins, Herbert, 262, 273, 274

Jennings, Henry, 82, 96

Jester, Clarence, 41

Johnson, Jack, 216

Johnson, Will, 150–52, 156

Jones, Meredith Ashby, 216–17, 246, 264

Jones, Sam D., 48; and interracial cooperation, 137–39; and temperance reform, 143

Jones, W. E., 95

Joyner, Walthal R. (W. R.), 137, 159

Kelly, Brian, 294 (n. 21)

Kennedy, John F., 272, 276

Key, James, 250

Kilpatrick, James D., 154

Kimball House Hotel, 88, 97, 144

Kimmel, Etheleen, 37, 38, 152

Kimmel, Knowles, 24

King, Lonnie, 274–75, 279

King, Martin Luther, Jr., 4; and sit-ins, 274–75; on "white moderates," 276–77; and Atlanta's image, 278; and Andrew Young, 280–81

King, Martin Luther, Sr. (Daddy), 4; and
interracial cooperation, 270–78
King, Primus, 268
Knight, Jack C., 123, 298–99 (n. 2)
Kuhn, Clifford M., 44
Ku Klux Klan (KKK), 36, 48, 85; modern
KKK, 265–76 passim, 308 (n. 1); and white
business leaders, 262–63

Ladies Visiting Board, 245
Langford's White Midway, 27
Lawrence, Ethel, 37, 39, 149, 152
Lawrence, Mabel, 37, 39, 149, 152
Leland's barbershop, 93
"Letter from a Birmingham Jail," 276–77
Lewis, David Levering, 69
Lewis, E. T., 257
Lincoln, Abraham, 183
Long, Zeb, 99–100, 106
Los Angeles Times, 111
Lunchrooms. *See* Restaurants, black cheap
Lynching: in Atlanta, 15, 36, 37; in cotton belt,
17–18; symbolic functions of, 33–34; white
public officials on, 36, 45–46, 51, 55–56;
and preriot white newspapers, 36–37, 57,
75; and white social status, 45–46; and
white religious leaders, 52; preriot black
criticisms of, 70–83 passim; East Point
lynching of Zeb Long, 99–100; southern
white defenses of, 115–16; national black
criticisms of, 124–27; national white commentators and press on, 128–32, 191–92,
200–203; and postriot rape trials, 147–52;
and threats against William J. White, 174;
and labor control, 176–77; and rates of
in Georgia, 184; averted via interracial
cooperation, 216; and Leo Frank, 260–
63. *See also* Antilynching; White mob
violence
Lyons, Judson W., 222

Mack, George H., 172
MacLean, Nancy, 22, 297–98 (n. 27), 308
(n. 1)
Maddox, Leola, 94

Maddox, Robert F., 137
Majette, Vara A., 54–55
Manhood: blacks as allegedly unqualified for,
23–24, 57, 116, 132. *See also* Chivalry; New
Black Men
—black men's ideas of: and New Black Men,
2, 61, 64–67, 70–72; and Booker T. Washington, 59–60, 121, 129; and John Hope, 62,
76, 142–43, 218, 263–64; and W. E. B.
Du Bois, 62–64, 124; and Jesse Max Barber, 66, 117–19; and Henry McNeal Turner,
70, 72; and Georgia Equal Rights Convention, 72–73; and Niagara Movement, 74;
and Atlanta race riot, 111; and black defensive violence, 111, 124, 130; and National
Afro-American Council, 130; and civic
leagues, 160–61; and Henry Hugh Proctor,
212–13; and Benjamin J. Davis, 222–23,
225–26
—white men's ideas of, 21–22, 39–40, 55–56,
187–88; threatened by urbanization, 22–
23, 43–44, 45; and Atlanta race riot, 109–
10; white claims to manhood challenged
by blacks, 116; and Charles T. Hopkins,
138–40; and William J. Northen, 163–64,
168, 184–85
Mankin, Helen Douglas, 268
Mansart, Manuel, 285–88
Manufacturers' Record, 177
Marietta Street, 28, 144; and Atlanta race riot,
90, 93–94, 96, 108, 260
Marion, Will, 93
Massive resistance, 269
Martin, T. L., 263
Martin, Thomas, 15
Matthews, William B., 70
Mays, Benjamin, 270, 273
McBride, A. J., 138–39
McClure's Magazine, 198
McCord, H. Y., 137
McGruder, Sam, 103
McLendon, Mary Latimer, 54–55
Men and Religion Forward Movement, 216
Merritt, Carole, 102
Metro Atlanta Rapid Transit Authority, 278

67, 184–85; on black rapists and white mobs, 165–70; and white women, 167; white press's responses to, 167, 175–78; and interracial cooperation, 168–69, 174–75, 216–17; and Atlanta's white ministry, 171–73, 178, 185; national black and white commentators on, 173, 190, 195, 196, 201; black elite responses to, 173–75, 185–86; and Georgia Equal Rights Convention, 174; white responses to, 175–78, 184–85; and disfranchisement, 177–78, 181–83; and temperance reform, 178, 180; failures of, 184–85; anger and violent imagery of, 185

Odd Fellows Headquarters and Auditorium, 224–26, 248
Odd Fellows Roof Garden, 224–26
Odum, Howard, 266
Ohmann, Richard, 198
Oliver, Terri Hume, 62
Olympic Games, 1996 (Atlanta), 278, 281
Organizations Assisting Schools in September (OASIS), 272
Outlook, 132, 187, 195–96, 204
Ovington, Mary White, 113, 199–200, 205

Pace, Harry, 246–48, 255
Page, Thomas Nelson, 24, 132
Page, Walter Hines, 187
Parks, Rosa, 272
Patterson, Eugene, 263–64
Payne, Billy, 281
Pendleton, John, 147
Penn, William F., 30, 62; and civil rights activism, 74, 182, 247; and black armed defense, 139; response of to Atlanta race riot, 138–39
People's Party, 44–45
Peters Street, 28, 82, 144, 229; during Atlanta race riot, 95–96, 108–10
Phagan, Mary, 260, 262
Philadelphia Tribune, 133
Phillips, John S., 198–99
Piedmont Hotel, 90
Pittsburg, 20, 26

Police: and regulation of race relations, 25–26; and Atlanta race riot, 96–98, 100, 103–5; proposal for black police, 157–58; and neglect of black neighborhoods and victims, 230, 243–44; Ku Klux Klan influence over, 262; and civil rights era, 270, 273, 274
Politics of respectability. *See* Black respectability, politics of
Poll tax, 248–49
Poole, Annie Laurie, 36, 50
Poor People's Campaign, 280–81
Populism, 44–45
Press: Atlanta newspapers' preriot racist agitation, 1, 23, 35–52 passim, 57–58, 74–85 passim, 289; national press on Atlanta race riot, 115–19, 130–34, 187–88, 197–204; and muckraking, 198; Atlanta press on Leo Frank, 260–62; Atlanta press's postriot caution on racial issues, 263–64, 270, 275. *See also specific publications, writers, and editors*
Price, L. J., 103
Proctor, Adeline, 212, 214, 236, 245
Proctor, Henry Hugh, 4, 141, 145, 238, 254, 264, 266, 273, 289; and Booker T. Washington, 2, 4, 187–88, 195, 196; and black respectability, 9, 77–80, 210, 254–56; and W. E. B. Du Bois, 62; civil rights activism of, 70, 76–77; threatened by *Atlanta Georgian*, 75; background of, 76–77; on white racial violence, 77; on black rapist, 78, 180, 224–25; and Benjamin J. Davis, 78–79, 161, 221–27; and opposition to saloons and dance halls, 78–79, 180, 224–25; and "black criminal element," 78–80, 82, 219–20; and civic leagues, 153–54, 156–59; and First Congregational Church, 159, 187, 189–90, 211–12, 218; criticized by blacks, 161–62, 220–21; on Atlanta race riot, 162, 187–90, 225; and William J. Northen, 163; and disfranchisement, 180–82; and Ray Stannard Baker, 188, 197, 201, 203; and Progressivism, 210–11; manhood ideals of, 212–13; on gender roles, 212–14; and black domestic workers, 219–20; intraracial isolation of,

Waits, Mittie, 37

Walden, Austin (A. T.): and NAACP, 253–54; and black voter mobilization, 268; and interracial cooperation, 270, 275

Walker, Alex, 154

Walters, Alexander, 119, 125–26, 205–6

Waring, James, 115

Washington, Booker T. (the Wizard), 4, 73, 288; and Atlanta's postriot interracial movements, 3, 133–34, 155, 166, 195–96, 207; racial program of, 58–59; and segregation and disfranchisement, 59, 131, 196; manhood ideals of, 59–60, 121; and Theodore Roosevelt, 60, 68–69, 131, 133–34, 194–96; opposition to, 60–61, 68–70, 72, 116, 119–22; and W. E. B. Du Bois, 63–64, 67–68, 121–22, 207–8; and John Wesley Edward Bowen, 65, 68; and National Negro Business League speech, 83, 120; and black defensive violence, 120; and Oswald Garrison Villard, 125, 127–28, 206; and National Afro-American Council, 125–30, 205; and T. Thomas Fortune, 130–31, 194, 196–97; and Law and Order Sunday, 155, 166, 196; and William J. Northen, 173, 195; and Henry Hugh Proctor, 187–88, 190, 195–97, 218, 232; and Brownsville, Tex., affair, 190–91, 194; and NAACP, 206–7; and black education, 245. *See also* Barber, Jesse Max; Interracial cooperation

Washington Bee, 61, 125

Watson, H. B., 227

Watson, Hattie Rutherford, 81, 238–39

Watson, John B., 81, 238–39

Watson, Thomas E., 25, 165; and blacks, 5–6, 44–45; and 1906 gubernatorial primary, 49, 51, 74; and Leo Frank, 261

Weatherby, Richard T., 153, 156, 181

Weatherford, Willis D., 264

Welch, Henry, 93

Welch, William, 90

Wells, Ida B., 169

West End, Atlanta, 100

West Side, Atlanta, 21, 100; social and environmental conditions of, 229–30;

and Neighborhood Union, 230–39, 244, 253

White, Deborah Gray, 316 (n. 10)

White, John E., 142, 239; and antilynching, 52; and prohibition, 137, 183–84; and racial commission plan, 164, 171–72, 177; and disfranchisement, 171, 183 84; on slavery and Reconstruction, 172–73

White, Walter F., 3, 7–8; and Atlanta race riot memories, 86, 88, 111, 112–13; and First Congregational Church, 218, 221; and NAACP activism, 246–48, 254–55, 266

White, William J., 114, 204; and Georgia Equal Rights Convention, 70, 73, 173–75; and interracial cooperation, 173–75, 183, 185–86

White business leaders: and Atlanta's national image, 14–16, 135, 177, 184, 262, 276; and white chivalry, 46–48, 139–40; and Atlanta race riot, 85, 86–88, 98–99, 111, 117–18; and Henry Hugh Proctor, 159, 215; and William J. Northen, 166–67, 177–78, 184–85; and Community Chest, 251; Atlanta race riot memories of, 258; and Leo Frank case, 262; and Ku Klux Klan, 262–64; and city politics, 268; and sit-ins, 274–76; and Atlanta Project, 281; and Neighborhood redevelopment, 282–83. *See also* Chamber of Commerce, Atlanta; Civic leagues; Committee of Safety

—interracial cooperation of: and postriot negotiations, 136–39; post–World War II, 268–70, 277, 280, 283–84; and Atlanta Urban League, 271–72; and Maynard Jackson, 278–79; and Andrew Young, 279

—and segregation: residential, 271–72; of public schools, 272, 279; of public accommodations, 274–76

White intraracial divisions and Atlanta race riot, 86, 88, 98–99, 109–10

White mob violence: and black voter mobilization, 10, 255; Henry Hugh Proctor on, 224–25; and residential segregation, 226, 270–71; whites' and blacks' shared fears of, 263, 270–72; Martin Luther King Sr. on,

273. *See also* Antilynching; Atlanta race riot; Interracial cooperation; Lynching

White primary, 52, 249–50, 268, 298 (n. 38)

White rioters: composition of Atlanta race riot mob, 98–99; and postriot trials of, 147–49. *See also* Atlanta race riot

White supremacy: and urbanization, 24–27; and black elites, 30–31; and Atlanta race riot, 107–10; and white economic jealousies, 108, 122

White women: "adrift," 14, 22–23, 31–32; and black men "adrift," 14, 26–30; and reform, 21, 54–55, 146, 179–80; employment of and gender relations, 21–23, 45; and William J. Northen, 167

White working class: and living conditions, 21–23; and leisure activities, 27–30; and white chivalry and race, 43–47; and Atlanta race riot, 98–99, 107–8; as target of temperance reform, 179–80; and Leo Frank, 261–62

White yeoman farmers, 17–18, 21–23; and white chivalry and race, 43–47; and disfranchisement, 181

Wichita Searchlight, 125

Williams, A. D., 220, 247–50

Williamson, Joel, 6, 98, 308 (n. 1)

Wilmer, Cary (C. B.), 106, 216, 217, 246, 264;

and civic leagues, 152, 157–59; and Ray Stannard Baker, 202–3

Wilmington Riot (1898), 1, 125

Witherspoon, Evelyn, 106, 257

Woman's Christian Temperance Union (WCTU), 21, 146, 179–80

Women's Registration Committee, 249

Women's Social Improvement Committee (WSIC), 244–47; and interracial cooperation, 245–46

Woodward, C. Vann, 5–6, 188

Woodward, James, 155; and Atlanta race riot, 88–89, 100, 135; and temperance reform, 143–44, 146

Works Progress Administration, 267

World's Work, 132–33, 204

World To-Day, 123–24

World War I, 216, 248

World War II, 258, 267

WRFG Living Atlanta Project, 257

Wright, Richard, 240–41

Wright, Seaborn, 179

Young, Andrew, 278–79, 280–81, 283–84

Young Men's Christian Association (YMCA), 79, 106, 221

Young Women's Christian Association, 81